*f*P

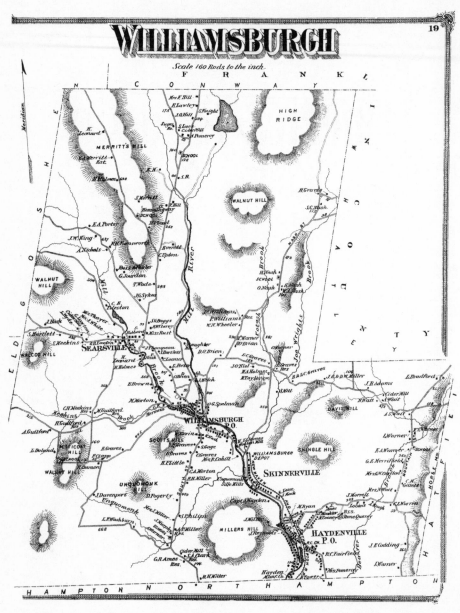

WILLIAMSBURGH

Scale 160 Rods to the inch

Map from the 1873 County Atlas of Hampshire, Massachusetts, by F. W. Beers & Co.

19

American Phoenix

The Remarkable Story of William Skinner,
a Man Who Turned Disaster into Destiny

Sarah S. Kilborne

Free Press
New York   London   Toronto   Sydney   New Delhi

Free Press
A Division of Simon & Schuster, Inc.
1230 Avenue of the Americas
New York, NY 10020

First Free Press hardcover edition October 2012

FREE PRESS and colophon are trademarks of Simon & Schuster, Inc.

For information about special discounts for bulk purchases, please contact Simon & Schuster Special Sales at 1-866-506-1949 or business@simonandschuster.com

The Simon & Schuster Speakers Bureau can bring authors to your live event. For more information or to book an event contact the Simon & Schuster Speakers Bureau at 1-866-248-3049 or visit our website at www.simonspeakers.com.

Illustration credits are on page 420.

Designed by Carla Jayne Jones

Manufactured in the United States of America

1   3   5   7   9   10   8   6   4   2

Library of Congress Cataloging-in-Publication Data

Kilborne, Sarah S.
American phoenix : the remarkable story of William Skinner,
a man who turned disaster into destiny / Sarah S. Kilborne.
p. cm.
1. Skinner, William, 1824–1902. 2. Industrialists—United States—Biography. 3. Silk industry—United States—History. I. Title.
HD9920.S56K53 2012
338.7'67739092—dc23
[B]
2012016151

ISBN 978-1-4516-7179-7
ISBN 978-1-4516-7181-0 (ebook)

For my Mother and Father

There is a tide in the affairs of men,
Which, taken at the flood, leads on to fortune,
Omitted, all the voyage of their life
Is bound in shallows and in miseries.
On such a full sea are we now afloat,
And we must take the current when it serves,
Or lose our ventures.

Shakespeare, *Julius Caesar*

Contents

Contents

Part I
The Flood

A man lived a lifetime before nine o'clock.
—*New York Tribune,* May 18, 1874

Chapter One

On the evening of May 13, 1874, a tall, robust Englishman walked through the door of Delmonico's restaurant in New York City. He was neatly dressed in a black suit with satin trim, bow tie, and embroidered waistcoat, the latter stretched impressively over his well-fed girth. While an attendant took his overcoat, he was greeted in the foyer by a host of familiar faces and several hands reaching out to shake his—an American custom to which he was, by this time, accustomed. In that genteel environment, however, his Cockney accent soon rang out like a clarion call at dawn, and one would have been hard-pressed to find even a well-trained staffer who didn't raise a brow at the brashness of the tone. Everything about William Skinner stood out—even his head, since he didn't like hats and chose not to wear them, despite their currency on the street.

Inside the restaurant, which was housed in the old Grinnell mansion on Fifth Avenue and Fourteenth Street, Skinner joined about seventy gentlemen who were filing upstairs to a private banquet room. They hailed from a great many places but they had one thing in common: silk. Here were the leading manufacturers of the American silk industry, along with several congressmen, some local politicians, and even a Japanese dignitary. Skinner wasn't the only Englishman among them, but at forty-nine he was one of the oldest, and he'd been specifically asked to give a toast this evening that would reflect on the past and honor the pioneers, like himself, who had turned American-made silk into an enviable addition to the marketplace.

Skinner hadn't wanted to be part of the line-up; he'd wanted to sit back and relax "without the thought of having a speech to make," but at least one of his colleagues had successfully talked him into it. If, having grown up poor and uneducated, Skinner quietly harbored a sense of social inferiority, few could match his formidable knowledge of the silk industry or his astonishing success therein. Further, he had a flair for the dramatic, and for all his instinctive hesitation to get up before a group of people, he possessed a natural ability to hold an audience's attention. This, along with the fact that he tended to keep things short, made him a popular speaker. Nor would he let his peers down tonight. As Skinner climbed the carpeted stairs toward the appointed dining room, chatting with friends and colleagues, at least part of his speech was already written out and tucked away in one of his pockets.

Anyone who read the papers or who knew anything at all about New York life knew that "to lunch, dine or sip at Delmonico's [was] the crowning ambition of those who aspire to notoriety." A presence in this establishment, "the most luxurious restaurant that had ever existed in New York," suggested irrefutable success, socially and financially. Banqueting here conveyed to the press and the public that this group of ambitious silk men had *arrived*. Their tireless, determined, and often brilliant endeavors had firmly established a silk industry in the United States and, at long last, a national organization devoted to their cause. Tonight these men were celebrating the second anniversary of the Silk Association of America and the exhilarating truth that "the American silk industry is, indeed, a power in the land."

Their private dining room had been festooned with flags representing all the great silk-producing nations of the world, with the U.S. flag and the flag of the Empire of Japan joined in symbolic solidarity at one end. Banners from every state in the Union were hanging throughout the room as well, reminding each manufacturer that he was indeed part of a *union,* an industry of thousands of which he was a vital member. At the center of it all floated a sea of colorful balloons above tables glistening with silver and crystal. Each balloon had been painstakingly tied with silk thread to the stem of a champagne glass and labeled with an industry trademark, advertising the breadth of American silk manufacture. Over here was "Corticelli." Over there, "Chinnacci." In another direction was "Unquomonk," the name of Skinner's own mill. Later on, with the toasts under way, the balloons served yet another purpose: the very ceiling would appear to rise up as the men raised their glasses in unison, elevating the occasion still further.

In keeping with the celebration, the menus had been printed on *American* silk, in purple, blue, and green with white fringe. Like miniature silk scarves, they were soft to the touch and elegant to the eye, their satin fabric casting off a rich luster under the glow of the chandeliers. On the front they listed the exquisite bill of fare, devised by New York's most famous chef, Charles Ranhofer, but with everything written in French, as on any given night at the restaurant, "all this of course was quite unintelligible to many of the gentlemen present." The backs of the menus, thankfully, featured more familiar English, since this was where the evening's toasts were listed. Down toward the middle was Skinner's speech: "Our Pioneers—Cherishing the recollections of the past, we emulate their example." By the time he stood up to present, a great deal of reminiscing would have already taken place, but his words, the organizers hoped, would put a flourishing cap on the topic. This dinner, after all, was nothing if not a jubilant reminder to all the men gathered that they were not only benefactors of the past but progenitors of the future. They too were making history.

• • •

The road for American silk had been a long one, longer than most cared to realize, since the potential for such a trade had existed for literally hundreds of years. By royal decree, silk arrived on the eastern seaboard in 1623, when King James I sent a shipment of mulberry trees and silkworm eggs to colonists in Virginia, along with copies of *A Treatise of the Art of Making Silke* and an order to abandon growing tobacco and begin the cultivation of raw silk. Dubbed "the wisest fool in Christendom" by his royal peer Henry IV of France, King James was maniacally opposed to smoking and obsessed with creating an English silk to rival the French and Italian. He had no interest in fostering silk manufacture in the colonies. The goal was simply "to compel [the colonists] to supply the cocoons, or the raw silk, to his manufactories in England, which was to be their only market for this product."

James had attempted to raise raw silk in England, but the damp climate had not produced mulberry leaves palatable to the delicate silkworm, whose digestion demands a temperate, crisp leaf. The Virginia climate, on the other hand, was perfectly suited to producing exactly the leaves that the silkworm demands. In fact, wild mulberry trees had been found growing near Jamestown by some of its earliest settlers, who were aware that they had in their environs an abundant supply of the natural food of the *Bombyx mori* and that raw silk might prove a worthy cash crop. Unfortunately, during their very first attempt to raise silkworms, the precious specimens—and all the profits to have been generated—were consumed by rats. After this the colonists had returned to growing tobacco, which was much easier. But this did not sit well with His Majesty. Thus when growing silk in England proved not possible, James resolved to clamp down on his Virginia colonists, ordering them to cover the landscape in mulberry trees and instructing them on how to cultivate silkworms. To lure them away from tobacco, he provided lucrative incentives to those who devoted the most land to his decree.

Yet silk culture, or sericulture, never took off with the colonists. Raising silkworms is extremely labor intensive. Not only must the leaves of the mulberry tree have a certain soft texture when they sprout in the spring, but silkworms must hatch at precisely the right moment in order to be fed the healthiest leaves. If the worms hatch too early or too late, they can die from lack of proper food. This is assuming that the eggs hatch in the first place, that they were successfully frozen through the winter after being harvested the previous summer, that Mother Nature has not played havoc with the orchards, and that rats or other animals have not eaten the worms. If at any time even one part of the equation failed, the farmer could lose his raw silk for the year. Compounding the struggle, raw silk made by the colonists was saleable only in Britain. They couldn't trade their product with other nations for political reasons, and they couldn't barter it at home for practical ones. Nobody in the colonies knew how to manufacture or even dye silk. Tobacco, on the other hand, was always in demand.

A few determined silk growers persevered, however. They turned their fields into orchards and their barns into cocooneries, learning exactly what it took to raise the unbelievably helpless silkworm. *Bombyx mori* is the only domesticated insect, having been so thoroughly cultivated since its discovery in China, circa 2700 B.C., that it can no longer survive on its own and must be raised and fed by humans. The farmers therefore lined their barns with shelves and tables and built scores of wooden trays to hold their giant silkworm populations. It takes two thousand to three thousand silkworms to produce just one pound of silk, and if these farmers wanted to make any profit, they needed to raise *a lot* of silkworms.

The silkworm is a caterpillar that produces silk proteins in its salivary glands. From the time it has hatched, at which point the little creature is no bigger than an ant, the silkworm eats voraciously around the clock. By its sixth week of nonstop feeding, the ravenous silkworm has increased in size about ten thousand times, to the point where it is as big as a sweet pickle, and it has produced a full sack of raw silk in its salivary glands. With this raw silk it spins a cocoon and enters the pupal stage, from which it will later emerge as a moth. The moth, however, is considered quite harmful to the silk; in its efforts to break free, it will tear an opening in the cocoon, ripping apart the silk and rendering it almost useless for production. Consequently only some moths are allowed to emerge, for breeding purposes; most are usually "stifled," or killed, while still in the cocoon. Steaming is one method of stifling, although many colonists would have used heat alone, literally baking the cocoons (with the pupae within them) in bread ovens.

Each cocoon is wound with one continuous strand of silk about half a mile long and, oddly enough, triangular in cross-section. Because of this triangularity, the strand acts like a prism, reflecting light like no other natural fiber. By itself, though, this one strand is so fine as to be barely perceptible. A single human hair is many times thicker. Great skill is required to unravel several cocoons at once while spinning or reeling the various silk filaments (or strands) together, thereby creating a stronger, denser raw silk strand, the precursor to all manufactured silk. The art of reeling raw silk had been passed down in China and Europe, where generation after generation had honed to perfection their closely guarded methods. For those on the American shore, thousands of miles removed from such arcane traditions, the art of reeling remained maddeningly elusive and the prospect of mastering it seemed as likely as King James puffing on a pipe.

Virginia silk growers, therefore, focused simply on growing the best crops of cocoons that they could, experimenting year after year with soil, light, shade, temperature, and a host of other variants until they were actually producing a very commendable grade of raw silk. Shipments of cocoons back to Britain became highly valued cargo. Rumor has it that either Charles I or Charles II commissioned a robe to be made specifically of *Virginia* silk. And so what had started as an experiment with sericulture in Virginia eventually produced silk that was, literally, fit for a king.

Sericulture slowly appeared in other colonies as well, with comparable, if only moderate, success. In the early eighteenth century Sir Thomas Lombe, "the most eminent silk manufacturer in England," pronounced a sample of raw silk from Georgia "equal or superior to any of the Italian." In 1755 Mrs. Charles Pinckney, one of the most distinguished women of South Carolina, personally boosted the American raw silk trade when, on business with her husband in England, she presented to Augusta, the Dowager Princess of Wales, a dress that had been made of silk from her husband's plantation. Mrs. Pinckney's silk "was pronounced in England equal to any imported into that country." Later Benjamin Franklin encouraged sericulture in Pennsylvania, sending dispatches from England in 1770 that included specific instructions from a French monk on the science of growing silkworms. Indeed, by the dawn of the Revolution, sericulture had been attempted in almost every colony.

Even at its peak, though, colonial sericulture was hardly a booming industry. Few met with the success of Mrs. Pinckney or the Georgia planters, who owned multitudes of slaves to perform the time-consuming work for them. And even Mrs. Pinckney had needed to take her raw silk to England to be woven by Englishmen, since no American yet possessed the skill. Certainly attempts to produce silk thread and silk clothing were made by nearly everyone who raised silkworms in the colonies, but without anyone to show these people *how,* they were quite lost. Their reeling was poor, at best, with "uneven" and "gummy" results. They had no recipes for cleaning or dyeing the silk, nor any techniques for spinning and weaving it. As the colonies grew, one might see a delegate at the Colonial Assembly wearing "a silk waistcoat . . . made from silk of his own raising" or "some grand lady appearing at a reception of the Colonial Governor . . . clad in a gown woven of native-grown silk." But such articles of clothing, which were markedly inferior to any manufactured abroad, were at best a statement of ingenuity rather than fashion.

With the onset of the Revolution came the demise of silk culture in the colonies. Trade with England having stopped, farmers were forced to turn all of their attention to growing cotton in order to provide uniforms for the army. At no great loss to the nation's economy, the mulberry tree and the silkworm were almost entirely abandoned.

For the next fifty years sericulture was relegated to a domestic art, pursued mostly in New England by farmers' wives. Agricultural fairs awarded prizes for exemplary cocoons, which must have been something of a novelty. Only one town continued to embrace the possibilities of native-grown silk. Mansfield, Connecticut, "seems . . . to have been the only locality where raising silk became a fixed industry." Orchards of white mulberries graced the countryside there, and, come springtime, scores of women and children could be seen plucking leaves for their tiny dependents. Despite the myriad challenges, "the silk obtained by a single family [in Mansfield] sometimes amounted to 130 lbs a season," furnishing many a farm with "a considerable income to its owner."

Meanwhile, Independence had created a vastly different America—socially and economically. "I find men and manners, principles and opinions, much altered in this country since I left it," wrote John Adams upon returning from France in 1788, after nearly ten years abroad on diplomatic missions. A new aristocracy was growing, ambition was on the rise, and in some circles money was more evident than integrity. At the same time, commercial relations had opened up with Europe, Africa, and the Far East, creating new opportunities for extending lines of credit. Well-heeled Americans, particularly in the North, began looking overseas as never before to procure the latest *modes* in apparel and décor, of which silk invariably played a major part. To create a fashionable lifestyle stateside, silk became an ever more necessary accoutrement, and in the decades following the Revolution importing silk became an increasingly profitable business. In fact in comparison to the exportation of staple commodities, which actually fell in favor, the importation of silk rose "in a fearful ratio."

In 1801 a formidable French agriculturist, Peter Delabigarre, who lived along the Hudson River in New York, declared to the New York State Agricultural Society, "Gentlemen, you have in your hands all the means requisite for success, and for enriching yourselves by the culture of silk." But nobody appears to have listened, in New York or anywhere else, until the 1820s, by which point the "fearful ratio" had become truly frightening. Americans imported roughly $10 million worth of silk goods in 1825, while exporting only $6 million worth of grain and flour. Not surprisingly, Congress formed various committees over the next several years, desperate to figure out how in the world it could get in on this silk business.

There was much talk of manufacturing silk, but that presented several challenges. First, nobody knew how to do it. Second, even if some of the nation's more enterprising men figured out how to build the requisite machinery—when no one in America even knew what silk machinery looked like—they would thereafter need a steady supply of raw silk to manufacture into silk goods. But where would this raw silk come from? The idea of manufacturing silk at a time when there was no established home industry for supplying the raw materials seemed like putting the cart before the horse. Philadelphian Peter S. Duponceau, another Frenchman eager to see the Americans advance, expressed the views of many when he asserted in a letter to a friend that American silk manufacture was not in the best interests of the country: "To do this would necessitate the importation of raw silk from France, Italy, or China. It is better for us . . . [to] make a perfect raw silk, and export it for years to Europe, than to commence manufacturing too soon."

No one—certainly no one in Congress—could have imagined the craze that followed. A new genus of mulberry tree arrived in the United States, in Baltimore, in 1826, and shortly thereafter "one after another of the experimenters in silk culture began to advocate the *Morus multicaulis.*" This mouthful of a name is the formal appellation of the Chinese mulberry tree. Unlike the red mulberry tree, indigenous to Virginia, or the white mulberry tree, growing happily in Mansfield, the Chinese mulberry grew from a seed (or even a cutting) into a decent-size tree in just one season, two at the most. Farmers and their families became starry-eyed with visions of instantaneous orchards and the thousands of silkworms that could thus be accommodated. Even those who didn't farm—doctors, lawyers, ministers, and others—wanted to get involved, and for the first time sericulture verged on becoming a national industry.

From Maine to Spanish Florida everyone seemed to want the Chinese mulberry, and speculators only fueled the market. Where in 1834 a hundred cuttings sold for $3, by 1839 the price had soared to $500. Unfortunately "the extravagant prices at which the cuttings were sold were entirely prohibitory of their use to feed silk-worms, since . . . the tree was [worth] more than all the silk that could be made from it." Finally, inevitably, the bubble burst that winter of 1839, and thousands of individuals who had invested in the tree, who had been told by some of the leaders of the day, "Plant mulberries in the full assurance that they will be wanted," found themselves bankrupt. Once the rising star of American agriculture, the Chinese mulberry became worthless as a weed.

Meanwhile, a few Americans here and there had begun to experiment with the actual manufacture of silk, based on some ideas learned from foreigners. Throughout the 1830s, as throngs of farmers were planting mulberry trees in their fields, a small number of men were laboring in machine shops with hammers, nails, wheels, and belts to come up with a feasible way to turn raw silk into a finished product, to spin, as it were, their own straw into gold. The resulting machines—winding, doubling, and spinning frames, as well as some weaving looms—were decidedly crude, but they worked, sort of, and presently a crop of silk mills appeared in New England. These mills were such novelties in their day that sometimes the workers couldn't get their work done because of all the visitors who came to see what they were doing.

The machinery gradually improved, thanks to the brilliance of one man in particular, Nathan Rixford, a Connecticut builder who dissected the existing machines and proceeded to build vastly superior models. Almost single-handedly Rixford created an industry for silk machinery, shipping his machines up and down the Connecticut River Valley as he received commissions "from different parts of the country." Yet none of the new mills, exciting and innovative though they were, survived for very long, because of two significant problems: amateur reeling and competition from overseas.

For the most part, American silk mills in the 1830s were using raw silk that had been grown and reeled at neighboring farms, and the quality of the reeling was so poor that the silk could not be properly fed through machines. In 1831 the French American Duponceau voiced his disgust at this situation in another letter to a colleague: "Our Connecticut women in 70 years have not improved their knowledge in the art of reeling." Not until the *Morus multicaulis* frenzy wiped out most local silk growers did New England silk men begin, out of necessity, importing raw silk from China. China had the cheapest raw silk on the market, and, since the Chinese had invented the art of reeling, American silk men could expect a more reliable raw material. A group of New Englanders even traveled to China—a journey of at least five months one way—to show the Chinese exactly the kind of reeled silk that American manufacturers (few as they were) needed back home. Consequently, with the dawn of the 1840s a quiet revolution had started to take place as "operations begun on the banks of the Yang-tse-kiang were completed on the banks of the Connecticut."

The greatest challenge now was the foreign competition. Not only were European silks sold liberally stateside, but most Americans preferred them, the general sense being that everything of refinement and taste originated abroad. Porcelain came over from France, Germany, and China, lace from Belgium, leather from Morocco, crystal from Ireland. Furniture, silverware, carpets, and paintings were similarly imported from foreign shores. Miss Featherstone, a character imagined by Harriet Beecher Stowe during the Civil War, exemplified the typical American female customer of her era. In one episode she complains to a clerk, "There is not, positively, much that is really fit to use or wear made in America—*is* there now?" And when the clerk presses her to consider buying American-made products, she has no idea where to start. "Well, but, *what can be got in America*? Hardly anything, I believe, except common calicoes."

Dressing in silk that had been manufactured in a New England mill seemed cheap and unsophisticated, not to mention imprudent and potentially embarrassing. Such a garment might develop an unseemly nappy texture; its color was liable to come off in the rain; and any part of it might split, crack, or tear before the end of one season. Moreover, foreign silks were actually cheaper, since the market for them was large enough to hold prices in check, while the American silk market, with just a handful of mills attempting to manufacture silk, enjoyed no such room to adjust pricing without risking collapse.

In these early years of production it was almost impossible for American silk mills to stay afloat, and yet there was a sense among men in the business that one day their efforts would be justified. In the fall of 1841, just two years after the crash of '39, a silk convention was held in Northampton, Massachusetts, drawing silk men from around New England, and with breasts full of optimism these delegates "expressed the belief that the United States might yet become a great silk producing nation." In some areas local tailors had become rather impressed with the products of nearby silk mills. In Northampton they had even declared locally made silk thread "to be a very excellent article, superior to the majority of the Italian silk."

These silk men convened again in 1843, this time in New York, and collectively agreed that American silk mill owners must make known their pride in their products. Despite home prejudice, they must strive to excel and persevere against the foreign competition. These men even made a powerful resolution never to sell their goods under foreign-sounding labels, a practice that was common among manufacturers in many American industries. "*Resolved,*" they wrote, "that we earnestly recommend to our silk manufacturers, now in the infancy of our enterprise, to set a good example to their brethren in other manufactures, by attaching their own name to their own goods." It was a triumphant call to action, if less than realistic. Indeed while many American labels—with unexotic names like Cheney, Jones, and Conant—bravely entered the general market, the most popular American silks by far were those whose designation implied a European provenance. The Italian-sounding Corticelli silks, for example, made an early, deep, and lasting impression on the trade. Consumers saw the name Corticelli, learned that these silks came from Florence, and naturally assumed that they had been manufactured on the other side of the world, in the Italian tradition. In fact they had been made by a New England manufacturer in Florence, Massachusetts.

• • •

When William Skinner arrived in the United States in 1845 at the age of twenty, the fledgling American silk industry, though passionate and full of heart, was in the midst of "the times which tried the souls of . . . silk producers and manufacturers." There were at most two dozen silk mills in operation, all in New England and all desperate for help from a foreigner like Skinner who came from a part of the world—East London—that had been producing silk for centuries. In particular Skinner knew the secrets to dyeing, and after establishing himself in Northampton, Massachusetts, where he turned locally made silks into brilliantly dyed threads, he encouraged both of his brothers to emigrate as well. Youths such as the Skinner boys, who began to arrive from abroad willing to barter their skills, helped give the nascent American silk industry the knowledge it lacked.

Yet more help came from abroad, in 1860, by way of politics. The British textile manufacturer Richard Cobden, who lived with the fantasy that a national "what's mine is yours" policy would bring peace among men, negotiated a horrifically unwise free trade agreement with France's Napoleon III. Following this, French silks saturated the English market and swamped the English silk trade. The Cobden treaty with France, as the agreement came to be known, "almost annihilated the silk industry in Great Britain." But Americans, suddenly able to purchase English silk machinery at bargain prices from mills that were going out of business, profited greatly from it. Even better, they could, at least for a while, remove the British from their list of competitors.

The Civil War brought still more opportunities to American silk men. "The war . . . compelled the government to levy heavy duties on all articles of luxury," which inevitably "proved of great benefit to the silk manufacturers." Tariffs on imported silk goods were put at 40 percent in 1861, and then, in 1864, as high as 60 percent, a rate that remained constant long after the South reunited with the North. In addition, the number of silk mills in the United States began to increase dramatically, creating more competition among American silk manufacturers, which in turn helped raise the quality and lower the prices (somewhat) of native goods. Though still considered inferior to the foreign article, American silk products at last became less objectionable to buyers.

Skinner's business alone testified to this. In 1855, shortly after he opened his own mill and ceased doing dye jobs for others, a state census recorded that he was making about six thousand pounds of silk thread per year. By the end of the war he was producing double that amount and making more than triple the profit. Indeed his annual production of silks was now worth $140,000—a staggering sum at the time. The growth of his business had even created a new community in Massachusetts. He'd built his mill in a rural area not far from Northampton, and by the close of the war it was surrounded by a bustling village that had come to be known as "Skinnerville." The very existence of Skinnerville testified to the rising success of American silk.

By 1870 American silks were everywhere, in coach laces, tassels, hairnets, ribbons, fringes, braids, hat bands, neckties, handkerchiefs, scarves, upholstery, vests, dresses, suits, shoes, and almost anywhere else fabric was found. They were present on the street, in the home, on the stage, in the lodge room, adorning brides and bridegrooms, actors and actresses, Masons and mothers. The Gilded Age, though not yet officially coined, was under way, and silk was more in demand than ever. Yet American silk manufacturers had no central organization looking out for their interests, no group to represent them before Congress, no agency to compile industry statistics. They were but a bunch of independent soldiers, battling more for survival than success. But the moment had arrived when they needed to unify for their common good, and, so, one day in June 1872, "forty-four firms and companies . . . held a meeting in New York City." By nightfall "the Silk Association of America [had been] organized."

That same year a small group of men from Paterson, New Jersey, who were now members of the Association, visited Washington to muster support for a stricter ribbon tariff (ribbons being the most common article used in women's clothing and hairstyles). Their goal was to make a case for American silk as a whole, since this tariff would eventually affect other branches of the industry. They took with them several samples of American silk to prove its quality and worth, and Representative John Hill of New Jersey, who supported the men's cause, showed some of the samples to his fellow congressmen. Merciless in their evaluation, the politicians immediately examined the silks under magnifying glasses. *Were there strands of other fibers in these silks? Cotton, perhaps?* They placed the samples in their mouths and tasted them for foreign ingredients. They sniffed the samples like bloodhounds, their noses on the hunt for adulterous chemicals. Finally, they pulled the silks to bits.

One congressman, after ripping asunder a specimen before him, concluded to Representative Hill, "Sir, it is pure silk." Then he challenged Hill: "Do you mean to say that this silk was manufactured in the city of Paterson?"

Hill confirmed this.

"I am astonished," the man remarked. "I did not know we were making an article of silk of so good a quality and fine a texture as this in the country."

The next spring, in May 1873, the Silk Association created a board of directors at its first annual meeting, and both Skinner and his brother George, who had become a silk manufacturer himself in Yonkers, New York, were elected to the board. Following the meeting Skinner, having been approached beforehand, made the lead toast at the Association's inaugural dinner. He began rather modestly, "I do not know why I have been asked to [make] this toast," but then assumed his position of authority. "I have been in this country thirty years," he proclaimed, "and I have seen the marvelous growth of the American silk trade." He told his audience that presidents and chief justices, men and women of every station, would one day all benefit from American silk. "The time is not far distant," he declared, "when, aided by the exchange of ideas and unity of interests which this organization secures, the silk trade will be made as great as the woolen and cotton trades of this country." The room erupted in applause.

The numbers backed up this bold declaration. At this point there were 147 silk establishments in the United States, employing nearly twelve thousand operatives. One of Skinner's closest friends, a fellow Englishman, Briton Richardson, announced that same evening, "People do not realize it, and you find it hard to convince them, that we make in this country over $33,000,000 worth of silk goods a year." Richardson was exaggerating, since the actual figure was closer to $20 million, but that was still a phenomenal achievement. Back in 1840 the annual output had been just $250,000. "No one need be ashamed of the silk trade of this country," Richardson crowed, building on what Skinner had said. "It has had a great many struggles. It has had a great deal of uphill work. But . . . when you look back and find that it has quadrupled itself in the last decade; when you remember that the silk trade of America, brief as is its history, has now in its employ more hands than the silk trade of France had after two hundred years of its existence, and has shown a progress that neither England nor any other European country can show . . . I think you will concede to me that the silk trade of America is a fact."

• • •

One can only imagine the menu that Charles Ranhofer had created for the second annual dinner of the Association in 1874. His meals routinely defied precedent. Both chef and restaurant in fact had recently made culinary history when they staged *le Diner des Cygnes,* or Dinner of the Swans, for the importer Edward Luckmeyer and his seventy-four guests. Akin to a tropical paradise, the setting for that meal began with a banquet table, down the center of which was a thirty-foot lake featuring four live swans on loan from Brooklyn's Prospect Park. While the swans glided to and fro, the guests dined on eight superlative courses, Ranhofer's menu building from some simple soups, *consommé imperial* and *bisque aux crevettes,* to a baked hors d'oeuvre, two kinds of fish (red snapper and smelt), a filet of beef, two entrées (fowl and duck), a "cleansing-palate" sorbet, two roast meats (capon and sheep), several vegetables, and fifteen selections for dessert. It's a pity that no menu from the Association's second dinner has survived, allowing a glimpse of its own splendid courses. But it is quite certain that the gentlemen were well fed and happily flushed (every course came with a designated wine) by the time the cloth was removed and the champagne poured for the after-dinner speeches.

First, the men lifted their glasses (and balloons) to "Our Country—the land of true liberty and refuge for the oppressed," after which someone in the back started singing "Our Country 'Tis of Thee," leading the room in a spontaneous chorus of patriotism. Next they honored President Grant and again broke into song, this time "For He's a Jolly Good Fellow." By now the balloons had become something of a nuisance, and more and more men were untying them from their glasses to let them soar aloft. Some balloons wafted to the corners, but others exploded against the gas jets of the lights. Loud *pops!* could be heard around the tables from time to time, and the exploding balloons seemed marvelously appropriate for a room filled with "anti-inflationists."

Representative John Hill, such a valued friend to the gathering, raised the next glass to "the American silk industry," which he called "a present credit, a future pride!," and began the third toast of the evening amid rousing applause: "Tonight, gentlemen, we may feel proud of this industry, that the work is accomplished, that we have achieved success, and that [silk] stands today so strong in the markets of the country!"

He couldn't have struck a more perfect chord. Earlier that afternoon

Secretary Franklin Allen had opened the Association's annual meeting with news of just how strong the silk market was, best measured by its solid survival of the financial crisis, begun some eight months before. On September 18, 1873, Jay Cooke and Company, one of the richest banks in America, had declared bankruptcy, and the effect on the nation had been catastrophic. The railroad market crashed; the New York Stock Exchange closed for ten days; Wall Street descended into chaos. The Panic of 1873 sent countless businesses into foreclosure, and thousands of individuals lost their jobs, incomes, savings, and fortunes as the country spiraled into a depression.

But America's silk men were averting disaster for one simple reason: they were in the silk business. "While many trades are languishing and some in ruinous disorder," Secretary Allen said, "the silk trade is well in hand." Despite the tough climate, luxury items weren't falling from favor. Nor were rich men and women the only ones still purchasing silks. Carriage makers needed silk for their cushions; the military needed it for uniforms; the theater needed it for costumes. Furthermore, from tailors to dressmakers, milliners, shoemakers, upholsterers, and even other textile manufacturers, absolutely everybody used silk thread. Thread remained the most stable branch of the entire industry and the one in which Skinner and the majority of his peers specialized.

Incredibly, when Americans had more reason than ever to be cautious, they were putting their faith in American silk, and there seemed no end to this trend, only greater rewards for all concerned. For Skinner, who had dedicated his entire life to silk and who was one of the first foreigners to join ranks with the American silk industry, this was an extraordinary moment to be alive and to be doing what he was doing, as Representative Hill only confirmed. "In times past," the politician said partway into his speech, "there were few people to buy these choice silks. Their use seemed to be almost exclusively for kings and queens, and princes and noblemen, and governors of states, and presidents of colleges, but the time is coming, my friends, when, on the free soil of our broad republic, where every citizen is a nobleman, and the sovereign is the sovereign people, including every class and order, the consumers of silk will be almost as numerous as the population of the country."

In fact, Skinner's own mill had produced more silk thread than ever in 1873—nearly half a million dollars' worth—and he had consistently employed about seventy people. Twice he'd even had to hire additional help, and as a result of his increasing business he had opened his first store on the corner of Broadway and Worth Street, in the heart of New York City's wholesale dry-goods district. Never before had he presented such a display of silk—cabinets of spools of all sizes and colors to choose from—to a wider variety of customers or for greater profit. With thousands of dollars of new machinery in the mill back home, along with a new dyehouse, activity had remained blessedly high. If 1874 proved to be like 1873, Skinner, like so many of his colleagues, would suffer no lasting effects from the financial crisis. His profits might be somewhat lower, but his business would still gain.

As part of his intended speech, Skinner had brought with him a letter to read. Written by an American woman in Paris, the letter was particularly telling because it expressed how far the American silk trade had progressed from a *lady's* point of view. This woman wrote that she had purchased some black dress silk from Cheney Brothers in Connecticut, and the firm had instructed her to give her new silk "hard usage" and to alert them at the first sign of any holes. Considering herself very patriotic, she was "exceedingly anxious that it should prove a success," because every dressmaker she knew "universally denounced American silks as worthless." As expected, she had a dickens of a time convincing her own dressmaker to work the silk, but finally her dress was made and she tried it on. She didn't love it. Feeling a bit of a sinking spell, the woman wasn't sure if she even liked the silk. It attracted dust, which was a nuisance, but she discovered that after a bit of dusting off, it was fine. Moreover it retained its luster impressively and over time proved positively indispensable. "At the end of six months," she wrote, "I should not have known how to do without it. I wore it everywhere, and kept on wearing it. . . . I crossed the sea with it and wore it throughout England . . . in Paris . . . in Italy. . . . It sailed on the Adriatic, was my constant companion during three months of adventures among the heathens of Vienna, and now that I've worn it back to Paris, and turned it wrong side out, hind-side before and up-side down, it is still my best gown, and the only friend I have that I have endowed with infallibility."

Skinner knew this letter would be a hit (especially the part where the woman complains about her only other silk dress, a French one, that takes on a "shining complexion" and "threatens treason at every turn"). It would also bookend nicely with another letter, one that Secretary Allen had read earlier that day, from the new chief justice, Morrison Waite. Acting on the belief that public officials should be seen wearing American silk, the Association had sent the new justice a silk robe that had been made in Connecticut, and Waite was thrilled with the gift. "It gave me great pleasure to wear the robe on the occasion of my qualifying to enter upon the duties of my new office," he wrote to the Association. "It furnishes the evidence of one of the greatest triumphs of American industry."

As bubbles fizzed in the champagne glasses and rogue balloons bobbed along the ceiling, as the chandeliers cast their warm glow over the tables and the waiters' footfalls fell silent on the plush carpet, as Skinner's friends—and even one of his own brothers—sat nearby on this celebratory occasion, Skinner's thoughts took to roaming across the Atlantic and Pacific, seeing limitless possibilities in the world. American silk would only improve. That was a given. So why wish to win over only Americans? Why not strive to win over the Europeans as well? Why not, even, aim to sell silk in the Orient, the birthplace of silk itself? Preposterous? Yes, but *why not*? A friend remembered that Skinner had a habit of "[saying] something so original and so searching that it would tear off whatever mask the topic might be wearing and let in a flood of light from an entirely new standpoint." During his speech this evening, Skinner did exactly that.

He stood before everyone, his superb frame easily commanding the attention of the room, and reiterated to his peers that their industry had grown to such an extent, in just three decades, that it was producing $20 million worth of silk goods annually. *Twenty million dollars!* "If we progress in the same ratio for the next thirty years," he said, "the trade will become something marvelous." To which he added famously, with arresting ambition, "I do not see why, in the next ten years, we cannot export silk . . . to China."

Two days later Skinner was on a northbound train, heading up the Connecticut shoreline on his way home to Massachusetts. According to his regular schedule (he visited the city nearly every month), he was on the last possible train of the day, which left the Grand Central Depot at 3 p.m. and put him on target to reach Skinnerville at 9:05. There was no dining car on the train—that amenity was as yet very rare—and there would be no twenty-minute meal stop at any station along the way. Unlike his glorious repast of two nights before, this evening's dinner would most likely be packed in a box or brown bag, just a few perfunctory victuals for a traveling businessman.

As the train sped along past the white church spires of various New England greens, the afternoon sun began falling toward the west and the temperature began dropping as well. The hill towns of western Massachusetts, of which Skinnerville was one, were known for their long winters, and the year 1874 had been no exception. It had snowed for days at the end of April, with heavy storms paralyzing the countryside, and there was still snow on the ground in patches. But for the moment, in that sun-streaked car, Skinner was miles from any lingering wintry weather. Outside the sky was clear. The tracks were clear. And he was rapidly winding down one of the most rewarding business trips he'd ever had.

Skinner had just been hailed as a pioneer in his field. His speech at the banquet had been so successful it was highlighted in the papers.

And his industry was considered by some to be one of the most exciting in America. Furthermore, his store downtown was filled with activity—he'd just hired a new salesman, a strapping young man named Fred Warner, to help his manager, James Peck—and he was getting ready to expand his business *again*. Skinner wanted to branch out into the manufacture of organzine this year, a thread used to make ribbons which were increasingly the rage. Skinner already had the requisite machinery on hand, had apparently erected an addition to his mill for the new department, and had even hired a local architect to design no fewer than eight new tenements to accommodate the new employees he expected to hire.

As much as business may have preoccupied his thoughts, though, he had something else on his mind this Friday, May 15, 1874. His eighteenth wedding anniversary was this very day, and hidden, protected, in his valise or suit, was surely a velvet-lined box from his favorite jeweler, Louis Tiffany, with something precious for his wife, Lizzie. Skinner, one of his granddaughters noted, "loved giving things," and on a similar occasion, when he'd been unable to be home on the day of his anniversary, he'd returned with a diamond scarf pin, carefully selected and beautifully wrapped for the woman whom he called "my darling."

Skinner relied on his wife more than anyone. Every bit as intelligent as her husband, Lizzie was, in any conventional sense, much better educated, having attended both elementary and boarding schools and having herself worked as a teacher for many years. There seemed nothing this exceedingly capable woman couldn't do, from laying linoleum to explaining mathematics. Following the birth of their fourth child, she even helped handle affairs at the mill while Skinner was away in England, and later she helped run the mill's boardinghouse. Like many rural housewives, she was intimately involved in her husband's business, but what set her apart was the fact that she was the wife of a rich manufacturer. There was no economic reason for her to be absorbing these kinds of responsibilities. She simply took them on, utilizing her "amazing genius for organization and development." More than a wife to Skinner, Lizzie was a partner.

Skinner's first wife had died young, leaving him a widower with two very small girls, but Lizzie had raised the children as her own and given birth to eight more as well. Of these ten children, seven were still living, and, adding to Skinner's sense of accomplishment, all were thriving. Nellie and Nina, twenty-three and twenty, had grown into smart, educated young women under their stepmother's tutelage. Nellie had graduated from a boarding school in Connecticut, where she'd studied French with none other than Georges Clemenceau, who was on his way to becoming prime minister of France. Nina had gone a step further, entering college with both of her parents' resounding blessing. She was attending Vassar in Poughkeepsie, New York. Lizzie's eldest, Will, seventeen, was about to close out his high school years at the prestigious Williston Seminary in nearby Easthampton, Massachusetts. Graduation was just a few weeks away—that is, if he could make it without being expelled. Will was charming, handsome, and, much to his parents' dismay, completely ambivalent about his education. Even so, Skinner hoped he would go on to Yale next year. Also enrolled in boarding school was Libbie, fourteen, who was attending the Grove Hall School for Girls in New Haven, Connecticut, but her school year had just ended, and she was back home again. Joe, eleven, and Belle, eight, were each eager for summer break. Getting ready for the summer games, Joe had bought a baseball bat the previous weekend. And the very youngest, Katharine, only six months old, had recently made her first appearance in public, with the world delighting in her just as much as she in it.

Skinner's train pulled into New Haven shortly before six o'clock. Departing passengers gathered their hats and bags and filed passed him out of the car, replaced by a throng of new faces coming aboard, each one looking for an available seat, preferably by the window if he or she wished to read in the last light of day. A couple of hours and a few stops later, the train pulled in to Northampton, where Skinner made his way to the exit and down the steps to the platform. Here he transferred to "a little one-car special hauled by a dinky locomotive" that took him the last leg of his journey, up the branch railroad of the Mill River Valley. The train passed the villages of Florence, Leeds, and Haydenville, the last aglow from gaslights that lined its streets. And then, at last, Skinnerville came into view.

There were some lights on across the river, as well as several windows softly illumined in the houses down by the road. The mill, however, was but a large shadow in the distance, nearly indistinguishable from the general darkness. The school and general store too were no more than ink spots for it was pitch black outside, owing to a new moon. Even in the dark, though, Skinner's own home—a three-story mansion set back from the rest, with tall French windows stretching from front to back—was quite identifiable, with several of its many rooms lit up in preparation for his arrival.

Through the air came the sound of his mill's bell, tolling 9 o'clock. At this moment Skinner didn't know who would still be up when he walked in the door. The baby usually went to bed at 7:30, and then the younger children around 8:30. But there was always a possibility that Belle and Joe might try to keep their eyes open to welcome Father home. And since Libbie had just returned from school, there was a good chance she'd have some callers this evening. Or she might have settled into a round of checkers in the sitting room with Mother, "a very expert player," while Nellie knitted by the fire.

As the train slowed in its approach to the depot at the northern end of Skinnerville, one of Skinner's employees, John Ellsworth perhaps, awaited him on the platform. The depot was about a quarter mile from the house along a dark, unlit road. Thus when Skinner stepped down from the car and into the cold night air, he would have found both driver and horse all ready for the short jog home.

The trip and this day were almost over, the anniversaries behind him, and a new year in the life of his marriage, his family, and his work was about to begin on the morrow. He was forty-nine years old, and the fabric of his existence had never been stronger. As he walked up the steps to his front door, there in the middle of Skinnerville, with the river flowing reliably behind him, the mill at rest across the way, the houses of his neighbors and employees all around, and a reunion with his wife and children just seconds ahead, there wasn't one clue, nor any sign, that the very next morning nearly everything in his world would be swept away.

Chapter Two

The rain began before daybreak, not much at first, but enough to render it a damp and cheerless morning by the time the first bell rang at the mill, at half past five. This bell served as the workers' alarm clock, alerting everyone at the boardinghouses that it was time to rise. Ellen Littlefield, who had boarded in Skinnerville for nearly seven years, was well used to the routine. A "packer" at Skinner's mill, she worked on the ground floor of the office building in a room filled with drawers of finished silk and stacks of boxes for shipping. Of the five or so packers employed at this time, Ellen was arguably the most experienced, given her longevity in Skinner's employ, and easily claimed respect as an old hand.

She was also, truth be told, fairly old to be working in the mill, having just celebrated her thirty-second birthday on May 8. Chances are, she marked the occasion with her closest friend at the mill, Aurelia Damon, who worked upstairs in the finishing room. At thirty-six Aurelia was Skinner's oldest female employee and his only female employee to own a home. By 1872, after more than twelve years of working at the mill, Aurelia had earned enough money to build a "very pretty cottage" on the opposite side of the river. Ellen was a frequent visitor at this house, where she and Aurelia could feel comparatively youthful in the company of Aurelia's infirm mother.

Most of the women that Skinner employed were in their late teens or early twenties. Many had come "seeking employment before marriage," drawn to the independence that millwork afforded as well as the opportunity to put some money in their calico pockets (for dowries, clothing, and even, on occasion, education). Only a handful worked at the mill for more than a few years; rarely did any linger past thirty, a dangerous age for a woman still to be single. But Ellen doesn't seem to have worried much about this, enjoying harmless flirtations with the likes of Tom Forsyth, that funny, handsome Englishman who worked in the winding room in the main part of the mill, or Nash Hubbard, "the widower," who was hired within the past year as Skinner's new bookkeeper.

As rain splattered on the windowsill, Ellen roused herself from the warmth of her bed, throwing off her heavy comforter and placing her bare feet on her large handmade rug. At this point in her career she'd graduated to having her own room—a rarity in boardinghouse life—and decorated it to *her* taste. Arranged here and there were books, magazines, and newspapers (she had a number of subscriptions), as well as her collection of photographs. Her melodeon, which she had been playing for about five years now, rested somewhere nearby, perhaps against the chair in which she practiced. And in one corner was a black walnut table made especially for custom sewing, of which Ellen did a great deal. Paper, ink, and letters lay about the room, awaiting Sunday, her day for correspondence. And curtains (made by her) hung in the windows, filtering the light on this cold, gray morning.

Gone were the days of sharing a bed with another boarder, in a room sleeping four or more. That was now the fate of the younger girls, most of whom boarded in the main house next door. The silk mill's two boardinghouses, which looked like regular old farmhouses, were managed by a well-known local, Fred Hillman, and filled with about two dozen operatives at this time. That number was going to swell once Mr. Skinner began hiring again. No one knew just when that would be, of course, as Mr. S. had put off his plans temporarily "on account of the dull state of the market." Even so, like the height of the river itself, such arrangements could change at any moment.

The Mill River was a modest waterway that originated in the mountains to the north and meandered rather pleasantly through Skinnerville. Unlike the mighty Connecticut, which flowed through three states, or the Merrimack, stretching from New Hampshire to Massachusetts, the Mill River was all of three towns long and forty feet wide. Still it made locals proud. "Seldom is there a river like our little Mill river," the *Northampton Free Press* had written just a few days earlier, "that has the power to propel so many water-wheels that drive so much silk, cotton and woolen machinery, so many saws and lathes for iron, brass, wood and ivory buttons, flour and corn mills, and also saw mills and other things." Indeed no fewer than sixty-four mills lined the river along its fourteen-mile run from the town of Williamsburg down through the town of Northampton.

Skinnerville, located within the township of Williamsburg, had been established in one of the river's more advantageous bends. Although the northern reaches of the valley were rugged, rocky, and hilly, the land opened up at this point into a lovely little plain. Nearly all the houses in the village, most of them built within the past fifteen years, were alongside the road and the river. It was a pretty road, shaded by elms, sycamores, and maples, and in back of most of the houses were gardens and fields divided by stone walls. Because it was so close to the river, though, the village flooded easily, particularly in the spring when freshets, or flash floods, most commonly occurred.

In February 1873 Ellen had received a letter from one of her sisters, asking, "Have you any fear that there may be a freshet there this spring? Mother said yesterday that the water would be apt to be high through those valies [sic] if it kept on raining." When springtime rains poured down, melting winter's snow and ice, the volume of the area's rivers naturally increased. Mill River became a considerable force, swollen and powerful, which was good for business since all that waterpower meant uninterrupted production at the valley's factories. But the river's swell could also rage out of control, back up behind ice jams, take out the wooden milldams, and otherwise cause a great deal of damage. To help ward against freshets and store some of that waterpower for later in the year, the manufacturers in Mill River Valley had built no fewer than four reservoirs, three up the west branch of the river and one up the east branch. These reservoirs were instrumental in controlling and regulating the area's natural watershed.

The reservoir on the east branch had never gained the trust of many townsfolk. Known as the Williamsburg Reservoir, it covered over a hundred acres, was a mile long, and contained about 600 million gallons of water. Almost from the start its dam had leaked, but supporters pointed out that the dam had been made with tamped earth and the rivulets of water flowing through it were entirely characteristic of earthen dams. A co-owner of all four reservoirs, Skinner drew on this one as a source of humor. Someone had asked him a few months back, "What do you have for excitement up here nowadays?" "Well," Skinner replied, "we occasionally have a freshet, then there is a general alarm that the reservoir has broken loose."

At ten minutes to six the second bell pealed through the early-morning air, just twenty minutes after the first. Ready or not, breakfast was being served in the dining halls, and the Hillmans' twenty or so boarders, Ellen included, rushed for the stairs, fussing with their clothes and greeting one another with groggy hellos. Then just half an hour later, the third morning bell rang. It was 6:20, ten minutes before anyone who worked in the silk mill, whether living in the boardinghouses or elsewhere, was to be at his or her respective post. Pushing back from the table, Ellen darted upstairs with the rest, donned her cloak and hat, and grabbed her umbrella and rubbers for good measure. In bad weather almost everyone wore rubbers over their everyday boots. Ellen had never seen any others like hers; they were "wired so the backs stood up about the ankle and one could just step into them." Though perhaps not the most comfortable, they were easy to slip on in a rush before heading outdoors.

The road through Skinnerville, sleepy just minutes before, was suddenly alive with men, women, and children hurrying through the rain and coming in from all directions but heading toward the same: Skinner's silk mill. The Cahill twins were coming down from the north, the Bartlett siblings from the south, the McGrath girls from the east. Close to sixty adult workers reported for work this morning, some forty women and twenty men, in addition to at least a dozen children and adolescents. Children were an integral part of the factory system in nineteenth-century America, composing their own class of workers within most industrial communities. Manufacturers benefited from their cheap labor, and families benefited from the extra income. The most progressive state in the union regarding child labor, Massachusetts had only two statutes for children under the age of fifteen: they couldn't work more than ten-hour days, and they had to receive three months of schooling a year. A decade earlier Skinner had pushed for the town to build him a school; it was, conveniently, two doors down from the mill.

In silk mills, however, unlike cotton mills, children weren't employed simply to run errands back and forth between departments or to replace full bobbins with empty ones on the spinning frames. Children stood before their own machines, finessing raw silk thread through tiny glass eyes and helping the brittle strands wind evenly, back and forth, on spool after spool. This was the very first stage in production at a silk mill, and it was generally considered ideal work for children, given their keen eyesight and nimble fingers. When discussing how John Ryle, mayor of Paterson, New Jersey, and one of the most eminent silk manufacturers in the country, began work at age five in a silk mill in England—an age too young even for most Americans—the trade journal *Manufacturer and Builder* was quick to explain, "The first process of silk manufacture is so light and delicate that it is adapted to the employment of very young children."

Several local families were represented among Skinner's operatives, with sisters and brothers growing up alongside one another in the mill. Henry Bartlett, for instance, who at twenty-five was a superintendent, had been in Skinner's employ since he was six. He followed in the footsteps of two older sisters and one older brother and in turn led the way for two more siblings. Of the twelve living Bartlett children, half had worked at Skinner's mill for a stretch of time, and four of them were still on the payroll.

Siblings were no less common among the boarders. Amid the throng of young women filing out of the boardinghouses this morning and emptying into the puddled street were five sets of sisters. In fact most of the boarders, Ellen included, had found work at the mill through a sibling. When Ellen arrived in Skinnerville for the first time, back in October 1867, two of her sisters were there to greet her, one older (Frances) and one younger (Lovisa). Neither was there any longer, each having moved on to another chapter in her life, but both Frances and Lovisa still had many friends in Skinnerville. Tom Forsyth had even named a dahlia after Frances, and Fred Hillman had made a special trip out of state to attend Lovisa's wedding. A feeling akin to family grew among many who worked in the mill, so closely did they live and work together.

Though many of the boarders were from nearby towns, a few, like the Littlefields, who were from upstate New York, had come from places much farther away. The Kendall sisters were from Bethel, Vermont, almost 130 miles to the north. At a time when the fastest mode of transportation was a train traveling thirty-five miles per hour and most people traveled by horse and buggy (at an average of seven miles per hour), 130 miles was a tremendous distance to cover. Exactly what inspired the Kendalls to make the long trek to Skinnerville is hard to say, when there were certainly mill villages closer to home.

But opportunity, in some form or another, brought them to Skinner's door.

Over at the mill Nash Hubbard stationed himself at a desk inside the main entrance and greeted each person who came in, noting his or her attendance. Umbrellas and raincoats dripped past him on the wooden floor as adults and children made wet trails toward their various departments. The foremen had already turned on the lamps, started up the machines, and begun feeding the furnace in the boiler house. Smoke was beginning to billow from the chimney, the turbine was beginning to churn in the wheelhouse, and the factory's countless belts, pulleys, and shafts were beginning to whip and spin into action. In a matter of minutes everyone was seated or standing at a station, and by the time the clock struck 6:30 a.m. Skinner's silk mill had started up for another day.

Those in the sorting room began picking through golden yellow raw silk from China, unfastening the large bales in which it had been shipped, removing the bundles of skeins, and then sorting the silk according to its fineness. Others were taking silk that had been sorted the day before, divvying it up into cotton bags, and lowering the bags into great boilers, softening the gummy silk to prepare it for winding. Over in their department the winders began winding the softened silk onto spools, while some of their neighbors were taking the spools just finished, fastening them onto cleaning machines, and running the silk through metal teeth to strip away any unevenness. From here the silk passed to the doublers, the spinners, and the twisters, who, on large spindled machines, doubled up strands of silk, spun them several times per inch, and twisted them tightly, sometimes in reverse, to create the strong, tensile thread that would bind men's suits and ladies' shoes. Then, finishing up this stage of the production, the reelers were prepping the thread for the dyehouse, taking it off the machine-specific spools and winding it back into skeins, or loose coils of silk.

Tom Skinner, chief dyer for his older brother, was starting his day as he would any other: washing out the tubs in the dyehouse to clean the pipes of any dirt that might have settled in them overnight. Dirt, after all, could ruin an entire batch of silk in the dyeing process, leaving it spotted and spoiled. At the other end of the mill complex, in the office building, the skeiners were beginning their day by taking some already dyed skeins, dividing them up according to custom orders, and arranging them into neat and orderly bundles. Traditionally all silk thread had been sold in skeins, but a manufacturer named Heminway in Connecticut had advanced the idea some time back of selling silk on wooden spools. This likely came about after the invention of the sewing machine, and spooled silk was now in great demand. Consequently, in a separate room, Skinner's spoolers were reaching for hanks of dyed silk and transferring them back onto spools. This was a job that took considerable care because these were the actual spools (presumably stamped with the Unquomonk label) that would go to market. Spoolers had one of the few mechanical jobs that didn't require them to be standing at a large spindled machine. Instead they sat six to a table, their feet working the pedals of their tabletop machines, as they wound the lustrous colored thread in even rows, back and forth, around and around the wooden bobbins. Finally, Ellen and the girls in the packing room were taking all that finished silk—skeined and spooled—wrapping it in paper, and carefully preparing it for transport.

By 6:45 the mill was buzzing with activity. Skinner had recently purchased a large supply of raw silk—one of the largest orders he'd ever made—so no one was idle at his or her post. In every corner of the mill women were sorting, cleaning, twisting, and reeling and talking to their neighbors all the while, discussing the depot's being cold as a barn or the need for better blankets at the boardinghouse or the likely winners at the next county fair. Some of the workers may have started wondering about the funeral for Lieutenant Governor Joel Hayden, which was slated for the next day, and someone else may have called out that black bunting had already been draped at the church down in

Haydenville. The mechanics meanwhile were already getting grease on their overalls, and the foremen were shouting over the racket in order to keep things running smoothly.

Up at the mansion, Skinner was tardily throwing off his sheets and getting out of bed. Though he aspired to get up with the second bell, at 5:50, he frequently overslept, a bad habit of his, and he seems to have turned over a few more times on this particular morning on account of his late return the evening before. Since Lizzie slept upstairs in a separate room with the baby, he had the master bedroom on the ground floor all to himself. After setting a fire in his fireplace, he likely stepped into his adjoining bath to wash and shave, taking the razor to his upper lip, which he always kept clean, and then, with a pair of fine scissors, trimming his dark beard. As for his thick hair, grayer than black these days, he kept it short, with a side part, neatly combed. Noting the steady rain this morning, he may have nodded with approval; rain was always good for a man who owned a mill along a river. It meant more waterpower. In time he put on a crisp white shirt, dark pants, suspenders, and waistcoat, left his overcoat for after breakfast, and slipped on socks and boots. Then, with a turn of the doorknob, he greeted the day.

About an hour later, as the clock approached eight, a dairy farmer named Collins Graves drove quickly into the village, cans of milk at his feet in his one-horse buggy. Decidedly off course from his morning delivery a mile to the north, he was hell-bent for the silk mill. When he saw his brother-in-law Willie Rhoades, next to Tom Skinner near the dyehouse door, he blurted out that the reservoir had given way— not bothering to specify which reservoir—and as alarming as this news ought to have been, it was so out of the blue as not to be believed. "Was this some kind of a joke?" the dyers wondered.

Unfortunately Graves didn't slow down to explain his bizarre exclamation but quickly moved on to Nash Hubbard, then coming out of Skinner's office, and exclaimed every bit as suddenly, "The reservoir

has given way and is right here. All you can do is to get out of the way!"
But there was no reservoir *right there*. A quick glance upriver confirmed
nothing of the sort. One simply saw the highway, rather empty at this
hour, with the same trees lining it to the north, the same depot up
the road, the same farmhouses nearby—everything indicating a normal
morning.

In the packing room, Ellen's eye caught some movement by the window, and she looked up from her station to see Graves driving away in
his buggy. But "he didn't drive any faster than usual as he started down
the slight grade" to the south, so Ellen didn't think much of it. Then
a voice behind her said, "The dam's broken." She jumped and turned
around, seeing "there against the door casing leaned Fred Hillman with
his legs crossed, grinning." He must have gotten a good laugh out of
that one, she thought, paying him no mind and returning to her work.

A few minutes later, an orphan named Delia Stearns looked out
the window and saw in the distance a voluminous mass that seemed to
take up the horizon, its black depth thundering down the valley. "With
great presence of mind" she "rushed to the alarm bell and rang it." In
an instant the mill's bell was pealing through the air, surprising everyone, and "all the machinery stopped" as the unbelievable news began
to spread from floor to floor.

Ellen had once made a plan with one of her friends to tie their favorite belongings to a tree if the dam ever broke, but she made no rush
to do that now. There was no time. Besides, the plan was never a serious
one; it was just talk. Ellen and her friend discussed it in the same way
one considers what to save in the event of fire and how best to save it
without possibly being able to know how dire the circumstances might
be. And so, instead of following any set course, Ellen simply ran outside with her fellow packers to see what was actually happening.

Down the street, Skinner had just begun breakfast with his family in the dining room when he heard the sharp clang of the factory
bell. The sound electrified him. His first thought was fire. He leaped
up and darted outside, whereupon he saw Collins Graves driving by

in his buggy. Graves shouted to him something about the reservoir, and Skinner, already rushing toward the mill, saw two things at once: an ominous darkness overwhelming the land to the north and, up the street, his operatives pouring out of the mill, many of them apparently confused and insufficiently convinced of the immediate danger. Ellen, for instance, had clearly understood that "something was wrong" when the machinery stopped, and in the street she "heard a terrific rumbling and saw a dark mass up the valley." But then, standing square in the path of a potentially deadly flood, she ran *back* into the mill for her coat and rubbers.

Others, taking in the sight to the north, were simply stupefied. Everything looked black. Indeed the sky above Williamsburg, a mile away, seemed filled with smoke as if from a fire. "They're all burning out up there," remarked one villager to another, having no idea what was happening. In fact a flood will often cause a fire, upsetting flammable objects that then ignite walls and buildings. But this was no ordinary flood. The water was twenty feet high, with spray soaring to forty feet in places. Any flame that dared crawl up a wick would have been quickly doused by the inland tide. That wasn't smoke in the sky above Williamsburg but the reservoir itself, crashing through the village with such force that its dark water was shooting up to the heavens.

"To the hills!" Skinner shouted as he raced down the street, waving his arms. "To the hills!"

The sight of their boss, still in his shirtsleeves, running down from his house in the rain and yelling at them at the top of his lungs, startled many a tepid foot to action. Skinner was a big, tall man, with a temper quick and fast. He always meant business. But never had he looked so wild. Soon nearly everyone was running across the street and up onto the railroad embankment, splashing through puddles and threading their way between houses. Some of the girls ran past Jerome Hillman's house, where his invalid wife, Sarah, stood in the doorway wondering what in the world was going on.

Back at the mill, in another doorway, dyer John Ellsworth was stuck, trying to save a bundle of silk that was too large to fit through the door. Spotting him struggling, Skinner "commanded him to drop the silk and run!"—surely the first time in his life Ellsworth had ever heard Skinner order anyone to drop silk and leave it. Silk was like gold. You didn't just leave it; you saved as much of it as you could. Elsewhere in the mill, possibly in the packing room, Hubbard had apparently already asked "one of the young men to put the boxes [of silk] on the higher shelves." This was protocol. In 1869, when the mill was being flooded by an autumn freshet—to the point where a section of the foundation was possibly giving way—"men & boys were running from one part [of the mill] to another wading through water up to their waists . . . moving silk & whatever water would damage." Ellen had witnessed the men loading as much silk as they could into a wagon and hauling it up to Skinner's barn. But there was no time for that now.

Within seconds the torrent was upon the residence of Lester Carr, a local carriage painter, who lived about a quarter mile above the silk mill. By chance Carr "happened to look out his door," whereupon he saw the monstrous wave and "the air full of sticks and boards." Having already swept away half the village of Williamsburg, the reservoir was a deadly cocktail of water, earth, wood, stone, and animal and human matter. It didn't look like water. It didn't look like anything Carr had ever seen. And its momentum created such a volume of air and spray that, well in advance of the headwater, his property was shrouded in a foul mist. He shouted to his family and they managed to escape, gaining a hill behind their house before the water could reach them.

Just below Carr's house, where the land curved slightly, debris in the roiling flood became jammed against some large trees, blessedly forming a momentary dam, and at least one of Skinner's female operatives saw the water held back. "It seemed to stop for a minute or so," she later recalled, but then it broke through and roared into the narrow expanse above Skinnerville, churning up soil, road, and hillside. The noise was deafening, as though an army on horseback were descending the valley.

With her husband still down at the mill, Lizzie Skinner was "terror-stricken" and "ran to the front piazza to urge him to escape," thinking he would be safer at home. She was promptly disabused of that notion once she stepped outside and took in the view to the north. Behind her, in their warm, dry dining room, her children were as yet unaware of the magnitude of the danger, though growing increasingly anxious as they watched "persons running and driving hurriedly across the lawn." Their father had only been gone for a minute or two, and in that time pandemonium had erupted. Not only were scores of mill hands charging uphill, but others as well, including George Smith, the fish peddler, who had passed Collins Graves in the street and instantly thereafter seen the "mountain" of water approaching Skinnerville. A one-armed veteran of the war, Smith used every ounce of strength in his upper body to turn his horse off the road, cut across Skinner's lawn, and "dash" up over the tracks.

Elsewhere in Skinnerville others had gotten wind of the warning—or simply glanced upriver—and were addressing the emergency in characteristically individual fashion. The widow Sarah Wrisley rushed into her garden to save her tomato plants and then, arms full of vines, rushed back into her house and climbed upstairs, as if her second story were a place of safety. Eli Bryant, a widower, scaled a ladder to the roof of a shed with his six-year-old grandson, leaving his daughter standing on the ground clutching a wrap for the child, begging them to come down and run for higher ground. Farmer Bartlett had been in his garden when Graves caught up with Smith in the road and heard the younger man call, "The reservoir's given way and is right here; all you can do is to get out of the way." Bartlett climbed a tree and began to sing hymns in its branches.

Another neighbor, Julia Kaplinger, who was also outside in a garden, ran to untie her dog from the barn, but her fingers couldn't undo the knot, and with so little time remaining she ran back into the house to save her daughters. Helen Hubbard, Nash's oldest, was making a squash pie when her little brother Jerrie burst in with the news. She abandoned the pie, grabbed some extra clothing, and herded her brother and sister outside, where the three of them ran for the railroad embankment at almost exactly the moment that their father did the same.

Delia Stearns was supposedly the last one to exit the silk mill—having evacuated everyone else—but it is unlikely Skinner saw her leave. As the reservoir closed in on the village, he was running back to his wife. With just seconds left he joined her in a mad dash through the house, shouting to Nellie, his eldest, to grab the baby and "fly to the hill!" He pushed the family of five out the rear door as the great wave swept down the street, slamming into the general store, crashing into the boardinghouses, and sweeping off building after building. Like several others before and after, the Skinners reached the safety of the tracks without a moment to spare.

By the time Skinner turned around, the village was underwater in a raging current that was clearing away everything in its path. The mill was no longer even visible, and his house, right in front of him, had been engulfed like an island. The water had filled the village up like a bathtub, flowing so far back that it surrounded Skinner's barn, where his horses were still in their stalls, and came nearly as high as the railroad tracks. It seemed to Skinner as though he were standing on the deck of a ship in a violent storm. Only this was no storm. Thirty-, forty-, fifty-foot trees were tumbling over one another like corn in a popper. Houses and barns were sailing by, the most improbable vessels there ever were. Bodies of men, women, and children appeared and disappeared in the water while some godforsaken souls were actually still alive, crying out as they were borne away.

"At one time," wrote Libbie Skinner afterward, "a house floated by with the smoke coming from the chimneys and two children were seen screaming for help at one of the windows in the second story." Others, too, reported seeing a house in the water with a smoking chimney.

Though hard to fathom how this could be, most of the houses were swept away at breakfast time, so there may have been one with a stove momentarily still smoking. The impossible was everywhere. Certainly this house would not have survived long. Few did. They collided with each other or with other matter and then split apart. Trees were like missiles in the swirling water. One soared right beside Skinner's house. Had the tree struck, it would have bored a hole into the parlor like a bullet in a man's stomach. Heavy machinery, too, was flying by as if on wings, and animals were somersaulting dreadfully in the mix. One little pig was carried off squealing, its cries intermingling with so many others, all being sucked downstream and out of sight.

Then, after what had seemed a lifetime, though it was no more than a few minutes, the torrent was gone. Described one reporter, the water "rolled on in its appalling force, a briefer time than many a dream."

Chapter Three

Of the four reservoirs sitting above the Mill River Valley, the oft-criticized Williamsburg Reservoir was indeed the one that had failed. At about 7:15 that morning its gatekeeper, George Cheney, had been finishing breakfast with his family when his father glanced out the window and exclaimed, "For God's sake, George, look there!" Part of the reservoir's dam was sloughing off and sliding downstream.

Cheney lived with his family in a "small, dismal-looking dwelling" that sat on a rise of land between the dam's spillway, on one side, and the riverbed, fifty yards to the east and forty-three feet below, on the other. Water surrounded the house on a regular basis; one had to cross a catwalk over the spillway to get to Cheney's front door. High up as it was, the place commanded a panoramic view of the reservoir to the north, the dam to the east, and the river and valley to the south. The location was terrible for farming, and Cheney was by trade a farmer, but he received $200 a year to keep an eye on the dam. Its west end began a short distance from his back porch, and the whole thing stretched between 500 and 600 feet—almost the length of two football fields—to meet the steep hillside across the valley. In truth Cheney couldn't help keeping an eye on the dam. Every time he turned around he saw it.

Constructed principally of earth, the dam was a huge artificial ridge between high flanking hills. Its wide sloping face was a bed of wild grass with cattails, ironweed, and goldenrods popping up in the spring. No water ran over the crest, only wind, gusting over the surface of the reservoir. When the reservoir was full, as it had been for several days, excess water drained through the spillway, eventually rejoining the river below. The spillway had been carved out of the western hillside, its channel smoothed so that the water, unimpeded by obstructions, rushed through it softly. The whole area would have been so quiet in fact that Cheney might never have known the dam was in danger had his father not looked out the window just then.

Cheney ran out the door and down a well-worn path to a shed in the middle of the dam, near the base. Inside the shed he grasped a wheel that stuck up out of the stone housing and threw all of his might into turning it to raise the gate, a valve in the drainage pipe that ran through the bottom of the dam. The drainage pipe had been closed to retain water in the reservoir since the mills below hadn't needed extra power, not with all the runoff from the spring thaw. But now, against his instructions to keep that pipe closed, Cheney opened the gate, hoping to relieve pressure building up against the dam.

This done, he paused to survey the dam and was "pretty well frightened" by what he saw. The slab that had disappeared downstream had left a crater behind, about forty feet wide, that stretched two-thirds of the way up the dam. Worse, rivulets of water were appearing in the exposed earth. The crater looked like a sieve. So severely compromised was this part of the dam that it seemed to be waterlogged from *within*, indicating that the saturation of the embankment was too great to have been occasioned by the rain. As Cheney could see with his own eyes, a number of insidious streamlets were percolating through the structure, stemming from a network that was likely growing vaster with each passing moment. Nothing could be more disastrous for an earthen dam.

Certain that the whole thing was about to give way, Cheney ran back to his house and told his family that he had to warn the people in the village below. He took off for the barn, a third of a mile away, yelling as he did so, "Keep off the dam!" He swiftly bridled his workhorse and told his father, who had followed down the road, to cut him a stick. The horse hadn't been fed yet, but it was too late for that now. Cheney leaped astride the animal bareback—he didn't own a saddle—and the horse, unused to being ridden, took off like a shot. Cheney held on, his knees gripping the sharp-boned back, and flogged the frightened animal to Williamsburg, three miles to the south. Galloping the whole way, the workhorse brought him there in ten minutes.

Cheney headed straight for the home of his boss, Onslow G. Spelman, general manager of the dam. In the yard stood the village butcher, making his morning deliveries, and Cheney yelled for him to get Spelman. The butcher later remembered that there was no denying the alarming nature of horse and rider. Cheney "looked white," and his unsaddled horse was "panting terribly."

"What's the matter?" Spelman wanted to know when he appeared. The night before, Spelman had been up at the dam with Cheney, investigating its soundness in advance of the spring, and everything had seemed perfectly fine.

"The dam's breaking away," replied Cheney, struggling to catch his breath, rain falling off his small straggly beard, his gaunt frame soaked.

"No, it ain't possible," dismissed Spelman.

Cheney repeated himself, and the two talked in circles for several more seconds. Given that Cheney was a farm laborer and gatekeeper, the latter job requiring almost no skill, he was considered by some to be "of little education and no more than ordinary intelligence." At this moment, Spelman clearly thought the man didn't know what he was talking about and simply believed that Cheney was merely "scairt."

A few years earlier, before Cheney was gatekeeper, someone else had spread a rumor that the dam was breaking, and the village experienced "considerable excitement," with people panicking, ultimately, over nothing. Spelman probably wanted to avoid that again. Nor was it exactly news to hear that part of the dam had given way. The previous spring "a load or two" of earth had caved in on the west side, and the resulting hollow, evidently considered harmless, had never been repaired. In fact Cheney had run past it this morning on his way to the gatehouse. By nature Spelman was conservative, and his thin, wiry frame remained as steely as ever.

Cheney would not give up, though. "The dam is breaking away!" he cried. And finally Spelman humored him with a small inquiry.

"What part?" he asked.

"The east part."

"No," Spelman exhaled. "You don't mean the east part, you mean the west part."

"No, I mean the *east* part," Cheney insisted.

This seemed to get Spelman's attention.

"Did you raise the gate?"

"Yes." Then Cheney suggested that someone sound an alarm. "Something should be done," he said. "Someone should go through to Haydenville."

"*You* go," said Spelman, taking no responsibility for the matter.

If he wasn't exasperated before, Cheney had ample reason to be so now. "My horse is not fit!"

Cheney's poor animal was frothing and sweating from a race it was never bred to run, and for the past three or four minutes it had been doing nothing but standing, heaving in the rain.

"Then go to the stable and get a fresh one."

Before Cheney could go, however, Spelman betrayed a growing sense of anxiety. "Did you see any water?" he asked.

"I did," said Cheney. "There was a stream running out of the bank as big round as my arm."

At this Cheney started for John Belcher's livery stable, 150 yards away, while Spelman went back into his house, and the butcher, who had witnessed the entire conversation, went to tell a neighbor what he'd heard.

At about the same time a young father named Robert Loud, who, like Cheney, had fought for the Union ten years ago, appeared at the top of the street, trying to run but barely keeping himself upright. About twenty minutes earlier he too had witnessed the chunk of dam falling away. At his farm high up on the mountain he had looked out his back door and seen the unbelievable off in the distance. He dropped everything and ran all the way to Williamsburg, two and a half miles from his farm. By the time he passed Spelman's, the men out front had gone and the street was quiet. Seeing no one about, he pushed himself to reach the grist mill, a hive of activity that would soon be in the path of the flood, and yet, when he finally got there and had people's attention, he was so out of breath that he couldn't tell anyone anything. All he could do was point mutely upstream, but someone suspected the news had to do with the dam, because, by then, others had spotted Cheney in town.

At Belcher's Cheney was met with the same incredulity as before. He knocked on the livery keeper's door to find the man still getting dressed and, naturally, a bit put out by being thus disturbed. Hearing the dramatic story, Belcher pronounced that it "wasn't possible." But if it was, he went on, hedging his bets, then Cheney should ride his own horse down the valley without wasting any more time. Cheney repeated that his horse could go no farther, but Belcher, who owned "one of the best barns in town," was not disposed to giving away free horses on a lark. In the end Cheney wore him down too, and the livery keeper started for his barn.

About this time, Collins Graves drove into the yard. He had seen Cheney ride over from Spelman's, and the gatekeeper's quiet sense of urgency had piqued his curiosity. "George, what's the matter?" the milkman asked.

"The reservoir has broken away and is coming down."

"Do you mean it?"

"Yes, it is coming right down."

Belcher now turned to Graves, and in a startling reversal of his previous stance, bellowed at him, "For God's sake, wheel your horse and let the people down the valley know what has happened."

Known for "'keeping his head' under excitement," Graves replied with familiar calmness, "If that's the case, I will go right down the river with my horse and alarm the people and you alarm them here."

Although the threat of flood seemed real, none of the men apparently believed that the reservoir was *literally* about to hit the village. Thinking it would take a few hours for hundreds of millions of gallons of water to drain out of its basin, Cheney supposedly intimated that the water wouldn't arrive till noon.

After Graves started off, Belcher finished saddling another horse, and a couple of minutes later Cheney was off too. Unlike Graves, however, he didn't get far. While waiting for his fresh horse, he lost his chance to warn people at the southern end of town, because the river rose suddenly, overflowing its banks and cutting him off. The only direction he could go was backward, toward the stable and higher ground, because just one road led south out of town, and it had entirely disappeared underwater.

Belcher ran to the nearest belfry, ringing the bell in the Methodist church, while others, witnessing the rise of the river, began running hither and thither spreading alarm. Even Spelman was on the move, over in the Congregational church to ring that bell as well. In minutes the sky to the north darkened and a thunderous rumbling drew near. One might have thought the thunder would help raise concern, but owing to the weather this morning, the sound of thunder wasn't anything unusual. Scores of people lived near the river, and they remained snug in their homes with no sense of the catastrophe about to befall them. When the flood wave hit at 8:03, according to a farmer's clock that stopped at that moment, its devastating arrival was mostly a surprise, and villagers had only seconds to get out of the way. People would later recall, "It was so sudden!" Many of Williamsburg's villagers drowned in their homes. Several drowned trying to escape. Others died trying to help. The reservoir carried off practically the entire southern portion of the village—mills, houses, barns, stores, sheds; people, animals, trees, gardens; tools, bricks, machinery, belting. Lives and the stuff of those lives were quickly intermixed with all that water and earth and transformed into death-dealing objects, hurtling forward in a great, tumbling rush toward whatever lay next.

In this instance, that was Skinnerville.

Given that Graves had a head start on Cheney, he was long gone by the time the river in Williamsburg overflowed, and he remained completely unaware of the fact that the reservoir was, quite literally, coming down the valley behind him. When he reached Skinnerville, he was only five minutes ahead of the wave, and he had absolutely no idea.

Still, in Graves's mind "there was not a minute to lose," which is why he was still in his buggy, having made the decision not to waste time getting rid of it. Similarly, in an effort to save time and energy, he didn't slow down at any of the houses he passed in Williamsburg, believing that Cheney and Belcher (and perhaps others) would take care of warning them. After all, Graves had the task of warning the people below, in Skinnerville and Haydenville. Unfortunately, many people in those houses died for lack of warning, for Cheney, unbeknown to Graves, had been cut off from reaching them.

Before leaving Williamsburg, however, Graves did make one crucial stop. Pulling up at the James Woolen Mill, at the southernmost edge of the village, he told one of the hands to find the superintendent and tell him the reservoir was coming, and to spread word immediately. This was the first time Graves bore responsibility for the news, and it must have sent a terrible thrill through him. Immediately thereafter he urged his chestnut mare into another run, and she responded instantly. Known as one of the fastest horses in the area, she covered the half mile to Skinnerville in just two minutes, the buggy flying so fast that milk cans flew out the side.

Directly upon entering the hamlet, Graves slowed down and pulled up to the silk mill for the same reason that he had purposely stopped at the woolen mill: he was worried that "the noise and din of the machinery would prevent the operatives from hearing any alarm in the streets." Also, in Skinnerville so many people worked in the mill that he was warning almost a third of the population right there. Then, believing (wrongly) that there was a decent amount of time before the reservoir would appear, he slowed down whenever he saw anyone to deliver the news.

Reluctant to be anyone's hero, Graves later said that had he known of the "great danger . . . so close behind [him]," his instinct might have been to save his own neck. He had a wife and two very young children, one just ten months old, who needed him back home, and while they weren't in any immediate danger—Graves's house was nowhere near the river—he was aware that he needed to take care of himself so as not to put their welfare in jeopardy. "I don't think I was specially frightened," he said, "and I surely was not aware that I was doing anything heroic."

Upon meeting George Smith, the fish peddler, Graves apparently drew up to a full stop. Smith wondered for a moment if the likable farmer, who was "somewhat known for chaffing," was trying to fool him, but Graves's urgent manner convinced him otherwise. The two happened to be in front of the Bartlett house, and Graves may have stopped so that old Thaddeus Bartlett in his garden might hear exactly what he had to say. As Graves left the village, he heard the mill's bell peal ominously through the air—his alarm was working!—and he urged his mare to resume her great pace. She coursed down the highway in the rain, covering another mile in good time, and brought her driver in his mud-splattered buggy safely to his next destination: Haydenville.

Haydenville was home to about eight hundred people. Like its neighbors to the north, it was a thriving little industrial community, very much awake this Saturday morning. In addition to a cotton mill, gas works, foundry, and tobacco works, the village boasted a brass factory that employed more than two hundred men, several of whom were the husbands and fathers of women who worked at Skinner's silk mill. One of the largest employers and one of the most significant enterprises on the river, Hayden, Gere & Company produced "thousands of water and steam valves . . . faucets, steam gauges, gas fixtures of every kind, and a multitude of other appliances for the utilizing of water, gas and steam," which were sold throughout the country as well as overseas. Just three weeks earlier the company had shipped a whopping six tons of finished brass goods in one day. As impressive was the actual brick and mortar, a giant complex of nine brick buildings, stretching six hundred feet along the river. Passing it, the average rider was in its shadow for two whole minutes.

Not Graves.

He sped past its many windows, its chimney belching black smoke, its fenced-in yard and hitching posts, and pulled up at the imposing office building at its south end. While his horse stood heaving, catching her breath, he dashed inside. Dripping on the marble floor, with several clerks watching curiously, he gave Samuel Wentworth, the superintendent, the same lines he'd been repeating for the past five minutes: "The reservoir's given way and is right here. All you can do is get away."

To Graves's surprise, Wentworth laughed at him.

"It won't be down here for four days," Wentworth said, "and when it does come the water won't come to our first floor."

Until now Graves had not had to defend his prediction. Having taken Cheney's word on faith, he expected others to do the same, as indeed most had. But he was now a long way from home, a good two miles from where he had started, and he was completely out of his element. He was probably the only farmer in the room, and this wasn't just any room: it had frescoed walls and mahogany furnishings, high ceilings and massive doors. The windows, unlike any he ever looked out of, were single-paned wonders of the purest French glass. The men before him were well-educated and cultured, with clean fingernails and tailored clothing.

In industrial communities, both urban and rural, there were strong class distinctions. A new arrival in Haydenville once remarked that an owner or superintendent of a mill "looks down on the overseers, overseers down on the foremen, they down on the hands generally, & so on." And farmers were lower on the totem pole than mill hands, because mill hands made a better living. Ellen, for example, the daughter of a dairy farmer like Graves, had left the farm first to teach, and then to work for Skinner, as had her siblings. Henry Bartlett, son of Thaddeus, had chosen mill work rather than farm work so that he could put more bread on the family table. Farmers were poor and, as such, often denigrated. For this reason George Cheney, the farmer-turned-gatekeeper, was painted in the press after the flood as being something of an idiot, and when Belcher came to his defense he didn't exactly praise him but said, as if to put the matter to rest, "[Cheney] is as 'smart' as the average of his class."

It is hardly surprising, then, that Graves, up against Wentworth, with all eyes upon him, felt suddenly at a loss for words. Truth was, he had no firsthand knowledge of whether the reservoir was actually coming. *He* hadn't seen it. *He* hadn't heard it. He had witnessed nothing out of the ordinary this morning. "If what [Wentworth] said is true," he thought to himself, "the people will have the laugh on me all right." He did not press his point about the reservoir but dripped out of the building, deferring to the sounder judgment of a man whom he believed had "more experience and greater ability" to know about such matters.

Still, something in Graves didn't let him abandon his mission altogether. He drove across the street to the barber's shop, notified them there, and to the butcher's shop, and then decided, doubt finally getting the better of him, to head back home.

He had just entered the dugway, a portion of road that had been cut out of the hillside next to the river, when a man came flying on horseback in his direction. "Turn around! The reservoir's right here!"

shouted Jerome Hillman, Skinner's night watchman. Behind Hillman a massive cloud of thick black smoke was entering into the dugway, about a third of a mile away, with a "roaring [like] rolling thunder." Graves wheeled his buggy about in a fury, and his little mare took off again, only this time she needed no prodding. She now knew what the men knew and was ready to bolt for her life. She and Graves raced into Haydenville, hot on the heels of Hillman and his horse, and both men shouted to everybody that the reservoir was "right here!"

Passing the brass works, Hillman, who had no idea that Graves had just been there, "shouted and gesticulated so that they thought he was crazy," but his "excited and violent" manner sufficiently scared the hell out of the men inside. Within seconds Wentworth had taken action, and the double hundred men in his employ began pouring out of their buildings. With the reservoir not only visible but audible, an inland tidal wave roaring around the bend of the dugway, workers bolted across the road, running for higher ground and the railroad tracks beyond, just as the villagers and silk workers had done in Skinnerville.

Hillman and Graves got as far as a hotel midway through the village when, in order to save their own skins, they had to abort their mission. A twenty-foot wave bearing houses on its crest was just behind them. The two men spurred their horses up a side street alongside the Congregational church where they parted ways—Graves driving his horse and buggy up to the tracks, Hillman dismounting, not even bothering to tether his horse, and running inside the church to ring the bell. Only moments earlier he had yelled at the sexton to do this very thing, but the man had evidently decided to flee. Hillman hardly got out a few peals before he too abandoned the building, which was fast becoming surrounded by water. "I had to wade to get to the hillside," he later remembered. Upon reaching the railroad tracks, he found himself in the company of scores of people, including Graves, and probably the hotelier and his son, their guests, and more. Of greater import, however, was finding his horse, which had fled like everyone else. To his relief, a man had caught him, and Hillman swiftly took back the reins.

Without pausing a second more, he jumped onto his horse and took off for Skinnerville on the railroad tracks, now the only accessible route north, with no desire other than to find his family—his wife, Sarah, and seven-year-old daughter, Clara—alive.

Behind him as he rode off, the flood was destroying everything in its path. Even the magnificent brass works, which some claimed to be the largest of its kind in the country, buckled under the force of the water and dissolved in the onslaught "like a pyramid of sugar in hot water."

Tragically Jerome's wife, Sarah, was almost instantly noted as one of the missing. When last seen by Ellen and the other girls, she had been standing in her doorway. Other reports varied. Some claimed she left the house with her daughter but ran back to get something and was then unable to escape. Another asserted that she was running with Clara and a servant girl and was trailing behind them, maybe ten feet or so, when the water pulled her down and she yelled to Clara to save herself.

This last story was just like the one told about Christina Hills. According to many, Mrs. Hills, who lived at the lower end of the village on the edge of the meadows, was running for the railroad embankment with her three youngest sons (the older ones being at work at the brass mill, with their father), when she tripped in a small brook and fell to the ground. One of her young sons stopped to help her, but she begged him to run for his life. The boy did as he was told and survived, but Mrs. Hills was swept away in the flood.

It's certainly possible that both Christina Hills and Sarah Hillman experienced similar deaths and last words, but following the flood so many stories became caught up in the rumor mill that Jerome Hillman must have heard several versions of his wife's final moments and must have agonized over what really happened. His only consolation would have been the fact that his daughter was safe. But he had no place to take her for warmth, no home in which she could dry off or gain comfort. Their house was gone, "the very turf torn off" where it had once stood.

•   •   •

The water had taken fifteen minutes to pass through Skinnerville, and when it was gone, so too was Skinnerville. Most of the houses had been swept into oblivion. Not a brick of Skinner's mill remained. Where half an hour before had been an enviable industrial village, busy with orders of colorful silk thread to be filled, there was now a mud-swept landscape strewn with timber and rocks, raked utterly clear of any trace of life. Skinner, like everyone else around him, could only stare at this wasteland in shock, unsure of what had just taken place, not yet aware of who might be missing, blinking in the continuing rain at the unfamiliar sight before his eyes.

Eleven of Skinner's fourteen tenements had been destroyed, including both boardinghouses, which had housed close to twenty-five people. More than half a dozen other homes, individually owned, had also been destroyed. Damages were extreme, and in many cases nothing was left of a building whatsoever. Like the silk mill, many houses had simply vanished. Others had been lifted off their foundations and pushed clear across the meadows. Several had tipped over. One landed in the middle of the road. Nash Hubbard's house had stayed where it was, but its façade was ripped off, exposing its wallpapered living room so that it suddenly looked more like a stage set. Trees that remained were stripped of their bark and denuded of leaves. Gardens and planted fields, with all that fresh topsoil, had been handily carried off, leaving giant craters in their wake. The wheel pit of the mill was filled with gravel. All the wells were choked with debris. There was plenty of water still about, on the ground and falling from the sky, but none to drink.

When interviewed a few days later by a reporter from the *New York Tribune,* Skinner pointed to a man who had lost his wife and children and said, "In comparison I have lost nothing, and have reason to be glad it is no worse." But this reporter, looking over all that Skinner had personally lost as the founder and patriarch of a village that had just been wholly eradicated, openly addressed the reality of the situation: "I question if the noon of that sad Saturday, whose morning found Mr. Skinner a prosperous manufacturer and a rich man, saw him worth a dollar in the world."

Part II
Before the Flood

Have you any distinct idea of Spitalfields, dear reader?
—Charles Dickens, *Household Words*

Chapter Four

William Skinner was born November 14, 1824, in London, England. When asked about his birth date, Skinner once replied that he was born the same year "in which Lord Byron died and in which the last execution for forgery occurred." Lord Byron was a hero to the British, and claiming connection with any part of his existence was a source of pride for a commoner like Skinner. As for forgery in Regency England, there were years in which someone was hanged in London practically every other week for possession of a counterfeit Bank of England note. To dissuade abuse of the new paper currency, forgery was a capital offense, but in far too many cases those who were convicted of this crime were poor people, completely unaware they'd been using fake money. Yet they were hanged nevertheless for breaking the law. It was a cruel time, and Skinner evidently liked to think that he came into being when the laws were changing, when one era was ending and another beginning. He hated the past.

Skinner grew up in the silk-weaving center of Spitalfields, in the city's grim East End. Both of his parents, John and Sarah Skinner, were silk workers struggling to make a living in what had become a crowded and ailing industry. At the time Skinner was born they were living in an alley called Vine Court, renting a dilapidated silk weaver's cottage. "Nature cast my lot in a silk district," Skinner later said, "and the first noise that attracted my attention in this mundane world was the throwing of the weaver's shuttle." His parents couldn't afford a crib so he slept on what was probably a bed of straw underneath his mother's loom and awoke throughout the day to the *clack-clack-clack* of the shuttle above, watching patterns of silk being woven above his head. Before he could even walk, Skinner had become intimately acquainted with the sound of labor, the color of thread, and the whirr of industry—all of which would dominate the rest of his life.

Little is known about Skinner's father other than that he was "not very strong" and came from an educated family that had fallen on hard times. He worked in a dyehouse, and he died in his late thirties or early forties, when Skinner was yet a teenager. Skinner's mother, Sarah, was descended from a tough stock of Londoners who had been silk workers "from generation to generation." Though weaving was typically the province of men, Sarah had learned the trade from her parents and was a weaver in her own right. She worked fourteen to sixteen hours a day, often seven days a week. She may very well have been the principal breadwinner in the family, even after giving birth to six more children. Skinner later "attributed his success in business" to the "industry and perseverance instilled into him by his mother." As one can imagine, this didn't come without its consequences.

Mrs. Skinner was her son's first employer. By the age of six, young Will was cleaning the warp on her loom and making the quills with which she wove. "The boys and girls of weavers who are unfortunate enough to follow the same calling," wrote Thomas Archer, a British journalist, "are first taught to wind silk on small pieces of reed placed on a spindle. These, when covered with silk or cotton, are known as 'quilles' (perhaps from quenouille) and are placed in the shuttle to supply the woof." Will would have wound the silk on a spinning wheel, using a small stool or a pile of bricks for a seat. At other times he would have bent over the well of the loom to remove "every knot and burr" from the long silk strands of the warp. With little variance he would have risen with his mother at 5:45 with the tolling of the Christ Church bell and labored by her side until the last of the candlelight in the evening. While she sat at the loom, both hands busy, he also would have helped care for his younger brothers and sisters, and in due course he would have taught them to wind thread and pick nibs the way he did. One of the few times Skinner shared aspects of his childhood, he mentioned that "all the household was obliged to assist" in the production of silk.

London's silk trade, almost entirely confined to Spitalfields, was a cottage industry, not at all indicative of the Industrial Revolution. Thread was manufactured in mills to the north, or imported from the Continent, and shipped to Spitalfields to be woven into fabric by hand. Unlike cotton or wool, silk cloth was too fragile for power looms, since rapid manipulation damaged the fiber. As for the Jacquard loom, a superior hand loom invented in 1801 specifically for the advancement of silk production, it was too expensive for any household to own. So the work carried on as it had for centuries: on old draw looms in light-filled garrets in individual dwellings.

Everywhere in Spitalfields were silk weavers' cottages. They were the most recognizable houses in the district, given their unusually broad windows on their topmost floors. These "long lights," as they were called, illuminated the garrets where the weavers and their children worked all day. Skinner recalled that his parents' garret comprised the third floor of their house, but this is somewhat misleading. Garrets weren't regular floors; they were large, unfinished attics, usually accessed by a ladder and a trapdoor. Mrs. Skinner's loom would have taken up half the room, and because of the loom's incessant clack and clatter, the floors would have been doubled in thickness to prevent vibration and noise from disturbing other boarders. By the early nineteenth century few weavers could afford to occupy a whole house. In addition to maybe one other room, most lived with their families in the garret, entombed in an isolated world of industry. Looking out the windows, one saw only "the blackened forest of chimneys."

In summer it was suffocating in this space, with sun beating in through the large windows, and winters were equally hard. Many garrets didn't have fireplaces—they were attics, after all—so families made do without or, if they had the means, installed a coal stove beside the chimney, piping it into the flue. Yet they had to be careful when burning coal not to let any black smoke discolor the silk. At all times they had to maintain a level of cleanliness, in spite of their impoverished circumstance, specifically so that "the delicate fabric upon which they work will come out from the loom without a soil."

There was probably a cupboard of some sort, or at least a shelf, for a few dishes and utensils. Given the need to work and little money to spend, Mrs. Skinner, like other women weavers, wouldn't have cooked. Rather, the family would have eaten bread for most meals "and perhaps a red herring, or a piece of cheese." On Sundays they might have enjoyed a bit of cooked meat—something a few halfpence might buy, such as cow's heels or sheep's head—from a nearby cookshop. Mrs. Skinner didn't leave off for meals during the week, any more than her parents and grandparents had before her. She raised her children to accept a life of "eating in one corner and weaving in the other of the same room." The only play that Will and his siblings would have known about was the kind to be dreaded. "At play" in a weaver's house meant "without work."

Along the broad sills would have been a few kinds of plants, something familiar in most garrets. Spitalfields weavers had once had a reputation for being master gardeners, cultivating flowers as exquisitely as they wove them, and the vestiges of that previous time were the pots and blooms on worn, sagging ledges. Weavers were known for their love of songbirds too. Even in the most straitened circumstances, they owned linnets, woodlarks, or goldfinches, raising them in birdhouses on the roof and keeping one or two in a birdcage in the garret. A visitor in the 1850s, riding an elevated train through the district, remarked on the "roof philosophy" of Spitalfields: all those birdhouses, all those long lights. "House after house presents, at the upper stories, ranges of windows totally unlike those of common dwellings, and . . . many and many a roof exhibits a piece of apparatus which on steady inspection is seen to be a kind of bird-trap."

In Spitalfields, songbirds lent music to an otherwise cheerless existence, and Skinner would revere them his whole life. When well into his sixties, sitting at the dinner table with some of his grandchildren, he listened quietly as one of his grandsons boasted about a cousin killing a scarlet tanager with a slingshot. The talkative boy, who was deeply impressed with his cousin's skill, now had possession of the bird and pulled the dead thing out of his pocket to show his grandfather. At this Skinner shut up the boy, and his cousin, with "a lecture on the wrongness of shooting songbirds" and ordered the child, "Take the bird to a taxidermist and keep it in your room as a reminder not to shoot birds."

The majority of silk weavers' cottages were mean, two-story dwellings, with damp foundations, poor ventilation, and little light except for that which illuminated the garret. Many houses had "more sheets of paper than panes of glass," rotten floors, and "walls and ceiling[s] sadly cracked." If the privy behind Vine Court was typical, the Skinners shared it with about fifty people. Worse, there was no drainage system in this part of town: "The water runs off as it can, and now and then the parish authorities send round a mudcart to gather up what becomes so thick as to block the way." Waste was supposed to be cleared by night-soil men, but when they didn't come around, which happened a lot, courtyards filled up with raw sewage, making the area prone to the spread of disease. In 1832, when cholera appeared in London, it showed up first in the East End, and when typhus swept through five years later, medical treatment there cost the city so much money that Edwin Chadwick, secretary of the new Poor Law Commissioners, "[argued] that it would cost less to improve living conditions than to provide passing relief for the sick." By the middle of the 1840s life expectancy in parts of Spitalfields had plummeted to sixteen years and infant mortality had soared to 22 percent. In light of this, the survival of all members of the Skinner family through the 1830s is not simply incredible, but miraculous.

Survival came at a cost, though. Young Will could expect to grow up looking much older than his years. Living hand to mouth in wretched conditions, silk workers were "more machines than active livers." They wore "grave and sorrowful countenances," their faces casting long shadows of deprivation. Rarely earning enough to pay more than their rent, they were constantly in debt. One local official called them, candidly, "miserable objects of charity." Mothers were known to be half-naked and "ashamed to appear in the streets," having sold their clothing to pay for bread. The population was so malnourished on the whole that a visiting hygienist would label the silk workers "a stunted, puny race." Said Sir Thomas Fowell Buxton, an advocate for their welfare, "It is not that some starve, but that so many are on the verge of starvation—it is not that a few suffer, but that so few escape."

Yet escaping a life of misery and finding fortune by making silk was one of the hallmarks of the silk workers' cultural history. Spitalfields did not start out as an almost anarchical and dangerous district, but as a courageous and ambitious community, where French Protestant silk weavers, fleeing religious persecution in France during the sixteenth and seventeenth centuries, introduced the silk industry to England and made silk a means for success under the Crown.

Back then, Spitalfields had been part of the countryside beyond the walls of London. An expanse of fields around an old medieval hospital, St. Mary's Spital, the area offered succor to travelers coming to and from the city, and when the French began to seek asylum in England, they found solace here in a settlement of "strangers" (i.e., foreigners) and "nonconformists" (i.e., Protestants) that had taken root on the outskirts.

The first wave of French men and women arrived in 1572, after the

St. Bartholomew's Day massacre in Paris, in which so many Protestants were murdered in the streets that the Seine flowed red with blood. Two decades later Henry the Great blessedly granted religious freedom to all French citizens through the Edict of Nantes, but French Protestants, still fearing for their lives, continued to leave in small numbers, often under the cover of darkness to avoid being caught, many following those who had successfully fled to England. Known to history as the Huguenots (possibly from the French *huguon,* meaning "one who walks by night"), their arrivals on the British coastline escalated exponentially after 1685, when Henry's grandson, Louis XIV, revoked the Edict of Nantes and reignited the effort to make France a purely Catholic nation. The attacks on the Huguenots were even bloodier and more severe than those of a century before. One of the king's missionaries bragged that sixty thousand men in the Bordeaux region alone had been suspended by ropes or suffocated with smoke until they "willingly" converted to Catholicism. (Those who did not convert were killed.)

Thousands of Huguenots fled France with only their skills and their faith. By 1700 a quarter of a million of them had left their homeland for other countries, so many taking refuge in England, at least forty thousand, that the word *refugee* entered the English language. Children were secreted in barrels on ships; parents hid themselves among cargo. Others crossed the channel in fishing boats, washing up along Britain's southeastern coast, cold, hungry, and desperate to get to London, where they could find sanctuary with other French immigrants and barter their valuable silk-making knowledge. An estimated fifteen thousand Huguenots arrived in London in 1687 alone, and the pleasant fields around St. Mary's Spital—the Spital's fields—succumbed to an explosion of development. The same kind of silk weavers' cottages that had graced the French countryside were soon lining newly built roads outside of the British capital.

As they rebuilt their lives in a foreign country, these Huguenot families—some of whom included Skinner's ancestors according to stories he heard—found salvation in silk. Prior to their arrival, there was no silk industry in England. A few "sylkewymmen" had mastered the art of making silk stockings, but that was nothing compared to the weaving of taffetas, velvets, and satins that the Huguenots introduced. They themselves had learned the secrets of making silk from the Italians, the finest weavers since the Renaissance. When France invaded northern Italy in 1521, victorious Frenchmen brought back with them a group of Milanese silk weavers to teach the French working class—the growing Protestant population—how to weave silk. By virtue of their intense work ethic, believing that labor promoted salvation, the Huguenots made remarkable inroads in the ancient art and presently began creating their own masterful silks. By 1685 their skills were so far advanced that they had even surpassed the Italians, and the brilliant silks that the Huguenots wove dictated much of European fashion. The Huguenots arguably created haute couture, which in the seventeenth century was not about designers but fabrics—their patterns, blends, and weight—and they helped establish a culture of fashion that meant "more to France than the gold mines of Peru to Spain." Consequently the exodus of Huguenots following the revocation of the Edict of Nantes was catastrophic for the kingdom; Louis XIV's action "nearly annihilated the silk manufacture in France." But it elevated the silk manufacture of England to unprecedented heights.

While the majority of Huguenots were silk workers, others were skillful in trades just as enterprising, and when tens of thousands of them began contributing to England's economy they advanced industries such as medicine, mathematics, goldsmithing, printing, and banking. Willing to work as hard as necessary to survive, they were powerful pioneers. Indeed, so influential was their industriousness and so exceptional their talents that those who settled in England, in Spitalfields and elsewhere, have been credited with helping to lay the foundation for Britain to become leader of the industrialized world.

One of the first steps toward this achievement involved silk. Because of the Huguenots, Britain stopped losing thousands of pounds each year to the French market for silk and became, incredibly, a competitor in the trade. Naturally this drew the attention of entrepreneurs looking for investment opportunities, and the most significant result was England's first textile mill. The savvy London merchant Sir Thomas Lombe observed that the primary expense of this growing industry was silk thread, which nobody in Britain yet manufactured. Until something was done about this, silk weavers would remain woefully dependent on the Continent for their supply of this essential material. And so Lombe, who had heard about silk mills in Europe, set out to build one in England.

First, though, he had to figure out how such a mill was constructed. In what was perhaps the first British attempt at industrial espionage, Lombe sent his nephew John, an adventurous young man "whose head [was] well turned for the mechanics," to Italy. Through bribery John Lombe gained access to a thread mill in Piedmont and made mental notes of everything he saw. When authorities discovered what he was up to, they set out to kill him, but he managed to escape on an English ship. Upon returning home, he designed Britain's first silk mill for his uncle, and it went up in the town of Derby, in 1717, to great success. Finally, Spitalfields weavers had an alternative to expensive imported thread.

After the disgrace in Piedmont the king of Sardinia was apparently "so incensed" that "he made it death" for any unauthorized person to uncover the invention of a machine in his kingdom or "to attempt to carry it out of the dominion." He wasn't the only one to clamp down on spies. In London, two years after Derby began producing silk thread with its copied Italian machinery, Parliament enacted a series of laws against the emigration of artisans, and it became illegal for any weaver, thrower, or dyer to leave the country or even travel abroad. Presumably the new laws would prevent any technology that the British might develop from falling into the hands of competitors, while ensuring that skilled workers couldn't be lured away by better prospects. As a result, those in Spitalfields were trapped. Only fifty years earlier it had been illegal for French silk workers to escape France; now it was illegal for their descendants to leave England!

The next chapter in Spitalfields' history thus began, a sad demise over the course of the eighteenth century. Although silk remained the most desirable fabric for those who could afford it, demand for silk declined after 1700, when Indian calicoes became the rage. Meanwhile the number of weavers had steadily increased as Huguenot families continued to grow, producing more weavers than there was demand for their products. The government had also instituted some protective acts that were more harmful than helpful. For instance, Parliament put such restrictions on the importation of foreign silks, lest they compete with local sales, that a wildly successful smuggling ring had developed along the coast. On the beaches where the Huguenots had once landed, contraband silks from France were now regularly coming ashore. The smugglers made a fortune, while the silk weavers in Spitalfields lost yet more business.

Unemployment increased, as well as frustration. There simply wasn't enough work to go around and not enough money to be made. Moreover, journeymen weavers increasingly felt that their employers, master weavers who managed the looms and assigned the jobs, were taking advantage of them, paying less and less as the years went by, while the masters disregarded loyalty because they too had to make a living. In the 1760s Spitalfields became a scene of violence. Journeymen rioted on several occasions, smashing windows, breaking apart looms, slashing the silk *in* the looms, and burning effigies of their masters in the streets. But the violence actually restored a simulacrum of peace in the district since it brought about a famous resolution in 1773, the first so-called Spitalfields Act, which fixed pay rates so that masters were forced to provide wages within a specified range.

After decades of struggle there was finally a minimum wage that the masters had to honor, but there was also now a maximum wage, or ceiling, which a master could not exceed when paying an employee. This ceiling was in place to prevent favoritism, but it made advancement in the trade impossible. Nor did the Act stop unemployment, foreign competition, or insidious undercutting. If two or more journeymen were vying for a job, or "web," a master weaver would still hire the individual who agreed to work for the fewest shillings within the specified rates. The new system even decreased the amount of webs being offered, since numerous masters left London in disgust over the regulations. Talent could not be rewarded, and no one could expect to make much of a living.

By 1802, when Skinner's mother was born, Spitalfields, the undisputed silk capital of the country, was also the most hopeless borough in the land. Weavers were no freer than the caged birds they kept, with just as little chance of being heard beyond the walls of their garrets. The thrift of old had faded, the earnestness of purpose had disappeared, and "the religious fervor which had distinguished the original Huguenot refugees [had] entirely died out." Spitalfields had become a faithless, poor, disease-ridden district, with no help whatsoever from the city. In 1806 a local silk manufacturer appealed to Samuel Whitbread, Esq., a member of Parliament, to do something, pointing out (as if Whitbread didn't already know), "This is the only district completely *shut out* from the benefits arising from the *spirit* of the poor laws. . . . Here *the poor literally support the poor,* and . . . [are] left to struggle on under an accumulation of extreme misery, unknown in any part of the country."

And yet the most beautiful silks imaginable were being transported from the streets of Spitalfields to the outside world. "Spitalfields silks" lined the walls of manor houses in the country, graced the figures of young ladies at court, and decorated the bedrooms of royalty. Exported to Europe, America, and the British colonies, they were internationally known and by this point had been revered for more than two hundred years. To be "as saucy as a Spitalfields weaver" meant to be proud of one's work. As late as midcentury Herman Melville would deride his manuscript of *Moby-Dick* as being anything but a popular work of art, saying that it was "not a piece of fine feminine Spitalfields silk."

In theory, the silk industry was England's most glamorous and "exotic" trade, but it was also by this time the most backward. Once the harbinger of the Industrial Revolution, silk had devolved into its bastard child, while cotton had steadily risen to become the nation's preeminent industry. Unfettered by tradition or artistic integrity, the cotton industry encouraged innovation and Richard Arkwright, for one, developed in this environment the water-powered spinning frame, which "in a single stroke . . . made the skilled hand spinner obsolete." If at any point the laws against the emigration of artisans were most strictly enforced, it was during the reign of British cotton when so many industrial advances occurred. And yet, just as the Huguenots once illegally left their own country, so too did an Englishman named Samuel Slater, who stole away to America in 1792 with the secrets of Arkwright's invention tucked away in his head. Slater wasn't escaping a life of misery but seizing an opportunity, and, because of him, the Industrial Revolution crossed the Atlantic and America commenced down the path to becoming an industrialized nation. While Americans later hailed the arrival of Slater, those in Britain slammed him as "Slater the Traitor." His story became a cautionary tale to manufacturers but an exemplary one to unsung laborers, demonstrating how valuable was their knowledge if they dared to share it.

In 1824, the year Mrs. Skinner became pregnant with Will, a great deal changed for the silk workers. The Spitalfields Act and its subsequent amendments (one of which extended protection to women weavers) were repealed to create a freer marketplace, while the ban on imported silk goods was lifted to spur competition. And the laws against the emigration of artisans were finally, and blessedly, stricken down, the ruling citing in part that "it was inexpedient to irritate the feelings of a valuable order of men by denying them the liberty of travelling which everybody else enjoyed."

Nobody actively tried to help the Spitalfields silk workers. There was no monetary relief from the government or the city. Officials simply wanted them to bring in more business, and, as a result of the actions just described, the silk workers did. When Skinner was a toddler, neighborhood looms were working feverishly to keep pace with all the new competition. They consumed a hundred times more silk thread than before. His mother, if given a web, probably worked harder than she ever had growing up. But that wasn't the whole picture. Even with the increase in production, only a third of the 100,000 people dependent on the silk trade in Spitalfields were employed in 1829. Furthermore, the average weekly earning was 9 shillings—in modern terms, the equivalent of about $65—for nearly eighty hours of work.

Young Will's first escape from the fate of his family occurred at about the age of eight, when he was sent to live with two of his father's sisters, Eleanor and Mary, to be their errand boy. This would have been a convenient way for his parents, who were welcoming their fourth child, to lower expenses at home while earning extra income from their son's employment elsewhere. Though perhaps unsettling, the move was a blessing for the boy. He was suddenly out of the confining garret, meeting people, making purchases, delivering goods, and, most exciting of all, *pocketing change*. One of Skinner's favorite paintings that he owned as an adult was *Counting Up* by J. G. Brown. The oil on canvas depicts a ragged shoeshine boy totaling copper and silver coins on a board before him, evidently "counting up" his day's earnings. The painting reminded Skinner of his boyhood and the tactile pleasure of a coin sitting in his palm.

Eleanor, known as Ellen, was a dressmaker who ran a small shop with Mary in a nearby parish. They seem to have been the most enterprising of John Skinner's siblings. (Another brother, William—after whom, presumably, young Will was named—was described as "never doing anything" but sitting around trying to look handsome.) Like John, Ellen and Mary had been "well-educated," or at least better educated than most, because someone clearly taught these women the classics. Unlike Sarah Skinner, who was illiterate and had to sign her marriage certificate with an X, Ellen and Mary could read and write with facility. According to one of Skinner's sons, "It was these aunts who persuaded Father to read Shakespeare."

Ostensibly, young Will had already learned to read by the time he moved in with his aunts. Since his mother certainly hadn't taught him, he may have learned to read from his father or possibly at a Sunday school. Such schools were not intended initially to teach Christian children the ways of their Lord; they were invented to teach laboring children, on their one day off, to read and maybe write well enough to sign their names. For the most part, though, Skinner's education wasn't in a classroom, but in the silk business, where, said a friend of his, "the curriculum is thorough, and the graduate can only get through by sleeping under the looms."

As a grown man Skinner was very self-conscious about his lack of formal study. He reprimanded his eldest son for not taking education seriously and was eager that the boy go to university: "It is my strong hope & desire that you will go through college, so that you can always feel you are an educated man." Influenced as much by his mother's illiteracy as by the advantages his aunts enjoyed, thanks to their accomplishments, Skinner supported education for girls and young ladies as well, at a time when this was not only unpopular but widely discouraged. A reporter recalled being "vividly" struck by Mr. Skinner's unusual belief that, "If my wife and daughters think a girl ought to have an education, she shall have it."

Of the two maiden aunts, Skinner was closer to the younger one, Ellen. She would have been about twenty-two, but this was not a young age in Spitalfields, especially for an unmarried woman. (Mrs. Skinner had been betrothed at seventeen.) In her few surviving letters, Ellen comes off as a tender, quiet woman who adored the company of children and who deeply appreciated even the smallest gestures. Given Skinner's lasting affinity for her, she had a much needed influence on him as a boy. By the time he went to live with her, he would already have developed some of his less favorable attributes: stubbornness, impatience, impulsiveness, and forcefulness. No doubt he was a very headstrong child, prone to outbursts, filled with pent-up energy, and probably bored to the point that he was on the verge of becoming a real troublemaker.

Moving into a household of adults could have been disastrous. As a lone child he could easily have been abused, but nothing of the kind seems to have happened. On the contrary, although taken in as a worker, he found at his aunts' a place of refuge, where he was challenged daily with new tasks, such as handling orders and money and learning about things other than silk. Ellen was a businesswoman, intelligent and articulate, and Will seems to have found in her a mentor that neither of his parents could be.

Within a year or two, however, at about the age of ten, he was old enough to work in the dyehouse where his father was employed. This meant that he could earn more money for his parents, but it also meant that he would have to leave his aunts' house. They couldn't afford to board him if he wasn't assisting them in their business. So Will moved back in with his mother and father and his now five younger siblings. Once more, he awoke each day to the tolling of the Christ Church bell, but instead of setting up at the spinning wheel next to his mother at her loom in the garret, he left the house with his father and walked through the early-morning streets, littered with detritus and heavy with London fog, to Vallentine's Dye Works on Blossom Street.

He started the habit of carrying a book in his pocket to memorize from daily, and there's no record of his father protesting, even when Will supposedly spent a portion of his earnings at the penny stand for more things to read. He devoured the famous, such as Lord Byron and Alexander Pope, whose *Essay on Man* he came to know so well that he considered it "a friend." Who knows whether Mr. Skinner ever told his wife the family was losing income on a regular basis to books. This may have been a secret the father kept for his son. Sarah Skinner would hardly have tolerated such a ridiculous and selfish habit, and this may have been another reason Will kept his books in his pockets: to hide them.

One may surmise that Will Skinner was a powerfully intelligent youth, voracious in his appetite for knowledge and almost militant in his eagerness to learn. How many children carry around books not simply to read but to memorize? As if afraid that at any moment his books might be taken from him. As if determined to be able to prove, anywhere, anytime, that he was in fact smart. He *was* smart, of course, and that was part of his problem. By the age of nine he was smarter than his mother. Every year thereafter his vocabulary grew bigger and his frame of reference wider, and he developed an intolerance of *her* "selfish" habits that boiled within him.

Although her hard work was impressive, Mrs. Skinner had some critical weakness that alienated her eldest boy, and that weakness may very well have been drinking—or abuse or gambling brought on by the drinking. In Spitalfields "drunkenness . . . [was] the regular and normal state of affairs," and alcoholism passed down through the generations as dependably as weaving and dyeing. Prior to the mid-nineteenth century, most of the water in London was too foul for consumption (one citizen described "highly-coloured deposits" in it), so just about everyone drank something else. In Spitalfields the cheapest two drinks were gin and beer. Will grew up on the stuff. "At this time," wrote a silk broker, "it was the daily custom for the London brewers to send round porter to the weaver's houses at noon." His mother would have welcomed the delivery, not only because it helped fill up her and the children's stomachs, but it provided something to look forward to at midday other than bread. "Fancy yourself," Charles Dickens remembered being told while on a tour of the district, "stewed up in a stifling room all day; imagine the lassitude into which your whole frame would collapse after fourteen hours' mere inhalation of a stale, bad atmosphere—to say nothing of fourteen hours' monotonous work in addition; and consider what stern self-denial it would require to refrain from some stimulant—a glass of bad gin, perhaps—if you could get it."

By eleven or twelve Skinner was slipping away at night to Drury Lane and Covent Garden, London's most famous theaters, to watch whatever production of Shakespeare was then on stage. His favorite actor was William Charles Macready, who produced and starred in one of the most legendary productions of *Othello*. When the curtain rose, Will was instantly transported to Renaissance Venice, with the Rialto Bridge arching in front of him, gondolas passing beneath it, and the Doge's Palace rising imperially in the background. This was not Spitalfields. This was nothing that Will (or most members of the audience) had ever seen. Will was so taken by the experience and so mesmerized by Macready that, like an actor himself, he studied Macready's every move and gesture, every pause and exclamation. Craving that sense of command, that dramatic ability to "[merge] intellect and passion into energetic purpose," he looked to Macready—and Shakespeare—to teach him how to act like a gentleman and lead like a senator. Indeed he would later credit the stage as the source of "much of his early education." It is impossible to say what Will's dreams were at this time, but they were certainly inspired by Macready and the beauty and loftiness of *Othello,* and they had little to do with the anonymous life of a silk worker in London. Will replayed the actor's scenes in his mind to the point where, even in his seventies, he could vividly recall them and reenact them for others. "Shall we ever forget," reminisced one of his friends in 1902, "that evening when he stood up in the corner of Mr. Hubbard's parlor and recited long passages from *Othello* in order to show us the style of Macready?"

Equally as affecting for Skinner was the indelible and decidedly unpoetic influence of William Cobbett. Cobbett was arguably the most radical, celebrated, and vilified journalist in pre-Victorian England. The son of an uneducated farmer, with neither money nor social connections, he became as familiar to the country as the king after founding the *Political Register,* a highly controversial newspaper that sold throughout England from 1803 until 1835. Famously antiestablishment, Cobbett had a "strong and implacable hatred of oppression of all sorts." He called the Lords a "prodigious band of spungers, living upon the labor of the industrious part of the community." He slammed the Bank of England as having exacerbated the problem of forgery by printing easily forgeable notes and accused it of being the murderer of all those who had hanged. He railed against increases in taxation, the high price of corn, and the soaring national debt as "a mass of blunders that covered [the] country in misery." He was fearless in speaking out for the workingman and made his paper the cheapest rag in town— once printing an edition that cost just 2 pence—so the workingman could afford it. He vowed to fight against injustice "until the last hour of [his] life."

To young boys like Will Skinner, Cobbett was a hero. He was a fighter and a survivor who couldn't care less what the authorities thought of him. He rallied back from bankruptcy and near total ruin not once, but several times, demonstrating that no obstacle was too great and no goal unattainable. Willing to "stand alone" and "never bend," he advised young men (in his book entitled *Cobbett's Advice to Young Men*) to do the same, letting no distinction of rank, birth, or wealth separate them from their aspirations. Of additional significance, Cobbett was wildly imperfect. Hypocritical, arrogant, and self-serving, he was by no means a saint.

Will too was hotheaded and impatient, and the older he got the more he felt he was right about everything. He cussed and swore with the best of them, unleashing foul language when frustrated, thwarted, or disappointed. Although capable of intense concentration and possessing great inner strength, he knew all about Cobbett's "turbulent passions" and, like this living legend, made enemies. Years and years later, when Skinner's eldest son, then a grown man, visited London on his own and sought out an old acquaintance (possibly an older relative) of his father, he was met with a door slammed in the face. "I know just who you are," said this person, "and you're not coming in."

Suffocating in London's East End, Skinner as a child took solace in the successes of Cobbett, and one cannot underestimate the impact that Cobbett's life had on his developing mind. Skinner would name his first son William Cobbett Skinner, and when, in his twilight, Skinner had to share a topic with a group of New England men at a private club, he chose "William Cobbett." For Skinner to speak about someone who had once proclaimed "I hate the United States and all their mean and hypocritical system of rule" to a group of Puritan descendants was both impolitic and potentially insulting. In the spirit of his boyhood hero, it was also provocative, challenging, and audacious.

The only stability Skinner appears to have had as a youth was found in books. His parents' circumstances were constantly shifting. By the time he was ten they were no longer living in Vine Court but moving around almost every year—a clear indication of economic distress. The neighborhoods grew worse with each move, many of the buildings they inhabited of such decrepitude that the city would demolish them in another ten or fifteen years. One address placed the family smack in the heart of the Old Nichol, a parish that "suffered from a death rate four times the national average." There was no church in this parish, just seventeen alehouses (and who knows how many gin shops) offering a different form of religion to its eight thousand inhabitants. The *Illustrated London News* described the Old Nichol as "a neighborhood as foul as can be discovered in the civilized world, [its] population, huddled in dark cellars, ruined garrets, bare and blackened rooms, teeming with disease and death, and without the most ordinary observations of decency or cleanliness, depressed almost to the last stage of human endurance."

After the Old Nichol the family moved to Whitechapel, familiar to history as the haunt of Jack the Ripper in 1888. Yet Whitechapel had long before cemented its reputation as a den of unrepentant vice, particularly about the streets of Flower and Dean, on a stretch that came to be called "the evil quarter-mile," from which the Skinners lived just two blocks. Prostitution was rampant, offering what was probably the most reliable pay a woman could expect in the East End. Little wonder that sixty brothels, with more than a thousand prostitutes, would eventually spring up in this area.

By the time the Skinners moved into Whitechapel, when Will was around fourteen, the number of employed weavers in Spitalfields had sunk to record lows. Of the twenty thousand looms in operation in 1824, fewer than half were still employed. Landlords continuously turned away silk workers, knowing full well they couldn't pay rent. And yet the majority of Spitalfields residents never left the district. They were poor, yes, but "greatly attached to their neighborhood," and "many old men [were] known not to have travelled during their long lives farther than King's-cross on one side and London-bridge on the other"—in other words, less than two miles in either direction.

As a result, the idea of emigrating to another country was not simply very rare but virtually unthinkable. Emigration symbolized a "virtual death" in the early nineteenth century. Those who left for life in another country knew that there would be little chance of seeing or communicating with loved ones back home ever again. Indeed the Irish used to hold wakes for people who emigrated, and Italian priests administered special benedictions. Said Cobbett himself, "There was something so powerful in the thought of country, and neighborhood, and home, and friends, there was something so strong in the numerous and united ties . . . that to tear oneself away nearly approached to the separating of the soul from the body."

Yet Will knew that some people got away. Cobbett, for one, had escaped imprisonment at one point by exiling himself in America for two years. And much closer to home, a silk dyer twelve years Will's senior, Edward Vallentine, had left Spitalfields for America in the summer of 1838. Vallentine's father owned the dye works where Will and his father worked, and it's reasonable to assume that Edward may have contributed, at least marginally, to Will's apprenticeship. Certainly the younger men knew each other well and shared a lot in common. They were both sons of dyers, and they both worked with their fathers in the same shop. They were both raised in the East End and baptized in the same church (Christ Church, Spitalfields). They were both from families of silk workers who had been in the area for generations, and they both claimed to be descended from the Huguenots, a mark of high honor in their circle.

Although the Huguenots had long since integrated with the English by the time Will and Edward were boys, vestiges of the old community were everywhere around them. The French were the ones who had introduced the cultivation of songbirds as well as gardening to Spitalfields. Blossom Street, Flower Street, Vine Court—all had been named by the Huguenots, who had aspired to create a "garden suburb." Rather ironically the Bank of England, the nemesis of most nineteenth-century weavers, had in fact been built up by a group of Huguenots, and a Huguenot paper manufacturer printed all of England's banknotes. Regardless of whether Skinner was actually descended from Spitalfields' original weavers, he always believed that "he had some French blood in his veins," and as a boy of little significance to the world, the connection made him feel important, perhaps even inspired. Long ago the Huguenots had left their homeland as well, willing to risk everything for freedom.

Edward didn't sail alone; he braved the Atlantic with a friend, Lewis Leigh, also a silk dyer. There must have been a great deal of chatter about whether Edward and Lewis would make it—whether they'd live through the journey, whether they'd survive in America. Given that they were almost certainly the first people Will had ever known to leave Spitalfields, he may have accompanied them down to the docks, helped them find their ship, and watched with others as the *President* left port and sailed down the Thames to the sea. Afterward, Edward's absence in the dyehouse would have been quite apparent. *The boss's son has gone to America.* Rolling up his shirtsleeves as usual, washing skeins and preparing vats of dye, Will must have thought about that a lot.

Six years later, Lewis was running his own dyehouse in Connecticut, and Edward was successfully established in Northampton, Massachusetts, the town that was "fast becoming the focus of the [New England] silk industry," with its abundant groves of mulberry trees and the promise of homegrown silk. Even more than Leigh, Vallentine was "remarkably" adept at "making a permanent black dye," and his business had grown to the point that he could no longer continue without qualified help. He needed a foreman and sent word to his father to send someone over.

No record remains of what exactly happened next, other than the simple notation, published in a biographical sketch, "William came to the United States to take the position." From this one might infer that Will was not the finest dyer in James Vallentine's dyehouse. After all, James could not have afforded to lose such talent. Yet Will "was noted for having a very good eye for color," and at age twenty was more than qualified to be a foreman, having been in the silk business for fourteen years. He would have been a logical choice for the post too on account of his intelligence, relative youth, marital status (still single), and unapologetic ambition. Said one relative, "Every time he had a chance to learn something he took advantage of it." At five-foot-ten he towered over most men in Spitalfields (who averaged five-foot-six), and with his dark complexion and black eyes, even his appearance burned with intensity. When James Vallentine received his son's request from America, he may have instantly thought of Will and even welcomed the excuse to discharge this competent but formidable and challenging young man.

Restless as Will was, accepting the position and deciding to leave could not have been easy. A lot had changed in his life over the past few years. For one, his father had died, and he had become the male head of the family, responsible for the welfare of his mother and six younger siblings. As the eldest son he was supposed to assume his father's place at the dyehouse, improve on it if he could, and generally look after the rest. Desertion on his part would be disastrous to what little security the family had. Moreover, leaving would mean asking his younger brother George, age seventeen, to take over as head of the family. George was already working at the dyehouse, as was their still younger brother, fourteen-year-old Thomas, but they did not yet share Will's seniority. Further, though his siblings were taking up their own mantles, they were simply less schooled in life than he was. They were, and always had been, more dependent. And some of them still had a lot of growing up to do in this very hostile environment. Apart from George and Thomas, there were Mary, fifteen; Betsy, ten; Sarah, eight; and Eleanor, who was just five.

If later behavior is any indication, Will made his decision quickly, instinctively. He may have sought counsel from Aunt Ellen or discussed the proposal with George, with whom he was very close, but having been raised to be self-reliant, he most likely made up his mind on his own. It's almost unimaginable that Mrs. Skinner would have supported her son's departure, especially after her husband's death, but John Skinner *was* dead, and whatever anchor he'd provided for the family had been sufficiently unmoored. In Will's decision one senses a desperation not only to get away from Spitalfields but also, finally, to get away from his mother. He wasn't the last to child to desert her, and in fact his emigration forged a path for the others to follow. Within the next five years four more of the Skinner children would leave home: George, Thomas, and Sarah would follow Will to the United States, and Betsy would move in with Aunt Ellen to apprentice as a dressmaker. Only Mary and Eleanor, it seems, remained behind with their mother. What became of them is unknown.

Will booked passage on the packet-ship *Toronto,* which set sail for New York on June 13, 1845. His ticket cost between three and six guineas—probably closer to three, as plenty of space was available in steerage for that particular crossing. Since he would not have had an extra three guineas lying about (that was more than £3, or more than $2,000 in today's dollars), Edward or James Vallentine likely paid the fare for Will to repay in America under Edward's employ. If that was the case, Will was about to enter a financial position that was far worse than any he'd known: in debt that was completely over his head. But he was prepared for whatever labor he might endure to free his name. Hard work, thanks to his mother, did not scare him.

The minute he stepped on that boat at the St. Katharine docks he turned his back on his childhood and faced, alone, much more than an open sea. What he felt at that moment remains a mystery. He was not one to pour his heart out on paper. He never kept a diary, and no account remains of his actual departure. Nevertheless he was not one to second-guess a decision, question his resolve, or look back. In all of his surviving papers he only once reflects on a moment in the past—the birth of his first child—and he does this only briefly when she turns forty-two. It is a rare, sentimental detour that lasts two sentences in a letter and ends abruptly with the words "but enough—." He was not raised to dwell on attachments; he was raised to survive.

The story goes that Skinner charmed the captain, Edward G. Tinker, into throwing a line off the stern in calm weather so that he might "take a bath" in the wake of the ship as it sailed along. It's a great story, one that paints him as an adventurous, carefree youth squeezing every moment out of life. Of course, it's probably apocryphal, but it made for good chatter and was certainly more innocent than what he was probably doing: hanging out with the crew ("the hardest kind of men").

Years later Skinner enjoyed seeing his grandchildren's eyes as wide as saucers as he talked about swimming in the middle of the Atlantic Ocean. What a vigorous young man he was! How inspirational, how independent! His fancied plunge into the waters reflected exactly the image he wished to perpetuate. He wasn't the lonely, unhappy young man risking everything for God knew what, desperate to escape an anonymous, wretched life. He was the intrepid young Englishman, daring to break out of a mold and follow in the footsteps of so many brave men before him. He was a dreamer and a doer, crossing the ocean with a book in his pocket, a small bag at his side, and nothing more valuable than the knowledge in his head.

Chapter Five

Will may not have "bathed" in open water, but his journey across the ocean was nevertheless eventful. The North Atlantic poses stiff challenges to any vessel that dares it, and prior to the age of steam this was especially true. In 1845 the seamen of the *Toronto* would have "fought their way . . . mile by mile" against the prevailing westerly winds, and those in steerage, like Skinner, would have suffered the battle in an airless, fetid cabin belowdecks. To make matters worse, Skinner was prone to seasickness—"a horrible feeling," he once wrote. On a later voyage he was quite frank about the nausea: "The air is so bad in the cabin I must now go on deck and put my finger down my throat and vomit again."

The *Toronto* was a member of the Black X line, "the only regular line of packets for New York," praised an advertisement in the London *Times*. She was a three-masted square-rigger weighing 630 tons, and in full sail she looked "very fine," to use Will's expression. By modern standards she was but a speck of a ship—the *Titanic* weighed over 46,000 tons—but the *Toronto* was actually large for her class, not to mention dependable and well known. On a legendary run from New

York to Portsmouth she made the 3,500-mile journey in just fourteen days. Most trips, however, took about a month. Unfortunately for Will, his crossing took a week longer than that, due to icebergs off the coast of Newfoundland that hindered progress and added to the danger. Indeed at the beginning of July Captain Tinker had to rescue the crew of a schooner, along with three thousand fish in its hold, presumably because the ship, like others before it, had "struck upon the ice." This would have created tremendous excitement on board the *Toronto*, particularly for those in steerage, where all of the unexpected guests would have been placed.

Tinker, a genial captain with bushy eyebrows and deepening crow's feet who hailed from Lyme, Connecticut, was likely the first Yankee Will ever met. Passage aboard the *Toronto* was certainly his first American experience. The ship itself was built on the East River in New York, outfitted with an American crew, and governed by the Puritan mandates of its New England owners. This meant, for instance, that it was a temperance ship, which must have been a shocking revelation to someone used to subsisting on ale. Another revelation would have been the ship's accommodations.

Aft of the mainmast were the first-class cabins, with gold decor and spacious berths, but Will didn't see anything so fine. Upon boarding the ship he was taken in the opposite direction, toward the cow house and chicken coops and led below to the cargo hold. Here, freshly cut, unfinished boards had been nailed to the sides of the ship in three rows, one above the other, providing just enough shelf space for thirty-seven passengers to sleep on—the number of people traveling in steerage on this journey. Immigrants at this time weren't yet big business. In 1845 most ships made money the old-fashioned way: transporting merchandise. Not that this made conditions much more pleasant. Regular cargo weighed a ship down, and "a deep ship, will, very probably, under ordinary circumstances, be very wet and uncomfortable, and the people will live up to their knees in water."

Steerage was a rank, "gloomy place." As with a silk weaver's garret, one needed a ladder to get to it, only rather than climb up, one climbed down, through the main hatch. Will was granted ten square feet of space to occupy, including his "sleeping shelf." Had he been able to put his feet on the floor, his head would have been two inches from the ceiling. As it was, there was no place to stand. An aisle about three feet wide divided the rows of boards, but one didn't walk through this aisle so much as crawl over it. Here were people's trunks, baskets, and bags, drenched in seawater that poured in from above. There was no separation of single men and women. There was no privacy. One relieved oneself in a pot or a corner. Daylight filtered down through the main hatch, when it was open, and at night the place was illuminated, if at all, by "a dip-candle hanging here and there in a horn lantern from the deck beams."

When Will sailed, those in steerage were expected to bring their own cookware and provisions, but most couldn't afford to buy a month's worth of food in advance. As a result, each received seven pounds of rice, potatoes, or flour per week, which was "supplied uncooked and . . . intended as no more than an insurance against starvation." Steerage passengers, responsible for cooking their own food, were allotted an open stove (more like a raised pit) on deck near the "farmyard." Given that there was just one stove for thirty-seven people and its unprotected fire was continually drowned out by the elements, no one enjoyed hot meals. The ship was also supposed to supply the steerage passengers with fresh water, but the prescribed allowance, often kept in old turpentine barrels, was horribly discolored when drawn and, as described by an earlier traveler, could have "[such] a rancid smell that to be in the same neighborhood was enough to turn one's stomach." The crew frequently smuggled liquor on board through a fruit vendor at the St. Katharine docks, and one can fairly assume that twenty-year-old Skinner, who distrusted water to begin with, bartered with them for some of their stash. Indeed the next time he crossed the Atlantic he took care to befriend members of the crew rather than anyone in his compartment.

There wasn't much to do on the *Toronto* other than daydream, swap stories, and play cards. This was torture for Will. He was trained to work, not sit still, and having nothing to do made him "uneasy" and "as nervous as can be." Finally, after five weeks at sea, the *Toronto* approached land, and one can hardly imagine the interest with which passengers crowded the railing to see American soil. In 1848 another immigrant described what it felt like to enter New York Bay: "Glorious morning! To the right is Long Island; to the left is Jersey State. What a fine country! Here at last is America. Yonder is Sandy Hook, with a lighthouse. What neat wooden cots by the water's edge! Observe those forests of trees, with a house here and there peeping through the foliage. The sight now before us compensates for all our toil and trouble."

Will and his companions enjoyed a glorious morning the day of their arrival. The sun shone bright and hot, but the city itself was far from glistening, and the air smelled of sulfur. The *Toronto* had arrived on Monday, July 21, 1845, two days after an explosion in a warehouse on Broad Street had shaken New York City like an earthquake, triggering the worst conflagration in a decade. Some three hundred buildings at the tip of Manhattan had been destroyed, and fires were still burning in more than twenty places when the *Toronto* passed through the Narrows. The piers along South Street were, however, unaffected, and the packet docked without incident, at which point Will disembarked to find the immediate vicinity deserted since everyone had flocked to the "burnt district." Consequently those in steerage walked off the boat unmolested by the usual crowd of hucksters. And as immigrant processing wouldn't begin until the following year, when ports became overwhelmed with refugees from Ireland, there were no officials waiting either. Will was at liberty to head wherever he pleased.

The fire wasn't the only story of the day. Will had arrived during a heat wave that had killed more than two hundred people in the preceding week. And then there was the storm. His first night in America was interrupted by "violent thunder" along with a torrential downpour. George Templeton Strong recorded in his diary that he had "rarely seen

lightning so continuous or vivid." Years earlier, when Cobbett was living in the States, he noted that thunder and lightning in America were
"tremendous" compared to what they were in England. Cobbett's wife
was "very much afraid" of American storms, and, having absolutely no
acquaintance with America, Will found himself dealing with not only
unfamiliar territory but alarming and harrowing weather.

This was hardly an auspicious beginning to life in the New World.
Yet the rain cooled off the city, dampened many of the burning embers,
and freshened the air. Then, following the storm, a full moon shone
down on the cobblestone streets, illuminating the rooftops and clean
brick façades (so unlike blackened London) and, much like a sunrise at
sea, as Will once described, made a "beautiful sight."

From New York, Will trekked up the coast to Boston and then took a
series of stages toward the western part of Massachusetts, finally alight-
ing in the small town of Northampton, several days later. In Northampton, he went looking for Vallentine and found him two miles farther
north, in a place called Broughton's Meadow.

Perhaps to Will's surprise, Vallentine was no longer just a silk dyer.
He was a silk *manufacturer,* with a silk mill that towered over the stagecoach road. Will, though, was used to the Vallentines running things.
After all, they owned the dyehouse in Spitalfields. They had money.
What may have caused greater shock, at least initially, was the rest of
Broughton's Meadow. In every direction lay a rough, rural landscape
of scruffy fields, entangled brush, and stubby trees. Sloping hills in the
distance penned in the interior, and only a handful of houses could
be seen, dotting unmarked, coarse country roads. The isolation and
solitude, the hot summer sun beating off the dirt, the flies, the flowers,
and the independence of it all might have been paradise to some, but
to a young man from the center of the industrialized world this must
have seemed like a sort of exile. Skinner was as far from home as he
could possibly be.

Although more likely to hear a cricket than a loom, Skinner had in fact landed in an area renowned for its influence on the American silk industry. There were three silk mills in Broughton's Meadow: one owned by Vallentine, one owned by a community of utopians who called themselves the Northampton Association of Education and Industry, and one owned by a former president of this community, Captain Joseph Conant. In the United States at this time, silk mills could be found in Massachusetts, Connecticut, New York, New Jersey, Pennsylvania, Indiana, and Ohio. However, there were only two dozen of them altogether. (By comparison, at least five hundred cotton mills were in New England alone.) As a result, these three silk mills in Broughton's Meadow comprised fully an eighth of the American silk industry in 1845.

This was no accident. The area had been intimately connected with the growth of American silk for some time, notably as the training ground for the most infamous proponent of the *Morus multicaulis* speculation, Samuel Whitmarsh. A city boy with deep pockets, Whitmarsh had become obsessed with the possibility of sericulture, traveled extensively throughout Europe to learn methods of both raising and manufacturing silk, and built a plantation in Broughton's Meadow in 1835 in order to realize his vision of "moth to cloth" production. His plantation included a brick silk mill, a cocoonery of 2 million worms, and a three-hundred-acre mulberry tree farm. Despite the fact that it was basically in the middle of nowhere, the plantation earned national press and garnered tremendous enthusiasm because of its bold, unprecedented investment in American silk. Daniel Webster, Abbott Lawrence, and James K. Mills, leading congressional advocates for the growth of American industry, trekked into the Massachusetts interior for a tour of this sensation-raising operation. However, Whitmarsh was apparently only interested in captivating visitors with "notions of wealth to be derived from silk culture" so as to "increase the sale of mulberry trees." When the mulberry bubble burst, and, as Skinner later put it, "the biters were bitten," Whitmarsh lost his fortune. Nevertheless he had put Northampton on the map. The first silk convention in the United States was held there, in 1841, and when Will arrived the town was still the pulse of the industry, small as that industry was, with Whitmarsh's plantation being run by the utopians.

If a man wanted to succeed in the silk trade this side of the Atlantic, Broughton's Meadow, on the outskirts of Northampton, was a better place than most. The market for American silk was uncharted at this point, and, in a collective effort to improve their products and business, Vallentine, Conant, and leaders of the Northampton Association were in constant communication with each other about trends, prices, suppliers, and so forth. The competition, they knew, wasn't each other's silk so much as it was the foreign article. The idea that "dear bought and far-fetched is good for ladies" absolutely governed the marketplace, with tailors and dressmakers pleasing their customers with foreign-made materials, such as Italian thread or Spitalfields silk. In order to fight the customs of the country, one needed to be a little bit foolish and a great deal determined.

Patience too was a welcome trait, given the hair-tearing frustration that came with the difficult task of producing silk in America. The proper machinery didn't yet exist, nor did the tools for even making the machinery. Everything was an experiment for these pioneering men and their peers. Moreover Conant, Vallentine, and the utopians didn't just make silk and then sell it. Rather, they offered samples to prospective clients and filled orders as orders appeared. Building a clientele took money and time, and meeting the demands of that clientele could prove even more costly. Not long after Will arrived, Captain Conant expressed the futility of recent efforts to produce a particular kind of thread for customers in Boston. "I have been . . . trying now for more than six months to have the silk twisted a little more," he wrote, "but I have tryed in vain. . . . Our silk is getting a bad name by not being twisted quite enough but I cannot help it." Conant's machinery was substandard, despite valiant efforts on the part of local machinists to improve it. Simply packaging skeins of silk proved fraught with struggle. "Don't laugh at the way they are done up," wrote one Association member to another, "for I did them and there is no one else that knows any thing about it to teach me."

In the matter of dyeing silk, however, Vallentine alone knew exactly what he was doing and just how to do it. His mastery of dyeing silk, hard won in Spitalfields, had made him extremely well known in New England. His early success in northeastern Connecticut, where he first showed his fancy colors and permanent black, had spread his name over hundreds of miles and sufficiently impressed Whitmarsh, then in full flush, to entice him to move to Northampton. Although Whitmarsh subsequently went out of business and, concurrently, the silk industry became wildly unstable as it transitioned from an agricultural to a manufacturing business, Vallentine had little trouble finding work. For every silk entrepreneur who failed, another entered the trade, and most mill owners, like the enterprising Cheney Brothers in Connecticut, "had no dyeing facilities and no knowledge of the dyeing process."

Working out of his own shop in Broughton's Meadow, Vallentine became capable of earning as much as $13 a day, dyeing more than a hundred pounds of silk a week. By contrast, a well-paid employee at the Cheney mill earned just 50 cents per day. "The only reason any lady ever married a dyer was for money," it was once believed, and true enough, Vallentine began to amass a small fortune. In May 1841 he purchased a house and forty acres in Broughton's Meadow for an eye-popping $1,200.

By most accounts Vallentine was the first master dyer in New England, but his monopoly on the trade was brief. In the fall of 1842 the Association, for whom he had been dyeing silk for several months, approached him with a proposition that he could have refused but didn't. Leaders of the Association had decided that their dyer should be a member of their community, which Vallentine was not, and in exchange for $100, they asked him to teach one of their members everything about dyeing silk. They wished for the training to be completed within four months, and if Vallentine didn't agree to their proposition, they were going to bring over another master dyer from England who would do as they asked.

In the first place this proposition was not simply bold but insulting, insinuating that Vallentine's expertise was knowledge that could be mastered by anyone within a matter of months. The member they had chosen Vallentine to teach, a Bostonian by the name of James Atkins, had no prior knowledge of silk, and the only dye he had ever touched was the ink at the printing press where he had previously worked. Second, a threat was hardly the sort of communication one would expect from a utopian society. Money, however, often speaks louder than ideals, and some of the Association's leaders believed, rightly, that they could both save money and make a lot of it if they could only dye their own silks. Also, one can fairly assume that they knew Vallentine well enough to know his ego would play into their taunt. Vallentine had made a big splash as the only master dyer in the area, and one can imagine that he wished to remain the only one.

On October 25, 1842, Vallentine accepted the $100, a comparatively small sum for him, agreeing to impart "all the information & practical experience I have had in said art & business up to the present date" and use "both by theoretical & practical illustration to qualify said Atkins [in every] process connected therewith with which I am acquainted." Although a brilliant dyer, Vallentine was clearly an awful businessman, neglecting to negotiate any benefits for himself in this transaction. Somehow he failed to recognize that his experience was valuable currency with which he could bargain. In the footsteps of Samuel Slater, who brought to America the knowledge of cotton-spinning machinery, Vallentine could have bartered his skills for a share in profit, stock, or both. He could have limited what he taught or drawn out the instruction for years. He could have simply demanded more money. Instead, he settled for a buyout that the Association could afford, and that acquiescence would cost him dearly.

News spread of the Association's coup, and soon the Cheney Brothers "followed up this entering wedge." To remain competitive, they wanted their own dyer too, one who knew "all the secrets of the art." Consequently, the brothers pushed a similar agreement on Vallentine, who proved slightly smarter the second time around, charging the Cheneys $300 and "[keeping] some of his knowledge in reserve." But the damage had been done. The Northampton Association and the Cheneys were big names in the burgeoning silk industry, led by some of the most ambitious men in the business, and Vallentine never recovered from his decision to sell them his knowledge. Observed the historian Linus Brockett, a contemporary of all these players, "The subsequent withdrawal of these two largest customers probably brought about Mr. Vallentine's failure in business."

Although Vallentine fought back by building a mill across from his house and expanding into manufacturing, making silk thread was not nearly as lucrative yet as dyeing it. Granted, he had more experience than most of his colleagues when it came to working with silk—and he was often appealed to for advice or assistance—but no one was getting rich in this business. Few of the silk mills then in operation made any kind of profit, and many owners subsidized their efforts with other investments. Captain Conant, for example, "also dealt extensively in real estate, buying old property, and repairing and disposing of it at a considerable advance." For their part, the utopians didn't just operate a silk farm and mill; they ran several other businesses, including both a lumber and a cutlery business. Indeed, when Vallentine decided to build a mill, he hired members of the Association to do the actual work, further enriching his neighbors.

Vallentine had no income outside of the silk business. Nor, being a foreigner, did he have a local network to draw on for financial support. So when he began to run out of money, he turned to his English connections, first appealing to his father to send him a dyer who could manage his dyehouse (and preserve the reputation he had established), and then entering into a partnership with Arthur Sowerby, an English merchant who fortuitously lived nearby. Though information on Sowerby is scant, records suggest that he had some connection to the silk trade. He bought 50 percent of Vallentine's business, and, by the time Will arrived, the company had become known as Vallentine & Sowerby.

Chances are Will had no knowledge before setting forth that Vallentine was experiencing any financial difficulty. "It is natural for persons who have adventured to leave home and to seek their fortunes in a foreign and distant country, to give highly coloured accounts of a success," warned the Irish Emigrant Society. And wishing to persuade another to follow, Vallentine would hardly have discussed, in any missive sent home, the fact that he was facing bankruptcy and had sold his own home to raise cash.

Still, Will's first impression of Vallentine was probably very favorable. After all, Vallentine was an esteemed member of the New England silk community, and he co-owned a silk factory and dyehouse on valuable property along the stagecoach road. He was building another house, this one next to Sowerby, and, though probably smaller than the original, it would have been bigger than any residence Skinner had known. As impressive, Vallentine had married an American, a woman with Connecticut roots, and was the father of four sons. With his extra-thick boots and fondness for tea, he appeared to be a comfortable, well-adjusted, and highly successful immigrant.

The illusion, of course, didn't hold for long, and Will witnessed firsthand that in the United States "making silk was not on the whole an easy task." Just over a year later Vallentine and Sowerby, confronted with insolvency, mortgaged everything they owned: land, houses, tools, machinery, the mill, and the dyehouse. Their silks had received awards, such as a silver medal for quality by the American Institute of New York in 1846, but they just couldn't get in the clear. Regardless of Will's help in the dyehouse and Sowerby's connections in the marketplace, the expenses of running a silk mill were proving insurmountable. Across the way the Association too was facing imminent dissolution, collapsing under $40,000 of debt and the weight of its own unprofitable mill.

In October 1847 Vallentine quit. He sold his share of the factory, transferred his property, and left Broughton's Meadow altogether. He tried to start over in Connecticut, relying on past connections, but his hitherto "robust constitution" began to fail him, and he died within three years, at the age of thirty-nine, his demise illustrating the harsh reality that "an emigrant might do well, or he might not." No matter how democratic the country was (or claimed to be), success in the New World was no easier than it had been in the Old. Prejudices abounded. Opposition thrived. Despite what anyone said, the streets were not paved with gold. As if Vallentine wasn't example enough, Sowerby became another. The merchant swiftly chose a new partner, James Munroe Grant, but Sowerby & Grant withered even more quickly than Vallentine & Sowerby. While Skinner labored in the dyehouse, creditors swarmed, and only eight months later the deputy sheriff of Northampton, Ansel Wright, seized possession of the property under court order.

Four weeks following, on July 27, 1848, almost three years to the date of his arrival in New York, when he had disembarked in that smoke-filled city with the good fortune of knowing that employment awaited him in a town called Northampton, Skinner served as a legal witness to the foreclosure of the factory. He and machinist Jason Sulloway were the last men standing.

Almost every advertisement for Skinner's later firm would proudly declare: "Established 1848." It is true that this year marks the date on which he stopped working for others and started working for himself, but he didn't exactly establish his own business. Rather, he began building his own reputation, operating under a personal maxim: "Succeed . . . you cannot afford anything else."

As it happened, Conant's silk mill, just down the road, was then "[undergoing] frequent changes." Conant's silk dyer, Harvey Holland, was about to become a partner in the firm, along with two other men,

Joseph Warner and Caleb Hartwell, and Conant was beginning to remove himself from the operation to pursue other interests. As part of their reorganization into Warner, Holland & Co., the men offered Skinner the run of their dyehouse, an opportunity he seized. Ironically one of his first commissions was from James Atkins, Vallentine's original apprentice. The Association had not survived its debts, and after dissolving in November 1846, Samuel Hill, the treasurer, had taken over the silk factory. He had kept Atkins on as dyer, but even after five years of practice Atkins was yet unqualified to handle certain jobs.

Silk dyeing is an art—an ancient, complicated, and highly intuitive art that requires years of apprenticeship. "A good dyer makes a manufacturer wealthy, happy and renowned," a member of the trade was quoted as saying in 1869, "while a poor one brings ruin, bankruptcy, and misery; and not considering the fineness of the cloth or the faultless weaver, the color sells the goods." This was especially true in the days before synthetic dyes, when colors came from nature, not laboratories, and were wildly variable. A dyer of long ago had to master the color vocabulary of the natural world. While some colors come from animals (the insect cochineal, when dried, produces "a perfect red"), most are obtained from plants and trees, and a dyer had to be fully conversant in the coloring properties of roots, leaves, blossoms, berries, and bark. Furthermore he needed to discriminate among shades of the same color. To make yellow he could use either St. Mary's thistle, safflower, French berries, fustic (a bark), or quercitron (another bark). Although he came from an urban slum, Skinner would have known more about the traits of various flora and fauna than many who had grown up in the country.

With few exceptions, organic colors fade quickly, and to remedy this dyers required an arsenal of chemicals at their disposal. These mordants (deriving from the French verb *mordre*, meaning "to bite"), such as alum, chrome, and tin, act as binding agents, enabling dyes to sink into fabrics and adhere to them. Without these binding agents, colors do not become colorfast. Yet "mordants, while necessary, were a challenge to master, especially as each produced different colors from the same dyestuff." Weld, a European plant that produced another yellow dye, was significantly altered depending on which mordant one applied to it, achieving "with alum a primrose-yellow, chrome a slightly deeper colour, iron a dull fawn and tin a warm yellow."

Matters were complicated further by impure, unpredictable ingredients. With most of the materials being shipped from thousands of miles away, a dyer rarely received perfectly ripe berries, freshly harvested wood, or newly ground alum. Consequently he "had to become adept in judging his dyes and chemicals, and their influence upon the dyebath." This was often done "by visual examination, taste and smell." Like a chef in a kitchen, a dyer had recipes that he followed, and at various points he might sample the mixture in his kettle to ascertain its development. He kept an eye on the progress of the brew, sniffed its (often noxious) aroma, tested the temperature with his fingers (a dyer commonly had hands burned from the toxic liquor), and remained alert to any change because, as one master dyer put it, "eternal vigilance is the price of success."

Recipes were the key to dyeing. Without them one couldn't do anything but stare at the bags of powder and matter, the vats and kettles, washboards and scales, and wonder how it all went together to produce brilliantly dyed silks. Passed down from generation to generation, from father to son, recipes were guarded and honored, preserved in the mind and refined through practice. They were rarely, if ever, written down, in large part so they couldn't be stolen. After all, the difference between one dyer's black and another's lay in which ingredients were used, which mordants were added, and precisely how long one devoted to each step. Complicating the process even further, dyers often dyed their silks first one color, then another, and this variable sequencing only increased the specificity of an individual's work.

Most silk-dyeing recipes that survive today were only recorded as late as the nineteenth century and, not surprisingly, leave a great deal of room for error. To create a black dye, for instance, one might use the following recipe:

> Take four pounds of good logwood, and two pounds of fustic chips, boil well; then add a quarter of a pound of blue vitriol, run your cloth one hour, or till the strength is well out of the dye, then sadden with two pounds of copperas, and one gallon of good old sig; run your cloth, and if it is not black, you must air and rince, and shift your liquor from your copper, and set another dye in manner and form as the first, and handle again. . . . But if it is attended with a rusty brownness, you may put in one quart of brown ashes, or two ounces of pearl-ash, and handle lively, which is necessary in all hot silk, cotton and linen dyes.

The ingredient sig refers to urine, specifically human urine that has been sitting around long enough to ferment, become charged with ammonia, and produce granular deposits of salt. In an alkaline state, urine is a powerful scouring agent and was used in countless recipes to cleanse and soften the fabric without spoiling its color. It was also cheap and readily available, and numerous professionals preferred it to store-bought ammonia, which was apparently "the only material that [could] be substituted for [urine] with any prospect of success." But the use of urine, as well as other acids and alkalies, necessitated that "the dyer, in effect, had to act as a bacteriologist without knowing anything about bacteria" since the preparations of his dyes "depended on close control of the fermentation process."

Dyers like Skinner could not simply rely on a visual grasp of color; they had to be scientifically minded about how they went about realizing the color. Their work required methodical experimentation, painstaking mental note taking, and the ability to reproduce results despite limited technical knowledge. While chemists would become a fixture in dyeing establishments in the twentieth century, there were none in the shops that dotted Spitalfields or, increasingly, the New England countryside in the 1840s. Experimentation was the domain of the master dyer who achieved reliable results based on empirical evidence and a storehouse of data that was only as rich as the stains on his skin.

Dyeing silk involved five basic steps—degumming, bleaching, adding mordants, dyeing, and weighting—all of which constituted an age-old process, little changed in thousands of years. Indeed the work in any dyehouse in the nineteenth century "would have been broadly familiar to the dyers of ancient Rome." The first step, degumming, consisted of boiling the raw silk in soapy water to cleanse it of its sericin, a gummy resin secreted by the silkworm as it spins its cocoon, rendering the silk sticky enough to form a dense, hard shell. Unless the sericin is removed, raw silk will remain stiff, lusterless, and impenetrable—and entirely unworkable for dyers who need it to be soft and absorbent.

At this initial stage "the age-honored long vat first comes into play, with its hot suds and many sticks, the dexterous handling of which constitutes so monotonous yet important a part of the daily routine [in a dyehouse]." The dyer used wooden sticks or poles, about an inch in diameter, which stretched across the vat and on which he suspended the raw silk. When "boiling off," as this first step was called, he slowly walked the length of the vat, turning the poles as he went, and he repeated this for about two hours, until the sericin had been dissolved. Then he took each of the poles outside and rinsed the silk in running water, which, in Skinner's new situation, meant rinsing them in the clean brook that flowed behind Conant's dyehouse. If, at this stage, Skinner had not been convinced the silk was clean enough, he would have subjected it to another boil-off, or two, before rinsing it again and finally laying it outside in some shade to dry.

While some dyehouses had separate, sheltered "dry-rooms," Conant's probably did not. Indeed there is no reason to believe his was any different from the average small-time shop, the kind that one mid-century dyer referred to as "a hovel." This particular New Englander went further, calling most dyehouses "hog-styes" that were "not fit for either man or beast." In summer the steam was suffocating, while in winter the moisture brought on bone-chilling cold. Condensation froze on the walls and floors. Few shops had stoves. Most were drafty. The air was thick with fumes. Surfaces were slick with chemicals. "As everybody knows," said a dyer in Paterson, "the dyehouse is the most dirty and unhealthy part of the silk industry."

Conant's dyehouse was most likely square and wooden, with slits in the roof to help ventilate the steam. There would have been shelves to one side, or perhaps some cupboards, for dyestuffs and supplies. Tools would have hung from hooks on the walls, and a sewer would have run down the middle of the floor, which was probably stone and sloped toward a center drain. Once he'd finished degumming, Skinner would have simply released a valve at the bottom of the vat and emptied the liquor onto the stone, letting gravity take care of the rest. For this reason the floor was constantly wet, like that in a bathhouse, and Skinner, like all of his predecessors, would have worn clogs to protect his feet, leather boots being useless in such an environment. One of the most recurring shouts he probably heard as a kid was "Shoes up!"—the warning cry in every dyehouse each time a bath was emptied.

Once the raw silk was clean, it was spun into thread at the mill next door, then returned to the dyehouse in skeins, whereupon a dyer like Skinner might have bleached it if he felt that was necessary (if, for instance, he was going to make the silk white or a delicate, pale color). Otherwise he went ahead to the next step: dyeing. After filling one kettle with a mordant and another with a dye, he deposited each in turn into a heated vat, sometimes steeping the hanks of thread in the mordant first, sometimes charging them with the dye and then with the mordant, sometimes infusing them with everything at once. It all depended on the recipe. At every stage he rotated the silk on the poles again, from one end of the vat to the other, making sure that each millimeter of silk was colored evenly. "A few moments of unnecessary immersion, or a slovenliness in the shifting of the dye sticks," as Skinner knew all too well, "might hopelessly ruin a tub-full of silk."

Given that he worked with extremely expensive material that he was subjecting to unpredictable dyestuffs, Skinner would have frequently tested a dyebath and its effect on a handful of silk before risking the whole order. Dyers could often be seen in their aprons and rolled-up shirtsleeves taking small hanks of silk outside and examining them in the sunlight. Was the color deep enough? Light enough? Rich enough? Was it even the right color at all? To answer this last question, sometimes a dyer had to let the sample rest a bit. When using indigo, for example, "the cloth when first taken out of the vat will exhibit a green shade; but being exposed to the air will become blue." There were particular ways to stand (with one's back to the light), particular angles and depths at which to examine the silk for greatest effect, and methods for relieving one's eyes from the strain of "matching off." Skinner would have learned early on that "relief and increased power of discernment are most rapidly gained by occasionally gazing steadily for a few seconds at a piece of cardboard or other material possessing the complementary colour of the samples under comparison." Thus when comparing reds, Skinner might have paused a second to look at a patch of green grass. When comparing blues, he might have sought some orange, burnished leaves to reorient his sense of perception. And he would have avoided direct sunlight at all costs; it was too yellow. Northern light was best.

Perhaps the most proprietary knowledge within any dyehouse was the method with which silk was "weighted." Herein lay the real wizardry of the trade. When the silk loses its sericin during the cleansing process, it loses about 25 percent of its weight; a hank of boiled-off silk is little more than a mess of flyaway strands. Skilled dyers had to know what dyestuffs to add to their baths to "reweight" the silk and make it "appear more solid, and thicker, and stronger than it naturally would be" without jeopardizing the quality and integrity of the fiber. Knowing that the heavier the silk, the more valuable it would be, dyers often "[took advantage] of this operation by the use of heavy dye-stuffs, and in many cases the fibre [was] almost painted with them." In ancient

Greece the verb *to dye* also meant "to deceive," and for centuries dyers had been adulterating their silks with cheap ingredients such as bacon fat and honey. Consumers could not tell the difference at first, only later, when it was too late. Cheaply weighted silk was likely to attract dust and become covered in unsightly specks. Its color was liable to flake after minimal usage. And being so compromised by additives, the silk itself was prone to fray and tear.

In Broughton's Meadow in 1848 deception appears to have been minimal. In fact Skinner began to reestablish the good reputation that Vallentine had started to build—that dyers, sweaty and stained as they might be, could become rich and make a respectable living if they remained true to their craft.

At twenty-three Skinner was in charge of his own operation, a very small one perhaps, as he may not have had a single helper, but he alone was determining its direction.

In keeping with standard rates he charged 37½ cents per pound for colors (green, blue, gray, brown) and 42 cents per pound for blacks. He boldly charged up to 87½ cents per pound for "high" colors such as crimson—a 30 percent increase over Vallentine's rate for the same. Yet even then his boldness matched the quality of his work. He swiftly established an account with the Boston firm of Ward & Boott, "Importers and Dealers in Dye-Stuffs, Oils, Soaps, Chemicals and Manufacturers' Articles." He stocked up on supplies such as sugar, soap, and ammonia (not favoring the man-made cleanser), as well as ingredients for his dyes, such as cochineal insects, which he may have special-ordered from an importer in Hartford. Wood and matches he purchased from a local supplier, as well as paper for letters (not bothering to buy ink since he could pretty well make his own). And in a small, leather-bound account book, with a handsome marbled-paper cover, he began to enter his transactions alphabetically. Then, just as quickly, he abandoned the alphabetizing (as well as his penmanship, which swiftly deteriorated) and spread out his entries. He put his main client, Warner, Holland & Co., up front and his smaller clients toward the back, with his purchases in the middle. Fastidious he was not—his tabulations could be quite sloppy—but he was organized. He knew precisely what was coming in and going out.

He worked incessantly, dyeing for three, sometimes four clients at a time, as opposed to Atkins, who dyed almost exclusively for Samuel Hill. Like Vallentine, Skinner handled upward of a hundred pounds of silk per week, often tending the vats overnight. Although he paid for a bed somewhere in the village, he would have spent most of his time at the dyehouse, consumed in his own world. However, his proximity to the silk mill of Warner, Holland & Co. exposed him to the workers there, about a dozen or so young men and women, and as his tenure increased, he became more acquainted with the partners, Joseph Warner in particular.

Warner was a steady, quiet man, "the better known, the better appreciated." He had been running his family's affairs since his father died eight years earlier, managing the family farm while earning extra income from the mill. One can only speculate how Skinner met Nancy, Joseph's youngest sister. Perhaps they crossed paths one afternoon when Nancy visited her brother at work. Or perhaps Skinner boarded at their house. Whatever the circumstances, after four years in America building a life for himself in Broughton's Meadow, Will, aged twenty-four, married Nancy Warner, one year his junior, on July 3, 1849, in Northampton's First Church.

The union cemented Skinner and Warner's business relationship; they were now family, doing business *together*. Crucially for Will, the marriage gained him social standing. In taking Nancy Warner as his bride, he married into the oldest local family in the area. The Warners had been the first to settle in Broughton's Meadow, back around 1778. The present family knew everyone, and everyone knew them.

Nancy was an attractive, vibrant woman, fair-skinned, with dark hair and eyes. Like Skinner's Aunt Ellen, she was educated and well-read. Both of her older sisters had been teachers. Joseph himself had been schooled to be a teacher. The Warner children had grown up reading Virgil, writing compositions, studying French, and attending both local and boarding schools. Though she may have dreamed of traveling like her favorite sister, Mary (who declared, "I don't mean to stay in Northampton all my lifetime"), Nancy found enough to do at home—supporting the antislavery movement, keeping accounts, painting the landscape—to keep her rooted there. Artistic, practical, and political, she was considered "the smartest in [the] family."

Nancy gave birth to their first child on September 19, 1850, in the old Warner homestead, where they were then living with Nancy's family. Exactly one month later, perhaps feeling enormous pride at being a father and wishing all the legal rights and privileges of other men, William entered the Court of Common Pleas in Northampton and became a naturalized citizen of the United States. Owing to the fact that he had been an unaccompanied minor when he arrived, with no subsequent criminal record, the process was quick, and from this point on in the eyes of the law he was no longer a foreigner. He was now an American.

The year 1850 also marked the arrival in America of both of Skinner's brothers as well as his younger sister, Sarah. Following in the steps of their older sibling, now established enough to be of help to each of them, Thomas had arrived in New York in April; George, Sarah, and George's first wife, Ann, in October. Thomas went straight to Broughton's Meadow, where he began working in the dyehouse with Will and made an instant impact. The dyehouse's earnings increased by 33 percent that year, reaching $2,000. George, on the other hand, sought work in the Mansfield area, no doubt relying on his brother's connections in Connecticut. Sarah, all of twelve years old, may have tagged along with George to Mansfield, or she may have gone to work for Warner, Holland & Co. next door to Will; her exact journey is unknown. In any event, after a five-year separation, during which they had minimal communication at best, these Skinner siblings were reunited, and what had once seemed an impossible dream—that they would all escape Spitalfields—had become a reality.

The end of the year brought still another big event for Skinner. In November he invested in his first bit of real estate, a small, triangle-shaped parcel of land across from the silk mill. Purchasing the property for a modest $6, he promptly set about building his first home. In keeping with his work ethic, or rather his inability not to be working, he even spent Christmas day managing the construction and shipping finished orders from the dyehouse.

At this stage Will felt far more comfortable in a dyehouse than anywhere else. He knew exactly what to do with a dipping pole; he wasn't nearly as smart with a knife and fork. A play called *The Spitalfields Weaver: A Comic Drama,* published a decade earlier in London, portrayed just how coarse and vulgar a man from Spitalfields might seem outside of his native parish—slurping wine like a dog, eating peas with a knife, chopping bread rolls as if splitting wood. The weaver in the play, who has married far above his station, is laughed at by his wife's friends (and especially her servants) and says to his beloved, "I'm miserable." But he's a quick study, and his innate "kindness and good nature," being someone who never adhered to protocol, endears him to the audience—as does the fact that he punches the lights out of an evil cad later in the story.

Skinner was sharply aware of the differences between himself and others. Joseph Warner, for one, was a college graduate (a striking accomplishment for any man of the period) and possessed "more than the ordinary degree of intelligence." No matter that Skinner could quote Shakespeare and Pope, Warner's refinement would have outclassed him the moment they entered a room. While others' speech was peppered with French and Latin phrases, Skinner's was peppered with dropped *h*'s, long vowels, and the irrepressible glottal stop. ("The 'orses dahn there need a drin' a wa'er," he might have said, sounding like he had pebbles in his mouth.) But Skinner knew a thing or two about survival; he was "a close observer of men and manners." In time he adapted. What's more, as his business took off and his family grew, others adapted to him as well, learning to respect his "rugged, forceful personality."

In 1851 Skinner's dyehouse continued its run of success. Unfortunately Warner, Holland & Co. did not have as good a return. Through word of mouth that traveled all the way to Pittsburgh, Warner's sister Eliza, who was living in that city with her husband, wrote to her mother back at the homestead, "I heard that [Joseph] had not turned off as much silk as usual this last year." The simplicity of the remark belies the significance of its meaning. If Warner's company wasn't producing as much silk, its number of clients must have fallen off, and if that had happened, Warner was losing money. American silk continued to be a damned hard sell to consumers.

By the end of 1851 Warner's partners, Harvey Holland and Caleb Hartwell, wanted out of the business, and Warner, Holland & Co. disbanded in December, with Warner "authorized to settle the affairs of the company." At this point, despite all that portended trouble, Skinner decided to enter into manufacturing and became his brother-in-law's new partner. The firm of Warner and Skinner began accepting commissions in January.

Considering the fate of his predecessors, particularly Vallentine and Sowerby, one might view Skinner's decision as almost willfully courting disaster. The risk was huge. Skinner paid $1,800 for a third of the company and had to go out on a limb to cover the cost. He was easily netting $500 or more a year, which was plenty to live on, but he needed a lot more than that to invest in a company. To buy into the silk mill he had to take on a mortgage of $1,300. What's more, the dyehouse's earnings would henceforth be merged with the mill's, so while legally an owner of the dyehouse, Skinner no longer had financial control over it.

Skinner didn't believe in luck ("Get all luck notions out of your head," he told his eldest son), but the fact remains that he bought into the company at a fortuitous time. Upriver, Samuel Hill, who had broken free of the debts of the Association but whose financial situation remained tight, was laboring to invent a more durable silk thread, something that would be suitable for a sewing machine. Given that the silk men of Broughton's Meadow were intimately familiar with each other's affairs, Skinner had to have known of Hill's latest venture, which, if successful, would create another market for silk thread. At this point, however, no one had any idea how big that market might be.

Sewing machines had been around for several years but were not popular. They worked in fits and starts, were difficult to use, and needed lots of repair. In short, they were more trouble than they were worth, and so the old, reliable hand stitch continued to be universally preferred. But in 1850 the failed actor and sometime inventor Isaac Merritt Singer was introduced to a broken sewing machine in a machine shop in Boston. As the story goes, he saw not only how to make it work, but how to make it better. Among other improvements, he replaced the model's curved needle, which moved in a rotary direction (the way a woman's arm moved as she sewed) with a vertical needle that moved straight up and down. He also introduced a tensioning system, enabling the machine to stitch continuously. However, no sooner had he succeeded in producing consecutive stitches than, as he put it, "the thread snapped." He had used common sewing silk, the strongest option available, but it was too weak for the rigors of his machine.

Thread was only one of Singer's worries. Shortly after obtaining a patent for his improvements on August 12, 1851, he was sued for patent infringement and became embroiled in a protracted lawsuit that did not end in his favor. While he poured his theatrical nature into defending his machine, Samuel Hill, back in Northampton, poured his conservative and tenacious spirit into producing a stronger thread. Traditional sewing silk consists of two strands of silk twisted together, but three-ply thread is more durable, as well as naturally smoother, and Hill drew on the expertise of Captain Conant and an energetic machinist named Lucius Dimock to help him manufacture a more reliable thread. Conant and Dimock had previously overcome the "great difficulty" of twisting together strands of silk that were "rarely alike in texture" after discovering a way to doubly—or triply—twist a single spool, and they either built or at least contributed to the design of the machinery that Hill employed. As a result, Hill was able to produce a three-ply thread that was "entirely free from slugs, knots, and uneven places" and that could pass through hooks and eyelets without breaking or snagging.

Sometime in 1852, the same year Skinner began his career as a manufacturer, Hill met with Singer and offered him a sample of his tricord thread. The famous scene that followed was recorded at the Centennial Exhibition in 1876: "The silk was handed to Mr. Singer with the request that he would try it. He put a spool upon his machine, threaded up and commenced sewing. After sewing sufficiently to enable him to judge of its merit, he stopped, and after examining the work it had done, exclaimed, '*Can you make any more like this? I shall want all you can make.*'"

Skinner entered manufacturing, then, at the very moment a revolution began to take place in the silk industry. Patent wars would bottleneck the production of sewing machines until 1856, but that didn't stop Hill from producing his new thread, now called, appropriately, "machine twist." Nor did it prevent others from capitalizing on what Hill had created. If Warner and Skinner tried to manufacture machine twist too, the results are unknown, but chances are they didn't. Warner "[made] the manufacture of sewing-silks a specialty" and was likely more intent on perfecting what they already sold than trying something new. While this may have been a prudent course of action, it would have been hard for someone as ambitious as Skinner to stomach. After all, as everyone would have known, Hill began to receive checks worth thousands of dollars from Isaac Singer.

Whether it was over machine twist or something else, Skinner's partnership with Warner soured quickly. Given the men's wildly different personalities, which of course dictated their fundamental approaches to business, this is not surprising. Warner's quiet nature was the result of acute shyness, an anxiety that had plagued him since childhood and that he had in part inherited from his father (who also suffered from crippling "bashfulness"). Warner was "safe" and "careful" in his dealings. He also worried a good deal, another family trait, and, at least when younger, tended to sleep a lot when feeling overwhelmed.

By contrast Skinner was fiery and energetic, rapidly evolving into "one of those go-ahead men who yield to no difficulty." He was disdainful of the "Warner hypo" (his nickname for the family's hypochondria), and with more than just a chip on his shoulder, believed that any man who couldn't rise to a challenge simply lacked internal fortitude. Although respectful of Warner's education, he probably dismissed it as useless and counterproductive in the office. Skinner acted on instinct. If he sensed the time was right to do something, he did it. He was "a man of action, who wished to see things accomplished, impatient of mere theory and debate."

Both Warner and Skinner were considered enterprising men, but their enterprise together dissolved within two years. In January 1854 Skinner sold his share of the company—at a slight loss—and parted ways with Warner, who remained, steady as ever, at the helm of the same mill he'd been running for years.

In the ensuing months Skinner decided to go into business for himself in the village of Haydenville, two miles north. Perhaps he was beginning to find Broughton's Meadow confining. The area was so closely associated with the silk industry that it was no longer called Broughton's Meadow. At a village meeting in 1852 citizens had decided to change the name of the place to Florence, after the famous Italian city known the world over for its silks. They had even proposed renaming the Mill River the Arno, but that proved too much for the modesty of most voters.

In the midst of starting over upriver, Nancy Skinner fell seriously ill. She had given birth to their second child, another daughter, in December, and seems never to have recovered. Her condition worsened to the point that she was driven thirty miles away to Ware, Massachusetts, to be treated by her sister Mary's husband, Dr. Worthington

Miner. But the medical attention did not help. She was diagnosed with "marasmus," a medical term that has no equivalent today but which defined a condition characterized by a visible and unstoppable "wasting away" of the patient. No matter how much Nancy ate or drank, she grew weaker and thinner, until, despite her hunger and thirst, she became physically incapable of eating or drinking. She died on July 28, 1854, at twenty-eight years old.

Records show little activity at Skinner's mill during the preceding weeks, indicating that Skinner may have taken several trips to be with his wife. July 3 had been their fifth anniversary, which he would have commemorated with some sort of gift. Yet during Nancy's very last days, Skinner was receiving shipments of machinery at the mill, suggesting that he wasn't anywhere near Ware. Since there was no telegraph in Haydenville at this time, the fastest news came through the mail. It's entirely possible that Skinner learned of his wife's death in a letter, delivered with the post after 4 p.m.

Nancy's premature death was devastating to Skinner. One can sense how deeply he missed her, and longed for her, by the epitaph inscribed on her tombstone in Northampton. Originally the marker had read simply "Nancy E. W., wife of William Skinner, born Nov. 5, 1825, died July 28, 1854." However, a year after her death Skinner read a recently published poem by Alfred Lord Tennyson and, sometime thereafter, had a portion of it added to Nancy's marker. Beneath her name one can still make out the following on the weathered stone:

A shadow flits before me,
Not Thou, but like to thee:
Ah Christ, that it were possible
For one short hour to see
The souls we loved, that they might tell us
What and where they be.

Chapter Six

Haydenville, the location of Skinner's new enterprise, was just over the Northampton border, in the town of Williamsburg. Though higher up the valley and deeper into the country, Haydenville had a larger population and a more developed industrial base than Florence. As early as 1809 two local brothers, along with two friends, had built a cotton mill here, and a gradual investment in manufacturing had grown from that time. Standing in the middle of Main Street in 1854—with a foundry, cotton mill, brass factory, pen factory, tin shop, boot maker, general store, and variety store lining the Mill River—one could safely declare, "The effects of trade and manufacturing, together with the convenience of the people, have wholly reversed the original tide of settlement." Haydenville was bustling. It even had a hotel.

The village had taken its name from the Haydens, an old Williamsburg family that seemed particularly blessed with a gene for invention and initiative. The two brothers involved in the first cotton mill were Haydens, and two of their nephews, Joel and Josiah, were largely responsible for the subsequent industrial growth of the area. By the time Skinner arrived, one couldn't step an inch without running into something that Joel or Josiah Hayden had built, be it a mill or a shop, a tenement or a foundry. Although Josiah wasn't living in the village at this time, his presence loomed large, not least because of the twin Greek Revival mansions the brothers had erected on a small rise above Main Street. Few houses in the valley could compare to their grandeur. The Hayden wealth was astonishing, and for an ambitious tradesman like Skinner, intent on making a go of it on his own, this was the kind of wealth he would have craved, the kind that reflected undeniable, incontrovertible success.

Skinner took over the untenanted J. J. Lewis place, a modest mill built in 1832 on the outskirts of the village. This two-story, wooden building had already been home to several businesses that had produced a variety of items—spoons, harness trimmings, hoes, tacks, metal frames—and typical of most mills of its era, there was nothing particularly industrial about it. In fact it was essentially a blacksmith shop, given all the ironwork that had taken place inside, but manufactories of the period were commonly set up in converted shops, barns, and sheds, even old schools. The Lewis place was straightforward, with four walls, a roof, a couple of floors, a waterwheel, and some shafting. It came with a mill pond, mill dam, raceway, and tailrace. Anyone with a mind for manufacturing could equip it with some machinery and start a business.

Technically speaking, the Lewis place was not in Haydenville but a mile up the road between Haydenville and the village of Williamsburg proper, in an odd little community that, because of its location, was neither here nor there. About a dozen families of farmers and laborers existed in this section, their houses lining one side of the road, against a backdrop of fields. Because the river flowed swiftly but not impressively through the area, manufacturing had not gravitated to this spot, and the Lewis place had remained the only mill. The small Unquomonk Brook entered the river north of the mill, providing some additional waterpower, but its contribution to the volume of the river was modest at best. In fact everything about this particular area was modest, and it was more remote and undeveloped than Florence had been ten years earlier. So while Skinner was theoretically moving to Haydenville and would presently sell his silks in the village, get his mail in the village, and buy supplies in the village, in reality he was going to be a good deal farther north, manufacturing in the midst of farmland, without another manufacturer in sight.

Although it would have made sense to move his family to Haydenville so that he could be closer to his new operation, Skinner continued to live in Florence. He may have been an entrepreneurial businessman, but he was also a widower with two very small daughters, and he likely stayed in Florence to remain near his mother-in-law and other relatives who would look after the girls. He spent little time with his children, but in a rare moment away from the mill he took them on a trip all the way to Boston, to have their pictures taken by the well-known photographer Elmer Chickering. This choice was no coincidence; their mother had once had her portrait taken here, perhaps on her wedding trip, and that portrait, the only such remaining, may have been the sole one taken of Nancy Skinner as a full-grown woman. Knowing the swiftness of death, Skinner was wasting no time capturing his daughters' likenesses.

In addition to several images of the girls alone, Skinner had a family portrait taken. He sits facing the camera, with the baby, Nina, balanced on his right knee, Nellie leaning up against his left, and his arms tucked round about them, hugging them close. The subjects of nineteenth-century photographs often look stern and serious, owing to the length of exposure of the film, but Skinner practically sears the camera with his gaze. He is at once mournful, calm, and powerfully resolute. As for his children, Nellie leans into him with a closeness that implies she felt protected by him and, like her father, stares straight at the camera with a magnetic directness. Little Nina, on the other hand, a little over a year old, appears terrified. Yet the overall picture, even for its time, is quite tender, revealing at its heart a proud father holding onto his young, vulnerable daughters.

Skinner dressed the girls up for the occasion, in matching plaid dresses and bows, and he obviously cared about his own appearance: he's wearing a fine dark suit with crisp white collar and cuffs. Embarrassed by the ill-fitting, soiled clothes he wore as a child, he now took pride in the fact that he could afford tailored suits. He had transformed himself into the clean, fastidiously attired man whom people would remember as "always neatly dressed." Though not yet rich, he had begun projecting himself as such, spending his money carefully and purposefully, cultivating his image. "He would never have bought an imitation pearl," remembered a friend, the novelist Adele Allen. "He would have waited until he had the money to buy a real one." Skinner could have had his girls' portraits taken closer to home, but Chickering was one of the finest photographers in Boston—indeed in the whole state—and photographs taken by him were a mark of prestige.

In Haydenville, Skinner commenced manufacturing with about twenty-five employees—five men, seventeen women, and a small number of children—most of whom he probably hired from nearby farms. Since Skinner didn't have a boardinghouse yet, his operatives had to live within walking distance. The arrangement would have benefited many of the area's families, since their children lived too far from other mills for employment. Although many of these young persons, especially the young women, may not have previously thought of working in a factory, the leap from farmhand to mill hand was not unusual since "the mill simply continued a long-standing attitude that children should help their families if they could." Moreover Skinner didn't need skilled labor except in the dyehouse. He could teach almost anyone how to sort, reel, wind, spin, twist, and skein silk thread, so his only requirements for employment were intelligence and a willingness to work. (He advertised simply for "smart, active girls.") And since his factory work was paid work, employment in his new silk mill became quite desirable.

Setting up the dyehouse took a little more effort. By this time

Thomas Skinner had fallen in love with a young woman from England, Rosamond Reece, whose family had arrived in Florence, and he had married her and settled down in that village. As a result, he would have been unable to tend the dye vats in Haydenville, as need be. In all likelihood Thomas remained chief dyer for Joseph Warner, which would have been as fortuitous for Warner as it was disadvantageous for Skinner. Unlike his brothers, Thomas had no desire to own a business; he was an artist in the true sense of the word and an outstanding practitioner of his craft. Losing such talent when Skinner arguably needed it most was a challenge, but he soon found a German dyer named Albert Köenig who was practically straight off the boat, and who became known as "Mr. King" when Skinner declared his name too difficult to pronounce. King was also descended from the Huguenots (those who had fled to Germany), with the silk trade every bit a part of his DNA. Despite the language barrier, Skinner and King spoke a similar vocabulary.

Skinner didn't have much capital at this time and, with no partner, actually started out with a startling deficit of investiture. Most men who entered the manufacturing business found investors or associates to help carry the initial financial burdens of the enterprise and to provide support as the business grew. The Northampton Association of Education and Industry had essentially been an association of investors. The Haydens had partnered with the capitalist Samuel Williston and later with a variety of others. Even Vallentine had sought the assistance of the merchant Sowerby. With such partnerships and capital, by the middle of the century few manufacturers operated with less than $10,000. In Haydenville the cotton mill had capital of $45,000, the pen shop $38,000, and the brass foundry $20,000. Skinner, on the other hand, had about $1,200—the sale price of his share of Warner and Skinner.

Fortunately, Skinner didn't need much capital because the silk business was run almost entirely on credit: raw silk was commonly sold on four months' credit, as was silk machinery, and the commission merchants, who brokered sales in the cities, also worked on credit. As a result, "a manufacturer [could] start in the silk business in a small way with little capital under these credit systems." He would also start out carrying a tremendous amount of debt. Skinner purchased $30,000 of raw silk his first year for a total of six thousand pounds of raw material. He evidently felt $5 per pound was a good deal, or else he was anxious to prove he could do more business than conservative Warner, who purchased a thousand pounds less. With this amount of silk Skinner should have been able to earn a profit of about $10,000, but after production costs, payroll expenses, interest payments, payments on the Lewis place, and miscellaneous expenses, his personal takeaway would have been negligible.

Moreover, the market for American-made silk thread was still in its infancy, and the quality of Skinner's product, which of course determined its marketability, was heavily dependent on the quality of his raw material, which was usually poor. During this period raw silk came from the Orient around the Cape of Good Hope, and the Europeans kept the best shipments for themselves. Thus American silk manufacturers "received the silk that Europe rejected." Inferior silk was a nightmare to work with and "the cost of picking out flaws and imperfections decreased [a manufacturer's] profits." Some, like the Haydens, whose interests were endlessly diverse, might have shaken their heads at putting so much effort into making something that generated so little return.

Without question, Skinner availed himself of the latest silk machinery to try to enhance the quality of his product. Having started out in the Florence community and worked with a number of mills in Connecticut, he was acquainted with some of the best regional machinists and their various contrivances to overcome the deficiencies of the raw material. Furthermore, he swiftly began to generate a network of peddlers to sell his products. Being a foreigner in business on his own, he could not rely on the local establishment to help him, so he did what few people in this age of modesty would do: he advertised his products, letting the countryside know that he was selling "a good assortment of all kinds of sewing silks, black and fancy colors . . . at the Subscriber's Manufactory in Haydenville."

Somehow, without any visible profit, Skinner's working capital grew to $7,000. By 1855, a year after starting over in Haydenville, the young manufacturer was proving that he "had more than an ordinary understanding of production costs" and that he was "a match for the thriftiest Yankee that ever lived." He was even able to purchase the Lewis place, having successfully secured a mortgage to do so. Estimates of his net worth varied between $2,000 and $4,000—still quite low for a manufacturer—but in a comparatively short time he had convinced area lenders that he was a safe bet for credit. They praised him as "an honest, upright straight forward man" who was "doing a good business." Furthermore, with his good looks, self-confidence, and rather amazing streak of independence, he was becoming something of a catch in the neighborhood. Everyone knew that he was a widower who needed a wife to look after his children.

According to family lore, Skinner met Sarah Elizabeth Allen when the horse pulling his buggy "suddenly stopped, and seeing the young woman William Skinner said to himself, 'That is the girl I am going to marry.'" The story is too romantic to be credible, but it is quite possible that Skinner had observed the young woman, nine years his junior, with an eye to marrying her. Lizzie and her family attended the same church as the Warners, and over the previous few years William and Lizzie had undoubtedly passed each other after services, possibly on several occasions. Just as likely, Lizzie had noticed the tall, dark-haired Englishman so unlike any of the other parishioners, who spoke rather coarsely yet comported himself superbly. They were married on May 15, 1856, in the familiar sanctuary of Northampton's First Church. He was thirty-one, she twenty-two.

Like Skinner, Lizzie was somewhat taller than most of her peers. She was nearly five-foot-seven, slender, with sharp blue eyes and very thick, curly brown hair. She had a heart-shaped face with a round chin, full cheekbones, and a large mole on her right cheek. A schoolteacher, keeping the school in Haydenville at this time, she was obviously educated. Yet as the daughter of a mill worker she was also acquainted with factory life. The youngest of seven surviving children, she was outgoing and self-reliant, and, of no small importance, she was believed to be of high moral character; she would not have been given a teaching license otherwise.

Lizzie had grown up in the village of Leeds, which sat between Florence and Haydenville. The first manufacturing village of any consequence in the valley, Leeds had originally been called Shepherd's Hollow, named for the Shepherd family who established here the Northampton Woolen Company, "one of the country's prominent woolen concerns in the first quarter of the nineteenth century." This company utterly transformed how locals viewed the Mill River, which had mostly been an agricultural asset. With the woolen mill it became a means of powering textile machinery, of joining the Industrial Revolution, and of generating wealth and prestige. In 1833, when Henry Clay, then a U.S. senator from Kentucky, was embroiled in tariff debates in Congress, he visited the woolen mill on a tour of the Northeast with his wife. They were greeted by more than two hundred operatives lined up outside, and Mr. Clay was "presented with [a] roll of broadcloth . . . made by this company, as a sample of the product of American industry." In 1849, justly proud of their small outpost and its contribution to the country's growing textile industry, the villagers of the Hollow changed the name of the place to Leeds, after England's great textile center. This influenced the naming of Florence a few years later.

Lizzie's father may have been one of those workers who greeted Senator Clay. Though Joseph Allen had inherited a family farm, he worked in one of the company's three mills during much of Lizzie's childhood. Of significance, this meant that he came in daily contact with English immigrants who had been recruited by the company to weave wool as only they knew how. Yet Captain Allen, as Lizzie's father was known, had fought against the British in the War of 1812, and so many of his great-uncles had fought in the Revolutionary War only sixty years earlier that the Allen family was famous in these parts for battling the redcoats. That Captain Allen not only worked alongside the English but also granted his daughter's hand to William Skinner was utterly symbolic of the changing times.

Even so, Captain Allen would not have approved of certain of Skinner's beliefs. Allen was a celebrated teetotaler, and Skinner not only drank freely but also believed wholeheartedly in the medicinal and nutritional value of alcohol. He thought nothing of drinking sherry when coming down with a cold or giving a lady some ale if she were feeling faint. He had no patience for the temperance movement; to the contrary, he aspired one day to have a wine cellar. Skinner also made no bones about the fact that he wanted nothing more in life than to make a lot of money producing silk. This, too, could have been off-putting to a man whose family, for generations, had been strict Calvinists, preaching that all desires for earthly gain were inherently sinful as they subjugated the desire to serve the Lord in heaven. However, Captain Allen had forsaken his inheritance as a farmer to make more money as a mill worker. Though devoted to his faith, he too had aspired to make a better living.

Like her father, Lizzie felt that the "chief aim" of her life should be "to glorify God and enjoy him forever." At sixteen she joined the Northampton First Church, and at twenty she became a lifetime member of the American Tract Society, vowing to abide by its mission "to diffuse a knowledge of our Lord Jesus Christ as the Redeemer of sinners and to promote the interests of vital goodliness and sound morality." One can only wonder what she thought of Skinner's upbringing in a neighborhood where people spent the Sabbath attending dog fights and, when asked, "had never heard of God." Skinner had been baptized, of course, but his early years were quite unobservant, and if Lizzie believed she might "save" him, she would have been partly correct. Her strong will was every bit a match for his, and in due time, with Lizzie beside him, Skinner would become a regular churchgoer, developing a very strong faith in the process. But he would always maintain, no matter what, that everyone was entitled to his or her own beliefs.

In marrying Lizzie Allen, Skinner once again married a woman of "pure American ancestry"; her family helped settle Northampton all the way back in the 1650s. Just as important, she was of notable intelligence. For her secondary school studies Lizzie had attended Williston Seminary in Easthampton (like Nancy Warner's sisters), and as one of the most precocious members of the Female Class of 1848, she graduated at the uncommonly young age of fourteen. At least as important, her intelligence included a marked resourcefulness. The life of a schoolteacher was a difficult one in rural America in the antebellum period. But Lizzie managed to work consistently, both near and far from home, making a respectable living for herself, every bit as industrious, in her own way, as both her father and the man she was marrying.

Coincidentally or not, Lizzie also had notable connections to the silk industry. Her grandmother Rhoda Parsons had been "the first woman in Massachusetts to raise silkworms; and moreover she did her own reeling and dyeing." More recently Lizzie's brother-in-law Marshall Hubbard and uncle William Parsons had followed Samuel Whitmarsh to Jamaica, after his debacle in Northampton, to try to establish silk culture in the Caribbean. (The experiment did not work.) Thus, over the years Lizzie had already heard many a conversation about silk. She would have been aware of the difficulties inherent in silk manufacturing, the high percentage of failure, the addictive nature of speculation, and, above all, the beauty of this unique thread. In other ways too she was well suited to understand the kind of passion that drove Skinner on, despite the odds. Two of her brothers had gone west to California in the great gold rush. One had even ventured to South America and as far away as Australia in search of gold. If either became rich, no one talked about it, which probably means neither made any real fortune, but the fact remains that they weren't leading ordinary or provincial lives. And neither, it seemed, would Lizzie.

Lizzie and William settled down to their wedded life in Florence, along with the two girls, now five and three. One might have thought that Lizzie would forsake her career as a teacher to assume the roles of mother and housekeeper, but she did not. Directly on returning from her honeymoon, she commenced teaching at a school in Leeds, about two miles away, which begs the question of who looked after the children while both their father and Lizzie were working, in two different villages, no less. In all probability the girls stayed under the governance of their Warner relatives, with whom Skinner remained friendly. When Lizzie gave up teaching a few months later, it was only because she became pregnant and was probably dismissed by the school committee. Her desire to teach after marrying demonstrates her willfulness and independence, characteristics perhaps to be expected from the youngest in a family marked by unconventional interests, but it also raises the possibility that she taught because she had to for financial reasons. Despite the fancy portraits and fine clothing, her husband's position was anything but stable.

In July 1856, two months after they were married, a local correspondent for the New York City–based Mercantile Agency, a well-known credit-reporting firm, filed a report on Skinner noting that he was a man of "good character and habits" but that he was "not supposed worth much, perhaps [$5,000]." Skinner was still operating with a minimum of capital with no cushion for failure, and failure remained a real possibility. In a strong market he could "keep his head above water," but if trade faltered for one or two seasons, the small-time manufacturer, operating largely on credit, could be "lost."

Even so, Skinner decided to expand his mill. He had outgrown the Lewis place and "was always complaining about being cramped for room." That facility had never been intended for textile manufacturing, and Skinner knew that he could not improve his business in a space that simply wouldn't allow it. In the spring of 1857 he moved forward with construction and erected an entirely new factory adjacent to the old one. The new building was three stories high, eighty feet long, and thirty feet wide. Unlike the Lewis place, it was specifically designed to withstand the vibrations and weight of textile machinery and to provide optimal space and light for the workers. Each story of the mill was an open, loft-like expanse to accommodate as many machines as possible, with windows on all sides for maximum light. The walls of the building were brick, which meant they were fireproof, and, being several feet thick, were much stronger than the plaster and lath construction of the old wooden mill. The flooring was probably a slow-burning wood, and the stairwell was enclosed in a tower that projected from the front of the building, another attempt to prevent the spread of fire from floor to floor. At the top of the tower was a bell, the area's first mill bell—as important for punctuality as for sounding alarms.

The windows, though numerous, were not intended for ventilation. They were operable, certainly, for egress in case of emergency, but they stayed shut to maintain the constant, slightly humid atmosphere inside the mill that kept the silk supple and cooperative. Fortunately for Skinner's workers, the need for fresh air in a silk mill was "not so imperative as in other textile mills." Cotton mills were filled with dust and a perennial haze of cough-inducing lint (which led to brown lung disease), and woolen mills subjected their workers to dust and effluvia not only from wool but also shoddy and mungo (a waste wool used to make cheap felt). Silk mills, on the other hand, managed to stay clean by virtue of the intrinsic cleanliness of the fiber. Skinner's mill, and the silk mills down in Florence, would have been among the healthiest textile mills in the valley in which to work. (They may have been the healthiest, period.)

Skinner's new complex demonstrated not only how far the American silk industry had progressed in twenty years, but how far he'd come in ten. He now owned one of the largest silk mills in the state, and, although there still weren't many silk mills around, that status provided it with a certain prestige. Skinner had a long way to go if he ever wished to have a mill as large as one of the famous cotton mills near Boston, along the Merrimack River, massive complexes of brick that were almost small cities unto themselves. But he wasn't out to be a titan of industry, just to be his own boss and as successful in his business as he could be.

With the expansion of the mill, Skinner finally moved his family to Haydenville. He purchased a small plot of land down the street from some members of the Bartlett family and proceeded to construct a sizable house, Italianate in style, with a low-pitched roof and broad eaves. Completely breaking up the monotony of the row of clapboard farmhouses, Skinner's new residence was the most fashionable house this section of town had ever seen. It wasn't necessarily bigger than the farmhouses, nor was it anywhere near as big as either of the Hayden mansions down in Haydenville proper, but the attractive, European-influenced home made exactly the statement Skinner wished. Here were wealth, worldliness, and real roots being planted.

As fate would have it, the nation's worst financial crisis in twenty years hit the marketplace not long after construction on Skinner's home was finished. The New York branch of the Ohio Life Insurance and Trust Company, a significant financial institution, suddenly and unexpectedly failed on August 24, 1857, precipitating the Panic of 1857. The New York Stock Exchange spiraled into chaos, and fear of widespread collapse set in as "prominent stocks fell eight or ten per cent in a day, and fortunes were made and lost between ten o'clock in the morning and four of the afternoon." Banks in the Northeast suffered the most, but the nation as a whole felt the crisis, and America now entered a recession that would last until the Civil War.

The impact on manufacturing was severe, as goods lay in surplus and orders diminished. Skinner's bold move to build another factory suddenly seemed to have been made at the worst possible time. An agent for the Mercantile Agency echoed a growing sense of unease within the local financial community, as everyone was on edge about credit. "[Skinner] has just put up a new factory . . . & is making a show of prosperity," the agent wrote, "but I don't know whether the profits justify it or not."

Toward the onset of winter Skinner was in such financial straits that he had to shut down the factory. His enlarged new mill sat empty and dark, with only the footsteps of the night watchman making any sound. Occasionally he had had to shut down the factory because the Mill River was so low that it couldn't power the mills, but that was always a temporary suspension, something the weather would fix in a flash. This situation was far more alarming, for the forces at play were strictly financial and completely unpredictable. Sure enough, as the situation progressed, Skinner began to fall behind on his payments.

He wasn't the only one suffering, as textile mills throughout the region were feeling the full force of this recession. Down the way, Joel Hayden and his partners had to close the cotton mill indefinitely. By January 1858 the *Hampshire Gazette & Northampton Courier* reported that both the silk mill and the cotton mill were up and running again, "but neither, we believe with full time or help." The partial resumption of business wasn't enough to keep Skinner in the clear. His debts to one firm in particular, down in jittery New York City, were such that no matter his appeals for an extension on his loans the firm "would not extend his paper." Indeed they ended up suing him, and Skinner finally experienced the danger of the inflated credit system on which he depended. If his products didn't sell, he couldn't pay his bills, and if he couldn't pay his bills, he couldn't get credit, and if he couldn't get credit, he was in trouble.

Hard to say, really, how bad things got for him, but one particular letter, written several years later, indicates how he approached the situation, as well as what he may have learned from it. Counseling an acquaintance on the verge of bankruptcy in 1868, Skinner wrote, "My advice to you would be to compromise with your creditors. You can then start knew [*sic*] where you are & start afresh. . . . I think this year [will be] a regular 57 & any man that is not well healed will go down. . . . There is no use in trying to patch up unless there is some foundation. I have had a good deal of experience in these matters." It would seem that Skinner handled the New York firm in exactly that way, perhaps agreeing to pay a portion of the debt up front and the rest in installments, with interest. To do so, of course, required capital, and Skinner quickly raised money, much as Vallentine had once done, by mortgaging his personal property, both in Haydenville and Florence. Unlike Vallentine, however, Skinner did not mortgage his factory, thus keeping his largest asset, even at this very low moment, entirely in his name. What "foundation" Skinner may have had—the kind that would have enabled him to negotiate with his creditors in the first place—is less clear. He didn't have a firm financial footing; otherwise he wouldn't have been sued. His factory, which was considered a "fine mill," provided him with worth, but the silk business was hardly the sort of stable industry that would have made creditors feel secure. What Skinner did have, though, was a solid reputation and, ironically, a good credit rating.

Today credit is approved or denied depending on a person's ability to make prompt and consistent payments. Skinner's credit standing, by contrast, had nothing to do with his financial history. Rather his rating was based on his perceived moral character, and those weighing in on this were his neighbors in Haydenville, Leeds, and Florence. In those days character was considered the primary barometer for judging a man's ability to meet his engagements. Reporters for the Mercantile Agency were always local men, who listened to the talk about town, made inquiries here and there, and based their reports on what others had to say. These reports were bound in volumes and filed in New York City, providing a centralized means for evaluating businesses and businessmen in the Northeast. Thus, the firm in New York that sued Skinner might have appealed to the Mercantile Agency for information on him and, in so doing, discovered that among his peers, presumably those who knew him best, Skinner was thought to be "safe," "easy in money matters," and, most important, "of good character and habits."

Skinner may have risked aggressively, but he was widely considered "meticulously honest," "sincere in purpose," and "untiring" in pursuit of any goal. Businessmen in Williamsburg and Northampton endorsed him as creditworthy, and, perhaps as a result, the New York firm was more willing to negotiate. By August 1858 Skinner had settled the lawsuit and was able to start anew.

The following year his mill entered its fifth year of operation. While not exactly booming, it was doing a "fair business" that kept activity lively about its grounds. Smoke belched from the smokestack, teams arrived with raw silk and departed with finished goods, the clamor of machinery rang from dawn to dusk. Skinner had weathered the storm of '57—better than a great many others in fact. The owners of the Northampton Woolen Company, the largest and most historic textile mill in the valley, had gone out of business, and all three of their mills had been sold (one of them to Samuel Hill for another silk mill). This failure alone made any manufacturer in the area who'd managed to survive the panic a bit more noteworthy. It was no accident, then, that in the summer of 1859, Skinner was elected a juror for the town of Williamsburg, his first civic duty, implying that his Yankee neighbors had begun to embrace him as a true member of their community.

Meanwhile, Lizzie had made a home for him in the house across the street, taken Nellie and Nina under her wing, and bravely started down the dangerous and often heartbreaking path of childbearing. On June 12, 1857, she gave birth to a son, William Cobbett, back in Northampton, choosing to have her first child at her parents' house, where she could have the assistance of her mother and sisters. Lizzie was thrilled to have a boy and, finally, a child of her own. "How pleased I was that you were a *boy*," she later reminisced to Will, "and how delighted I was that I could call you mine." Unfortunately Will was not an easy baby. Nor was this an easy time, with the onset of the Panic, and, like many new mothers, Lizzie experienced considerable anxiety after his birth. She soon enough found her bearings, however, and two years later, on July 15, 1859, gave birth in Haydenville to a daughter, whom they christened Elizabeth Allen (after Lizzie) but whom they eventually nicknamed Libbie. The family was growing.

The same month Libbie arrived, Skinner sold his property in Florence and paid off that mortgage. After these transactions he had no more material connection with the village of Florence; that part of his family's life was over. He and his wife and children were now permanent residents of the town of Williamsburg, living in the village of Haydenville.

By 1860 Skinner was thought to be "doing well." The *Hampshire Gazette* reported, "His silks are noted for their excellence," and, in a blush of exuberance, added, "[They] have always found a steady demand in the market." Demand may not have been exactly steady, but certainly Skinner had had an unmistakable impact on his surroundings. In the six years since he'd moved into the Lewis place, its neighborhood, once a sleepy part of town, had taken on a life of its own, the population doubling to roughly 120 people. Nearly every home in this section housed one or more silk operatives, and an older couple in the area, William and Mehala Jenkins, had even turned their home into a boardinghouse. Aurelia Damon was one of their boarders now, as well as, for a while, Skinner's little sister Sarah. New houses had begun going up along the tree-lined road, and when Skinner finally built his own there, he became more than just a mill owner. He became the backbone of this growing community. People began to refer to the stretch of highway between Haydenville and Williamsburg as "Skinner's village," a moniker that was authenticated by the *Hampshire Gazette* on July 17, 1860: "Mr. Skinner [knows] no such word as fail. Under his management quite a little village has sprung up about his factory and the place is now called Skinnerville."

Skinnerville! Did Skinner take any satisfaction knowing that, in his adopted country, there existed a community (albeit a tiny one) bearing his name? Unfortunately, there's no way to know what he thought of this tribute or whether he even had anything to do with it. Skinner was not shy about promoting his products, so he would hardly have been reluctant to attach his name to a place, further enriching his reputation. What's certain is that he didn't read the *Gazette* on July 17, 1860, when it was delivered to his house with the mail that day. Perhaps feeling, as some others still did, that he "should have more capital to give perfect ease" and sensing no growth in the market as the nation spiraled toward civil war, he had decided to invest in a speculation overseas. When "Skinnerville" made its debut in the press, Skinner was actually thousands of miles away, in a second-class cabin on a steamship bound for Liverpool.

Chapter Seven

During the 1850s, when little headway was made in convincing Americans of the value of American silk, there was nevertheless a great deal of progress going on in the trade's machine shops. Machinists continued to tinker with existing machinery, making improvements and advancements in the twisting, sorting, and cleaning of silk, as well as the speed and accuracy of machines. Machine twist proved the greatest innovation of the decade for silk men, but there were others that drew excitement, a few of which could be attributed to Lucius Dimock, the Florence machinist who had once worked with Captain Conant and who had probably inspired Samuel Hill. Skinner knew Dimock too, and when in 1860 Dimock invented a machine for improving the luster of silk, Skinner made a radical investment in it. He struck a deal with Dimock in which he purchased the British patent rights for the machine and then sailed to England with a model of it, hoping to reap a sizable return on the investment.

Then as now, international patent rights had to be acquired separately, by territory, and most small-time inventors had little interest in crossing the ocean to navigate foreign patent laws in countries with which they were wholly unfamiliar. Further, they had no way of defending their patents abroad once they returned home. Nor would most machinists, being day laborers, have the money to make such a trip in the first place. If possible, it made more sense to sell the foreign rights upfront to a speculator like Skinner, creating a win-win situation for both inventor and investor. Dimock received a few hundred dollars without ever leaving home, for a patent he wouldn't have pursued anyway, and in exchange Skinner received the rights to make, potentially, several thousand dollars on something he didn't invent. Indeed in the six or so weeks that Skinner anticipated being away, he believed he might be able to make anywhere from $3,000 to $5,000 on the machine. Not only would this be some of the quickest money he'd ever earned, but it would greatly free him up to make additional investments in his business.

Speculations are unpredictable, but the smartest investors typically have some very good reasons for betting on the risk. Skinner certainly did. Six months earlier England and France had signed a free-trade agreement that enabled French silks, among other fancy products, to enter the English market essentially duty-free. Suddenly British silk manufacturers needed ways to make their products more attractive and competitive, and Skinner anticipated that Dimock's machine, which increased the luster of silk thread, was something that these manufacturers, in their state, couldn't afford not to buy.

Skinner was to depart from Boston on June 13 on the steamship *Arabia*. He was so nervous beforehand that he lost the ticket for his trunk on the train from Northampton and was overwhelmingly grateful when the conductor let the issue slide. His brother George, now a silk manufacturer himself down in Yonkers, New York, traveled more than a hundred miles to see him off—which says a great deal about the brothers' respect for the gravity of a transatlantic voyage. Even if lost ships were rare, the reality was that any ship could go down, never to be heard from again. In 1836 an Irish emigrant, fearful of the voyage to America, expressed what many felt generally: "If it was any place I could *travel* to by *land* I would not mind it so much . . . but I feel a kind of *terror* of the *sea.*"

To think that he, William, was risking his life again, as well as the welfare of his wife and children, to go back to England, after all he had been through to get away from that place, made both brothers want a drink. Unfortunately the ship left too early in the morning for them to find one, and Skinner was sorely disappointed that they couldn't at least toast his health. He needed the boost. "I am mighty nervous," he wrote from his hotel near the depot, "but after I get on board ship I hope to become cool." George comforted him as best he could, assuring his brother that he would look after Lizzie and the children in the event that Will never returned.

Apart from his trunk, Skinner had some sort of crate in which was carefully packed a full-scale replica of Dimock's New and Improved Machine for Stretching and Glossing Silk. Like a modern steam iron, Dimock's machine did two things at once. It simultaneously stretched and steamed recently dyed hanks of silk, thereby removing kinks and wrinkles and adding luster and brilliance. Part of the appeal of the machine was that it was portable and easily manipulated by hand. In appearance it was a fascinating-looking box on short, squat legs, and Skinner intended taking it to "all the silk dyers and manufactures" in and around London. He planned on showing how the dyed silk was placed inside this contraption and looped over two bars that would gently separate from each other while steam was admitted into the chamber. The box was shut tight during the entire operation, and the operator, through the use of a hand lever, would be responsible for both the degree of stretch and the pressure of steam. Skinner also planned on keeping something of a journal about the machine, to "[write] down all the facts [he could] gather," possibly to pass along to Dimock, who would be eager to know how the machine fared on its first trial.

Skinner's second voyage on the ocean was markedly different from his first one. "What a wonderful thing steam is," he wrote, as the ship cut through the waters. "The *Arabia* is 345 feet long & has twin engines of 500 horse power each & consumes from 95 to 100 tons of coal per day." He ate his meals at a dining table with table service, and the only unpleasant aspect at mealtimes was the lady who sat opposite him, who, he complained, "eats like a Hog." He joked, "It is having to see her eat that has taken my appetite away," but the truth was he was seasick. After one nasty bout of retching, he wrote to Lizzie, "If I ever get back no *speculative* but an *undoubted* certainty will ever tempt me to cross again."

His nerves did not, as he had hoped, become cool as the ship made headway. He worried about Lizzie and the children. ("You cannot think how much I am continually worrying about you.") He worried about the mill and, since King had left to start his own business elsewhere, about the dyehouse as well. Imagining what Lizzie might be doing back home, he wrote, "I suppose you are up to your eyes in business & I only wish I was—this confining me with nothing to do is as bad as being in a prison." He couldn't read; it made him seasick. So he talked a lot with the crew, with whom he felt most comfortable, and observed his fellow passengers. "We have a fighting man on board—named 'Dublin Tricks,'" he dryly remarked. "There is no doubt but Sing-Sing is where he ought to be." On another occasion, probably the first time he was ever called a "Yankee," he amused himself at the expense of some southerners, whose growing hatred for the North he found very unimpressive.

As the *Arabia* steamed farther away from America, he wrote home on one of the tables belowdecks. Surrounded by strangers and damp, inhospitable air, he told Lizzie, "Absence will make my heart grow fonder." But in truth that was hardly possible. He loved his wife, as he said, "with all [his] soul." He stared at her picture. He wore the vest she had made for him "all the time." "I often shut my eyes & get out of my body & come & see you & kiss you," he wrote at one turn. But he also kept telling her what to do, demonstrating his inability to stop being the boss. He wanted her to send him updates on the mill. He expected her to oversee a large painting job while he was gone and pushed her to "have things done up in shape" so that he would be "satisfied." Even when offering encouragement he retained an authoritative air. "I must now say my darling that you are the woman to see after things & I hope you will show yourself to all the folks that you are smart."

Near the close of the journey Skinner's resolve was challenged in a violent storm when, for hour upon hour, "all the poetry of fair weather [was] gone." But even as gale-force winds whipped up the sea and waves crashed over the bow of the *Arabia,* even as seasickness tested him again and again so that he felt miserably alone and an eternity from home, he remained as driven as ever, finding strength not in God or family but in the thrill of success. "I would give a good deal if I could but see you," he wrote to Lizzie during the storm, "but the love of gain is the reason I am now away."

After ten days at sea, on June 23, Skinner arrived in Liverpool, and after a brief delay at the customs house headed south to London in the rain. He had a stopover in Manchester to change trains and found himself with several hours to spare, but he didn't visit any silk mills in the area. One might have thought this an excellent opportunity to meet some of the manufacturers in the North and begin generating interest in his machine. However, due to British patent laws, Skinner had to keep the machine completely secret. Unlike the American system, the British granted the first party to file for a patent the legal claim to the idea, regardless of where it came from. Skinner had to hide his invention until registering it with the London patent office or risk the possibility that someone might steal Dimock's idea. Holding back was not in Skinner's nature, and all he could think about was the time he was wasting. When he finally arrived in London, the first thing he wrote was, "A week has nearly passed & I have hardly got under head way with the machine."

His frustration was not helped by the weather. The rain persisted, and by now he was "[suffering] every day with cold," cursing himself for having left his best overcoat at home, and his boots were getting so dirty they were becoming an embarrassment. He would have to buy another pair.

In London, Skinner threaded his way to Chancery Lane, where he found the patent building—an edifice he never would have seen as a child—and in the presence of a bunch of well-spoken English clerks, handed over Dimock's diagrams, now carefully labeled as his own. Then he had several days to kill while he waited for the application to be processed. Walking about, he was "struck with the general improvement that has taken place with the people," finding that "they dress entirely different & look more intelligent than they did when [I was] here before." He was impressed that the beer had improved. "There has been quite a change in the drink of Londoners since I left," he explained to Lizzie. "Bitter Ale is the drink & it is very good. I have been compelled to love it." He also went shopping for presents for Lizzie and the children and, of personal significance, reunited with some of his family.

Skinner rented a room on Great Winchester Street, in the same house where his aunt Ellen lived, and subsequently spent evenings with her. One can only wonder at Ellen's interest in the richly transformed life of her oldest nephew, the boy who had once run errands for her, whose restless mind she had helped tame with the works of Shakespeare. Skinner next visited Betsy, possibly his favorite sister, who welcomed him to her home (nowhere near "the evil quarter-mile") and introduced him to her two young children, whom Skinner found "bright as a button."

Betsy didn't recognize him, he was so changed, and neither did their mother, whom Betsy took him to visit. Upon seeing his mother Skinner had such a visceral reaction that he was apparently unable to speak. Perhaps she was drunk, diseased, blind from so many years at the loom, or suffering from dementia; it's impossible to know. But in response to her brother's discomfort, Betsy lied and told their mother that she had come with her husband, Captain John Child Burroughs. It's hard to imagine what Skinner felt after this visit, but his mother certainly felt nothing remarkable. She remained completely unaware that her firstborn son had come home after fifteen years.

Though it was essential to keep Dimock's improvement a secret, Skinner nevertheless hired a cab one day and took the machine in its crate to a particular dyehouse in Spitalfields. Here he showed it to a chemist named Jim Keith, with whom he must have had a previous acquaintance or a very good reason to trust him. After Skinner demonstrated the ease of the machine, its portability, and its effects, Keith was on board to help sell it, using his many contacts within the current silk community. "Jim Keith thinks well of it," Skinner reported to Lizzie, "& we shall have it in full blast Monday & next week I hope to write you a flattering report of the prospects." The patent came through two days later, on July 4, and he and Keith immediately began demonstrating the machine to prospective buyers. Success was instantaneous. Skinner excitedly informed Lizzie, "[Parties] that have seen it work think it is the greatest thing they ever saw."

What Skinner needed now was a partner, someone to whom he'd hand over the machine in exchange for 50 percent of its profits. The price of one machine would be £100, or roughly $500 at the time, so he and his partner would each make $250 per machine, less manufacturing and delivery costs, presumably. This was a very good deal, and given the incredible amount of interest the machine generated in just a handful of days from those who saw it, Skinner also, swiftly, found a business partner.

The identity of the man is not certain, but the name "Thomas Keith in London" appears in one of Skinner's ledgers beside a few entries for freight, patent expenses, and royalties. Thomas Keith (who was almost certainly related to Jim) was a well-known silk dyer whose recent experimentation with artificial dyes had sent shockwaves through the silk trade. In 1857 he had accepted the request of a teenager named William Perkin, another East Londoner, to sample a kind of dye that Perkin had invented. Perkin's dye, a shade of mauve, was entirely manmade from coal tar, and Thomas Keith became the first dyer to use it successfully. The idea that silk could be dyed using nonorganic colors was a groundbreaking concept, with extraordinary implications for the future, and Skinner and every other dyer and manufacturer worth his salt would have been closely following the advancement of these "aniline dyes." That Keith, who was on the forefront of this revolution, would invest in Skinner's machine might have made a considerable difference in its ongoing popularity.

Skinner and Keith needed to secure twenty buyers to bring in $10,000 in order for Skinner to reach his goal of earning half that, and they had to find these buyers quickly, both to generate interest and to make good on their investment. The machine was not going to remain a novelty for long. Skinner's window of opportunity was small and he knew it. "I must make the thing go ere I leave," he told Lizzie.

Back home, Lizzie was making do and, like Skinner, discovering just how much she appreciated her other half. On June 28, with still no word of whether the *Arabia* had reached Liverpool, Lizzie had written him, "Again I am about to address you but words are inadequate to express my feelings towards you. . . . If I am ever again permitted to enjoy your society . . . I shall certainly know how to appreciate it. My thoughts are constantly with you." Sounding a lot like her husband, she added, "If it were not for my household cares I should be *very very lonely*. How much better it is for people to have enough to do."

Skinner received Lizzie's first letter in the same post that he received word from employee George McFarlane at the mill. "Everything is working like a charm," McFarlane told him right off the bat. "Much better than expected. The help all appear to be doing their duty." The dyeing that Skinner had been worried about was going very well ("no blunders yet"). The silk was coming out with an excellent weight and a "very good shine." (Knowing Skinner would question this, he added, "You will see it and then you can give your verdict.") As for orders, there were plenty. "[Mr.] Hovey wants 7 cases 11 oz. . . . I sent off today a 50lb case to Foster & Libby—The day after you left we rec'd a letter from Merrills & W Slatering. They were in a great strait for twist. . . . I think you will be pleased when you come home."

Once Skinner had the patent he spent most of his time promoting the machine. In so doing he learned just how desperate the silk trade in England really was. Although Britain's silk workers hadn't known prosperity since the eighteenth century, their future had never been so uncertain. In London, Skinner wrote, "the silk trade is very dull—men half employed." In Leek, he wrote, "the silk trade is very dull in all its branches." In Macclesfield, the city that manufactured so much of the thread used by weavers in Spitalfields, "all the people look half starved & in fact they talk of opening up soup kitchens—so bad is the silk trade." He couldn't believe that pay was as little as $1.75 a week—for a full sixty-hour week—for *skilled* labor. (He paid $3.)

The fact that Dimock's machine, an *American*-made machine, would be something that British silk men welcomed—and that some of them acquired—demonstrated how drastically the silk industries in the two countries were changing. While one was suddenly threatened and foundering from years of stasis, the other was innovating, driven by a desire to earn market share. For an opportunist like Skinner, the climate was more than ideal for introducing technology and profiting from a crumbling state of trade. Of course, one might think this was a small bit of revenge for him, given his childhood, and it may have been.

Skinner made a decision during the second week of his stay to visit his mother one more time. He evidently now felt the courage to speak to her; he may have even wanted to give her some money. This time he went by himself, and in what must have been a cramped, poorly venti- lated room, he told her what she could not see: that he was her eldest son, William, back from America. Almost immediately he seems to have regretted it. Her reaction appears to have been as wretched as the circumstances in which she lived, and after less than an hour Skinner found it unbearable to be with her any longer. As he walked away down the street, he felt debilitating disgust. "I felt such a contempt for her," he wrote Lizzie afterward, "that I was sick the remainder of the day."

But Skinner hadn't come to England to revisit the past. He had come to make money. And the experience had proven to him not only that the original risk was worth it, but also that he had made the best decision of his life when he bought his ticket for a berth on the *Toronto*. "I have seen nothing here," he concluded well into the trip, "that would tempt me to leave America."

As it was, America back home was about to enter a period of unfathomable instability. The Republican Party (of which Skinner was not a member; he was a lifelong Democrat) had nominated Abraham Lincoln as their presidential candidate on May 16, 1860, and following Lincoln's win of the highest office in the land, South Carolina (whence came those southerners on the *Arabia*) and ten other states seceded from the Union to form the Confederacy. The resulting four years of war, beginning with a Confederate attack on Fort Sumter on April 12, 1861, and ending with the surrender of General Lee on April 9, 1865, created the bloodbath that left no one untouched.

Like most of the Northeast, the town of Williamsburg was firmly in support of the Union. As one local historian put it, "Williamsburg was too far north and too 'New England' in sentiment to have room for any disunity over the slavery question and the Civil War." The Stars and Stripes, which began to fly continuously above mills and post offices, became a daily reminder of the struggle, and throughout this period one couldn't walk ten minutes in any direction without encountering some evidence of the war. The town of Williamsburg furnished 250 men for Lincoln's army ("twenty-nine above its quota") and consistently raised money to outfit its soldiers, provide them with a monthly wage, and care for their families in their absence. After the president's call for troops in July 1862, "the largest and most enthusiastic meeting ever known in Williamsburg" took place, and Skinner, along with Joel Hayden and Lewis Bodman, pledged a total of $800 "on the spot" to help support whoever came forward to serve. Records show that Williamsburg's citizens ultimately paid $20,000 in aid for its volunteers and their dependents, and suffered, on average, the loss of one in ten soldiers. Skinnerville, small as it was, contributed fourteen men to the war, which was nearly half the number of eligible men in the village. "Occasionally the pulse of patriotism beats as high in this little village as in other places of larger growth," wrote the *Hampshire Gazette*.

Lizzie attended and hosted sewing bees to make clothing for the soldiers, but as the wife of a manufacturer and the mother of children too young to serve (Willie was five in July 1862, and their second son, Joseph, was two months old), she had the luxury of participating in these events without being directly related to anyone in uniform. Nor did the children ever have to worry about their father going off to battle, and Nellie, for one, who was a teenager during the war, would have understood exactly the implications of this blessing. Indeed so small by comparison was the family's involvement in the war that, through the ages, members had to resort to exaggeration. A grand story would emerge that Skinner's brother-in-law Captain Burroughs was a blockade runner for the South (which he may well have been) and that somehow, for a time, Skinner hid the man in the house in Skinnerville, lest he be captured by Union forces. This story provides the family with a rather daring exploit during the crisis, but the likelihood of Skinner's having done such a thing is zero. For Skinner the war became a turning point in his career and social standing, and he never would have jeopardized such gain to harbor a man affiliated with the enemy, even if that man was his dear sister's husband and even if the man's life had been at stake. Skinner would have seen Burroughs as a threat and wanted nothing to do with him.

The war years made Skinner both rich and reputable. As devastating as this period was for most communities, it was also—as conflicts often are—propitious for industry. When the federal government needed money to finance its cause, "one of the ways was to levy a war duty on all silk goods," ultimately raising the tariff to 60 percent. Having witnessed the deleterious effects of free trade on the British silk industry and having labored for years without any concerted protective measures at home, Skinner had declared to Lizzie while abroad, "We must have a high tariff if we ever want to develop the [resources] of [our] country in manufacturing." Captain Conant had gone to Washington back in 1846 to win support for protection, as had others at various times, yet nothing proved so advantageous to this cause as the war effort. "It is an undeniable fact that [the rise in the] tariff was the great stimulus to domestic silk mills," observed the silk historian Shichiro Matsui, "and it is reasonable to state that the real foundation of the silk industry in this country was laid during [the civil war] period."

The fact that all levies on the tariff had to be paid in gold only enhanced the effect of this protection. The price of gold skyrocketed during the war, causing inflation to set in, and most luxury goods suffered as a result. In the past, inflation would have greatly harmed the American silk trade, since most consumers simply were not willing to spend even a pittance on native silk, let alone an inflated price. However, with both the tariff and the price of gold significantly elevating the costs of already expensive foreign silks, American silks suddenly became more appealing.

In December 1864, while fighting raged on in the South and at least one of Skinnerville's soldiers, William Bartlett, struggled to survive in a Confederate prison, a reporter for the Mercantile Agency noted for the first time, "Wm Skinner [of] Haydenville . . . has made largely in silks" and "he is supposed to be rich." In the spring of 1865 another wrote that Skinner's credit was "very good," that he had "made money," and that sources close to him estimated his worth at $50,000. This was a far cry from a decade earlier, when his assets had amounted to a tenth of that. By the end of the war Skinner's mill was consuming $100,000 of raw silk per year, more than triple what it had initially required, and it was producing at least twelve thousand pounds of sewing silk annually, valued at an estimated $140,000. Skinner's taxes had also grown to be among the highest in town, and his success became hard to ignore. The *Hampshire Gazette* reported at one point, "We notice that

Wm. Skinner, Esq. Sewing Silk manufacturer, has up a new building every time we drive by, and judging from the amount he contributes to Uncle Sam's crib every month, he must be making a large quantity of goods, or else disposed to be very generous to his adopted uncle." As a direct result of the war effort, Skinner became the second wealthiest man in town, trailing only Joel Hayden.

By this time Skinner was taking advantage of a broad network of businesses that had spread throughout the valley, all catering to the area's growing industrial base. He purchased spindles and paper in Northampton, soap and boxes in Florence, machinery in Leeds, and metalware in Haydenville. To care for his family in the event of loss, he had begun to purchase fire and life insurance policies from local agents of national companies, and as for the money coming in, he deposited his earnings in the oldest bank in the valley, the Northampton National Bank. As one might expect, Skinner became a valued customer to this institution, and its stockholders, counting among them some of the most distinguished capitalists in the area, came to know him well. His account at this bank thus spread his reputation in exactly the kind of circle in which he liked to be known: one of influence that could be of service to him later.

Not surprisingly, Skinner's civil clout had grown in proportion to his escalating profits, and in January 1863 the town of Williamsburg voted to build him a school in Skinnerville. This was good news for all the families in the village, bringing education within reach of every child, but it was arguably even better news for Skinner. As production increased at the mill, he needed more child workers, but by law any child who worked for him had to attend school for a minimum of three months a year. In the past this had been a challenging requirement for the children to satisfy. Skinner's youngest workers had to walk fully a mile to the nearest grammar school in Haydenville, which had cut into the time they could spend working on the family farm. The new schoolhouse, then, made employment at Skinner's mill easier and more desirable, now that satisfying state requirements wasn't so taxing.

Then came a bit of scandal.

Miss Martha Brown, a young woman who had been working for Skinner for at least five years and who lived at the boardinghouse, disappeared on Wednesday, July 30, 1865, sometime after 5 p.m., having last been seen walking along a road about half a mile north of the mill. She did not come home that evening, or the day after, and presently search parties were sent out in all directions. Ponds were dragged. Woods were canvassed. Finally, after six days of "much excitement in the neighborhood" but no success in finding her, it was "generally understood that she had wandered away and died." The *Hampshire Gazette* noted, in closing, "Information concerning her whereabouts will be rewarded by Wm. Skinner."

A week later, with still no news of her, information emerged that helped fill in the gaps. Someone divulged that Miss Brown, a girl of "sensitive disposition," had been seeing a young man whom she had hoped to marry, only to have been lately "unceremoniously discarded." The implications of this would have sent imaginations atwitter, leading many to wonder if Miss Brown had been acting "immorally." Had she discovered she was pregnant, only to be rejected by her lover? Had she run away in shame? She was discovered at last about half a mile south of the factory, in some woods, exhausted and in shock. Her recovery was slow, during which time the truth of the matter must have been revealed to certain parties. But what happened to her during her disappearance and why she had left in the first place were never disclosed publicly. From this point on her story was hushed, and once Miss Brown was well enough to be on her way, she disappeared again, this time into obscurity.

A scandal of this sort could reflect quite badly on a mill. Since the early days of industrialization in New England, factory owners had striven to create wholesome environments for their workers. When the first textile mills opened there was great prejudice against them owing to the reputation of their English counterparts, famous for their wretched working conditions, which were considered breeding grounds for immorality, disease, and corruption. Few believed the American factory system would (or could) be any different. Thus when Francis Cabot Lowell, one of the most forward-thinking men of his time, built a cotton mill in Waltham, Massachusetts, in 1814, he knew that no American parent wanted his or her daughter to end up in any place remotely similar to an English textile mill. He also knew that in order to work his power looms he needed dexterous, intelligent young women, precisely the sort who had grown up on New England farms, who were better educated than most, and who were naturally hard-working. Lowell therefore established clean, safe boardinghouses for his workers, often run by respectable widows or wives, so that women from afar who wished to earn more money than they could ever make at home needn't fear leaving their family to go work at a mill. Nor did they need fear becoming trapped in a lifestyle from which they could not extricate themselves. They were encouraged to return home whenever they wished.

His approach worked and was nowhere as evident—or famous—as in the city that was modeled on his designs and posthumously named for him: Lowell, Massachusetts. When Charles Dickens visited Lowell on a tour of America in 1842, he was struck by the extraordinary differences between it and the manufacturing centers in England. "Many of the circumstances whose strong influence has been at work for years in our manufacturing towns have not arisen here," he wrote, "and there is no manufacturing population in Lowell, so to speak: for these girls (often the daughters of small farmers) come from other States, remain a few years in the mills, and then go home for good." The women whom Dickens observed in Lowell were not slaves to industry. They were "healthy in appearance, many of them remarkably so, and had the manners and deportment of young women: not of degraded brutes of burden." As for the boardinghouses, Dickens noted with interest, "The owners of the mills are particularly careful to allow no persons to enter upon the possession of these houses, whose characters have not undergone the most searching and thorough inquiry." Anyone who failed to live up to the company's expectations for modesty and morality was "removed" and their position "handed over to some more deserving person." In this way the reputation of the mill owners, and that of their mill hands, remained above reproach.

Lowell's success as a model manufacturing community (even if it was, in truth, far from idyllic) ended a few years after Dickens's visit, following the influx of Irish immigrants fleeing the potato famine. The enormous supply of cheap labor that landed on the doorsteps of the city was rapidly taken advantage of by increasingly penurious mill owners who traded social consciousness for profit. Within a decade the feel of the city had entirely changed. Gone were the days of loom sheds filled with respectable farm girls, who were, in turn, respected. In their place were desperate immigrants, with accents so strong they were barely understood, whose poverty emboldened others to treat them poorly. No longer was Lowell a place for "worthy and virtuous" New England girls.

Yet the positive view of mill work that had been so well nurtured in previous years did not disappear elsewhere. On the eve of the Civil War, Anthony Trollope visited America and beheld the legacy of Lowell: "Employment in a factory is now considered reputable by a farmer and his children. . . . Factory work is regarded as more respectable than domestic service [and] those now employed have a strong conception of the dignity of their social position." There were scores of New England girls who still wished to escape the farm, wanted to earn money of their own, and hoped to find work in a mill. As a result, in their attempt to avoid cities like Lowell, they tended to migrate to smaller industrial communities, to places like the Mill River Valley and, specifically, to mill villages such as Skinnerville.

Skinnerville was reminiscent of the early days of manufacturing, when there existed a shared feeling of responsibility between owner and worker and when care was taken to protect and preserve the morality of the workplace. Hidden away in the hills, the village offered its patron little opportunity to hire cheap immigrant labor, since few immigrants, other than the highly skilled and expensive kind, were ever going to find their way to him. Consequently it behooved Skinner to offer that which would attract a more discerning, American workforce. His boarders originally stayed in a large farmhouse (not unlike their own homes) and were cared for by an elderly couple, the Jenkinses. Then, sometime in the early 1860s, Skinner built a proper boardinghouse, which from the outside wouldn't have looked much different from the Jenkinses' home but on the inside offered a larger dining room and significantly more beds upstairs. He hired a widow to manage the place, Mrs. Sears, who, judging from accounts in some of the boarders' letters, inspired great affection from the girls. There were rules to follow, curfews to respect. Skinner's desire for the village to have its own schoolhouse also played into the "model mill village." Here was a place that supported learning as well as honest work. The boarders were offered education as well. For a small fee they could take a writing class in the dining room to improve their penmanship, a valued skill for any boarder who wished to correspond with family and friends back home. Fifteen classes cost $1.75; the materials were free. Like other mill owners, Skinner lent his employees books from his personal library. He even drove them to church on Sunday. (But whereas others required their employees to attend, Skinner, no Puritan himself, did not.) Women could expect to come to his village, work for him, and leave, their pockets richer, their talents broader, and their virtue intact.

Martha Brown brought the mill its first negative publicity, right when Skinner was in the midst of planning a major expansion, getting ready to enlarge the mill and the boardinghouse, the latter to help accommodate a greater workforce. That he offered a reward for information about her is understandable, but it also displays the degree to which he hoped the whole matter would go away, and quickly. It was bad for business. He wouldn't have wanted the poor judgment of one worker to affect, even slightly, his ability to hire others. In his mind neither he nor anyone else (such as Mrs. Sears) was at fault for whatever had happened to Miss Brown. Nor did any potential hire need fear that she would end up the same.

Skinner viewed his world in black and white. You were either with him or against him; you helped him or you hurt him. This could make him an extremely unforgiving employer. By the postwar era he had been managing people—scores of them—for more than a decade, and some lifelong patterns had been set. If he suspected that he'd been crossed, manipulated, or deceived by someone, he fired that person. In his own words, "Such a man I have no use for." And if that person had relatives who worked in the mill, he might fire them too.

Even so, Skinner was an employer who inspired great loyalty among his employees. Like others, Aurelia kept a picture of him in her house, as if he were part of her family (or she a part of his). He may have been tough and inflexible, but he was honest. At the mill "he was straight-forward and apt to be blunt, but one could take his word for anything." If he said he was going to do something, he did it. If he told you what he wanted, that was what he wanted. If he gave you a compliment, he meant it. A reporter summarized, "At times he was not diplomatic, to say the least, yet one always knew where [one] stood [with him]."

Though possessed of an exceptionally large ego, he had none of the pomposity that often goes along with that. He never forgot where he had come from, and he didn't care at all where others were from. "There are just as intelligent Irishmen . . . as Americans, or Frenchmen or Germans," he once exclaimed. "I don't care who the man is, be he an Englishman or a Turk, if he is competent." All of this was bracingly refreshing in the workplace. Skinner admired hard work and respected a person on the basis of it. "As an employer," said one, "he was kind and considerate, never forgetting his own coming up from the rank and file [in] labor."

Following the enlargement of the mill, Skinner began to attract boarders from farther away. In 1866 the Tower sisters from Chester-field, Massachusetts, ten miles north of Williamsburg, who lived at the boardinghouse and worked in the mill, recommended the mill to their visiting cousin, Lovisa Littlefield, from upstate New York. Lovisa secured a position at the mill and noted in one letter home that she wasn't the only girl from out of state; sitting next to her was "a girl from Vermont." Within a few months Lovisa was recommending the mill to her sisters. Frances arrived during the middle of winter, in January 1867, further noting that "Skinner's boarding house" was "a very good boarding house," and Ellen followed ten months later, in October.

On Ellen's first night she was assigned a spot in the "sky parlor," or attic, at the boardinghouse, sharing one of several beds and acclimating to the dim light and lack of heat. The place was very cold, but she and her sisters, along with the rest, huddled together under soldiers' blankets, willingly sacrificing the comforts of home for the freedom of being away from home and earning their own living. Within six months of Ellen's arrival she had earned enough to take a trip to Northampton, where she splurged on a hat ("a white hat, had it trimmed with black lace") for $3.50—almost twice the fare of the stagecoach that had brought her to the mill.

Although small by any standard, Skinnerville was full of life in comparison to the remote, isolated farm where the Littlefield sisters were from. It was more colorful too, the sisters learned, as they became familiar with its various characters. Captain Hayden was the regal veteran who walked with a limp as a result of his horrible wound during the war. John Christopher, an illiterate Irishman who worked in a mill in Williamsburg, was known to stumble down the street drunk. Jerome Hillman was a master rat catcher. Thaddeus Bartlett, patriarch of the Bartlett clan, was a religious zealot. Miss Gardiner, the schoolteacher, was perhaps the most popular person in the village, with her incredible knack for "teaching the young idea to shoot." And Tom Skinner, Mr. Skinner's younger brother, who, in the end, had moved up to the village with his family, was an exceptional gardener and "always had a pleasant smile for everybody." Tom had finally taken over the dyehouse during the war years and was responsible for the sterling colors the girls spooled and skeined each day.

By the fall of 1867 Skinner's estimated net worth had leaped to $150,000, and Skinnerville, with its population nearing two hundred people, no longer felt like an outpost. "By comparing the past with the present," wrote one newspaperman, "it is evident that at no very distant day it will be one of the most prosperous villages in town." Each morning a large number of men in Skinnerville donned their overalls smelling of metals and oil and walked south to the brass works, while their sisters and daughters headed off in the opposite direction, to the silk mill. The village was supplying labor to more than just one industry and positively enriching the overall community. Said Skinner at a local celebration in 1867, "Nature affords us many a contrast: but never a pleasanter one than when she gave us the American who is an Englishman, and placed a Silk Factory and a Brass Foundry side by side."

When the railroad came to town Skinnerville gained still more notice, becoming the terminus of the Northampton-Williamsburg line. Those in Williamsburg proper were unable to come up with the financing to extend the branch track a mile farther, so Skinnerville became the final station on the road. This put the village on the map. Soon people from all over were embarking and disembarking at the Skinnerville depot. Traffic wasn't tremendous by city standards, but it was respectable enough to inspire a local merchant to open a general store in the village.

As the village grew, so too did Skinner's family. By 1868 the family consisted of six growing children—Nellie, Nina, Will, Libbie, Joe, and baby Belle—and Skinner and Lizzie decided that they had outgrown their Italianate house. To build the family a bigger, more impressive residence, Skinner hired a Northampton architect, William Fenno Pratt, who knew Lizzie's family well, having traveled with some of them to Jamaica when all were much younger. Since that time Pratt had designed the City Hall in Northampton, the home of Emily Dickinson's brother in nearby Amherst, the Northampton National Bank building, the residence of Onslow Spelman in Williamsburg, and other buildings throughout the region too numerous to count. For Skinner and Lizzie, Pratt designed a three-story, five-chimney, Second Empire manse, with a piazza out front overlooking a half-moon drive. Construction of the house cost between $20,000 and $30,000—an enormous sum at the time. For perspective, Skinner's workers earned less than $500 annually; it would have taken them over forty years to earn $20,000.

Set back from the road and diagonally across from the mill, the place was a staggeringly ostentatious display of wealth and, even as the frame was going up, a spectacle of wonder. "Wm. Skinner . . . is building just the tallest kind of house for this section," declared the *Hampshire Gazette*. When construction was complete, one correspondent was given a tour of the place, after which he was so puffed up by the privilege that paragraphs of fulsome praise poured forth from his pen. "Mr. Skinner's residence . . . is one of the finest mansions in Hampshire county, and is probably equal, if it does not excel any other private residence in the number and spaciousness of its different departments. Nothing is lacking in the way of taste, elegance or convenience; its various appointments are perfect in every respect, and taken as a whole, it not only reflects the great credit on the taste of the architect, but speaks well for the munificence of the enterprising owner also."

Commensurate with his growing stature, Skinner became more involved in town affairs, serving on the school committee for Haydenville and Skinnerville, the jail or "lock-up" committee in Williamsburg, the singing committee at the Haydenville Congregational Church, and in 1871 the centennial committee for the celebration of Williamsburg's hundredth birthday. With Joel Hayden he had established the Mill River Reservoir Company and, with Hayden and others, the Williamsburg Reservoir Company, both founded in order to build reservoirs upstream to increase the waterpower of the Mill River. He became a director of the Northampton National Bank and a cofounder of the Haydenville Savings Bank, serving on the latter's influential finance committee. He was elected to be a financial representative for Williamsburg in charitable matters and also elected to help settle the affairs of the Northampton-Williamsburg railroad. With plenty in reserve, he became the second largest supporter (behind Hayden) of the Haydenville Congregational Church and spearheaded the establishment of a waterworks in Skinnerville to provide fresh water for household use as well as "for the extinguishment of fires." Skinner served as a fire warden, became a frequent speaker at local events, and, not surprisingly, as his political power grew, found it hard to stay away from politics.

In 1872 Skinner led a local campaign for Horace Greeley, who was running against Ulysses S. Grant for the presidential election that year. At the same time, he ran for state senator from Hampshire County. Republicans in power were riddled with scandal, and Skinner clearly felt there was an opening for someone like him, of "independent character," who could "dominate the situation." In contrast to Joel Hayden, though, who followed his success in manufacturing to a seat in the state legislature and a prestigious post as lieutenant governor, Skinner lost his bid for the senate—by a lot. His willfulness and impulsivity were "an argument against him" at the ballot box and, though unhesitatingly straightforward ("Mr. Skinner is a blunt, plain man to whom a spade is a spade"), he was uncomfortably self-righteous. Rough around the edges, direct, hasty, and unapologetic, he had none of the Puritan reserve of his colleagues and was deaf to a great many of their subtleties. In most political circles he would have been a liability.

Skinner was simply better suited to business, wherein he thrived specifically because he was "original, forceful, masterful." Here his energies were better deployed. He continually succeeded at "breaking down sales resistance and securing greater distribution for dyed silks." With his unflinching candor and genuine passion for his product, he "not only had the faculty for getting new business, but knew how to retain an account once he got it on his books." Some even considered him a "merchandising genius." Certainly he was a savvy marketer. For instance, every other mill in Williamsburg was associated with the name of its founder or partners: the Hayden, Gere & Co. Brass Works, the Onslow Spelman Button Mill, the Henry L. James Woolen Mill, and so forth. Skinner, by contrast, called his factory the Unquomonk Silk Mill. The name of the brook just north of his factory, *unquomonk* was an Algonquin term meaning "ending place" or "border," and long ago the nearby Unquomonk hill, from whence the brook flowed, had helped define native territory in these parts. Skinner was the only immigrant manufacturer in Williamsburg and, intentional or not, naming his mill the Unquomonk Mill stripped it of a foreign association and made it undeniably local. The name also curried favor with town residents, since the Unquomonk Brook was a popular fishing spot. When they saw spools of thread stamped with the Unquomonk label, they felt a direct connection, as if the silk were somehow theirs too.

Yet using this kind of trademark was a dicey move in the silk business, with its stubborn preference for European goods. Downstream, Samuel Hill had reorganized Whitmarsh's Northampton Silk Company into the Nonotuck Silk Company, but he often discarded the name Nonotuck when it came to selling his silk, preferring Italian-sounding labels. Wrote a chagrinned visitor to the Florence mill in the summer of 1866, "I saw only one thing that I did not like, and that was the envelopes in which the sewing silk is put up for sale. . . . They bore the inscription: *Giovanni Lapamo Monticelli, a Firenze*. This, I was informed by the small boy who showed them to me . . . was thought to have a marketable value." In brand names too Hill preferred those with a Latin flair, the Nonotuck's famous Corticelli line being just one example. His approach, of course, was completely standard. Among other American-made silks in the marketplace were Hovacci, Vittorelli, Bellini, Metz, and Chinnacci silks.

"Unquomonk" would have sounded like a veritable clunker in this mix, to say nothing of abysmally American. Just the same, its Native American provenance would have set Skinner's silks apart while still conveying a sense of history. Unlike many of his colleagues, Skinner did not place the Europeans on a pedestal; proud to be an American, he was just as proud to sell American silk. Some time after the Civil War he began using the image of an Indian's head as his logo. He may have taken his cue from other businesses that capitalized on native imagery, not the least of which was the U.S. Mint, the image of an Indian head being pressed into every penny at this time. Apart from the bald eagle and the American flag, it was about as American an image as one could find, and ever since that penny went into circulation in 1859, the image of an Indian head had literally become connected with a sense of worth. Consequently, Skinner's Indian head logo transmitted the subtle message that his silks had value too and were within reach of everyone. Inelegant though the name was, the Unquomonk brand worked and became easily recognizable in the trade.

As the business grew and aged, so too did Skinner. Over the years his hair became flecked with gray, and he grew a beard that he kept neatly trimmed, framing the bottom of his face in the style favored by Lincoln. No longer youthful or thin, he was instead "a man of striking appearance . . . tall, broad shouldered, benevolent and at the same time powerful looking." For all of that "superb strength," however, he had a highly sensitive stomach and suffered from chronic digestive problems, no doubt partly attributable to his poor nutrition in childhood. He sought water cures for his condition at well-known springs. In Saratoga, New York, in 1866 he stayed at the ultrafashionable Grand Union Hotel, where he started each day drinking sixteen glasses of water before breakfast. Every hour thereafter he drank a glass of Columbian Water, which was considered "of great value" to those with "irritable and weak digestive and assimilating organs." The treatment helped him feel immeasurably better, as witnessed by his brother George. George, who had accompanied him to the Grand Union on this particular trip, proclaimed that he "never saw such a change in a person." If the brothers hadn't been able to drink water as children, growing up in Spitalfields, William more than made up for this as an adult. George, though, never took to the water business. He preferred to stick with alcohol. "Saratoga agrees with me," Skinner told Lizzie, "but it does not with George."

Even in his forties Skinner was still carrying a book with him every day, and he frequently peppered his speech with historical and literary references and aphorisms. He preferred, really, to use the cultivated words of others whenever possible, rather than his own plain speech.

Not only did such quotations reflect well on his intellect; they hid his inability to come up with the words himself. "Mind is the standard of the man," he wrote to his son Will, quoting Dr. Watts. "Actions is eloquence!" he once told a group of voters, invoking Daniel Webster. Poetry dropped from his lips just as easily, and Shakespeare and the Bible were always on the tip of his tongue. "At his office," remembered Adele Allen, "he quoted Shakespeare and the Bible, as he was engaged in other occupations. If you came to ask a favor, he would reply in a line from Shakespeare. If it were only, 'Speak, man, speak,' it was Shakespeare."

If Skinner was the patriarch of the village, Lizzie was by his side as its matriarch, presiding over the grand mansion that sat square in the center of it all. Said a friend, "It would, in my judgment, have been impossible for [Mr. Skinner] to do the work which he did . . . without the aid of his devoted wife." She divided her attention between home, church, and the mill's boardinghouse, where she stepped in as disciplinarian as needed. (Mrs. Sears's authority went only so far.) Lizzie may have assumed this role on her own, but it's entirely possible that Skinner expected her to do so. In a patriarchal mill village laborers were the equivalent of children, and none more so than boarders who lacked any familial instruction. And so, just as he left his own children's upbringing to Lizzie, Skinner left the disciplining of the mill girls to her as well.

Disciplinarians are not always well liked, of course, and, at least on one occasion, Lizzie severely clashed with the boarders. She "expected obedience" from her charges, no matter the circumstance, and the spring of 1870 marked an extreme example of this. The boardinghouse was full that season. Not only were several of the beds filled with about ten girls who worked in the mill, but some rooms had been given to men now affiliated with the railroad, and still more space was occupied by other men (about six or seven) recently hired by Skinner for some stonework. In all there must have been upward of twenty residents in the boardinghouse at this time, and Ellen Littlefield, who had outlasted both of her sisters at the mill, was among them.

152

According to Ellen, the female boarders had been getting short shrift for a while. Production had been down at the mill, and this had affected life over at the boardinghouse, where the quality of the board had plummeted. "The board would be called good generally I suppose," wrote Ellen, "but it is the same thing over and over. I don't pretend to touch the meat. I don't think it fit to eat." She complained to her mother that the meat was so "raw" it ran "bloody" on the plate and that "bread and butter is all I have to depend on." To be deprived of edible meat was a physical and psychological hardship; it was the central component of the boardinghouse diet. Observed Anthony Trollope, "To live a day without meat [for an American] would be as great a privation as to pass a night without bed." Ellen became increasingly hungry and agitated, working ten-hour days, six days a week, and paying for untouchable food.

When it became clear that unrest was brewing among the girls, Lizzie asserted her influence to keep them in check. Her involvement only worsened morale. "I have been so 'riled up' and indignant for more than a week that I dont know what to do," Ellen wrote home in May.

> We have been used most awful mean. From week ago Friday noon till Tuesday night we had sour bread put before us, *so* sour that we could not eat it . . . and while we had sour bread, they [the men] had sweet bread. . . . But that is not the meanest part yet. Tuesday night the girls got so starved out and indignant that there was an outburst at the supper table and Mrs. S. came in and talked to us in a way to make the men think we were horrid creatures. . . . I cant tell all she said but 'twas "unladylike." . . . And now, after all this meanness the Mrs. goes to a young girl with threats, that if we dont behave better we shall [lose what] privileges as we have had.

In the privacy of her letter, Ellen then added, "I should be very much pleased to know what privileges we have now that we *can* be deprived of." The girls had to clean their own rooms, empty their own slops, and stoke their own fires. They had to do their own washing and ironing and sewing—all of which they had to do at night, after work. Nor was their supply of wood a constant: "Sometimes we have a few sticks of wood to heat the coal and sometimes we have none." Furthermore, all the washing took place in the dining room, where the stove was, and this room was often unavailable for household chores. Ellen had been living in the boardinghouse for almost three years at this point, and none of this had previously made much of an impression on her. She'd grown up on a farm and was used to a life where labor, and its challenges, never ceased. But when one feels injustices are taking place, as Ellen now did, suddenly a great many things turn objectionable.

As if Lizzie's threats weren't enough (What "privileges" *was* she talking about? Their "privilege" of a job?), she also, it seems, lied to the girls. During the "scene" in the dining room, she insisted that they had good board, received all they paid for, and that their outburst was particularly inexcusable since they had received exactly the same kind of bread as the men. "Well," fumed Ellen to her mother, "that estimable, injured lady no sooner turned than I took a slice from each table (not waiting for the women to clear) and I wish *you could have* seen them." This was the moment when Ellen discovered, with incontrovertible proof in her hands, that she and the other girls were being cheated. Not only that, but they were being cheated by *Mrs. Skinner.* Adding salt to the wound, everyone knew that Mrs. Skinner wasn't suffering any deprivations herself. Just two weeks earlier she had splurged on a $50 carpet, a marble-top stand, and two chairs.

An incident like this exposed the baser sides of those whom the girls were meant to look up to. Skinner and Lizzie may have enjoyed positions of leadership in the village, but that did not mean they always led effectively, or appropriately. And yet, over time, even these tense situations became memories that served to deepen attachments to the mill and the village. Despite the fact that she and the other girls were treated horribly that spring, Ellen did not leave Skinner's employ. She could have gone back to being a teacher, which was how she'd made a living before becoming a mill girl, but she didn't want to be off by herself in some one-room schoolhouse. Nor did she seek work in another factory. She had become too much a part of the family of Skinnerville, too much a part of the silk mill, too accustomed to her lifestyle in the village—with all the good and the bad it had to offer. Like any family, Skinnerville had developed its share of stories, in the boardinghouse and elsewhere, some involving the Skinners and some not, but each serving to tighten the fabric of the community, with each memory, over time, deepening everyone's relationship to the place.

To lend at least some perspective to Lizzie's side of the bread affair, she had given birth to her seventh child a few months before, but the little girl had soon died, at barely five weeks old. This was the second baby Lizzie had lost. From her irrational behavior in the boardinghouse, she was clearly trying to get back on her feet and take charge again but failing miserably to do so.

In total, Lizzie gave birth to eight children between 1857 and 1873, three of whom died—two as infants, one as a toddler. Infant mortality may have been more common in the nineteenth century, but losing a child then was no easier than it is now, and Lizzie and Skinner were devastated by the deaths of their children. After their first daughter passed away, of whooping cough at two months old, Skinner submitted a poem with her obituary to the paper. This was not a customary thing to do, even among the well-to-do, and bespoke the gravity of the loss. Six bittersweet lines, from the seventeenth-century English poet Robert Herrick's "Epitaph upon a Child That Died," appeared below the announcement of Mary Louisa's death in 1864:

> *Here she lies, a pretty bud,*
> *Lately made of flesh and blood:*

Who as soon fell fast asleep
As her little eyes did peep.
Give her strewings, but not stir
The earth that lightly covers her.

The Skinners' next loss was little Louise, who died in March 1870. Then, two years later, came the hardest blow of all, the death of their bright, smart, and charming four-year-old, May Emma. "Little May," as she was called, died of "inflammation of the bowels," brought on, so they believed, by eating too much popcorn one Saturday night. She commenced vomiting the next day, was unable to keep anything down thereafter, did not improve, and died a week later. Lizzie, reeling from the shock, took out a small journal in which she recorded the milestones of her children and dutifully recorded the last week in May's life, all the while finding it impossible to believe that she was recording May's death: "Oh the sweet little child. The pet of the household, so bright, so active, so full of life and frolic. Can it be that we shall behold thy sweet face & form no more on earth! Yes it is ever so and the only consolation we have is that thou are with thy savior who can be better for thee than earthly parents." In the absence of Little May's voice, she remarked, "[the] house is desolate."

Skinner's children often used his old ledgers as scrapbooks. His payroll ledger from the late 1850s had found its way into Little May's hands at one point and was covered with her scribbles and crayon drawings. She had also practiced writing her name, perhaps following the lead of her older sister Libbie, who practiced her handwriting there as well, writing the names of Skinner's employees over and over again. When Little May died, it was probably Libbie who wrote, at the top of one page, "This page dedicated to our Little May," and who covered over all of Skinner's once important entries with clippings of poems relating to death and children. One in particular stands out, for obvious reasons, and amplifies the magnitude of the death of this one child:

Little Chatterbox

They call me "Little Chatterbox"—
My name is Little May;
I have to talk so much because
I have so much to say

And oh! I have so many friends—
So many! And you see
I can't help loving them because
They every one love me

I love papa and my mamma—
I love my sisters, too;
And if you're very, very good,
I guess that I'll love you.

But I love God the best of all—
He keeps me all the night;
And when the morning comes again,
He wakes me with the light.

I think it is so nice to live,
And yet if I should die,
The Lord would send his angels down
To take me to the sky.

The following year Lizzie became pregnant with her eighth and last child, and the focus in the household shifted from death to birth. Katharine arrived on November 6, 1873, joining surviving siblings Nellie, Nina, Will, Libbie, Joe, and Belle. Libbie, who was away at boarding school, wrote to her brother Will, also at school, "Isn't it splendid having seven (7) in the family? I think it is perfectly splendid." Baby

Katharine restored a sense of fullness to the family, and Lizzie, who had lost her two previous daughters in a row, became terrifically attached to the little girl.

Katharine was born in the midst of the Panic of 1873. Prior to the banking regulations of the twentieth century, banking crises occurred in some form or another almost every decade during the 1800s. As before for Skinner, this panic followed a period during which he had made an aggressive expansion of his operation, opening his first salesroom in New York City, installing $8,500 worth of new machinery in the mill, building a new dyehouse, and purchasing still more property for additional tenements. As if that weren't a lot to take on, he was soon to receive his largest shipments of raw silk ever, totaling about $75,000 worth.

Despite the current worry in the atmosphere, however, and his substantial, ongoing outlays, Skinner had little cause to lose any sleep. He had been in the American silk trade so long by now—almost thirty years—that he was not only a pioneer but also a survivor, with tremendous hope for the future. He believed that as long as the nation continued to grow—and there was no stopping it now—so too would the demand for silk. Silk symbolized prosperity. Everyone wanted silk. At the first annual dinner of the Silk Association of America, in May 1873, he had told his peers, "This is a country of great growth. . . . There is not an Irish servant girl who comes over to this country whose ambition is not to wear a silk dress." And the demand for silk thread—Skinner's specialty and the basis for all silk creations—never went out of style, even during lean times.

Nina Skinner, who was attending Vassar College in the fall of 1873, wrote to her brother Will in December, "I am afraid on account of the panic Christmas presents will not be very flourishing." Due to her father's business, she still had the luxury of being able to think about presents, and yet she wondered. "Do you think Father really lost very much by the great Crisis—you always know if any one should." Indeed young Will paid close attention to his father's business, perhaps already anticipating that he would one day follow his father into the trade, the way Skinner had followed his father. But Will wasn't the only one paying attention to the machinations of the mill in Skinnerville. The silk mill had become an integral part of the valley's economy, as much a facet of life as the very river that flowed through it. Rumors spread that Skinner had invested in some "wild cat" scheme and lost a fortune in the Crash. But it was not true. As the new year of 1874 rolled around the *Hampshire Gazette* reported, "William Skinner . . . is running his sewing silk manufactory to its full capacity, full time, and full pay, with a good demand for the finished product. Long may he grow!"

Part III
After the Flood

Of all the inconveniences, shortage of water is the most to be avoided.

—Vannoccio Biringuccio, 1540

Chapter Eight

In Easthampton, Massachusetts, twelve miles south of Williamsburg, the biggest news of the morning on May 16, 1874, was the continued financial crisis ("No marked increase in the volume of legitimate trade") until a messenger on horseback flew into town, making straight for the telegraph office. The man carried a telegram in his pocket for Henry L. James, proprietor of Williamsburg's woolen mill, who was down in New York City about to sail for Europe. The messenger handed the telegram over just before 9 a.m., directing it to be sent to the manufacturer's hotel. Written by James's bookkeeper, the slip of paper read:

> The Williamsburg Reservoir gave way this morning and washed away half the village. Our factory stands. Don't sail. Answer here. Spelman and Skinner's factory gone.

Within seconds the messenger was besieged with questions and a crowd began to form. When Will Skinner came out of his Latin class at nearby Williston Seminary at about 10:30 a.m., he "noticed that the men were all standing around in groups on the street" and was instantly summoned to the headmaster's office. He naturally assumed that he was in trouble again, "especially as the headmaster appeared very serious when [he] walked in." Instead the headmaster told him that the Williamsburg Reservoir had burst and that his father "was reported to be lost." Back out on the street, Will was called over by the hotel proprietor William Hill, who told him not only that the reservoir had destroyed Williamsburg, Skinnerville, Haydenville, and Leeds, but also that *twelve hundred people* had died. Now "very anxious," Will set out to find a team of available horses, and Hill, eager to help and concerned for the boy, agreed to drive Will home.

Returning the way the messenger had come, Hill and his charge reached Williamsburg about an hour and a half later. As the village came into view, they must have thought they'd reached the end of the world. To the south almost every vestige of life had been scraped off the earth, leaving an apocalyptic expanse of mud, sand, water, and wreckage. The river was now flowing where the road had been. People were crawling over the ruins, calling out names, searching in the rubble. Inside the town hall, which had survived the flood and been turned into a morgue, men were laying out corpses as quickly as they were brought in. At least two of Will's friends, Susie Nash and Minnie Bodman, were there cleaning the dead and covering them with sheets. Although some of the bodies appeared to have only slight injuries, most were in terrible condition, mutilated, bruised, gashed, and torn. Blood dripped onto the floor. None of the bodies had been identified as William Skinner.

With the main road under water to the south and not a path to be seen anywhere, Hill could drive Will no farther. The teenager's only option was to continue on foot the rest of the way. His feet sank into the mud. He had to wade across the river where the bridge was gone. He had to climb over boulders, toss aside furniture, and dexterously step from rock to rock, from wood plank to broken door, for at least another mile. When Will finally arrived home sometime in the afternoon, he saw in disbelief that the reports of everything being swept away were true, and that his family's house was "very nearly the only one standing."

Because of its size, the mansion had acted like a dam in the midst of the surge, the water backing up against it and then rushing around its sides with even greater force. Part of the front piazza had collapsed, its supporting columns knocked out. Windows were broken. The foundation had been partially destroyed. And in the rear of the house one corner was almost entirely ripped off. But the house still existed, unlike the silk mill, and having been told that his father was dead, Will apparently believed that he needed to take charge of the situation and "confusedly resolved to carry on his father's work," vowing to "rebuild the mill." He noticed a rescue crew across the river and called out to them as they were working away. A man's body had been discovered over there by two fingers poking up out of the ground, and, perhaps, Will thought, they had found his father. Then he heard several of them calling back to him, including his father. If the story is true, one can only imagine what Skinner's voice meant to the boy at that moment.

Over at the house Will found the rest of his family—his mother, sisters, and brother—miraculously safe as well, but he quickly learned how many neighbors were still missing. There were several children, friends of his younger siblings, who had supposedly been "away from home at play, and did not get the warning." A gang of men was pulling at the monstrous tangle of debris that had accumulated on the mansion's upstream side, searching for bodies. A number of remains had already been discovered near the depot, including the badly disfigured body of Williamsburg's doctor, Elbridge Johnson. Inside the house fifteen men were helping to shovel out the mud and water that was several feet deep downstairs, a task that needed to be done quickly so that more damage didn't ensue. Already under the weight of all that slurry the floor of the library had given way, its furniture falling into the basement, including the family's piano, which landed on top of the sodden heap below. Beneath the library had been Lizzie's food storage, so that, as one reporter later put it, "potatoes and pianos, pictures and pork, books and bacon became terribly mixed" in the flooded cellar.

Lizzie would have had her hands full, directing the men in their cleanup, ordering her children to gather blankets and wraps for survivors, and handling all the people who suddenly showed up at the house. Apart from the ad hoc rescue crews, neighbors began appearing at the back door (the front being blocked by debris) seeking information, comfort, community, and help. Indeed the house quickly turned into a kind of headquarters. Damaged as it was, it no longer seemed intimidating or imposing but just another survivor of the terrible flood, and more people than ever found themselves within its protective walls. "All day," Libbie Skinner recalled, "people poured into our house to tell their narrow escapes and to offer their sympathy. One man who was very nervous and excitable said, 'When I heard the mill-bells ring, my knees began to shake, and my head began to swim. I could see nothing, so rushing into my house I grabbed my mother-in-law; left my wife to follow and ran to the hills. My little dog who was right at my heels was carried away and lost.'"

Scores of animals died. Nearly every household in the village had had a cow, a few had had horses and pigs, and there was no trace of any of them. The Skinners' stable appears to have been the only outbuilding to survive, and the family found their horses—Jim, Kate, and Major—all alive but in need of immediate rescue. They were "buried in mud and water up to their heads."

The only unaffected parts of the village were on the very outskirts. Since the flood had not topped the railroad embankment, the tenements that Skinner owned above the tracks were still there, with their gardens and livestock. The bluff across the river had also been above the water's reach, so that the houses over that way, including Aurelia Damon's, were only as wet as the driving rain had made them. But elsewhere all was ruin, with thousands of pieces of broken and split wood scattered across the landscape. Rocks too were everywhere, more rocks than one could possibly imagine, carried down from the mountainside above, and deep gullies filled with detritus and dirty, brown water gruesomely pockmarked the ground.

Unable to get their bearings, many villagers walked about aimlessly. Others "sat upon the tracks and knolls, homeless and bereaved." Skinner's boarders were all over the place. Mary Kendall, who had "escaped from the [boarding]house, thinly clad, without either shawl or hat, dressed in a light wrapper with thin shoes," started going "from house to house in the rain with hundreds of other half-distracted people, looking for friends who were supposed to be lost." At some point Ellen Littlefield waded across the river to take solace with Aurelia. Other silk mill employees started for their homes in neighboring villages, frequently finding that those homes no longer existed. Delia Stearns, the young woman who had wisely rung the bell at the mill, was an orphan who had lived with an adopted uncle in Williamsburg, but her uncle and cousins were missing and the house was gone. Alone she sought refuge at a nearby farm. "Well do I remember that morning," wrote the farmer's daughter years later, "when Miss Delia Stearns, with all she had left . . . came to [our] home."

Skinner was as stunned as everyone else. A neighbor overheard him muttering, "I worked for what I had and now it is all gone." In the driving rain he walked the length of the former factory site, searching in vain for reminders of it. All that remained was the rim of his steam engine's flywheel, broken sections of the penstock half-buried in mud, and some bits and pieces of machinery. The shell of his stretching and glossing machine—the one for which he'd secured a British patent—lay on its side in front of his house. To show just how insignificant these remains of the factory were, James Peck, the manager of Skinner's New York store, would later report that a bucket was also found.

Back in his house Skinner set up a makeshift office upstairs, in an alcove overlooking the front drive. By noontime the telegraph office in Haydenville was up and running, and Skinner had to send telegrams to his creditors, informing them of what had happened. The most important cable would be for Abiel Abbot Low, magnate of the shipping firm A. A. Low & Brothers. Skinner owed Low most, if not all, of the $75,000 that he'd recently spent on raw silk, every bale of which had been swept away. Normally Skinner would have repaid Low with the proceeds of his summer and fall seasons, but that was now out of the question. He also telegraphed a partner of Low's, Edward H. R. Lyman. Originally a Northampton man, Lyman still kept a house in town, but this morning he was in Brooklyn, a world away. Skinner sent dispatches as well to his store in New York, his brother in Yonkers, and other associates and relatives, including his former sister-in-law Mary Warner Miner. He informed Mary and her family that a "great disaster" had taken place, that a "reservoir broke flooding Williamsburg, Skinnerville, Haydenville, Leeds and Florence," but that the Skinners were "all safe."

Skinner also began fielding inquiries from incoming telegrams. In response to one asking what was left of his fortune, he replied succinctly, "My Head."

Taking charge of the domestic crisis, Lizzie had to figure out how to feed her family. The stove had to be dug out. Fires had to be lit. Food had to be found. The baby had to be nursed. And when members of the press began coming around, looking for her husband, Lizzie, her curly hair falling into her face and her arms and hands filthy with mud, answered them as best she could. Sometimes she knew where Skinner was; at other times she had no idea. There was just so much going on.

Reporters from the *Hampshire Gazette* and the *Northampton Free Press* appeared at the house within an hour or so of the flood, having dropped every other assignment and hastened to the upper villages to get, as the *Free Press* put it, "as rapid a general view as a prime quality of horse flesh would permit." Shortly after noon six reporters from the *Springfield Daily Republican* boarded a train for Northampton, and by four o'clock several of them had passed through Skinnerville, "gathering every detail from original sources." These men were the first in an entirely different kind of wave that Skinner, his family, and the village were about to experience. Reported the *New Haven Register* at midday, "Reporters from New York and from all important cities and towns in

New England are rapidly making their way to unfortunate Williams-burg, and Leeds."

Although people immediately began to flock to the devastated val-ley, only a handful, apart from intrepid local newspapermen, made it to Skinnerville on Saturday. Part of this had to do with the rain, which caused delays in travel, but mostly they were impeded by conditions on the ground. Above Haydenville teams could pass only "with great difficulty, on account of the almost complete destruction of the roads and adjoining fields." Volunteers who came down from the north set to work in Williamsburg, where there was more than enough to be done, and volunteers who came up from the south generally stopped in Flor-ence, to tackle the search for bodies in its monumental field of debris. Few made it past Haydenville. Consequently, those in Skinnerville were left to their own resources and pretty well isolated as a result. Only neighbors went back and forth, mostly to retrieve and transport corpses. Compounding the isolation, the 10:20 a.m. train did not arrive. Nor did the 2:22 p.m. train. The tracks had been washed out in Leeds.

Surely one of the more surreal things Skinner did that afternoon was shake hands with the press. Only a few hours earlier he had escaped death, he had witnessed his life's work swept away, and then, in the pouring rain, men with notepads began asking him to talk about it. Over the course of the next few days he would repeat his story: "I was just sitting down to breakfast." He would catalogue how much he'd lost: factory, goods, tenements. And to those who were strangers, who noticed his British accent and asked about his origin, he would also re-tell where he came from and how he had built the place up from noth-ing—emphasizing this last bit considerably. He had been a self-made man. He had received favors from no one. And unlike most of his peers in the valley, he had little, if anything, to fall back on.

Skinner estimated his personal losses to be upward of $125,000, which was such a huge figure that disclosing it was almost bragging. The amount demonstrated just how rich he had been and how thor-oughly unusual his position now was. Sometimes he put the figure at

$150,000. In truth he had no idea how much he'd lost since his records were in his safe, which was missing like everything else, and even someone as dramatic as he couldn't have imagined that he was underestimating the amount. When all was said and done, Skinner's losses totaled nearly $200,000, the equivalent of roughly $35 million today. No one else in the valley would suffer a greater personal financial loss from the flood. But even in these early moments following the disaster, it was abundantly clear to some that Skinner was "the heaviest loser by the flood." As anyone could see, there wasn't "a single brick left" of his mill.

Skinner made such an impression on the reporter from the *Republican* that the man considered his story not only uniquely stirring but also uniquely American. "The ruin of Mr. Skinner's property is a matter of peculiar hardship and regret. His career is one of those splendid examples of strong steady development of a business and reputation, by industry, earnestness and honesty, so characteristic of our land." The journalist went on to say, "[Skinner] had built this handsome factory and deservedly prospered in it, and a few years ago erected a spacious and elegant house . . . where, amid his delightful family, he seemed as enviably situated as is often granted to man. He has simply lost here the results of an honorable and strenuous life-time, and has to start anew, with the valuable capital of his good name alone."

From reporters Skinner learned about some of the extensive damage elsewhere. In Haydenville the brass works had disappeared almost as entirely as his silk mill. All that remained of the nine brick buildings was half of the "upper shop," which was more or less shredded. The Haydenville Savings Bank, of which Skinner was a vice president, was also gone, as was the Haydenville Masonic Lodge, of which he was a cofounder. The tobacco factory, gas works, and part of the cotton mill were gone. The shops along Main Street were gone. Tenements and houses in the central portion of the village, just the day before so conveniently located along the river, had been scattered to kingdom come. All four bridges were gone, and part of the church had been converted into a morgue, just like the town hall in Williamsburg.

Down in Leeds the ruin was equally overwhelming. Scores of people were missing, and more than thirty buildings had disappeared, including George Warner's button factory, the only telltale sign it had existed being its chimney, which stood alone in the open air like a finger pointing to the sky. One of the more fortunate edifices belonged to Skinner's longtime competitor, the Nonotuck Silk Company. Though shattering the silk mill's dam, upturning its boardinghouses, flooding its wheelhouse, and knocking out its bridge (with several operatives on it), the water spared the actual complex.

Farther south, in Florence, the damage was mostly flooding, the water having leveled out with the land and spread out over the alluvial plains just north of the village before flowing much more slowly onward. As a result, the water at this point wasn't so much destructive as oppressive, and the staggering sights were not what had been taken away but rather what had been left behind. Once an expanse of fertile farmland, some of it owned by Skinner's former brother-in-law John Warner, the Florence meadows had been submerged in a sea of debris as high as a man is tall. When reporters reached Skinnerville in the afternoon and saw nothing remaining, more than a few would have deduced where much of the village could be found: in the Florence meadows.

The Nonotuck's Florence mill lost a portion of its dyehouse, an older wooden building, and the gable end of its main factory. Other companies lost sheds and outbuildings and suffered the loss of stock and machinery. All three bridges in Florence had been washed away, and farther south, in Northampton, still more bridges had been carried off and even more manufactories had been affected, much of the damage relating to canals and dams. Indeed from the top of the valley on down, nearly every milldam, penstock, wheelhouse, and turbine had been ruined, rendering the region powerless.

By nightfall the small body of five-year-old Robbie Hayden, son of Captain Hayden and his wife, Isabel, had been found in Haydenville, the discovery bringing wrenching grief to his parents. His grandfather Eli Bryant was still missing, however, as was Christina Hills, a mother of six, and Sarah Hillman, Jerome's wife. Jerome had searched for Sarah all day without success, even as others in Skinnerville—all those children, for instance—had blessedly turned up. When Williamsburg's town selectmen came around tallying the list of survivors, Skinner was able to report that everyone in Skinnerville was believed to have survived except for Mr. Bryant, Mrs. Hills, Mrs. Hillman, and Robbie Hayden.

That so few villagers actually died in Skinnerville was miraculous, because nowhere else was the destruction so thorough. "It was at Skinnerville," observed one man later, "that the destructive force of the flood was most impressed upon [me], for it seemed to me as if practically the entire village had been wiped out of existence." One correspondent remarked that the village was "a perfect picture of devastation and desolation," and another concluded, "The village of Skinnerville has been absolutely obliterated from the face of the earth." Little wonder that many people had assumed that Skinner and all of his operatives had instantly perished with the mill.

By day's end it had become clear that thousands of people had not died and that the number of dead might be under two hundred. Even so, a triple-digit death count represented an "appalling loss of life" and instantly distinguished the flood "above all others" in the history of the Northeast. Dam failures were not uncommon, but most prior instances of "runaway ponds" had resulted only in land damages, not deaths. "In the United States," reflected an editor at New Jersey's *Paterson Daily Press*, "floods and freshets are common enough, but a sudden deluge like that which has fallen upon Massachusetts has hardly any parallel in American experience." An editor at the *New Haven Register*, who read in disbelief the dispatches that kept coming in from the flooded district, proclaimed to his readers, "It begins to be understood that no previous casualty happening in the country bears any comparison to this truly appalling calamity."

Over the course of the next few days officials would confirm that the greatest number of deaths had occurred in Williamsburg, where almost sixty people had died. Fifty more villagers had died in Leeds, and about twenty-five in Haydenville. No one perished in Florence or Northampton, where buildings had been flooded but few swept away. As for the survivors, one newspaper reported, "In Haydenville 37 families demand succor, in Williamsburg about 20, and in obliterated Skinnerville there are 26, along with 21 girls who lodged in the silk factory boarding house." In other words, about eight hundred people were homeless as of Saturday evening, in need of shelter, food, and clothing.

In response to this cataclysmic situation, relief meetings were hastily organized, the closest to Skinnerville being held near nightfall in the Haydenville Congregational Church, which was to have been the scene of Lieutenant Governor Hayden's memorial service the following day. Although Hayden had died in November, his service had been postponed until the spring, when the weather would be pleasanter. Already draped in black bunting, the chapel's funereal atmosphere was eerily suited to the grimness of the hour. As it happened, Acting Governor Thomas Talbot had arrived in Northampton the night before to assist in preparations for the memorial and was therefore rather serendipitously in the valley when the disaster unfolded. He gave an "electrifying" address at the Haydenville relief meeting, speaking "to those who could aid their needy fellows," immediately donating $200 himself, "all the money he had with him." By meeting's end committees had been organized to raise subscriptions for relief, bury the dead, clear debris, and search for the missing.

At what point Dr. William Trow stood up to speak is unknown, but he turned everyone's attention to a different matter altogether. The only physician left in town now that Dr. Johnson had been killed, Trow called for an investigation into the cause of the disaster. Throughout the afternoon those who had had their wits about them had begun to wonder what exactly had happened up at the ill-fated reservoir, and many were beginning to conclude that "somebody [was] responsible, either through carelessness, stupidity, avarice or ignorance." Nothing extraordinary had occurred to explain the dam's failure. There hadn't been a freshet. There hadn't been record-breaking rain. There hadn't even been an unusual amount of snowmelt. Spring was so late this year that none of nature's usual suspects could have precipitated a disaster so sudden and extreme. No, the dam gave way "at a moment of not unusual pressure." Human error had to be involved.

Elsewhere, a journalist for the *New York Tribune* was putting together a summary of what he had learned about the reservoir. "The reservoir . . . is said to have been carefully constructed, but people declare now with great freedom that they have long regarded it as unsafe, and that of late it had been unusually leaky. How much truth there may be in the charges made against the companies responsible for its safe condition, it will perhaps be prudent not to determine until the excitement has died away and the facts are more accurately known." Up in Williamsburg a journalist for the *Springfield Republican* was conducting an interview with Lewis Bodman and acquiring even more details.

Bodman, "a fine-looking old gentleman of great dignity," was one of the original progenitors of the reservoir, along with, reporters would find out, Skinner and Governor Hayden. In April 1865 these three had received a charter from the state granting them authority to form the Williamsburg Reservoir Company. The valley already had one main reservoir at this point, northwest of Williamsburg in the town of Goshen, and a smaller one, also on the west branch of Mill River, in Searsville, but they had proven insufficient to supply the valley's mills with adequate waterpower during the dry season. Thus, with permission from the state, a third reservoir was built in 1865 to the north of Williamsburg and paid for by the newly formed reservoir company, whose shareholders, ten in all, ran the major manufacturing interests on the river. Bodman revealed to the reporter quite openly that "the proprietors were not satisfied with the [third] reservoir when it was built, and felt that it was not safe." In fact the reporter learned, "Mr. Bodman had accompanied the late Lieut. Gov. Hayden when the reservoir was first filled . . . and says that they both expected to see it go off at that first trial. It manifested no special weakness, however, and at various times subsequently it was strengthened." Bodman was no longer an owner of the reservoir, having sold his mill with its interest some years ago to Henry L. James, but he kept an eye on things and had been very pleased with the reservoir lately. Had anyone asked him whether the structure was sound, he would have "unhesitatingly replied in the affirmative." Furthermore the current owners apparently felt the same way. Recorded the reporter, "This opinion of its safety, Mr. Bodman says, was coincided with by all the manufacturers, who, he remarked, had most reason to feel anxiety if there were any ground for it, as having most at stake in the matter."

Outside of the relief meetings "nearly all [were] distracted by the loss of family, or friends or property or occupation." An inquest and the matter of culpability were the last things most survivors were concerned about, and most of the mill owners, as they struggled with the ruin upon them, hotly resented any supposition that they were somehow responsible for this day. Skinner certainly did. The only conceivable reason he might have supported an inquest at that moment was to find out who had done this to him.

Chances are that few villagers left Skinnerville as night wore on. It was simply too dangerous to walk about without a road to follow and with no idea what one might run into or step on in the darkness. The rain stopped early in the evening, but "the night that followed was black." There was no moon. Both sky and land were as dark as pitch. Here and there in Skinnerville one may have seen a few fires lit up beside wrecks, with families huddled together about the flames as "owners preferred to remain near the remnants of their homes to going to neighbors' houses." Whatever property endured, regardless of condition, was closely protected, and several men stood guard with lanterns long after the hour of sleep had passed. Others, those for whom no vestige of a home survived, not even a doorframe, slept in the Williamsburg depot or in barns that had been luckier than houses. Jerome Hillman and his daughter, Clara, moved in with the Skinners, as did, eventually, the Hibbert and Van Vechten families. When exactly these two other families moved in is unclear, but if indeed they all slept in the house this evening, the Skinners would have had an additional eleven people under their roof, swelling the number of adults and children in the place to eighteen.

Given that the mansion had two capacious upper floors untouched by the flood, one could argue that eighteen was actually a modest figure for the number of people the house could have held. But Skinner's home, even with its large dry bedrooms, would not have been an inviting place to stay. The house was flooded, after all, and quite damaged. Worse, it reeked of fetid matter, infusing the lower story at least with an inescapable rotten odor. In the mid-nineteenth century disease was thought to spread through smell, and one can reasonably assume that most people, given any other choice, would not have slept in that house.

With Skinner's first-floor bedroom uninhabitable, he likely moved up to Lizzie's room, though he may not have stayed there but sat up much of the night in the alcove at the end of the second floor. The adrenaline and anxiety from all that had happened made sleep impossible, and his stomach, which acted up even under normal circumstances, was certainly no help to him this evening as the minutes went creeping by.

Down in Northampton a reporter for the *New York Times* noted, "The whole county is awake and waiting for morning." And up in Williamsburg, tucked away on a farm, the river out of sight, Delia Stearns, whose uncle was confirmed dead and whose home had been swept away, wrote down in a small diary, "How many broken hearts and homeless ones there are tonight." To which she later added what many, including Skinner, would have been thinking: "Such a sad, sad day as this has been. Why was it permitted? God only knows the end."

The following morning brought "a cool, sweet Sabbath dawn" and "a blue sky flecked with fleecy clouds." Robins and bluebirds sang in the trees while sunlight dappled the muddy ground. Survivors were grateful the rain had stopped, but the beautiful weather was "jarring." Nature was not in concordance with everyone's reality.

With the coming of dawn, Skinner had a multitude of things to confront. Throughout his house windows remained broken, floors were on the verge of collapsing, everything downstairs was wet and muddy. The cellar was underwater; storage was lost. None of this had disappeared overnight. His buggy had to be dug out of the stable. His horses needed hay. His family was in shock. And three of his villagers were still missing.

Beyond all this, which was enough for any man to deal with, whenever he looked out the window he saw "his empty mill site, the few tenements [of his] that [had] not been swept away, overturned, uprooted trees, huge piles of driftwood and debris." What was he going to do? What *could* he do? Rebuild? It had taken him decades to create what he had lost the day before. How was he going to afford building a new mill and a brand-new dam, millpond, and raceway? The riverbank would also need to be rebuilt, but he didn't think that was his responsibility, as it was public property, and the river rechanneled. Who was going to cover the cost? And what about the road? Parts of it had been jettisoned into neighboring fields.

Skinner would need to build new tenements and boardinghouses. He would need a new school. He would need all new machinery and supplies. Of immediate importance, he was going to have to salvage from the miles of debris as much raw and unfinished silk as he could in the hopes of being able to sell some of it. A large stock of finished goods had been stored in his safe, but he needed that safe even more for its other contents. The safe held all his stock certificates, railroad bonds, and some cash, as well as almost all of his accounting books. Moreover it contained at least one life insurance policy toward which he had already deposited thousands of dollars at interest. Were anything to happen to him now, that policy was all his family had left.

By eight o'clock teams of horses began coming into view down the road—an incredible sight after the isolation of yesterday—bringing carriages that neither Skinner nor anyone else in the village recognized. Wrote a local reporter, "Lumber wagons, buggies, carriages, express wagons, everything in the shape of conveyance, were brought out, and a multitude which could not be numbered nor correctly estimated, crowded the entire route of the disaster." Thousands of people were on their way. Some came to volunteer. Some came to scavenge. Most came to see the destruction of this record-breaking flood. Exclaimed another reporter, "Such a Sunday surely never before was seen in a New England community. . . . An unknowing person would have argued a cattle-show, circus, college commencement or other country-fête day, so miscellaneous and entirely un-Sunday-like was the procession." Nobody was going to church. The valley's carnage was a mightier sermon on the brevity of life and the afflictions of humanity than any preacher could hope to match this morning. Someone calculated that "the number of teams going towards Williamsburg averaged 350 per hour during the greater portion of the day." Every ten seconds, then, another vehicle was passing the Skinner mansion.

Few cared that the highway was washed out. Determined to see every inch of the devastated valley, these visitors cut paths wherever they could, jostling precipitously over the waterlogged, pockmarked terrain, heedless of the risks in doing so and at times paying for their exuberant curiosity. Near the depot "several teams spilled their occupants into two or three feet of water." Manure piled up in front of the mansion when traffic came to a standstill, sometimes for as long as forty-five minutes in "exasperating blockades." The wheels of so many carriages and the hooves of so many horses caused more damage than had already been done. "My carriage wheels passed over a beaten and battered [serving tray]," said one passenger. "It may have been made of silver for all I know. A little further on they ground into fragments a triangular piece of marble from some fine lady's dressing case."

The ultimate goal of most was the reservoir. "Nearly all the visitors went to the reservoir about three miles above, to see if it was possible to detect or find the cause of the disaster," recorded a journalist from the *New York Times*. And during their passage through Skinnerville, as through other points, these visitors called out to residents to ask all manner of questions. "What was here before?" "How much farther to the reservoir?" And perhaps more pointedly, "Are you Mr. Skinner?" Whether Skinner had patience or pride enough to answer one can only guess. There he was, his boots and pants covered in filth, big hollows under his eyes from lack of sleep and anxiety, his house a sad spectacle behind him, his mill now an exercise for the imagination, talking to strangers whose only worry was whether they might tip over in the mud as they indulged their fascination. "It is true," wrote a reporter from Greenfield, "that these afflicted ones may have been annoyed by the questions of the curious and have suffered other intrusions upon their sorrow, but . . . generally it was a well-behaved, respectful and sympathizing assembly."

Fortunately in the mix came some welcome faces. During an interview with Eli Perkins of New York's *Daily Graphic*, Skinner's brother George arrived, stepping out of a hired carriage with as warm a smile as he could muster. He had traveled all the way from Yonkers to be at his brother's side, and Perkins later described the ensuing scene between the two in a noteworthy piece about William. As famous a humorist in his day as Mark Twain, Perkins boasted a large following of readers but found nothing laughable to offer them in the current crisis. The only thing he could find to exaggerate even was Skinner's social status. Unlike other reporters, who seized on Skinner's rise from poverty as adding currency to his present fall, Perkins portrayed him as a gentleman manufacturer "of culture and European travel" who had lost not only his factory and all of his records, "[but] also souvenirs and works of art gathered from all over Europe." Skinner's "European travel," of course, had been confined to England, and one wonders what souvenirs Perkins might have been alluding to. Still, the effect Perkins wished to convey was real enough: the flood had been a leveler of fortune, and, as Skinner's suffering demonstrated, the wealthy are no more exempt from tragedy than anyone else.

Perkins knew Skinner personally, along with George and Henry L. James, having met them all in Saratoga some time before. In talking to Perkins, then, Skinner wasn't so much talking to a reporter as an old acquaintance. Perkins wanted to know everything that had happened both before and after the flood, and Skinner told him.

"I looked back and the factory was gone," said Skinner. "It went like lightning—bricks, irons—everything. It was a sea of foam and houses. I've been on the Atlantic in a storm. That was it, a big wave dashing over the deck, but on the top of that wave, yesterday, were houses, trees and lumber."

"But I don't see a single brick left," Perkins said, pointing to where the factory had been. "Where are the bricks?"

"Gone sir! floated down the stream. Why, my big safe, my big Marvin's safe, has floated off too, and we've been looking for it all day. I wouldn't be surprised if we should find it floating around on the Connecticut River or maybe out on the Sound." At this Skinner began to laugh, and soon after, George arrived.

"Now, Bill," George said jestingly, stepping into the conversation, "you won't have any of these bonds troubling you any more. No more Saratoga—no—" George presumably meant to joke that, without a mill and its debts to cause him stress, Skinner wouldn't have to go to the springs ever again to restore his health.

But suddenly Skinner couldn't laugh anymore and stopped his brother before he could continue. "No, George, it's all gone. The work of a lifetime—$150,000 yesterday and today not a cent."

"But you have your wife and children, Bill," George said more soothingly. "You're all right."

Perkins recorded that the brothers' eyes then filled with tears, they clasped each other's hands, and "their laughing faces became long with sympathetic sorrow."

George's arrival was of no small consequence. Though neither as shrewd or instinctual as William nor as thoughtful and talented as their brother Thomas, George was nevertheless wildly successful—some might have said lucky. Within the past few years he'd invested in the manufacture of organzine, emerged from near bankruptcy by doing so, and accrued colossal wealth in the process. Word on the street was that his company in Yonkers was worth between $300,000 and $400,000. Given his taste for extravagance, he probably looked like a prince in Skinnerville that day, and he had arrived with a full billfold ready to help.

Alongside George was his business partner and brother-in-law, William Iles, and not far behind came another friend and fellow silk man, the broker Briton Richardson. Each of these gentlemen, seeing the magnitude of destruction and the pitiable state of the survivors, made cash subscriptions "on the spot," jump-starting Skinner's campaign for relief that he hadn't even realized he was starting. His store manager down in the city, James Peck, showed up as well, along with Fred Warner, a recently hired salesman who had deep connections in the valley. Fred's brother George had owned the button works in Leeds, and only a few months ago Fred had been his brother's bookkeeper. If he had still had that job, he might have drowned like the new bookkeeper had, and Fred must certainly have thought, if only fleetingly, "There but for the grace of God."

A messenger also pushed through the crush and delivered a telegram to Skinner from Abiel Abbot Low, who expressed sympathy for his predicament, conveying to him that appropriate consideration regarding his debt would be granted to him in the present crisis. A heartbeat later Edward H. R. Lyman showed up from Brooklyn to reiterate in person the firm's generous position. This was almost too much for Skinner. "Directly after breakfast I drove out to Skinners," Lyman reported to Low. "I saw Skinner at once. He had only received your telegram a few minutes before & was quite overcome upon seeing me."

As one might suspect, Lyman wanted to assess the damage and determine just how bad things were. He informed Low that the situation was in fact dire. "[Skinner's] mill and everything connected with it are swept clean away, even his safe [has] not been discovered. . . . The newspaper accounts that I have seen are not exaggerated. No one can realize the extent of damage done without seeing it." Lyman was stunned by the condition of Skinner's house, with a foot and a half of mud downstairs, water in the basement, and the gaping hole in the library floor as perilous as ever. Lyman told Skinner that, first things first, he had to get his house in order, "for the comfort of himself and family." Second, he had to start thinking about the future. Did he have any thoughts about how he might rebuild? No, Skinner didn't have any idea. Lyman then said that he would come back in a day or two, after Skinner had had time to "think [things] over calmly and quietly after the heat of the excitement had passed off." Lyman was confident that by that time Skinner would know "what he wanted to do and what he thought he could do."

Barely twenty-four hours had passed, and the pressure was already on for Skinner to strategize a way to repay his debts. Because that, really, was what Lyman's visit was all about. If A. A. Low & Brothers were going to see any of the money that Skinner owed them, they needed to push Skinner back on his feet. During his brief visit Lyman made it clear to Skinner that he "had friends" and that no matter his predicament "he should have help." Skinner was grateful to hear this, but he understood too how vastly different were Lyman's and his own sense of time at the moment. Lyman had to get back to Brooklyn; he had business to attend to and was ready to discuss options and trades and manufacturing. Skinner, on the other hand, was having a hard enough time finding a pen to write with. Lyman was ready to come back the next day, to bring about a close to their discussion, but Skinner asked him to wait until Tuesday, explaining that he needed as much time as possible "to think and be more collected." Whether or not he believed he'd actually be ready to begin solving this crisis by then, Skinner nevertheless promised to "express his wishes" at that point. Lyman reported to Low that Skinner "appeared as well as a man could do under all of the circumstances."

Others with interests in Skinner's credit showed up on his doorstep as well, including representatives of the Northampton National Bank. The bank's president and vice president alike assured him of their full cooperation in sorting out his difficulties. He also received a visit from an agent of the Mercantile Agency, who reported to his superiors that Skinner's financial situation had indeed been severely compromised, but that the silk magnate's state of mind, anxious and easily threatened even in the best of times, wasn't helping him any. "[Skinner] claims to be poor now," wrote the agent, "but he is inclined always to picture the dark side of things and hopes are entertained that he will be able to get on."

Losing everything was all Skinner could think about. "I said to Mr. Skinner," remembered a local minister, "'You have a good character left. The high name you have ever had and deserved among manufacturers has not been taken from you.'" And a correspondent for the silk industry would report, reassuringly, "The feeling on his behalf is such . . . that he will get another and perhaps a better start than most ruined men would be likely to experience at the hands of their creditors." Yet for Skinner at this moment it was cold comfort to be reminded that all he had left of any value, after nearly thirty years of work, was his name, meaningful though that may have been to others.

Skinner was by no means the only manufacturer suffering from shock. In Williamsburg Henry L. James, whose youthful brow belied his forty-five years, was reeling from the deaths of several of his employees and was in a state of utter disbelief at the destruction of his many tenements and the sudden inoperability of his woolen mill. The river, which had previously run behind the mill, was now running down the street in front of it, and the building, though standing, was ruined inside. A reporter for the *Hampshire Gazette* observed that the fate of Skinner's silk mill and James's woolen mill would likely depend on the speed at which these proprietors could wrestle themselves out of their grief. "When, if ever, these factories will be in operation again cannot be told. Mr. Skinner and Mr. James, though usually plucky men, seem broken with the terrible loss which has befallen them."

"What will be the end?" Perkins had asked Skinner, and Skinner answered in effect that this *was* the end—unless the state intervened and provided financial assistance. He had no insurance against this type of disaster. None of the manufacturers had flood insurance (indeed even today it is rare), and contrary to the effects of a fire, "the flood has taken everything—buildings, contents, foundations." Furthermore even those whose property had survived were not exempt from misfortune. "When a factory, which is the life of a village, ceases to run, and is gone forever," said another reporter, "the loss cannot be measured by the loss of that mill alone. For, on its successful operation depended the value of all the surrounding property. Every house and every acre of land in the village, though untouched by the flood, is largely depreciated in value by the loss of the mill; and they are actually large sufferers who have apparently lost nothing."

Estimates for damages ranged between $1 million and $2 million (or in the range of $300 million today). Roads, bridges, and dams had to be rebuilt, which would cost the town of Williamsburg tens of thousands of dollars, and hundreds of people now qualified as paupers to be cared for out of the town's treasury. Compounding the misery, state assessors had completed their annual assessment of property taxes on May 1. Countless people owed taxes on property that effectively no longer existed. In consequence of all this, the Williamsburg selectmen circulated a petition on Sunday that asked the legislature to "send up a committee to view the desolation of the town" so that a bill might be introduced relieving Williamsburg, and also Northampton, of some of the burdens now forced upon them. About a hundred men in the valley signed the document, including Skinner, who affixed his towering, slanted signature to the congested list of names.

In a move that many may have considered rash, Skinner also "dismissed his operatives . . . telling them that he would pay their wages on Monday." Rather than bring everyone together at this moment of crisis, thereby encouraging a sense of unity that could prove crucial for recovery in the days and weeks ahead, he chose to disband his industrial family. Many of these men and women had worked for him nearly all their lives and would have done everything in their power to help rebuild the business. But Skinner claimed he couldn't afford to be their leader anymore. He said that he had just enough money in the bank to pay them their previous month's wages, a total of $3,400, beyond which he was broke, and he rather gracelessly told his employees that paying them would cost him further ruin. "It is stated that Mr. Skinner informed his workmen that he would pay them what he owed, but that it would take his last dollar."

Worse, though normally true to his word, Skinner did not pay his workers on Monday. In all likelihood he wasn't willing to divest himself yet of what little cash he had left. A week would pass before he wrote anyone a check.

Henry L. James, for his part, had no intention of letting go of his workforce. He may have been feeling undone by his bad luck and wracked with grief over the deaths of seven of his employees, but he wasn't about to compound the situation by cutting the strings of his most dependable ties. Reported the *Springfield Daily Union,* "Mr. H. L. James notifies his help that he wishes them all to remain with him, and that he shall resume operations at his mill as soon as possible." Down in Haydenville a similar but even more uplifting story was unfolding. Joel Hayden Jr., age thirty-nine, who had taken over as president of Hayden, Gere & Co. following his father's death, met with his partners, Collins Gere and Sereno Kingsley, and decided to rebuild at once. "I have lost all I had," Hayden told a reporter matter-of-factly. "But up and at it again." Another item quoted "one of the firm" (probably Hayden, since he had recently assumed the presidency) as saying, "We have but just begun—Do you think we are going to give up? We shall be running again in less than six months." On Sunday morning copies of the following notice appeared throughout Haydenville:

NOTICE

Having decided to rebuild our works at once, we hereby give notice that we wish to employ a large force of workmen to clear away the debris, &c., and preference will be given to those previously in our employ. Application may be made at once to S. C. Wentworth, for particulars. All wages due our workmen will be paid just as soon as we can make up the accounts, and any one heretofore in our employ who is in need will receive aid by leaving name and wants with H. M. Brewster.

We would ask as a favor, that all material, books, papers, &c., that may be found by any person, belonging to us, be returned, or we be informed where they are and we will defray all expenses.

Office at present at home of H. M. Brewster.

HAYDEN, GERE & CO.

And so, while brass workers stepped into Mr. Brewster's home to apply for jobs and wages, Skinner's silk workers did the only thing they could do: help themselves and each other. They continued to sift through debris for artifacts of their former existence and search for bodies in the environs of the mansion, all the while being gawked at by strangers continually driving by. "One can have but a faint idea of the number of persons who visited the village today," wrote one correspondent. "At 12 o'clock there were lines of teams both going and coming for three miles."

Sent up on immediate assignment, illustrators and photographers also began making their presence known. The photographers, who would continue to appear throughout the following week, set up their big cameras in front of the mansion, across from it, next to it—one even got inside of it—and ducked their heads under big black cloths to shoot frame after frame of stereoviews, pairs of pictures that created three-dimensional images. Looking at stereoviews was an enormously popular form of parlor entertainment in the nineteenth century, and collections of them, especially those that captured current events, were highly prized. One paper advised that views of the flood "should be purchased and preserved as they represent one of the most tragic events of Modern times."

The illustrators perched on flats and rocks, took out their sketchpads, and tried to capture what they saw and heard for the audience at large. Milton Bradley of *Frank Leslie's Illustrated* imagined the moment the reservoir engulfed Skinner's mansion, showing water surging past the edifice up to the second story. Another artist, Theo Davis, from *Harper's Weekly,* walked the length of Skinnerville with great concentration, documenting its geography along the river for inclusion in his widely publicized map, a bird's-eye view of the destroyed valley. For readers who had no idea where the Mill River Valley was or what it might even look like, Davis's rendition provided them with the perspective they craved.

Some people, of course, came to help, including Mary Warner Miner and her husband, Dr. Worthington Miner. Miner may have felt his services would be needed, given Dr. Johnson's death, but in one of the numerous strange and inexplicable twists the disaster occasioned, there were in fact few people who needed medical assistance. People had either died or lived; few had been hurt. Charitable donations also began to appear, but at this stage there was no rhyme or reason to them. "On [Sunday], charity offered its assistance to those who had lost their homes," Libbie Skinner recorded. "One man must certainly have had a peculiar idea of what would be acceptable for two barrels of rolling-pins came into our possession to be distributed among the people."

The only good these pins would have brought was maybe some comic relief, which would have been appreciated. Frequently people simply had to laugh, because otherwise the grief was too much. At one point Skinner was observed "jestingly searching for a single brick of his once magnificent structure," while elsewhere in the village, one of his neighbors "laughingly remarked that it didn't take him long to pick up his things after the flood, as he couldn't find a single article that belonged to him."

By nightfall the safe belonging to Hayden, Gere & Co. as well as the safe belonging to the Haydenville Savings Bank had been found in the river south of the brass works. Skinner undoubtedly hoped that his safe would turn up there as well. It didn't. His boiler, though, was found near the wreck of the brass works "lying in the placid current." That his boiler, which weighed several tons, had been swept half a mile downstream like some inconsequential wood chip spoke once more to the extraordinary force of the reservoir. A great deal from his mill had actually gotten stuck in Haydenville, though most of it was mangled with other debris about the bases of trees and houses, and "in some places so firmly [was] it embedded that yokes of oxen had to be employed . . . in pulling the heterogeneous mass away." Unfortunately, when something like a silk spinning machine was found, it was usually so broken as to be useful only as scrap.

The dark of night once more brought little rest and complete exhaustion. The valley had been overrun as if it were the grounds of a county fair, and now all the people had gone but those who couldn't leave: those who had been, as it were, the main attraction. The quiet seemed almost cruel. Gathering her family upstairs, Lizzie may have tried to remind them that today was still the Sabbath. There had been no church, of course, and the family's Bibles, along with other books from the library, were likely a mess of pulp, floating in the bilge in the basement. But Lizzie didn't need a Bible to preach her faith. The flood afforded this Christian woman her greatest confirmation to date that the "utmost importance" was to be "on the Lord's side." Death could come at any moment, but, as she once wrote, "if we are only prepared we shall say whenever my Father calls, I am ready." For his part, Skinner didn't fear death or the afterlife; he feared poverty. And for the first time in his life he might have repeated the biblical verse from Job that every family from Spitalfields knew by heart: "My days are swifter than a weaver's shuttle, and come to their end without hope." None of his hard-won success had spared him the sudden loss of his life's work.

Chapter Nine

On Monday all the reporting that had been done over the weekend finally hit the stands. Stories of the flood and of the dam "exhilarated the morning meal" in homes near and far, including numerous explanations of why the dam had failed. One theory had to do with muskrats: they had "honeycombed" the embankment and thus compromised its integrity. Another theory involved the effects of a possible strike during construction: "There was a strike among the workmen and, inasmuch as the strikers were unsuccessful, they intentionally weakened the reservoir in completing it." And one man "familiar with the case" had asserted to a Boston reporter, "The frosts had started the earth so that the water had found numerous little courses through which it finally carried off the first mass of earth . . . and at once precipitated the catastrophe."

Perhaps because he knew many of the reservoir's owners, Perkins, for one, abstained from blaming them for wrongdoing. "I cannot attach particular blame to any one," he wrote after his visit. "The men whose mills were destroyed, and who have been made beggars—Mr. James, Mr. Spelman, Mr. Skinner, Mr. Hayden, and Mr. Warner—

were the directors of the Williamsburg Reservoir Company. They owned it. They had so much faith in it that they risked their own lives and property. If they built their factories and residences in its path no one can accuse them of bad faith. Their good faith was backed by their works, by every dollar of property, and by their wives' and children's lives. Who shall charge them with neglect, with insincerity, or anything but lack of knowledge?"

Who *didn't*, might have been a better question. Few shared Perkins's perspective. "Whatever may have been the cause, it seems clear that there was a criminal carelessness on the part of the owners of the dam in failing to see that it was made secure," concluded one reporter for the *New York Herald*. "They cannot plead the excuse of ignorance of the existing danger for, years ago, the late Lieut. Gov. Hayden of Williamsburg, and other residents in the vicinity, pronounced the work unsafe, and expressed the fear that it would some day give way and that the villages would be inundated."

Lewis Bodman's interview Saturday evening had proved especially damning. When pressed about his views on the construction of the reservoir, he had confirmed that "the work as a whole was not satisfactory" and that the central core wall of the dam had been "slovenly built." Bodman strongly hinted that the contractors were to blame. They had "hurried up their work as rapidly as possible, with too little regard." He tried to put the onus on the superintendent, who was "sick some of the time and did not exercise so constant and close a supervision as his position demanded." Bodman even went so far as to implicate the county commissioners since they had examined the dam and pronounced it acceptable. But the bottom line, as many saw it, was that the owners had known all along that the dam could give way any moment and still they had let it stand.

Skinner's thoughts on the reservoir had been few. He "did not take a great deal of interest in it"—apart from its usefulness to him. Built in the summer and fall of 1865, the reservoir was intended to increase the power of the river during the dry seasons, when the river would reach "the very lowest of low water marks" and be reduced to "a mere bed of rocks and mud." At times like this manufacturers lost money from the inability to continue production and often had to lay off employees. One year the *Hampshire Gazette* reported, exasperated, "Scarcely one of the mills is running full-time, and unless we have rain soon the prospect is that still more inconvenience will be the result." The level of the river was integral to the industrial life built along it. Even a teenager like Will Skinner would inquire in his letters home, "Does the mill run or not for want of power?"

The first reservoir on Mill River was built about 1840. Located northwest of town, at the head of the river's west branch in neighboring Goshen, this was known as the Goshen Reservoir, and Skinner, after he'd moved to town and started manufacturing, became a principal shareholder of the Mill River Reservoir Company that owned it. By the end of the Civil War, however, this reservoir could no longer supply enough water during the summer for the growing number of mills on the river, and, as had happened in other industrial valleys, additional power became necessary to keep pace with the war boom. Indeed Skinner's support of another reservoir probably stemmed from the fact that he required a bigger mill to meet the growing demands of his market, and naturally a bigger mill would require more waterpower.

Industrial reservoirs were a uniquely American advancement. Unlike most of England, the American Northeast is blessed with a vast watershed system, making it an ideal environment for trapping and storing water for industrial pursuits. Credit goes to Zachariah Allen, a Rhode Island manufacturer, for organizing the first American reservoir company in 1823. Allen's frustration with losing labor and money during the dry season inspired him to form a collective of neighboring manufacturers to build a reservoir expressly for the purpose of helping to power their mills year round. Increasing both production and profit for everyone, the reservoir proved to be "an experiment . . . so successful that it was replicated on industrial rivers throughout the world." By the time of Lincoln's inaugural address, reservoirs had become as familiar to the New England landscape as the white-steeple church and the red-brick mill.

The site for the new Williamsburg Reservoir was due north of town, at the head of the east branch of Mill River. Some of Skinner's colleagues had selected the site the year before, and Onslow Spelman had gone ahead and purchased the land: 111 acres, perfectly positioned to collect the runoff from the surrounding hills and providentially situated above a steep slope. In April 1865, with the site confirmed and ideas already forming about the design of the dam, Skinner, Bodman, and Governor Hayden applied for a charter from the state to form the Williamsburg Reservoir Company for the purpose of building another reservoir and establishing a corporation "with all the powers and privileges, and subject to all the duties, restrictions and liabilities set forth in all general laws which now are or may hereafter be in force relating to such corporations."

Corporations like the Williamsburg Reservoir Company were not at all like modern corporations. Indeed "the notion widely held today that corporations are private enterprises would have appeared nonsensical to any American up to the end of the 19th century." Historically, as America was being colonized, all corporations within her borders had to serve the interests of the king of England. Following the Revolution corporations no longer had to serve the king, but most Americans believed that corporations had to be of service to the new democracy, advancing the public good. As a result, they were not entrusted with autonomy. State legislatures had control over them and could go so far as to determine the issuing of stock, the raising of capital, the handling of debt, the voting of shareholders, even the distribution of profits.

Nevertheless state legislatures had a vested interested in staying out of the affairs of corporations, because corporate assistance was too valuable to economic and industrial growth. The country was expanding by leaps and bounds in the nineteenth century, and state legislatures could hardly keep up with the demands for new roads, bridges, canals, dams, and other infrastructure. They welcomed private capitalists whose investments enhanced the country's framework, and the Williamsburg Reservoir Company was just another example of capitalists pooling their resources for a beneficial public work.

But when Skinner, Hayden, and Bodman applied for a charter for their reservoir, they weren't being civic-minded. They were seeking permission to promote their own interests within the confines of the law. That the public would also benefit was secondary to their concerns, though it was surely emphasized in their application to the state legislature. Building a reservoir on the east branch of Mill River would significantly affect everything around and below it, presumably for the better. The legislature approved.

Once Skinner put his name on the charter, he had no other role in the Williamsburg Reservoir. There is no evidence to suggest that he participated in any further organization of the company or the raising of stock. When shares were allotted, he was the second smallest shareholder, presumably because his mill (even an expanded one) would require less power than others. He had nothing whatsoever to do with the actual building of the reservoir. Nor did he participate in most company meetings after the inaugural one. Once, after he was voted in absentia to the board of directors, he communicated to the secretary that he declined the nomination. Skinner's interest in the reservoir, and in reservoirs in general, was purely financial: he invested for gain only.

At the company's inaugural meeting, May 8, 1865, at the Mansion House hotel in Northampton, shareholders voted on the plan for their reservoir's dam. Yet in actuality the plan was a done deal before the meeting. Over the previous winter a sort of building committee had formed, consisting of three Northampton manufacturers: William T. Clement, William Clark, and Lucius Dimock, who had risen to become a partner at the Nonotuck. These men had already solicited several proposals, one of which called for the dam to be faced with "ornamental" stone, which, though impressive, would have cost about $100,000—more than triple the amount that anyone intended to spend. Another proposal, from a Holyoke engineer, called for a plain earthen dam with a core wall of brick and would have cost the company only $24,000, but it too was rejected. The brick wall probably had something to do with this. There was no reason to order bricks and pay to have them shipped when the surrounding countryside was filled with stones that could just as easily be used for a core wall, should the dam require one. The building committee thus decided at some point that they could design an earthen dam as well as anyone, if not better, and if they designed it themselves, they wouldn't have to contend with someone else's wasteful or impractical ideas.

An earthen dam is little more than a mound of excavated earth piled high and wide across a riverbed to stop the flow of water. Sometimes earthen dams have an inner wall of stone or brick to enhance the strength of the structure, but the necessity of such walls was debatable among the committee, as well as among other shareholders. Clement and Hayden, who were for it, argued that a central wall would not only cut off any seepage that might percolate through the dam from the reservoir but would also inhibit the burrowing of animals, like muskrats and eels, whose inclination to tunnel through earth could compromise the integrity of the structure. But with the support of at least one shareholder, Dimock argued that such walls added nothing more than expense. An earthen dam properly built would be impervious to the flow of water and entirely unwelcoming to animals. In the end Clement and Hayden's argument won out, and the committee designed an earthen dam with a core wall of rubble masonry.

To draft their plan the committee hired Lucius Fenn, a railroad engineer who was a friend of one of the committee members. A cross-section of the proposed dam made it look like a pyramid, with earth sloping down on either side of an interior stone wall. The dam would be 43 feet high in the center, about 600 feet across, and roughly 145 feet from front to back. The stone wall would be bonded mostly in grout, its solid face interrupted only by a drainage pipe that would run through the bottom of the dam just above the original streambed.

According to the committee's design, the wall was to be set in a trench roughly three feet deep to secure its foundation. And the top of the dam would be a level roadway, wide enough for farmers to transport teams and livestock to and from neighboring pastureland.

The only aspect of this design that seemed unusual to Fenn was the inside, or upstream, slope, which was to be unusually steep. Fenn questioned whether that was wise, as the horizontal pressure from the reservoir's impounded water was going to be significant, and a gentler, more graduated slope would better resist that kind of pressure. Most inner slopes were no steeper than 2.5:1. In England the preferred pitch was an even more moderate 3:1. But the committee wanted a pitch of 1.5:1, a thirty-four-degree angle from the horizontal, because building it would use less earth and cost less money. Nor was the committee concerned that its approach was novel or experimental. These men were used to trial and error; they tested machinery and engineering all the time. If the inner slope proved too sharp, they told Fenn, "We can fix it afterwards."

In contrast to the other proposals, the committee's plan was the safest financial risk. Their earthen dam would cost as little as $21,000 to build, roughly a fifth of the most elaborate design. Further, since the company's charter entitled the manufacturers to raise $30,000 for their reservoir, they would have an additional $9,000 left over with which to repay Spelman for the land and cover maintenance, repairs, and contingencies over the long term. Even Clement and Hayden, who initially wished for a "stronger, larger and more expensive dam," approved of the cost-effective design. They were Yankees, after all; a compulsion for thrift was in their blood.

Yet the proposed plan was not merely thrifty; it was a downright steal. Skinner barely felt a pinch in his pocket. The second smallest shareholder, he owned fifteen shares, or 6 percent of the company. Building this particular reservoir, he learned, would only cost him about $1,400, payable in installments according to the progress of the project. Nobody, least of all a man who prefers to do business on credit, wants to spend more money than is necessary, and Skinner would have appreciated the fact that this extremely important investment wasn't actually going to cost him very much.

Just as critically, at the inaugural meeting shareholders outlined the corporation's by-laws and elected Dimock, Clement, and Clark to be the company's directors, putting them officially in charge of building the reservoir, with Dimock becoming the unspoken "boss engineer of the enterprise."

Though a man of "considerable experience" in mechanical engineering, Dimock had, as far as can be ascertained, no experience in civil engineering nor any prior experience with large-scale engineering works. No matter. He had a thorough understanding of water-power as it pertained to machinery, as did the other directors, and collectively these three men had decades of experience with smaller mill dams. In the early to mid-nineteenth century mill owners were almost categorically considered men with "common engineering knowledge" and just as capable as those who called themselves professional engineers, if not more so. Not yet a specialized field, civil engineering was at this time merely another trade, and few who practiced it had any particular degree or educational background that would have qualified them over anyone else. Consequently there was no reason to think that Dimock, Clement, and Clark, all highly intelligent and reputable men, couldn't manage the construction of a sound earthen dam. Moreover these men were as dependent on the dam's success as any. No one doubted that they would attend to it with due care and concern.

The dam was officially completed on January 11, 1866, and that spring the reservoir was allowed to fill in slowly. At least, that was the intention. One Sunday after heavy rains the reservoir began to fill so rapidly that the drainpipe was unable to release water fast enough to keep the level down. Workmen who happened to be on site grew alarmed. If it continued to rise, the reservoir could swamp the dam. Also, the men noticed that the embankment on the west side of the dam was becoming soggy beneath their feet, as if water was saturating the structure. They worried that sections might slough off at any moment, whereupon the whole thing might collapse.

By this time the contractors, Joel Bassett and Emory B. Wells, had been paid and gone on to new jobs. The directors would have to solve the dam's problems with other laborers. First the west side had to be stabilized, which was soon accomplished by driving timbers down into it. Then the slope had to be graduated, as the original pitch had proven too steep to resist the wave action and mounting pressure of a steadily increasing volume of water. "Earth," the directors found, "would not lie in water at so sharp an angle; it undermined and slumped down." As an immediate remedy, they directed workmen to cover the inside slope with hemlock boughs to stop the waves from washing more of it away. Once the reservoir began naturally to recede, workmen added more earth and decreased the slope to a thirty-degree angle, or a pitch of 1.73:1, still considerably steeper than was customary. They also rebuilt the spillway. In total these repairs cost the company between $1,200 and $2,000.

Word of the dam's weaknesses spread quickly, and at this point Skinner began to take notice. Like others, he didn't like what he heard, especially the part about the dam possibly leaking. Not only did the west side remain "wet and slushy," but streams of water had materialized, coming through both sides of the dam at various points. The general consensus was that the dam wasn't leaking—that these streams of water were natural springs forced into new courses by the construction of the reservoir. Even Governor Hayden, who had helped build the earlier reservoir in Goshen, supported the "natural spring" theory. Still, there was nothing reassuring about a brand-new dam oozing water, and Spelman, Bodman, Skinner, and Hayden, their mills being closest to the reservoir, began quietly to fear for the safety of their operations. Loss of property was the main concern. In the event of a dam failure they anticipated destructive flooding that would wash away bridges, damage mills, and ruin stock. They did not envision—there being no precedent for such a thing—a flood of such catastrophic proportion that it would annihilate whole villages and take people's lives.

The company hired the livery keeper John Belcher to tackle the job of stopping the water from flowing through the dam. Belcher specialized in horses, not dams, but he had a fine reputation for succeeding in a great many things. Unfortunately, it turned out, this wasn't one of them. He made an especially strong effort on the eastern bank, digging a trench where the spring flowed, puddling the earth therein, and then compacting the earth to make the area watertight. This seemed to work well enough, until the reservoir filled in again the following year and the spring resurfaced. Nobody had a proper explanation.

Everyone wanted to believe the spring was harmless, but seepage through an earthen dam under any circumstance must be regarded with suspicion and carefully monitored. Was the inner slope proving too weak and suffering from erosion? Why wasn't the stone wall stopping the seepage? The directors got their second taste of alarm in the spring of 1867, when the downstream embankment experienced its first slide. On the western slope, which was now so well known for being wet that men watered their horses there, a section of earth eight feet deep and forty feet long disappeared downriver. Once again Belcher was hired to attend to the problem, and he proceeded to layer in stones and drive in timbers to anchor the embankment.

Following this second alarm, the reservoir company itself began to feel mounting pressure. Several people wanted the county commissioners called in to inspect the dam, and if the directors of the company wouldn't petition the commissioners, there were others who would do it for them. The dam had never been officially inspected. In fact county commissioners were not allowed to inspect dams unless they received a written request from a concerned party, and in order to dissuade alarmists and reduce the number of unnecessary visits to perfectly fine dam sites, anyone who petitioned for an inspection found himself liable to pay a fee in the event that the commissioners found everything acceptable and the visit unwarranted. The law purposely limited the amount of bureaucratic oversight to which a corporation like the Williamsburg Reservoir Company might be subjected, in part to encourage such capitalists to take on public works projects.

At their annual meeting in May 1867 the shareholders of the Williamsburg Reservoir Company voted to consult with a lawyer "concerning the personal liability of stockholders in case of damages or loss by the breaking away of the reservoir & to take such measures as are necessary to relieve them from the same." One such measure was to call in the commissioners and procure a report that would be "admissible evidence in the trial of any issue involving liability." This annual meeting was one of the largest attended, and Skinner was the only shareholder *not* to attend. He would soon claim that "he knew nothing of the meeting for calling the county commissioners to examine the dam," but this was a rather masterful brushstroke over the facts. Like everyone else, he'd received a written notice of the meeting a week before it was held.

It's possible that Skinner avoided the meeting because he didn't want to be associated with any sense of wrongdoing—which a vote to secure indemnity in case of a lawsuit might have been seen to imply. What's more realistic, however, is that he simply couldn't be bothered. A few years earlier he had received a summons for jury duty to serve as a grand juror in criminal cases, but he never showed up, and finally the court dismissed him, noting that he "hath neglected and refused to appear in pursuance of said summons." That he didn't attend this meeting proves just how much he assumed others would take care of the dam. Had he known that assessments would be discussed at the meeting, he may have been more likely to attend. Money matters, after all, rarely failed to attract his attention. The directors wanted approval to pay for whatever repairs the three commissioners might require and to purchase land and build a house for a live-in gatekeeper to watch over the dam. But Skinner didn't vote on the assessments, just as he didn't vote to consult with a lawyer or hire the commissioners.

When the commissioners visited the dam several months later, they promptly rejected it. The directors then invested about $600 or $700 in additional repairs before calling the commissioners back the following summer. The commissioners rejected it again. What concerned these officials was the existence of water on the downstream slope—in other words, the continual seepage. After this second rejection—and after more than two years of difficulties—the company went all out on repairs, hiring Belcher again, along with one other laborer, and investing between $5,000 and $10,000 to strengthen the dam throughout. This included extending the breakwall on the troublesome western side as well as bolstering the inner slope with considerable rip-rapping and blanketing it with more layers of stones to prevent any further erosion. Finally, in October 1868, after their third visit, the commissioners approved the dam.

Once the dam received its official approval, fears about its integrity died down, and it receded into the background of daily life. Indeed as time wore on and it stood without incident, "the reservoir [was] considered as enhancing, rather than deteriorating the value of property in the valley below." A year after the final repairs, Skinner even credited the reservoir with saving a great deal of his property. A freshet in October 1869, brought on by torrential rain, caused considerable damage to his mill. Ellen Littlefield, then in her second year on the payroll, wrote to her mother, "Mr. Skinner thinks the great reservoir above here is all that saved us because it was so nearly empty before the rain." In this instance the reservoir had held back disaster, filling up with water that otherwise would have intensified the river's flooding.

Only a month before the fateful flood of 1874, the river had been dangerously high, "as high as comfort will allow . . . without 'slopping over,'" reported one local. Thus when Skinner left for New York at the beginning of May, his greatest concern was a freshet, while the reservoir seems hardly to have warranted a thought. Nor was the reservoir much in the thoughts of anyone else, except for Dimock and some other directors. A small group had planned on visiting the valley's reservoirs on Friday, May 15, for something like an annual inspection. However, they spent so much time in Goshen surveying the valley's original reservoir as well as another, built in 1873, that they didn't have time to visit the one in Williamsburg.

Interviewed about this on Sunday, the day after the disaster, Dimock admitted that he and his fellow directors had missed an opportunity to inspect the Williamsburg dam before it gave way. "But if we had gone over to it we should not have seen anything amiss," he said, "and if we had, I don't see how we could have helped ourselves. That reservoir contained enough water to run all the mills on the stream for a whole summer, and if we had opened the escape pipe as wide as it could be, we should not have been able to lower the water six inches in a whole night." In other words, neither Dimock nor the other directors would have wanted to lower the reservoir, given the abundance of power it was storing, and even if they had, they wouldn't have been able to do it fast enough to stave off disaster. There was simply nothing that could have been done.

Following the flood, a rumor circulated "that numberless suits for damages on account of life and property" were going "to be commenced against the association of manufacturers which built the flimsy dam." Yet it was a delicate situation for any villager to speak out against a mill owner, and no one went on record challenging the so-called establishment. Members of the press, though, owed little allegiance to the capitalists.

"[The] sadness of the event is intensified," proclaimed the *New York Herald*, "by the agonizing fact that the calamity is the result of the conceptions of Lilliputian souls of grasping corporations." Stated the *Boston Daily Globe*, "Owners of property cannot be trusted. . . . Should they [the owners of the reservoir] be proved to have been aware of its insecure condition, we trust nothing will be allowed to shield them from condign punishment." The *Hartford Courant* said simply, "If it be true that the owners of this dam have for years been distrustful of its strength, they, evidently, are responsible for the affair."

As with any colossal disaster, especially one like the Mill River Flood, then considered the worst of its kind in the history of the country, there arose impassioned cries for sweeping changes to be made in a system that could allow for such a tragedy. Some called for legislative reform, arguing that "proper safeguards against failure [of such dams] should be provided by law and rigidly applied." The "incapacity" of public officials to inspect such works before they were completed and their limited accountability afterward had to be made things of the past. The time had come for the legislature to step forward and become actively involved in overseeing industrial developments under its stewardship. A board of engineers was called for. "While the state provides for the inspection of steam boilers," wrote the *Worcester Gazette,* "there should be a competent board of engineers to examine such immeasurably greater engines of destruction as these large reservoirs of water in manufacturing districts."

Talk of change was one thing. Dealing with the here and now was another. A writer for the *Hampshire Gazette* contemplated the enormity of the situation. "There are many reservoirs in various sections of the state, perhaps no more secure than this one was, though deemed to be safe. Who has charge of them? Who inspects them? Who knows beyond a doubt whether or not they are safe?" It had become glaringly obvious that no one could vouch for the integrity of the reservoirs scattered over the Massachusetts landscape. But reservoirs were not only in Massachusetts. "In certain parts of hilly New England" everyone knew that "all the valleys have reservoirs of this kind for the use of the mills." And if such a horrific disaster could happen in Massachusetts, a state that had the reputation of being "the model American commonwealth," then a disaster of equal magnitude could happen anywhere.

Though localized in a valley that many outside of it had never heard of, the Mill River Disaster swiftly became the nation's biggest news. Word of it spread across the ocean to England and across the plains to California. The first transcontinental telegraph line had been completed in 1861, but wires throughout the country were still being laid down, and the concept of "national" news, or of local news becoming national, was still something of a revelation. Lines were buzzing night and day with fresh dispatches from the flooded district. "Nothing since war times has equaled the excitement," wrote the *Berkshire County Eagle,* while Samuel Bowles's desk at the *Springfield Republican* was "littered" with reactions coming in from all corners. Bowles even deemed it necessary to devote an entire column to "the Universal Damning of the Dam," presenting excerpts from various editorials excoriating the construction of the reservoir and lambasting nearly everyone who had anything to do with it. "As the newspaper is becoming more and more the pulse of public feeling and opinion," he wrote, "these scores of leading articles and editorial paragraphs . . . reflect pretty accurately the impression [the disaster has] made upon the country." The calamity, Bowles felt, was "a very profound one," and he advanced, "No event of the sort within our remembrance, not even the Chicago fire itself, affords a parallel for it."

Curiously, Boston papers seemed more inclined to take an innocent-until-proven-guilty approach in regard to culpability. "It is a grave matter upon which no journalist should risk a premature judgment," pronounced the *Boston Journal.* Seconded the *Boston Pilot,* "It is proper to await an investigation of the subject before fixing the blame of criminal neglect upon any." Governor Talbot was an extended member of the Hayden family, having married one of the late Governor Hayden's daughters, and some editors may have thought it politically prudent not to be too hasty in giving their opinion. At least one paper, the *New York Tribune,* asserted that finding out who was responsible was not the thing to focus on now. That could wait until everyone in the devastated valley had been properly cared for. Coincidence or not, one of the *Tribune*'s correspondents, Charles Webb, was a friend of both Henry L. James and William Skinner and thus, like Perkins, very much on the side of the manufacturers.

The *Tribune*'s editors had some harsh words to say on the state of "our national recklessness" but were quick to inform readers that the disaster wasn't as bad as it might have been. Although unable to cite anything of equal or worse consequence in America, the paper mentioned several events in Europe, recalling in particular England's Great Sheffield Flood of 1864, almost exactly a decade earlier. The Sheffield flood occurred when a large earthen dam gave way in South Yorkshire, unleashing a reservoir of water that eviscerated the countryside and killed nearly 250 people. Owned by the Sheffield Water Company for the purpose of powering mills in the area, the reservoir had covered about a hundred acres, holding roughly the same volume of water as the Williamsburg Reservoir. No one at the time understood why the dam gave way when it did, and the exact cause of the failure would never actually be determined (or, rather, agreed upon). Even so, everyone agreed that this flood was overwhelmingly disastrous, one of the worst in the century thus far, and the *Tribune* believed that people needed to be reminded of it to help put the Mill River Flood in perspective.

But that wouldn't have made anyone in the Mill River Valley feel any better. Moreover there was a belief among many that England's industrialization was a dirty business, lacking morality and integrity, and if a similar disaster had now happened here, what did that say about American industry? Nor did the *Tribune*'s suggestion to halt the discussion of responsibility pass muster with most people. The matter of responsibility loomed large for the public, with people generally blaming the mill owners first, then the contractors, the commissioners, and finally the state legislators. They spared no one, with one significant exception: God.

In years past God would have been central to the conversation, the disaster being perceived as punishment from on high for the insubordination of man. In eighteenth-century New England, for instance, Jonathan Edwards famously preached that people were "sinners in the hands of an angry god." Edwards, a Calvinist preacher, sparked the first religious revival in America, also known as the Great Awakening, from the pulpit at the Congregational church in Northampton, the very same in which Lizzie and Skinner were married. In fact Lizzie's great-great-grandfather Joseph Allen had been one of Edwards's most ardent supporters. Edwards's fire and brimstone sermons, contentious even in his own time, had a lasting impact on New England, as well as other parts of the country, and even in the early nineteenth century a disaster—certainly one in the form of a flood—would have been considered a manifestation of God's supreme displeasure with the grasping human condition. Yet coinciding with the dawn of the industrial age there emerged a startling new interpretation of His role in the affairs of men and women. Henry Ward Beecher, then the most famous preacher in America, repeatedly proclaimed from the pulpit of Brooklyn's Plymouth Church (and elsewhere) that God wasn't angry. God was loving, expansive, even nurturing. He was a merciful Father who wanted only the best for His children, and America, growing by leaps and bounds, was a shining example of a nation blessed by God's guiding hand. Though the concept of original sin persisted, it was leavened by the conviction that God was here to help.

An editor at the *San Francisco Chronicle* reflected on how times had changed. "Public opinion," he wrote, "is growing more and more determined in this land to hold to strict accountability those who by their negligence or willfulness sacrifice the lives of others. We have got past the days when the explosion of a steam-boiler, and the slaughter of people in its vicinity, was indifferently looked upon as a 'mysterious dispensation of Providence.'" There was certainly little belief in western Massachusetts that God had anything to do with the failure of the Williamsburg Reservoir dam. A week later the *Springfield Republican* would report, "The same general tone seems to have pervaded all—a rejection of the superstitious theory that such a calamity is the judgment of God, and an assertion of man's sole responsibility for it." Reverend Gleason of the Congregational church in Williamsburg would become increasingly adamant, insisting, "We cannot charge God with man's ignorance or neglect." Gleason lost thirty members of his congregation in the flood, and long before God could hold anyone to account in the afterlife, Gleason wanted accountability in the here and now.

To his and others' satisfaction, an official inquest, called for by Dr. Trow, was about to begin. "It is hoped," reported the *New York Herald,* "that the Coroner's investigation which is to commence tomorrow will result in defining the path of duty for the Grand Jury and the Judges of the criminal courts of Massachusetts."

Though Monday had dawned cool and wet, with rain once again falling on the stricken valley, the crowds did not abate. A New York reporter who'd opted to walk up the valley rather than drive, perhaps on account of the congestion, confirmed that the number of "curious visitors" was "nearly as great as the day before," and that on the roads "everything in Northampton, from a landau to a hay-cart, was in use." Libbie Skinner recorded what it was like to have to contend with all these people: "For a few days our valley was completely filled with visitors. Some had come to help remove the debris and search for the bodies of those who had been drowned. Others came from sheer curiosity, and like curious people everywhere they were only a trouble. They had no sense of propriety. They would walk through our house as if it was a public building and every small article which happened to be in the rooms on the first floor, they felt perfectly free to appropriate. One man was found trying to take a silver knob from a blind in order to have something to aid his memory in recalling this deluge."

All existing property was subject to theft. In Florence, the Kendall sisters tried to find some of their possessions, and in a stroke of good luck Nettie spied her sewing machine in some debris. This was an expensive item for a mill girl to own, and now, without the mill to provide employment, Nettie needed that machine more than ever. But just as she saw it someone else did too, and, despite her entreaties, the machine "was lugged off by a relic hunter before her eyes." Other thieves attempted to steal a coat of Jerome Hillman's with some silver in the pocket while he was preoccupied digging for his wife. Everyone victimized by the flood became increasingly worried about his or her belongings. Skinner was exceedingly nervous about his safe and its contents, as well as all the silk that was swept from the mill, lying God only knew where. Hayden was anxious to recover as many of his patterns and items of brass as possible. James wanted his wool, and George Warner and Spelman their buttons. Such goods were easy money for the unsavory, and, as the manufacturers would soon learn, stores of their materials were in fact being recovered surreptitiously and "secreted in dwellings."

So great was the threat to property that "appeals were immediately made for police protection," but the number of officers available in the valley proved insufficient to discourage the looting; the militia had to be called out, and a journalist from the *New York Sun* observed, "The entire line of the valley from Haydenville to Williamsburg is now picketed [with soldiers]." Skinnerville and Haydenville fell under the protection of Captain David Maguire from Company F of the 2nd Regiment. By Monday afternoon more than ten uniformed men, muskets at the ready, were patrolling Skinnerville, and what had previously been a free-for-all gradually became somewhat more civilized.

Of the four missing Skinnerville villagers, two had been found by Sunday evening—Mrs. Hills, mother of six, and eight-year-old Robbie Hayden—and a third was discovered on Monday. The body of Eli Bryant, an elderly resident, was recovered after some workmen heard Bryant's dog, a St. Bernard mix, barking and digging at the ground some distance from the river. The men took over the animal's work, and when they uncovered Bryant's face, the dog "seemed for a second overjoyed, but when a cloth was wrapped around the rigid form and the removal was begun," noted an onlooker, "the noble creature seemed bowed with grief." The body was far from where searchers were looking for remains, and while the dog's discovery was a heartbreaking story of loyalty it was also a warning. "It is reasonable to believe," wrote a Boston man afterward, "that some now missing are [buried deep] beneath the sand beds . . . their bones to be found in after time by accident or by the changing of the course of the Mill River." Only one more Skinnerville resident remained missing at this point, Sarah Hillman, and her husband Jerome, wracked with grief, couldn't have stopped thinking, *Where is my wife?*

At least one critical facet of everyday life reappeared in the village on Monday: the train. The tracks had been repaired over the weekend, and with engineer Van Vechten of Skinnerville working the controls, a small locomotive came whistling around the corner through the rain, puffing its way into the depot. This was excellent news for the survivors, as supplies would henceforth arrive a great deal faster, and, with the railroad resuming its familiar, reassuring schedule, a small bit of normalcy would return to the devastated village. But talk of rebuilding was still fantasy; Skinner told a reporter his losses were so great "that he would be unable to build up even a house for his family."

Skinner's visible lack of enthusiasm, combined with the dispiritedness of Spelman, James, and Warner and the total loss of manufacturing capital on the river, was creating the worst possible scenario for an industrial valley, one of crushing immobility. Only one enterprise seemed a likely candidate for rebuilding any time soon: the brass works. Hayden Jr. was also the only afflicted proprietor who openly bristled at the suggestion that he was in any real financial distress. Indeed he sought to assuage everyone's fears with a bold declaration of solvency. To a reporter from the *New York Times* he said "that the statement made in a New York paper about his having lost every cent is untrue. He is very well off, all things considered, and owes no man anything."

Unfortunately Hayden wasn't telling the whole truth. In the wake of his father's death, he had aggressively moved to consolidate the interests of the company. While this had seemed like a good idea just a few months before, the company's obligations were now spectacular. Governor Hayden had left behind ten heirs, no will, and, apart from other investments, $150,000 worth of stock in the brass works. In cooperation with Collins Gere (whose interest in the firm was minuscule, about one eighth) and his silent partner Sereno Kingsley (whose interest would have been equally small), Joel Hayden had bought back all of his father's shares from the heirs. Consequently the heirs lost nothing when the brass works disintegrated in the flood, having just disposed of their stock, while Hayden still had ten big checks to write. In addition, then, to recouping the firm's losses from the disaster, estimated to be in the range of $75,000 to $80,000, and settling any outstanding operational debts, Hayden had to reconcile the firm's additional liability of $150,000 to his father's heirs.

Hayden was in deep, but he remained utterly sanguine, even stubbornly proud, claiming on Monday that nobody had to worry about the care of families in Haydenville, that "the immediate necessities [of the homeless and bereaved] would be relieved by Hayden, Gere & Co." This was an astonishing statement given the magnitude of the need, and one can only wonder where he expected to come up with the funds.

Skinner, on the other hand, began acting more like a clerk than a proprietor, soliciting people in towns near and far for the supplies that his villagers needed. He sent one request to Springfield "for clothes for seven boys—ages 6, 10, 11, 14, 15, 17, 20—and six girls—ages 16, 6, 5, 4, 3, 2—and some baby clothes." Skinner was absolutely specific about what was needed in Skinnerville. With so much wanting, neither he nor Lizzie wished to receive yet another barrel of rolling pins. In concert with Franklin Allen at the Silk Association, he also opened a bank account in New York City where donations coming in from the silk industry for the valley's silk workers could be deposited. From this fund Skinner began to pay for relief items, such as sixty dozen pairs of socks and stockings, and assumed leadership of the relief effort for both his and the Nonotuck's silk operatives. For whatever reason, no owner of the Nonotuck stepped forward to help him. From the beginning he was the valley's only silk manufacturer addressing the needs of its more than eighty destitute silk workers.

Within the silk industry Skinner's name quickly became synonymous with this disaster, not only because of his relief efforts but, more significantly, because of his overwhelming personal loss. So many silk men were talking about what had happened to their colleague that an editor at the *Paterson Daily Press* even suggested that they help him start over. But Skinner made it clear that the best way to help him was to provide for his operatives, something he could no longer do. More than half of his female workers had been boarders, and they had lost all of their possessions. They had no way to pay for food or clothing or transportation out of the flooded district. Skinner himself did not want any personal assistance. At one point he received an extremely generous note granting him an immediate loan of $1,000, but he returned it, "saying he was under a great strain and did not know what might happen to him." Taking money like that, even in the form of a friendly loan, would have felt like taking charity, the acceptance of which is almost always abhorrent to a self-made man. He did not want to owe any of his friends anything, but he would gladly take money for his workers.

The Mill River Flood occurred in the days before there were any volunteer, state, or federal organizations to help victims of catastrophes. The American Red Cross, for instance, would not be established for another seven years. Nor was there any precedent in the long history of Massachusetts for governmental assistance to citizens in crisis. The petition that had been sent on to Boston asking for a reprieve from taxation and money to help rebuild the towns was akin to a shot in the dark. The citizens of Williamsburg and Northampton were asking the legislature to do something it had never done. As for federal aid, Congress had passed the Federal Disaster Relief Act in 1812 to grant free tracts of land to the sufferers of an earthquake in the Missouri territory, but this had the unintended consequence of inspiring fraudulent land claims and turning the territory into a jackpot for speculators. Moreover the Relief Act had been instituted to help a territory, not a state, and most people believed the federal government should stay out of state affairs. Efforts from officials in Washington to secure money for local communities in crisis inevitably boiled down to backroom politics: who would back whom, for how much, and for what in return. One congressman from Vermont tried to rally support for the Mill River Valley survivors, but he found no enthusiasm among his peers. His was the only effort at the federal level.

Knowing they were on their own, valley residents banded together over the weekend to form various committees for relief, but these committees were scattered and small, and in a few places like Skinnerville they didn't even exist. In consequence of this, on Monday evening a "mass meeting" was held in Northampton's town hall to organize a central relief committee and better coordinate the valley's relief effort. Good intentions aside, it was also a way for Northampton officials to take ownership of an effort that could potentially bring in tens of thousands of dollars to the valley. Charles Delano, a prominent Northampton lawyer, proclaimed that it was time for "men of means and business and leisure" to assume responsibility for the valley's wants, and by the end of the night a twelve-member general relief committee, consisting of *only* Northampton men, had been elected to "take the entire charge of the [relief] work." Despite the fact that Williamsburg had endured far greater devastation and would need the majority of aid, not one Williamsburg citizen was put on that powerful committee.

Following the meeting the general relief committee elected subcommittees on supplies, labor, police, and finance, filling these with Northampton men as well, with one exception. The finance committee would be composed of well-respected financiers from each affected village, men who would solicit and collect donations for their villages and deposit that money into a central relief account in Northampton. All donations would henceforward be pooled so that they could be used to greater advantage for everyone, with the finance committee assigned to manage the money. Skinner naturally was chosen as the representative for Skinnerville; joining him was Lewis Bodman for Williamsburg, Joel Hayden Jr. for Haydenville, and General John L. Otis for Leeds. The banker Luther Bodman (Lewis's brother), born in Williamsburg but a resident of Northampton, was elected chairman and treasurer of the committee.

Not having attended this relief meeting, Skinner must have learned of his appointment to the finance committee late in the evening, when the few Williamsburg men who had gone to the meeting passed by his house on their way home. Skinner had stayed in to talk with George about what was arguably more important to him than the politics of relief. Edward Lyman was coming back the next day, and Skinner needed to figure out what to tell him. It is impossible to say what, if anything, the brothers resolved, but by the time George left it was still raining, the darkness outside as intense as the night before, and only one thing was clear. In order to start over Skinner needed money and waterpower, and his objective had to be finding them wherever he could.

Chapter Ten

A legislative committee from Boston, consisting of three senators and seven representatives, arrived in Northampton at about 9 a.m. on Tuesday, May 19. They spent the morning slowly making their way up the valley, talking to survivors, stepping into the morgues, and witnessing innumerable scenes of sorrow. When they arrived in Skinnerville, where there was so little for the eye to fall upon that the mind had difficulty imagining a village, Skinner joined the growing entourage.

The committee's carriages took a sizable group to the ruined reservoir, including selectmen from both Northampton and Williamsburg, the original contractors for the dam, a civil engineer from Boston, an assembly of newspaper reporters, and several of the area's manufacturers. About two and a half miles north of Williamsburg drivers had to abandon the road and direct their teams across a field, following a path that led to the gatekeeper's house. Ironically George Cheney's house, sitting practically on top of the dam, was one of the few dwellings the committee had seen all day that didn't need to be hauled off as recycled lumber.

The empty reservoir and broken dam left most of the group speechless. Where only the week before had been a magnificent lake was now a flat expanse of mud, tree stumps, and puddles. The committee had an unobstructed view through the massive gap where the center of the dam had been. It was an astonishing opening, 250 feet wide, framed on either side by two jagged towers of stone, which more closely resembled the remains of some ancient ruin than the dam's core wall of which they had once been a part.

One after another the men descended the hillside into the gap, where they quietly inspected what had once been the base of the dam. For the next several minutes "a careful examination was made of the bottom, the wall, the earth, the fillings and the surroundings." At one point someone muttered, "Child's play," and at another "A boy's dam." The contempt was audible.

Not the least bit happy to be the target of what he believed were unwarranted judgments, Joel Bassett, lead contractor for the dam, felt that many among these well-heeled men were drawing conclusions about matters they knew nothing about. As members of the group gathered close to him, he drew out the original specifications for the dam, drawn up by Lucius Fenn in the spring of 1865, and attempted to exonerate himself and his partner, Emory B. Wells, by showing that they had built the dam according to these specifications and were not to be blamed for its failure. A rugged sort, thick-set, with a large, open face from which descended a small curtain of whiskers that crudely brushed the tip of his collar, Bassett was blunt and direct. He unhesitatingly asserted that Fenn, who wrote the specifications, and the county commissioners, who approved the dam, were the ones most responsible. To support his claim Bassett told his audience that a solid core wall had been built into a trench on a hard and firm foundation exactly as specified by Fenn. Given that most of the wall no longer remained, Bassett was probably banking on the fact that his audience would have to take his word for all this. However, one member of the group did not: Colonel Henry W. Wilson, a civil engineer from Boston whom the legislative committee had asked to accompany them on this visit.

1

Sarah Elizabeth "Lizzie" Allen (1834–1908), William Skinner's second wife and the mother of his eight other children. Lizzie was a schoolteacher before she married Skinner and shared his ambitious spirit. Skinner called her "the woman to see after things."

2

Nancy Edwards Warner (1825–1854), William Skinner's first wife and the mother of Nellie and Nina. Nancy was a sister of Skinner's first business partner and came from a well-known, educated family.

William Skinner with daughters Nina and Nellie in Boston, circa 1855. Just as Skinner was establishing his own business, his young wife Nancy died, following the birth of little Nina. This family portrait was taken shortly after Nancy's death.

3

4

Thomas Skinner (1831–1922). A master silk dyer, Thomas was the youngest of Skinner's two brothers and the second to come to the United States. He ran the dyehouse at the mill in Skinnerville and then in Holyoke. His expertise was rare.

5

George Benson Skinner (1827–1891). George arrived in the States a few months after Thomas and made a small fortune manufacturing silk in New York. After the flood, he offered William advice and may have loaned him some money.

6

Ellen Littlefield (1842–1936). Ellen came to Skinnerville for the opportunities that factory work provided. At the time of the disaster, she was working for Skinner as a packer; then through the summer she helped salvage flood-damaged silk. She moved to Holyoke to work in the new mill, and eventually married Skinner's bookkeeper, Nash Hubbard.

Map of Skinnerville, 1873. "W. S." denotes property of William Skinner.

7

Lovisa Littlefield (1846–1935). Lovisa was the first Little-field sister to work for Skinner. She arrived in Skinnerville in 1866 and quickly became "an expert spooler." After she married, she had wanted to return to Skinnerville to visit, but decided it would be too difficult emotionally after the flood.

8

9

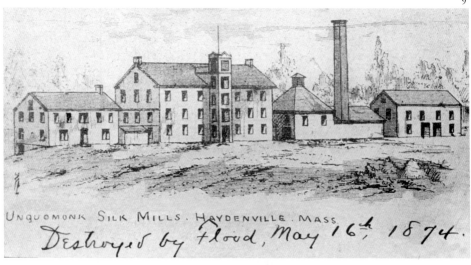

Skinner's Silk Mill in Skinnerville before the flood. He called his factory the Unquomonk Silk Mill, popularizing a local Native American term, and adopted the image of an Indian head as his logo.

George Cheney (1844–1918). Gatekeeper of the Williamsburg dam, Cheney rode his horse bareback three miles to town to tell his boss that the dam was giving way.

11

Collins Graves (1840–1910). Graves, a dairy farmer, rode his buggy (with the milk cans still in it) down to Skinnerville and Haydenville to spread the warning. Credited with saving hundreds of lives, he was praised as a hero and immortalized in poetry.

12

"The flood at the residence of Mr. Skinner." Within hours of the disaster, New York newspapers were sending artists to the devastated region to interview survivors and imagine the event for readers far away. In this drawing, the water is depicted surging past the Skinner mansion. From *Frank Leslie's Illustrated Newspaper,* May 30, 1874.

"Miraculous escape of a child from death at Williamsburg." From *Frank Leslie's Illustrated Newspaper,* June 6, 1874.

13

14

"The valley of death—scene looking from the suburbs of Williamsburg towards Skinnerville—the flood subsiding." From *Frank Leslie's Illustrated Newspaper,* June 6, 1874.

Remains of the west side of the dam. This image is from a stereoview, one of hundreds taken after the flood, and shows spectators climbing a portion of the dam's broken wall.

View of Skinnerville, looking downstream. Skinner's house is in the center with the caved-in piazza. The silk mill had stood along the river and extended well to the north (or left) of the mansion. A small portion of its foundation is visible.

Remnants of Skinner's mill. Men examine the silk mill's flywheel after it had been cleared of debris. So little of the mill survived that one of Skinner's employees would proudly report a bucket was also found.

One of Skinner's tenements, tipped over amid wreckage. Of the fourteen houses Skinner owned for his workers and their families, eleven were lost in the flood. The shell of this particular house survived; most were entirely swept away.

19   20

William Cobbett Skinner (1857–1947) and Joseph Allen Skinner (1862–1946). Will was at boarding school when the flood occurred and rushed home that afternoon. Like his father, he had a keen sense of business and marketing. Joe fled from the water with the rest of the family, running up the hillside. Scientifically minded, Joe was intensely interested in the production of textiles. The brothers took over their father's company when he died and successfully steered it through the turbulent 1920s and 1930s.

21

22

Elizabeth ("Libbie") Skinner (1859–1927). Libbie had just returned home from boarding school for summer vacation when the disaster occurred. She recorded vivid details of the flood and its aftermath.

Ruth Isabel ("Belle") Skinner (1866–1928) with baby Katharine Skinner (1873–1968). Belle, eight at the time of the flood, grew up to be a noted philanthropist. After World War I, she rebuilt the French village of Hattonchâtel and received awards for her relief efforts, including the Legion of Honor. Katharine Skinner was just six months old when the flood occurred. Unlike her siblings, she had no memory of the disaster.

PLAN OF THE NEW CITY OF HOLYOKE.

Map of Holyoke. This early depiction shows the design of the city's ingenious canal system and layout for manufactories. The Holyoke dam is to the upper right, crossing the powerful Connecticut River.

The Holyoke dam, as pictured in Harper's Weekly, *1869.* Built with "four million feet of sawed timber," as well as concrete, gravel, boiler iron, and "abutments of massive masonry," this impressive dam was heralded as producing "the finest water-power in the country."

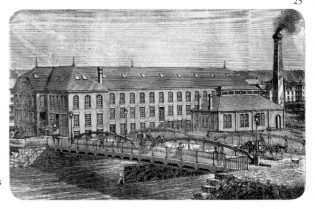

25

The Unquomonk Silk Mill, 1875. Skinner's first mill in Holyoke opened November 16, 1874, exactly six months after the flood. The one-story building to the right is the dyehouse. As the company grew, the mill was enlarged, more property was purchased, and greater buildings were constructed.

26 *William Skinner & Sons Silk Mill, 1912.* The central building was a thousand feet long, stretched over three city blocks, contained more than five acres of floor space, and required "a walk of several miles" to tour its many departments. It was considered the largest silk mill under one roof in the world.

30

Good Housekeeping, 1907; *Photoplay,* 1931; *Esquire's,* 1943; *Charm,* 1951.

Skinner's was one of the first textile houses to branch into consumer advertising with an ad in *Ladies' Home Journal* in 1903. Ads for the company appeared in every major American magazine for the next fifty-eight years.

The Skinner family home. The picture on the left shows the house just days after the flood, damaged, with visitors in front of it. Skinner had the house taken apart piece by piece and rebuilt in Holyoke, where it became known as Wistariahurst for the wisteria vine that Lizzie planted along it. The house stands today as a museum and is listed on the National Register of Historic Places.

33

William Skinner and his family, 1884.
Standing: Libbie, Lizzie, Will, and Nellie.
Seated: Belle, Nina, Skinner, Katharine, and Joe. The family flourished in Holyoke. On May 16, 1941, Joe wrote: "Anniversary of the Mill River Flood—67 years ago . . . we have grown well. Father established his business in Holyoke and his success and our success has been amazing."

Skinner and Lizzie on the porch of Wistariahurst, circa 1898. Said Skinner, "We all stand equal in the race for success."

Wilson was a trained engineer "of high repute" whose work included a reservoir at Hartford, Connecticut, which had been in existence for twenty years. A tall man of imposing bearing, with a "massive" head, black curly hair, and a black goatee and mustache, he reminded people of the famous actor Edwin Forrest, though unlike Forrest, Wilson was not inclined toward the dramatic. "Frank, ready, [and] decisive," he swiftly discredited Bassett's claim. Had the construction of the wall faithfully followed Fenn's plan, he explained, it would have been set within a trench at least three feet deep, all the way down to hardpan. No trench was to be seen here. On the contrary, the wall appeared to have been laid on top of whatever surface was convenient, be it rock, gravel, or loose earth. If this was the case, the wall would not have been secure at all and, to quote one of the stunned onlookers, must have "slid off as though the ground was greased." Bassett presumably protested that the trench itself had been washed away, but Wilson would have none of it. "This dam was not built according to the specifications of that paper in your hand," he told the contractor, plainly.

"But, Sir—" Bassett interjected, attempting to hold his ground.

To which Wilson immediately responded, "Excuse me, Sir, you are talking now to a man who fully understands this kind of thing and can see just how it is. Mr. Bassett, we are standing on your own witness and its testimony condemns you."

Wilson proceeded to take over the examination, pointing out that the contractors had failed as well to build the embankments according to the specifications. These were supposed to have been cleared of all perishable matter, stumps and roots in particular, that could decompose over time, creating avenues for seepage. The banks were also to have been rid of "all sods, muck and everything of that character," which could not be compacted to the point of being watertight. The central wall was to have been a classic New England stone wall, bonded with cement, "as strong as a single shaft of granite." Wilson stepped up to one of the stone towers, took out a knife, and with the back of its blade "scraped [the cement] out from between the stones like so much new cheese," concluding that not a square inch of proper cement had been used in the wall. Additionally, he observed, many stones were mismatched and had not been carefully arranged to fit together. Properly laid stone walls have minimal gaps. This one was built like a sieve.

Given the construction, water from both the reservoir and the natural springs on the upstream side would have been able to penetrate and weaken the dam, first through the embankment, which remained porous with roots and other matter, and then through the center wall, which had been grouted with permeable cement and improperly laid. Most dangerous of all, water would have seeped, and later flowed, *under* the center wall, through the gravel and loose earth that composed the bulk of its foundation. "The accident which has desolated this once fair valley was inevitable," concluded Wilson in disgust. "The only wonder is that it did not occur before."

When Wilson pronounced the construction of the dam criminal and its failure equivalent to murder, Skinner lost control of himself. No longer caring about propriety—everyone to this point had been quite civil—he walked right up to Bassett and Wells and told them they ought to suffer for what they'd done.

"Look here," said Skinner, his black eyes filled with rage. "If you want to know what I think of you two, I'll tell you that you ought to have a rope around your necks and something ought to be done with the rope, too."

Everybody heard him. He was loud and clear, and he had, in effect, just publicly accused Bassett and Wells of manslaughter. Wilson may have called the dam's failure a murderous crime, but he had stopped short of calling anyone a murderer—in part, perhaps, because there was still a lot to learn about this dam. There were many people involved in its construction, after all, not least of which were the all-important building committee and the tightly knit group of shareholders to whom that committee had been answerable. Had the specifications been carried out properly, Wilson believed, the dam probably would not have failed. All the same, the specifications themselves "were not what they should have been." The plan had been a bad one from the start, even before Bassett and Wells were hired. But Skinner heard what he wanted to hear.

A reporter from the *Boston Daily Globe* questioned whether Skinner had really meant what he said.

"Mr. Reporter," Skinner responded, "you may say that William Skinner said just that thing, and that he sticks to it."

Following the visit to the dam, the large group returned to Williamsburg and dined, probably at the Hampshire House hotel, after which they moved to a room upstairs for some concrete discussions about the monetary needs of the valley. The legislators listened, asked questions, and made some computations, but promised nothing to Skinner or anyone else. Having now seen the extent of the damage and suffering that the flood had caused, the legislators understood only too well why they had been called in to help, but they also realized that the valley needed extraordinary amounts of money. Hampshire County's own Senator Edson figured "the loss to the town [of Williamsburg] . . . at but little less than a million dollars, and that of Northampton, which takes in the village of Leeds and Florence, at nearly the same amount." In Williamsburg some predicted "a damage to highways and bridges of $115,000, and a loss in real and personal property of $500,000." The road through Skinnerville alone was going to cost approximately $25,000. But no one could say with any accuracy how much money the afflicted towns would actually need, and the legislators were not going to offer assistance in a vacuum. Furthermore these politicians were more than a little hesitant even to entertain the concept of state aid for fear of future ramifications. "So far as the committee has been able to ascertain," one of the senators would write, "there is no precedent [for this]." And regarding personal suffering, a number of senators felt that "it would not be prudent or safe for the Legislature to enter upon the distribution of charity to relieve cases of personal hardship and distress."

Rebuilding roads, bridges, riverbanks, and water privileges were municipal expenses, but if the legislature didn't provide Williamsburg with the assistance to take care of those things, men like Skinner, who was previously the largest taxpayer in town, were going to be stuck with the burden. Without question the bulk of repairs in Skinnerville would fall squarely on Skinner's shoulders. Like his fellow citizens, he was hoping for encouragement from Boston, but he received only sympathy—and that wasn't going to help. Although there was a reasonable chance that the legislature would ultimately, somehow, support the recovery effort with funds from the state treasury, this would take time, and Skinner needed to begin making decisions *now*.

When exactly Edward Lyman returned for his follow-up visit is unknown, but the silk trader reiterated on Tuesday that Skinner had very strong support in the trade and that, from the standpoint of A. A. Low & Co., he could depend on both leniency and assistance. He didn't need to worry about his current debts, nor his lack of money to purchase new materials. The question Skinner needed to be asking himself, according to Lyman, was not *if* he could rebuild, but *where*, and whether Skinnerville could be the answer. They decided that it could not. Reported the *Springfield Republican* in next morning's paper, "Mr. Skinner states that the water privilege [in Skinnerville] could not again be utilized without enormous expense, the washing out of the former channel rendering it almost useless. Mr. Skinner will probably either lease or erect a new factory elsewhere, and is looking about for a favorable location." The paper then added, "Probably he will not go farther than Northampton."

Lyman, of course, was an old Northampton man, born there in 1819, and he almost certainly suggested investigating his hometown's possibilities. The flood had wreaked havoc on its village of Leeds, but elsewhere, in Florence and below, trade was expected to recommence in a reasonable amount of time. Somewhat fortuitously the town had a share of available water privileges, and local capitalists were beginning to awaken to the opportunity this disaster might occasion them. Not a few would have appreciated the fact that Skinner's mill, were it relocated to Northampton, would consolidate the valley's silk manufacturing within its borders, providing it with a glimmer of its earlier prominence in the silk industry. Furthermore, if Skinner relocated here, he wouldn't have to abandon the valley—only move to the safer end of it.

The issue of waterpower remained a critical factor, however. Yes, Northampton boasted available water privileges, but with the Williamsburg Reservoir gone, would there be enough power during the dry months? A *Boston Globe* correspondent heard a mouthful from one man whose identity, for whatever reason, remained anonymous: "A manufacturer who had suffered severely stated to your correspondent, today, that he doubted very much that any of the factories, with the exception of Hayden, Gere & Co., would be rebuilt. He said that the prejudice in this section against reservoirs will be so great that it will be impossible to run mills by water, and that steam power is not what is wanted in the work, besides being too expensive."

The man quoted may have been Skinner; the sentiment certainly mirrored his own. He had invested in a steam engine in Skinnerville, but only used it when absolutely necessary. Fueling a steam engine required coal, which was expensive to ship, and keeping the engine running smoothly required costly maintenance. When available, which for most of the year it was, waterpower was free, and the cost of maintaining a water turbine was nominal. Skinner also required the use of a lot of water in his business—to clean, boil, dye, and rinse his silk. Were he to be limited in his ability to capitalize on the Mill River due to fears or circumstances resulting from the disaster, he would be unable to run his mill successfully. No matter his attachment to the area, his business would be better off someplace else. Moreover, steam engines commanded stiff prices, and Skinner couldn't afford one right now, not with everything else he was going to have to purchase if he was going to build another mill.

• • •

Seventeen miles away, in the city of Holyoke, Massachusetts, Edwin Leander Kirtland, the editor of the *Holyoke Transcript,* finished a lengthy editorial on the flood to be published the next day, exemplifying the spirit of opportunism that the disaster was inspiring elsewhere. The piece began leisurely, "The pitiable condition of the Mill River valley . . . is a theme for varied comment," but then it quickly zeroed in on what was important to enterprising spirits: "To the visitor, to day, the restoration of the [devastated] region would seem impossible."

Only a week earlier the *Transcript* had run a small but prominently placed advertisement that read as follows:

Wanted.

A score of small manufactories. Holyoke needs them, and they can thrive here, if they can anywhere. Water power is cheap, and rents are dear. Outsiders have an idea that our immense water power is intended only to drive mammoth wheels of large manufactories, but there are grand chances for small manufactories. . . . We will welcome all who wish to live in an enterprising city and under an economical city government.

Holyoke was an up-and-coming city, with an ingenious canal system for supplying waterpower to factories in an urban environment. Before any space in the paper was devoted to describing the destruction in the Mill River Valley or enumerating its current suffering and need for relief, Kirtland, who was almost certainly in concert with Holyoke capitalists, made a sales pitch to the devastated manufacturers with his editorial pen.

First, he catalogued advantageous reasons for leaving the valley. Since people's fears were acute, nothing but extensively reinforced dams of very expensive masonry were ever going to be able to be built there; thus "the present restoration of these sites and the power would doubtless cost more than the original improvement." Then there was the matter for patriarchs like Skinner of having to restore their communities: "They must not only build dams and re-grade for and build mills, but they will be compelled also to restore chiefly the habitations of the operatives and other agents and auxiliaries upon which the prosecution of their enterprises depends." All this would cost time when it was most inopportune. "These men have established trades and patronage to which interruption will be a serious drawback." But the situation should not be considered hopeless or even overwhelming because nearby manufacturing centers had invested in development projects over the previous winter that were now ready for occupancy and "awaiting conditions of trade favorable to new enterprises." Lest anyone have any doubt, Holyoke was just such a center.

Kirtland then brought in the locals, informing old and new readers that Asa Willard and Mosher, Wait & Co. had "new and commodious buildings, with power suitable for large or small enterprises." What's more, if one wished to start from the ground up, there was opportunity for that as well, since the powerful mill builders D. H. & J. C. Newton had "room for rent, and abundant facilities for the speedy erection of mills of every class and kind upon sites owned or controlled by themselves or others."

From the get-go, the smaller manufacturers of the Mill River Valley seemed likely to be the easiest fish to catch. Kirtland mentioned in passing that Hayden, Gere & Co. had "declared their intention of rebuilding" on their original site, and he more or less wished them well, remarking, "Immediate restoration won't pay." Then brushing them aside (for the moment), he targeted those enterprises that had known more modest success, and, though he didn't name them specifically, it was evident that he was speaking to George Warner, Onslow Spelman, and, of course, Skinner. They were the "unfortunate proprietors" with so little to fall back on, and Kirtland wanted them to know that, despite Holyoke's reputation for going after "mammoth enterprises," their businesses would be heartily welcomed. "We could truly fix a date within which these washed out manufactories could be all comfortably located here and elsewhere, that would astonish even those enterprising manufacturers themselves." Skinner, Spelman, and Warner had only to name the day on which they hoped to be back in business, and, according to Kirtland, Holyoke men would make it happen with something like the snap of their fingers.

Kirtland feigns a bit of restraint in his concluding remarks, but only briefly. "We are not pleading for the total abandonment of the water-cursed valley; its power will sell for what it is worth whenever the market requires it; and the towns . . . will yet partially recover their own [industries]." Then he continued: "But it is within the bounds of possibility; that a larger part of the concerns which have been started there will be transplanted elsewhere, that many of them, to avoid long interruption of business, to secure safe location, constant power and space for limitless expansion, will bring their button shops and silk factories to Holyoke, and leave the scene of the struggles and triumphs and disasters to those who have new enterprises to build, for which the deserted valley may furnish just the opportunities desired."

Farther down the road in Springfield, Samuel Bowles seems to have gotten a clear whiff of the dust that Kirtland was beginning to kick up. There was little love between the cities of Springfield and Holyoke. Though they had few competing industries, they were equally eager to advance their manufacturing bases, and Bowles let fly an obvious jab at Holyoke's engineering as he summed up the need for a state board of engineers in the wake of the disaster:

> There is a wide range of duties and cares which might be intrusted to such a board, in connection with the dams, canals, reservoirs and natural basins and streams in the commonwealth, not only with reference to their general security, but also with a view to prepare for and prevent the spring freshets which periodically devastate some of our narrow valleys. Nobody can call to mind the miles upon miles of heavy canals in this commonwealth, overhanging cities as those at Holyoke, without apprehensions of their security.

Despite the fact that some Springfield investors were every bit as eager to lure the valley's ruined businesses to their city, Bowles refused to take Kirtland's approach. He was too invested in journalistic integrity to see his paper become a tool for municipal interests. Rather, he strove to sow seeds of doubt about Holyoke, for which he had little regard, and then let it be known to all concerned parties that, contrary to what anyone else had to report, the future of the Mill River Valley was not nearly so bleak as had been supposed. One of Bowles's reporters had learned that Spelman, who only a day or so earlier had emphatically told the *Hampshire Gazette* he could never rebuild, would in fact be rebuilding his button mill in Williamsburg. Henry L. James too had decided in a blush of newfound enthusiasm not only to rebuild but to "considerably enlarge his capacity for manufacturing," while in Haydenville, Hayden and his partners were already drafting plans for a new establishment. A local investor had come forward with $25,000 toward a new button mill for George Warner in Leeds, and the Nonotuck and Emery Wheel companies were reportedly on the move to repair their facilities in Leeds as well. Bowles even had some sanguine words for Skinnerville, though its recovery appeared hopeless at present: "Its time will come by and by; if not through its present enterprising and greatly afflicted proprietor, then through younger and fresher men in the work of life."

On Wednesday, the coroner's inquest continued its preparatory phase. A jury of six local men had been selected by Northampton's district attorney, and these men, along with Coroner Ansel Wright, convened at Williamsburg's town hall Wednesday morning to view the body of one of the flood victims. John Atkinson, a forty-eight-year-old husband and father, originally from England, had been the foreman of the weaving room at the James mill. Atkinson's body had been found the day before in a meadow three miles south of Williamsburg, "crooked around a tree" with $23 in his pocket. As the jury gathered around his decomposed remains, Coroner Wright gravely asked for their word of honor: "Do you solemnly swear, that you will diligently inquire and true presentment make, on behalf of this commonwealth, when, how, and by what means, the person whose body lies here dead came to his death; and you shall return a true inquest thereof, according to your knowledge and such evidence as shall be laid before you; so help you, God?"

The six jurors were all distinguished valley residents. The *Hampshire Gazette* praised their selection as "a very intelligent body, in whose judgment the public will have full confidence." Yet the truth was that the majority of them were on very friendly terms with the owners of the reservoir company. Apart from caring for them as their physician (and knowing them intimately in ways others never would), Dr. Trow, for instance, had helped found the Haydenville Savings Bank with five of the owners. He had also served with Skinner and Joel Hayden on committees too numerous to recount. To say that there might have been several conflicts of interest with men like this on the jury would be an understatement, and one wonders how the *Gazette* or anyone else imagined they could possibly reach an impartial decision. For someone like Skinner, on the other hand, who didn't believe the company had done anything wrong, this was exactly the kind of jury that was called for. Following the viewing of Atkinson's body and a group visit to the dam site, the jury recessed until the following Monday, at which time the inquest would officially begin at the Northampton courthouse.

Wednesday was Joe Skinner's twelfth birthday, but there would be no celebration this year, not when there was so much mud and debris to be cleared around the house and when the predominant conversation at home was how his father was "ruined." Nor was Skinner around much even to tousle the boy's hair. He was engaged much of the day in talks with potential donors for relief. The Reverend George Phillips of Worcester, an old friend who had once been pastor of the Congregational church in Haydenville, arrived with more than a thousand dollars at his disposal, the balance left over from an 1871 relief fund for victims of the Chicago fire. Skinner impressed on Phillips the peculiar hardship in Skinnerville, and such was the impact of their meeting that Phillips would ultimately earmark nearly half of Worcester's relief fund just for Skinnerville.

Skinner also went to Williamsburg to meet with members of the Connecticut legislature, who had come to discuss their astounding pledge of $10,000. At the home of Henry L. James, the lawmakers entertained ideas of how best to spend their money, and Skinner proposed that a portion should be earmarked for providing all those "operatives and young girls thrown upon the world" with new clothes that would give a sense of some permanent relief. Most of the women had been wearing the same filthy shift for days and were dependent on donations that in most cases were ill-fitting cast-offs. He understood all too well the importance of clothing when one had little else, and he proposed that the most cost-effective approach would be to give the young women fabric, something that for them was more desirable than anything ready-made because they could then make their own apparel exactly as they wished. His suggestion to spend a portion of the $10,000 bequest on good-quality fabric struck everyone as a good idea, and a reporter in attendance noted, "No doubt such a plan will be adopted, with the ladies to manage the details."

After the meeting Skinner probably wrote several of these legislators, as he surely wrote to Reverend Phillips, thanking them for their time and generosity. As a member of the finance committee and the leader of Skinnerville, his correspondence at this time was voluminous. Every donation required a thank you; each day he needed another donation; and anytime he needed supplies from the general committee he had to send in a written request. He engaged Fred Warner to help with the paperwork, often dictating and, one suspects, barking out orders to the young man. Skinner also had to keep a record of all the monies he was receiving. One of the largest checks so far, for $1,100, was from the Silk Association. Members of the silk industry were proving to be one of the most generous groups of businessmen on the finance committee's roster, and Skinner would have duly deposited their donation into the central relief fund.

Little did Skinner know, however, that the general relief committee was disbursing the money that he deposited into that fund without approval. Since the general committee had established the central fund, its members felt entitled to appropriate every dollar within it, evidently considering the finance committee to be little more than fund-raisers and bookkeepers. Nor did Skinner yet know that at the rate those men were starting to spend the money (for relief efforts mostly within Northampton), the fund would be depleted before even a penny was dispensed to the silk operatives. Unbeknown to anyone at this stage, the finance committee was on a collision course with the general committee, and, contrary to all efforts to form a unified coalition, the valley's leaders were about to begin feuding over the very reason they had come together: money.

While Skinner was managing, soliciting, and discussing donations with officials, one of his workers was down in Haydenville, searching for objects from the mill and poking the ground with a cane when suddenly he hit something "which sounded like iron." The man immediately began to dig at the ground and, after realizing what he had uncovered, called for a lot of help. Skinner's big Marvin safe was soon unearthed, loaded onto a stone boat, and hauled north to the mansion. This was no small deposit box, but a steel room large enough to step inside and weigh bales of silk on a scale. That such a large object had been buried in sand so that no one could find it for five days proved once again the power of the flood and the need for total perseverance in prosecuting any kind of search.

The safe was brought into the house, probably through the double-wide front doors, and maneuvered into the sitting room, whereupon began the complicated task of how to open it. It was still locked, its key long gone, and the top had been crushed in so badly that the door was otherwise inoperable. Someone presently got hold of a crowbar and, after a good deal of struggle, managed to wrench open a portion of the steel, which then unleashed a torrent of water into the room, redrenching that floor. What also tumbled out, though, was a slew of soaking-wet papers and books—almost all of Skinner's records. This was extraordinary news. Without his accounting books, Skinner had been completely unable to tally his debts to his creditors or collect outstanding bills, not to mention that calculating his employees' wages with any accuracy was impossible without his payroll ledger. Without his cashbooks he had been helpless to document what bills had been paid. He was also unable to redeem his railroad bonds, or use them as collateral, without certificates of ownership. Similarly, without proof of his life insurance policy, neither he nor Lizzie had a record of the thousands of dollars he had put into it.

Having sat in muddy water for five days, the books and documents were a mess of bonded, pulpy paper covered in gunk. Everything needed to be washed and dried quickly. It was a perfect job for the children, who worked under Fred Warner's supervision and who, in helping with this task, found a sense of purpose during this uncertain time. They spent hours in front of a huge open fire, laying out papers and propping open books, careful not to burn or soil with ash what they were attempting to save. Some of the pages they dried to a crisp; others they smeared with more mud while wiping them down. Some papers were impossible to unglue. But eventually they managed to clean and dry the lot.

Within hours of the safe's being recovered a rumor began circulating that Skinner's life insurance policy, which was for $100,000, was about to come due and that he would soon be able to cash in on that money. Suddenly his financial situation seemed less precarious. Wrote one reporter, "What Mr. Skinner will do with this sum of money which has come to him so opportunely in the midst of disaster is to be decided by the gentleman himself; but it is hoped and believed that the village that bears his name may be benefited by the reestablishment of industry within its borders." Alas, the policy would not mature for another ten years, when Skinner turned sixty, and if he made no further payments until that time he would be entitled to only the $60,000 already deposited. Wrote another journalist, "To use [Mr. Skinner's] own expression, the endowment will be of very little use to him in the present crisis."

Down in Leeds there was another longed-for discovery, when the body of Sarah Hillman, the last person missing from Skinnerville, was pulled from a large mound of wreckage near a bridge. Her naked body had been revealed in the noonday sun by a group of volunteers with pickaxes and shovels. Unlike the other bodies recovered that day, many of which were impossible to identify because they were "so shockingly mangled and mutilated," Sarah's corpse was recognizable, and that, at least, was a blessing for her grieving husband, Jerome. The identification of her body also reduced the total number of missing. At the start of the day about fifteen bodies had remained unaccounted for; by twilight the number was down to about seven.

This particular evening "was spent by the survivors in safety and comparative comfort. It is true that many of them had to sleep in barns and depots, on beds provided by the charitables. [But] the majority were better situated, being housed by the hospitable neighbors as before." Skinner's household remained full and chaotic, but with the discovery of Mrs. Hillman's body, there was a significant reduction in anxiety, and with the added discovery of the safe, there was a sense of relief. That night, in contrast to the previous ones, Will noted that both Jerome Hillman and his father felt noticeably "better."

Chapter Eleven

Five days after the flood, on Thursday, May 21, volunteer laborers arrived in Skinnerville for the first time—more than 150 men from the Boston & Albany Railroad. When they appeared in front of the Skinner mansion in the rain, Will and Fred began to direct a number of them in cleaning out the cellar. In the meantime others started to clear away the snarl of matter that still ringed the house like a choker, while more fanned out across the meadows to help clear debris around the wrecks still standing. Despite the miserable weather—the rain was much heavier than earlier in the week—the railroad men did an impressive job, "considerably improving the appearance in [Skinnerville]."

Skinner spent the morning in Northampton with an old friend in the silk trade named Hovey, on what was certainly a business trip to look at potential sites. Hovey was from out of town, had no allegiance to Northampton, and his visit had an unexpected result. By Thursday's end the likelihood of moving to Northampton had faded, with people speculating that Skinner was more attached to staying in Skinnerville than he'd previously conveyed. This positive impression was further impacted by the improvement to Skinner's house by the railroad men, their work revealing that the building wasn't as compromised as it had seemed.

"Mr. Skinner has a natural pride in re-establishing himself in the village which he once built up," wrote a *Springfield Republican* reporter enthusiastically, "his old neighbors and friends are most anxious for him to stay, his fine residence after the necessary repairs will furnish a new tie to bind him to the spot, and, with the capital he needs at his command there is everything to encourage him in a determination to stay." Furthermore a closer survey of the land damages that afternoon suggested that they were not as insurmountable as Skinner had initially thought. "The great obstacle has, hitherto, been the apparent impossibility of utilizing the water privilege," the reporter went on, ". . . but thorough investigation by careful men leads to the belief that this difficulty is not insuperable. There is thus, it will be seen, good reason for believing that Skinner's case is by no means so hopeless as it has seemed."

As night wore on, however, only those as far away as Springfield were able to think about such things as the future. Those in the valley were once again trapped in the present. The rain came down in sheets, as it had been doing for much of the day, raising the level of the river as well as the water in the two reservoirs up in Goshen. Villagers in Skinnerville huddled together up near the railroad tracks, under trees and blankets, fearing another flood. "More than half the people living on the route of the river left their houses," reported one local, "and retired to safer quarters on higher ground." To the north, men were stationed along the road to Goshen at half-mile intervals with ready-bridled horses and loaded guns, with orders to fire at the first cause for alarm and break into a relay. Elsewhere "torches and lanterns were made ready and placed where they could be had and lighted at a moment's notice." Charles Webb, who was staying with the Jameses, went to sleep like many men that evening: on top of his covers, fully clothed, with his boots on, weakly joking that he "never did like to have to dress in a hurry." Darkness enveloped the valley. Rain pounded on the windowpanes. And no one could sleep, dreading a flood that never came.

Nothing seemed secure anymore. If the Williamsburg Reservoir had burst, others could too. A rainy day was no longer just a rainy day and, for many, would never be again. In a letter to Will more than twenty years later, Skinner commented, "It has rained all day—this is just the kind of weather we had in 1874." After the flood, weather became directly relevant to one's sense of safety and aliveness.

Friday dawned lovely and sunny, bringing the crowds again. More than three hundred gentlemen from Connecticut arrived to view "the full horrors of the scene" and, in their top hats and frock coats, made such a presence that the villagers, for once, were doing the staring, not the other way around. The fine weather continued on Saturday, as did improvements to the village. The railroad men fashioned a make-shift bridge of planks and rope across the river "to connect the divided people," and tents arrived from the adjutant general's office for the homeless. Though hardly places to call home, these sturdy canvas quarters, pitched in the former Kingsley meadow, made all the difference to those who received them. Observed one correspondent, "They came most opportunely."

Even if others were speculating that Skinner might rebuild in Skinnerville, however, there would be no work here for a long time, and many of his boarders began to leave the area on Saturday, after Skinner finally paid them their wages. This was fulfilling what many had feared: that the valley was going to lose its industrial base or at least be severely compromised by an exodus of labor. As a result, many felt that the relief effort needed to pay these people a sort of modern-day unemployment compensation to keep them in the area until their jobs returned. But since there was no telling whether their jobs would return, dispensing the relief fund that way was not practical. With money at last in her pocket, Ellen Littlefield left the village on the afternoon train, to stay with family in New York as she assessed her options. Like so many others, she hoped Skinner would find a way to start over in Skinnerville, but she too had to get on with her life.

Down in Holyoke, Kirtland was shaking his head at what he perceived to be the folly of wanting restoration when there was real opportunity elsewhere. "It is now written that Williamsburg, Hayden-ville, Leeds and probably Skinnersville will be speedily restored," he reported. "[Yet] to restore the truant river to its original bed and re-build the territory, to say nothing of the buildings, will be found a gigantic work, and will take time. . . . The pleasant associations of the valley homes were matters of slow growth, and whoever expects a restoration of the familiar places and things existing before the flood, will have to wait long and in vain." In other words, no matter how desperately one wished that the flood could be overcome, the villages rebuilt, and the suffering erased from memory, the valley would never be the same. If one needed proof, one only had to look back a couple of days to the panic that set in during the rainstorm of Thursday night. Didn't Skinner and others see that? Elsewhere in the paper was a small advertisement with an unmistakable message:

> The inhabitants that live alongside the goosepond streams that are fed by elevated reservoirs, shamly dammed, are trem-bling in their boots for fear that their houses and families will be swept away without a warning. Come to Holyoke, where you can live happy and not be murdered by water power.

On Sunday churches in the valley resumed their services, albeit on a reduced scale. The Haydenville Congregational Church was open for morning worship, and the Skinners, as on so many prior Sundays, drove down to attend, their buggy in nearly as bad shape as the road. Nobody could enter the sanctuary without thinking of all the bodies that had been brought there, and Reverend Kimball aptly preached from Psalm 90, "Thou carriest them away as with a flood." Many of the congregants broke down at the mere sight of one another, for "until to-day it required almost as much searching to find many of the living as it did the dead." Whatever warmth was felt at seeing an old friend, however, was smothered by the leaden absence of those missing. Delia Stearns, attending services in Williamsburg, recorded how difficult it was to be at church that day, the familiar ritual anything but comforting: "The vacant pews of the lost were draped in black and white. I wonder if we shall ever smile again."

Standing in his pulpit, Reverend Gleason, after a heartbreaking remembrance of the week just behind, rallied in the last throes of his sermon to raise support for the valley's manufacturers. Disregarding all the accusations in the press of wrongdoing by these men, Gleason focused on their humanity. These were good men, outstanding citizens, who had profoundly shaped their communities and who needed to be put in a position to rebuild here in the valley. They were not to be condemned but assisted, and he boldly asked his congregants, most of whom were utterly bereft, to find the wherewithal in this trying time to help provide *for their leaders*. He called for a "generous tide" of donations, a tide of benevolence large enough to roll up the valley, "setting the lathes and spindles in motion," so that Warner, Hayden, Skinner, James, and Spelman might not have to struggle so hard to climb out from under "the burdens of this dire disaster." At Skinnerville, he went on to say, this tide of generosity would have a particularly profound effect, and everyone who donated to its renewal would feel in his soul the great reward of Christian charity.

Let it rise to Skinnersville, and there . . . find something still higher. As the tall corn ships entering the harbor of ancient Rhodes sailed beneath the colossal statue that bestrode the harbor, so must this benevolence flow through the desolated field covered by the large heart of William Skinner. If but a moiety of the wealth which has for many years flowed through the channels of piety to our churches, colleges, and schools, should return, like "bread cast upon the waters," to the generous givers, the valley would again be made glad, and the prayer go up from every home, "God bless the donors!"

There was, after all, no telling how significant Skinner's business and the village of Skinnerville could yet become. Only ten days earlier Skinner had declared that the silk industry held such promise that American silk manufacturers might one day export silk overseas, and talk around town was that Skinner himself "intended to be one of the pioneer exporters." Everyone knew that Skinner was fiercely ambitious and hoped to be as large a silk producer as Hayden, Gere & Co. was a brassware producer, and that he might still achieve that someday had to be deeply considered by those in the valley. The departure of his business, if that came to pass, would forever affect the history of the valley, denying it considerable potential. According to one man, everyone who was concerned with the valley's "position in the county and state" needed to be addressing this matter.

Over the course of the next few days, local citizens began to respond. In Williamsburg, Skinner was offered "for a small sum" an old water privilege with land for development, in addition to a temporary lease on an empty woolen mill untouched by the flood. Almost as soon as these offers were made, the grapevine quivered. Someone reported that Skinner "[didn't] propose to remain idle" much longer and that, fortunately for Williamsburg, he was going to resume his silk business there, in the available woolen mill, "as soon as the necessary machinery can be procured." But there is no record of Skinner's doing any such thing, and if he considered relocating to Williamsburg he doesn't seem to have considered the prospect long. At this point there was little incentive to move from one devastated village to another, within the same bankrupt town, when there were other propositions to consider, many coming in from major industrial centers.

Hayden, for instance, had begun receiving offers from Brooklyn, Jersey City, Hartford, Providence, and even Omaha, Nebraska. Within the Connecticut River corridor, he was beginning to hear from Springfield, Turner's Falls, Miller's Falls, Collins Depot, and, as one might have guessed, Holyoke. Hayden and his partners, though, continued to insist that they were staying put. Clarence Sumner Luce, a Boston architect who had grown up in Haydenville, had been hired to draft plans for their new mill, the design of which Hayden soon publicized to illustrate the majesty of the future enterprise. As described in the *Springfield Republican*, "The main building will stand about 25 feet back from the roadway, and will have a frontage of 350 feet. It will be of brick, two stories high, with a roomy attic lighted by dormer windows, and will have two graceful towers, situated about 87 feet from each end of the building." Hayden couldn't get the construction started fast enough. In the meantime he and his partners had decided to convert their foundry building, which had survived the flood, into a makeshift factory that would be powered by steam. The place would be able to accommodate up to one hundred employees, and, in a matter of days, the company hoped to begin filling orders.

On Monday, May 25, nine days after the disaster, the inquest "concerning the death of John Atkinson" began at the Northampton courthouse. Coroner Wright planned on calling more than forty people to testify, including all living directors of the reservoir company, the contractors of the dam, the designing engineer, the superintendent, four of the builders, the county commissioners, gatekeepers past and present, two of the messengers whose warnings in advance of the floodwaters saved hundreds of lives, a number of local witnesses, and several key experts on reservoir dam construction. A special stenographer had been sent for from Boston in anticipation of the amount of recording to be done. This proved to have been a wise decision. Although an inquest can be as short as a few hours, this one would last a week, and the testimony would take a month to transcribe, filling 1,118 pages of legal paper.

Although for the most part Skinner would keep his distance from the inquest—it wasn't a priority of his, and, in his mind, he already knew who was guilty—he did appear at court on at least two occasions, the first day being one of them. Most of the mill owners felt it prudent to appear as a sign of respect since their dam was the biggest thing on trial. They sat at a table in the front of the courtroom, their lawyer, Daniel W. Bond, at their side. Also up front were the jury and the lawyer Charles Delano, whom Coroner Wright had appointed as cross-examiner. Delano was something of a dandy—he tied his briefs with ribbon and, whenever entering a room, fixed his hair "in a dainty manner"—but he was a shrewd and relentless interrogator, and having twice served as a representative in Congress, enjoyed a fine reputation as an orator. Captain Enos Parsons of Northampton was foreman of the jury and had been given authority, somewhat surprisingly, to speak on behalf of the reservoir company, the owners of the dam having been granted special permission to ask questions of the other witnesses, so long as they did so in writing.

This first day's witnesses included the three most famous men connected with the flood: George Cheney, the gatekeeper who sounded the original alarm; Onslow Spelman, the manufacturer who didn't believe him; and Collins Graves, the farmer who did. They attracted a considerable audience and gave the inquest an air of celebrity. By this time Cheney had received hundreds of people at his house who had come not only to look at the grim gap in the dam but also to look at him and, just as important, his horse. The poor animal was quickly losing most of the hair in its tail because amateur collectors were taking strands as souvenirs of this great moment in history. Spelman, on the other hand, had become almost a pariah, many believing that more lives could have been saved if he hadn't dismissed Cheney's warning. As for Graves, he had become *the* hero of the flood. His name had been immortalized in countless poems published in numerous newspapers, often on the front page. This was a golden age for poetry, and readers especially devoured poems that romanticized current events. John Boyle O'Reilly, an Irish writer and editor with a large following in Massachusetts, composed one of the more popular poems, a ten-stanza dramatization entitled "The Ride of Collins Graves." To Graves's mortification, O'Reilly compared him to both Sheridan and Paul Revere and closed his verse with these lines:

> *When heroes are called for, bring the crown*
> *To this Yankee rider: send him down*
> *On the stream of time with the Curtius old;*
> *His deed as the Roman's was brave and bold,*
> *And the tale can as noble a thrill awake,*
> *For he offered his life for the people's sake.*

Never mind that the poetry about Graves was generally awful. It was everywhere, to the point where one editor quipped, "Whittier and Longfellow may as well hang their harps on the willows. The subject and the rider are both exhausted."

To begin the day, Delano called several witnesses to identify the body of John Atkinson and confirm the death that was the basis for this inquest. Next he established the timeline of the flood and a bit of history about the dam, beginning with the Cheney family. George's father recalled "sorter throwin' his eye out the winder" during breakfast and seeing part of the dam give way. When the whole thing began to burst, George's mother, who had fled up the hill with her grandchildren, recalled being unable to look because the sight "made her sick," but George's wife witnessed the entire failure. She "took a seat near the door and watched the dam . . . burst all at once." It sounded "like an earthquake."

When Cheney took the stand he retold his experience on that morning and boldly stated, with Spelman staring straight at him, how Spelman had not believed him about the dam. He also explained in simple terms how the dam had leaked "year in and year out" all along the bottom, with one particularly large stream poking through the eastern side. He suggested that he had always believed the big stream on the eastern slope was dangerous and told the jury "he had, within the month, said that the dam would break where it did."

Robert Loud, who ran all the way down from his home in the hills, followed with his story, as did others. When Collins Graves was called, his name sent "an electrical stir" through the courtroom, but there was nothing dramatic about his delivery. He humbly recounted his ride through Skinnerville and on to Haydenville, after which Myron Day, an "older and more serious looking man," described racing downriver in his express wagon to warn the people in Leeds. Thus concluded the timeline of the flood.

In the afternoon Eugene C. Gardner, the architect hired to survey the dam's construction, illustrated the basic design of the dam, and, finally, ending the day's session was conservative, wiry Spelman. Spelman was the first owner to be called up and, despite his reputation of being "very clever" and "sharp," proved to be a mess. He stumbled over nearly everything he said, as if he couldn't get the whole experience over fast enough, and he often looked ready to apologize, but to whom, and for what, it was never clear. From the moment he opened his mouth, people knew they were in for something interesting.

"You are a mill owner in Williamsburg," Delano began simply, to which Spelman swiftly replied, "I *was* a mill owner in Williamsburg."

Spelman had been treasurer and secretary of the reservoir company since its inception, and Delano, producing the company's ledger, asked Spelman to read his minutes aloud. Delano wanted to determine who had been on the committee in charge of building the dam, and the company's ledger seemed a logical place to look. Perhaps because he knew what was missing, Spelman was so nervous that he could barely hold the book, let alone read it, and Delano "out of mercy" finally took the volume back and read from it himself. There was no mention of the company's electing anyone to a building committee; it was as though the dam had built itself. When questioned directly about who had been in charge, Spelman professed that he "did not know who were the building committee," but, when pressured by Delano, at last admitted that directors Lucius Dimock, William Clement, and William Clark had "acted in such a capacity" and were later assisted by Governor Hayden.

Spelman then gave "a long roll of answers" to Delano and the jury "in continual attempt to avoid the suspicion of having had any special authority or responsibility in the construction of the dam." This rather stretched credulity as Spelman, who lived nearest the dam, had been on site three or four times a week during the dam's construction. He also insisted that he "never knew what the contract [with the contractors] was; never had it in his hand; had no idea as to the width of the wall, at bottom or at top; never measured it; never questioned its strength."

Determined nevertheless to get some valuable testimony out of this man who, as secretary and treasurer, had been a key member of the company, Delano returned to the ledger. He opened it to the minutes of the meeting of May 14, 1867, and handed the book back to Spelman, who this time, "in obedience to the jury," managed to read the following: ". . . moved that Mr. A. T. Lilly be a committee to consult with D. W. Bond Esq concerning the personal liability of stockholders in case of damages or loss by the breaking away of the reservoir & to take such measures as are necessary to relieve them from the same."

More than at any other time Spelman probably wanted to apologize to his peers sitting opposite, but he couldn't erase his own words. He denied that they suggested that the owners had been worried about liability, but the evidence was there in print. They had even resolved to talk with a lawyer and "take such measures" as would absolve them in the law's eyes from any culpability should the dam ever fail. Delano may have been unable to extract any meaningful answers from Spelman out loud, but he was nevertheless able to use Spelman's own words as damning evidence.

As Skinner walked out of the courtroom and climbed into his buggy to go home, one could practically hear him seethe, as he did on a later occasion, "I am now convinced the motto on Puck is correct, 'What fools these mortals be.'" Spelman hadn't spoken an intelligent, defensible word the entire afternoon. On the contrary, his jittery, often convoluted testimony had supported the premise—which the press had been declaring for a week now—that the owners of the dam were as connected with its failure as anyone.

Two days later, on Wednesday, May 27, Skinner returned to the inquest to testify himself. Wednesday was a "very hot" day, and with the celebrity testimony ending on day one, only those "vitally interested in the question at issue" were present. Skinner's name wasn't called until the afternoon, so he had to sit through the morning as the mercury rose, watching, among other people, the man who he thought should be hanged.

Joel Bassett talked at length about his working relationship with the building committee, which, according to him, had been a good one. He described in detail the dam's design and construction, the overall superintendence of the work, and the amount of money he had made on the project, which he claimed hadn't been nearly enough. For a man decidedly in the hot seat, his confidence was remarkable. But when grilled after lunch by the jury on how he and his partner Wells had built the core wall, Bassett became evasive, defiant, and downright uncooperative. Dr. Trow wanted to know in particular how Bassett could square his assertion that he'd built a trench for that wall since the ground, for a distance of twenty feet on either side of where the wall had been, seemed perfectly level. Finally, "after the most wearisome repetitions of the question," Bassett admitted, cowed, "I can't tell, sir."

When Skinner assumed the stand afterward, he was all business. His testimony was "terse, characteristic and satisfactory" and, in the opinion of one reporter, provided a "refreshing contrast to the rambling explanations of Mr. Bassett." Unlike Bassett, who was described as "rough-and-ready" and "full of habit," Skinner appeared "a handsome looking man," with a clean face framed by "full dark whiskers" and "fine grey hair." Also unlike Bassett, who appeared the fabled version of the untrustworthy and deceptive laborer, Skinner came off as the proprietor beyond reproach. He answered each question without the slightest hesitation and left no margin for error in understanding what he meant. A reporter for the *Springfield Republican* recorded the start of Skinner's testimony:

> He had nothing to do about deciding the plans for the reservoir . . . nor with building the dam, which was completed before he saw it; he did not want to use much water, and so didn't take much interest in the matter. . . . He had been in the habit of removing the silk from his mill when apprehending a flood, but did not do so with any thought of the possible breaking of this reservoir; he had felt with the rest that the dam was unsafe, but some six or eight months ago Gov. Hayden had reassured him by telling him that the dam "was all right now." . . . He had heard Messrs. Hayden and Dimock complain of the contractors, and knew that there was generally a pretty hard feeling between them; it existed while the dam was being built.

Dimock had a rather staggering reputation for being "the most profane man in the state of Massachusetts," so it was not surprising when Skinner next remarked that Dimock was "always cussing and damning the contractors for slighting the work." In Skinner's mind, Dimock's disgust with the contractors further supported the argument that the latter were to blame for everyone's troubles. But Skinner's testimony at this point actually contradicted Dimock's. The day before, "the boss engineer" had been called in for questioning and proved an even less reliable witness than Bassett. A man of ferocious intelligence, Dimock had suddenly had amnesia, remembering absolutely nothing about the construction of the reservoir. Charles Delano, undeterred, maintained a line of "quiet but persistent questioning" that implied profound disbelief in Dimock's lack of recall. "The witness was asked if he had, as a director, stockholder, mill-owner, or person having a memory, any idea as to when the reservoir dam was decided upon." Dimock had no response. He "could not answer the question. He did not remember whose plan was accepted; he could not recall any time when the contractors were employed; he knew as a fact that they built the dam, but had no recollection of having employed them." If Dimock couldn't even remember working with Bassett or Wells, how could he possibly have cursed them for negligence?

A member of the jury asked Skinner "if he was present when Mr. Dimock made a different statement at his recent examination." In particular, was he present the day before, when Mr. Dimock "stated that he never had complained of the contractors"? Skinner addressed the juror with a calm, swift finality. He didn't know what Dimock had said, but "he must have forgot himself. This is the truth now."

The jury also wished to confirm whether Governor Hayden had participated in Dimock's strong use of language, and Skinner responded that, while he had never heard the governor "exactly swear," he had heard him agreeing with Dimock. That Governor Hayden, an esteemed politician, had supported the damning of the contractors intensified the argument for many about the guilt of the contractors and the comparative innocence of the mill owners.

After this Skinner was excused. He stepped down from the stand and returned to his seat at the front of the courtroom. No doubt his approach had been to say as little as possible, just as he wished others would do. "Mr. Skinner takes the matter very quietly," the *Springfield Republican* noted on another occasion, "and advises his friends to do the same." He served mainly as a character witness for the reservoir company, his straightforward testimony illuminating nothing other than a sense of integrity—depending on whether one wanted to believe the company could have any.

Although the courtroom was no longer filled with spectators, it remained full of reporters since there was a feeling in the press, at least initially, that the disaster might have larger implications than just a monumental demand for relief. Reform—a word detested by every capitalist of the day—might come out of it. Or not. Either way it was news. The *Boston Morning Journal* prophesied that the investigation would be "one of the most important inquests held in New England for a century," and Samuel Bowles at the *Republican* explained that the inquest was especially striking because "it has to deal, not with recognized ignoramuses or swindlers, but with . . . Massachusetts manufacturers and builders." He asked, "How can we dogmatize about Troy and Stonehenge when we search the Connecticut valley in vain to find the responsible builders of a dam not ten years old?" Here, in the industrial heart of America, was an example of how the creators of modern capitalism could fail society.

As the inquest proceeded and the details filled in over the course of the week, no one in his right mind could deny the egregious flaws in this dam's construction. It was, the public learned, built without any contractual obligations. In fact the contractors had refused to sign the contract they were initially presented, disagreeing with its terms, and the company simply never drew up another. The contractors then worked for the most part without proper supervision. Fenn superintended them at the start, but he was a railroad engineer, not a dam engineer, and his last day at the site was August 1st because he had another job to attend. The building committee then asked Eugene C. Gardner, an architect, to "give such superintendence as he could." But Gardner came down with some type of ailment that kept him in bed until almost October, and he was off the job for part of November as well due to a death in his family. During his last testimony, Dimock sheepishly admitted that "he supposed it was not right to leave such work without [proper] inspection" but Fenn's specifications had required only that the dam be superintended, not that it be superintended by any one especially qualified to do so.

Obviously, the specifications were faulty, and Fenn, their author, took heat for them. However, Fenn stated in no uncertain terms that he would have certainly been more definite on any number of issues "if he had had any power to enforce a single idea." He claimed that the committee had completely disregarded him when he told them that the steep pitch of the inner slope was dangerous and "that he would not trust this work to any contractors, even if they were his most intimate friends." More alarming still, Bassett testified that he too had considered the design to be "defective," declaring that he had also told the committee "that there was great danger to be apprehended from that dam, and that if they raised the water on that bank as it was, he wouldn't give a dollar for all the property in the valley."

Neither of these men was paid for their opinions, so few could fault them if the committee disregarded their input. However, several in the courtroom were unable to stomach Bassett's revelation that he, a contractor, had built a dam he *knew* would probably burst.

"There wasn't a great deal of conscience in that?" Dr. Trow demanded from the jury box when Bassett was last on the stand.

"I don't know what you mean by conscience," Bassett retorted. "I don't know why conscience should hinder me. If the dam had to be built, I don't know why we shouldn't just as well build it as anybody else."

Money played a significant role in the failure of the dam. The contractors wanted to make some, so they took the job. And the committee had wanted to save some, so they designed a cheap dam—and hired cheap workers into the bargain. The committee also chose to spend as little as possible on repairs, and only after the county commissioners had twice refused to approve the dam did the committee invest in extensive improvements.

The public learned too that the county commissioners could have called in a professional engineer to help investigate the matter, but they did not. They could have summoned all of the directors to the site for a thorough inquiry, but they did not. They could have questioned the contractors, the surveyor, and the designing engineer in the interest of the public, but they did not. One commissioner explained that he didn't feel any of that was necessary because dam engineering wasn't particularly complicated, and "he thought they knew as much about it as any three men." So they had just walked around the dam, making notes to be given to the company about how the earthwork was "not . . . just right." Such an investigation hardly constituted an adequate inspection, but there was little else to be done. The dam had already been built; all anyone could do was stare at it. When called as an expert witness, Henry Wilson remarked on the futility of such an exercise, "You cannot tell how a reservoir is built by looking at it, any more than you can tell what lumber is in a house by its painted outside."

While the inquest played out, and while the matter of rebuilding loomed large, Skinner found himself involved in yet another complicated situation: the battle over relief. Only a few days after the finance committee had been organized, its chairman, Luther Bodman, had sent telegraphs to Springfield and elsewhere stating in no uncertain terms that "over one hundred thousand dollars" would be needed to meet the demands of the moment. Almost eight hundred people qualified as destitute, most of whom were dependent on mill work that no longer existed, all of whom needed food, clothing, pillows and blankets, and numerous other daily necessities. But with the country in a national depression this was not an easy time to raise money, and many outside of the valley considered the appeal for $100,000 to be unwarranted, even potentially exploitative. Several of the gentlemen from Connecticut who had visited on Friday were members of the Connecticut legislature, and they had come not merely to satisfy their curiosity but to judge whether their legislative appropriation had not been made too hastily. Fortunately for the finance committee, "the party left feeling satisfied that the most highly colored descriptions of newspaper correspondents had not been overdrawn, and that they had done right in voting an appropriation for those who had suffered so terribly."

By the time the inquest began, the finance committee had received subscriptions of over $65,000, but only $20,000 had actually been received and this money was being swiftly depleted on expenditures with which the finance committee increasingly did not agree. The cost of labor, for instance, was proving very high. With so many people rendered jobless, those who volunteered in the cleanup efforts were being paid for their services, but this was taking an enormous toll on the central fund, and Skinner, for one, would have been infuriated that some of these volunteers, many of whom didn't even live in the valley, were receiving wages that were higher than he'd paid his skilled employees. That smacked of imprudence and shortsightedness. As for the wagonloads of supplies being purchased, they too seemed excessive, and villagers in Skinnerville weren't even guaranteed a fair share of them since the nearest official supply depot was a mile away in Haydenville.

The *Hampshire Gazette* later explained, "The general relief committee went forward and did what seemed to them to be necessary. . . . They argued that a 'relief committee' was of little use without money. . . . So they ascertained what was wanted, and drew upon the finance committee [i.e., the relief fund] to pay the bills." The finance committee did not like this arrangement in the least and argued that "if this course was to be followed, the funds in their hands would be speedily gone; that claims were [being] presented which were unjust and exorbitant; and that it was *their* business to say to whom the money should be paid and for what purposes." They demanded a stop to the spending, but the general committee simply didn't want to listen to the finance committee. "From this difficulty between the two committees there sprung considerable feeling," and, reaching what appears to have been an impasse after only a week of this business, Skinner, Hayden, Otis, and the Bodman brothers took matters into their own hands.

On Tuesday May 26, in a hotel up the street from the courthouse, the finance committee met over supper and resolved that only cash would be given out from now on, only members of the finance committee would make dispensations, and only sufferers would receive dispensations. No policeman, nor any volunteer laborer, would receive money from the fund anymore. A large stock of donated goods would remain available through the supply committee in Northampton, since material donations were still coming in, but no more supplies would be purchased. From this point forward "money will be given wherever practicable in preference to clothing and provisions."

A modern-day expert on disaster relief has said, "If you give somebody a tent, they ask for more goodies. But if you give them a hammer and nails, they build something." Indeed, following the flood, someone suggested that the relief fund should help the destitute "build cheap houses and furnish them modestly," and it was readily understood how avidly men would work for their board "when each knows that he is preparing a home for himself and his family." But with so many people clinging to the relief committee's skirts, the finance committee felt it wisest to set these people free with money of their own and let them, in the spirit of self-sufficiency, rebuild their own lives.

During their meeting Skinner and his colleagues organized the sufferers into four classes: single men, single women, families, and widows who had lost their husbands in the flood. Then they settled on a lump sum for each group. To single men they would give $50 each, or roughly the equivalent of one month's work, plus a supply of clothing. To unmarried women, whose position in society was more compromised, they would give $100 (about three months' pay), plus a trunk filled with clothing (or cloth), stockings, and shoes. To families the committee first apportioned $200, then upped that to $300, and to widows they would give $500. These amounts were intended to compensate in some small measure for loss of income and household possessions. There could be no compensation at this time for loss of real estate; such losses were beyond the scope of the committee's resources at present. "These sums are . . . thought to be more judicious and more truly charitable to help these poor people to their feet again once for all," Skinner explained in a letter to Reverend Phillips, "with a reasonable assurance that they will then be able to provide for themselves, than to keep them dependent upon a daily or weekly dole." Dispensations were to begin immediately.

Editors at the *Springfield Union,* speaking for many on the general relief committee, condemned the new resolution, claiming, "[It] changes entirely the aspect of relief distribution and leaves the general relief committee rather out in the cold. . . . We can but think that this action is unwise, as it is impossible that the money should go as far and buy as much when expended in small sums by the beneficiaries." They had a point; supplies are cheaper to buy in bulk. But the finance committee didn't want to hand out supplies; they wanted to give people money and put an end to the discussion of who needed what. They did not want providing relief to be an ongoing affair.

Skinner had to testify at the inquest on Wednesday, but on Thursday, back home in Skinnerville, he set himself up in the sitting room and began writing checks to survivors. Twenty boarders lined up before him, their boots scraping across the bare wooden floor of the once carpeted interior, and across some sort of table, wiped down from mud, Skinner gave them each $100—probably the largest check they'd ever received in their lives—after which their names were "stricken from the relief book." No doubt he worked from a list, as did other members of the finance committee, requesting that each recipient sign for his or her compensation, with a third party, perhaps Fred Warner, witnessing each transferral. The room would have been very crowded, as families showed up too, and by the end of the day Skinner had handed out $4,000.

No less subject to favoritism than his peers in Northampton, Skinner took liberties with the funds at his disposal. Ten recipients in his records received the widow's share of $500 or more, even though no one had been widowed in Skinnerville, and four people received as much as $800 or more. Skinner also, ultimately, gave additional sums to the highest taxpayers in the village to help address losses in real estate, despite the fact that the finance committee had agreed this was currently unwise. Furthermore he gave his brother Thomas one of the largest dispensations in the village, $825, when Thomas didn't qualify for more than $300. Exactly when he handed out these larger sums is unknown, but as he faced his neighbors, and even his own brother, across that table, Skinner proved incapable of being impartial.

Hayden didn't distribute money any more equitably in Hayden-ville. Noted the *Springfield Union* with disapproval, "The disbursement of relief under the new plan adopted by the financial committee—a money gift to each of the suffering families—is not quite uniform in the different villages. . . . in Haydenville the disbursements vary according to the size, needs and previous condition of the family." The Bodman brothers, too, handed out money according to their own calculus.

The reality was that the finance committee wasn't any better equipped to handle the situation than the general committee had been. Skinner and his colleagues had no experience in disaster relief and, like the state, no precedent on which to act. Their objective was to treat individuals in like categories the same, regardless of age, income, background, social status, number of dependents, or extent of loss. They wanted to avoid inequitable dispensations, which could lead to unfairness, but when it actually came down to it, most of these men felt it was their authoritative right to say who should get what. Observed one man later, in a statement that could apply to everyone involved, "The generous contributions of those days exhibited the best side of human nature, but the disbursements in some directions exhibited the very worst phases of human nature."

After receiving their checks, more of Skinner's workers left town. Several women were driven to the depot on Friday with their trunks and their checks and, as others had done earlier in the week, departed for the Heminway Silk Company in Connecticut, which had offered them positions. While other manufacturers might have been loath to lose more employees, Skinner probably didn't think it was such a bad thing. Fewer mouths to feed actually lifted his burdens. He even went so far as to help some of his workers leave, securing passage for the Hibbert family on a ship back to Liverpool. Originally from England, the Hibberts had decided that they couldn't face the uphill battle of trying to make it again in America, although at least one member of the family, James, hoped to return someday to Skinner's employ.

Within Skinner's house, too, the landscape was shifting and the situation easing. Jerome Hillman and Clara had left, moving up to Williamsburg, leaving only the Van Vechtens—Edward, his pregnant wife, Cathaline, and their three young children—occupying the two back rooms above the kitchen in the ell. And so, after two weeks of using his home as a shelter, relief center and supply depot, Skinner finally had the space to begin using it in a more generative fashion—as headquarters for salvaging his silk and his business.

Chapter Twelve

By this time, almost the beginning of June, a lot of Skinner's silk had been found in the valley, some of it as far as four miles away. Will and Joe Skinner and Fred Warner had retrieved several bales in Florence, including "a great many of organzine and raw spooled silk," and when all those railroad men had swarmed over the property, cleaning up and clearing away the tangles of branches, planks, beams, and other debris, they had uncovered an impressive quantity of silk in the sand just south of the mansion. Reporters noted with some surprise that the silk was "in good condition," but silk always had a strong chance of surviving the elements, the tenacity of the fiber being one of its great hallmarks. A strand of silk "is said to be little inferior to that of a good quality of iron wire of equal diameter."

Yet the floodwaters were a beater and, while a reporter might have thought the silk looked good, Skinner's trained eye knew better. All of the silk had been soaked and "damp silk is less tenacious and more elastic than dry silk." Given that the silk would have been thrashed around in the water, tangled like hair, and brought into contact with all kinds of serrated edges, many strands would have been pulled to their utmost and snapped. Even spooled silk, which had a greater chance of surviving the waters than loose, skeined silk, was not impervious to the assault. Nor is there any telling what percentage of Skinner's raw silk had already been boiled off or cleaned, and cleaned silk is highly susceptible to shrinkage and swelling. This swelling, of course, is what the dyer plays with when dyeing silk, but silk's readiness to soak up organic materials presented a challenge for Skinner here, since his silk would have absorbed all kinds of excess from the slurry. That which had been buried down on the flats would have also taken in "the slimy deposits which had been so many years accumulating in the numerous milldams," to say nothing of the fluids that might have oozed from nearby corpses and carcasses. Those bales that Will, Fred, and Joe carried back to the house would have been filthy, disgusting, brittle, and *heavy*.

Skinner too searched for his silk. One visitor to the flood-ravaged valley later recalled being mesmerized watching Skinner down on his knees, tenderly pulling a clutch of silk from the sand. The visitor had no idea who this bearded man was. Stripped of his coat, as he surely must have been, with his sleeves rolled up and his hands plunging into the ground like a laborer, Skinner did not fit the image of a patriarchal manufacturer. Moreover he wasn't paying any attention to the visitor, his companion, or anyone else around, but focused solely on the matted clump of silk he had found. The visitor was struck by Skinner's undivided attention to "what might seem to another a bit of dirty waste," and asked his companion, "Who is that gentleman?" As the strangers looked on, Skinner "drew forth from its covert the bunch of silk and held it as though it were something sentient, worthy of revivification, and bringing to perfection."

Unfortunately, though a lot of Skinner's silk was being recovered, much was being stolen, confirming his fears that theft was a genuine issue. One officer searched fifty houses and ended up with a treasure trove of "silk and silk soap belonging to William Skinner, patterns belonging to Hayden, Gere & Co., and much bedding and clothing belonging to other parties." In their wanderings Will and Fred had confronted a particular resident suspected of stealing "quite a good deal [of silk]," and some men came to the mansion with "several hundred dollars worth that they found in Haydenville in a Frenchman's house under the bed." Skinner had had to take out fourteen search warrants so far.

Like his books and ledgers, whatever silk was recovered had to be washed, cleaned, and dried. None of it would have been thrown out since, even soiled, the silk was too valuable. It would have been stretched, gently, and re-reeled on a spinning frame, then skeined by hand into old-fashioned coils. Some of the silk would still have been too compromised to be salvaged for thread but was nevertheless sellable as "waste silk" to a company like Cheney Brothers, who had discovered a way to weave uneven silk into products like ribbons and handkerchiefs. Skinner's children might have helped with the unwinding and washing of the silk, but to operate a frame and skein silk, Skinner needed skilled professionals. He thus sent word to Ellen Littlefield that he wanted her back, and she seized the opportunity for employment again. He also rehired Aurelia Damon and a handful of others. The spinning frame was set up in what seems to have been the only habitable room downstairs, the sitting room, and tables for skeining were arranged on the third floor.

No sooner had the house filled with silk workers, however, than Skinner left them (under Lizzie's watchful eye). While his manufacturing peers were knee-deep in repairs and reconstruction—James had men cleaning out his penstock, the Nonotuck was installing new machinery, Hayden was converting barns into tenements for his workers—Skinner boarded a train at the Skinnerville depot on Monday, June 1, and passed out of sight for several days. Quick to investigate his departure, a Springfield correspondent reported that Skinner was leaving "[on] a business trip of a few days, which will extend as far as Philadelphia." The correspondent further noted, "By the time he returns [he] will probably have made up his mind whether to rebuild in Skinnerville or accept one of the many offers to locate elsewhere."

Skinner was gone for a week, during which time he stopped in New York City to meet with his creditors. One can only imagine what it was like for him to step off the train at the Grand Central Depot, into the hustle and bustle of city life, everybody on their way to someplace else, everyone so far removed from the desolation and stagnation he was living in at home. These people had such freedom. They could buy oysters on the corner, hail a cab, step into a shop, and not think once about the disaster that had occurred in Massachusetts just two weeks earlier.

His creditors were most anxious to hear from him personally. "There is no knowledge in this mar[ket] of his present condition," wrote an agent for the Mercantile Agency. "[Yet] there is a kindly feeling entertained towards him by the entire trade who have tendered him any credit he may want without knowing what shape he is in or how badly damaged by the late flood."

Also on the agenda for Skinner would have been a visit to Franklin Allen at the Silk Association's office, during which he no doubt provided the secretary with an in-depth account of the disbursement of the relief fund. Allen would have reciprocated with some news of his own, filling Skinner in on the passage of an important amendment to the Customs and Internal Revenue Laws. Imported silks, so long the bane of the American silk manufacturer, were to be taxed regardless of their "classification," the U.S. House of Representatives finally being persuaded that some silk goods entering the country were passing through customs without being subjected to the requisite silk duty. Importers were adding a touch of cotton to silk ribbons, for instance, so that the ribbons couldn't be classified solely as *silk* ribbons, and thus subject to a silk tax. Now such classification was void. Given that Skinner had been intending to expand into the manufacturing of organzine, a silk thread used to weave silk ribbons, this could prove to be an important turnabout down the road. The stronger the market for American silk ribbons, the better his business would be. But of course at this moment talk of his business was of a much different cast. While it was certainly helpful to be reminded of the doings of his trade, and necessary for him to remain informed, the tariff bill, recently a major topic of discussion among the Silk Association's board of directors, may have seemed almost otherworldly to Skinner. He probably would have been thrilled if the foreign competition were the biggest thing he had to worry about.

At some point during the day Skinner would also have visited his own store on Broadway. Emotional man that he was, he may very well have teared up at seeing the shelves of his wares and the astonished and grateful faces of his salesmen. There they all were, just as he had left them. Incredible though it seemed, some things in his life hadn't changed.

And yet, looking at his manager, James Peck, and all the displays and signs around the room, Skinner probably wondered how he was going to keep this store. How was he going to pay its rent and payroll? Did it make sense even to hold on to it? As for business, he surely had a list of questions for Peck, starting with how much money was in the register. Was there enough stock on hand to fill current orders? If not, how many orders had been canceled? How many new orders had been turned away? Had his clients been informed yet that the mill was gone? What had they been told? Skinner was about to lose a lot of business to his competition. Already he was losing workers to them. Other mills were definitely benefiting from his misfortune. But, he would have told Peck, don't give up on orders for the kinds of thread being salvaged back home. Soon he would be ready to start shipping that silk for the store to sell.

The rest of his trip was devoted to investigating prospective mill sites, and two facts became clear to anyone following his steps: Skinner was willing to consider moving far away from the Mill River Valley, and he was willing to entertain the idea of rebuilding in a city. Anyone who was familiar with Skinner's personal history would not have been surprised by the former. He wasn't afraid of change, no matter the personal cost. The second realization was probably more surprising.

Why would Skinner, the former patriarch of a successful factory village, want to rebuild in a city?

But there was a great deal to be said for the idea. The industrial landscape of the country was shifting. The Civil War had necessitated such a tremendous increase in production, across so many industries, that the modest mill tucked away in the hillside was no longer an inspiration, but more of a carryover from earlier times, confronting more and more limitations. The cost of shipping was greater. The labor pool was smaller. And upland streams were so unpredictable that the mill owner never knew, from one season to the next, if his mill would be running full time. While independence might have been the biggest advantage of the rural manufacturer, it was slowly becoming his greatest liability. Pulsating urban areas that were serviced by railroads, populated with laborers, rich in real estate, busy with commerce, and often specifically engineered to support numerous mill powers were attracting ever more manufacturers.

Skinner took the ferry to Brooklyn, an increasingly powerful city within half an hour of his store and his primary market. The New York area on the whole "possessed plenty of labor and easy access to both raw materials and finished products." Moreover, many silk men lived in Brooklyn, such as A. A. Low, Edward Lyman, and Skinner's old friend and silk broker Briton Richardson, who lived in the lovely sounding Carroll Gardens. But the water privileges Skinner saw in Brooklyn were not merely disappointing; he was "awfully disgusted" by them. If they were along the Gowanus Canal, Brooklyn's main industrial waterway, this would have been unsurprising and exemplified one of the reasons *not* to move to a city. The Gowanus Canal was polluted with raw sewage and industrial waste, and Skinner wasn't about to use contaminated water to dye his silk. Furthermore the real estate was expensive and the taxes high.

Skinner may have toured additional sites in Yonkers, where his brother lived, or Paterson, New Jersey, across the Hudson. Paterson had become known as the Silk City of America, with more than four hundred citizens employed in about twenty silk mills. If any city was advantageous to manufacturing silk, Paterson had to be, at least in theory. It offered an astounding number of skilled silk workers, the majority of whom had come over from Macclesfield, England, in the 1860s—lured, as Skinner had been, by the prospect of better work in the American silk trade. Paterson also had some of the finest silk machinists in the country, specialists he could draw on when outfitting his new mill. But Paterson had suffered terribly from the Panic, dipping into such an economic depression that it was said that the only workers making any kind of money were the children. Emigration to the city had slowed noticeably, and the population had actually started to decrease. Though water privileges would have been available at low prices, Skinner would not have wanted to relocate from one disaster into another.

In Philadelphia, Skinner probably met with his colleague, the local silk dealer Franklin Hovey. Philadelphia had a rich history in silk, dating back to the days of Benjamin Franklin, an enthusiastic proponent of sericulture. Explained an early advocate, "The city was most suitable for silk dyeing operations, because of the lightness of the Schuylkill water, which quality greatly contributes to the beauty of silk." The city also had a bright future. With the Centennial Exhibition coming to town in less than two years, it was certain to experience an explosion of business. Skinner would have been pleased to hear that his family wouldn't actually have to live in the city; Hovey and his family, for example, lived across the Delaware, in picturesque Beverly, New Jersey, where many of the top hats lived. But something about Philadelphia didn't sit well with Skinner. With the Centennial Exhibition on the horizon, rents might have been exorbitant and water privileges too expensive. He considered Philadelphia for about as long as he considered Williamsburg: only briefly.

Coming home on Friday, Skinner was joined on the train by his son Will, who boarded the car at Easthampton. Will had returned to school and was preparing for final exams. Seeing his father on the train and listening to him talk of business was a lot more fun than studying Latin, so he took in an earful. The good news was that Skinner had settled with his creditors, everyone showing him "sympathy and consolation." Perhaps he had received extensions on his loans in return for a higher rate of interest on them. Whatever the terms, he didn't have to pay anyone anything right now, and he once more had credit, enabling him to buy raw silk again. The key to his future, the Skinner men discussed, lay in finding the best and most economical situation in which to rebuild, where construction costs, land expense, and water fees wouldn't be so hefty that he would drown before having a chance to swim. So far, though, Skinner had seen nothing in New York, New Jersey, or Pennsylvania that would do.

The following day, Saturday, June 6, Skinner went to see Holyoke. Ten miles south of Northampton, on a bend in the Connecticut River that had been known for generations for its powerful falls, the city had a noteworthy history. In 1847 a group of mostly Boston capitalists invested $2.5 million in the area with the goal of creating another mill city like Lowell, which had already brought them considerable returns. Known as the Cotton Lords for their reign over cotton manufacture in the Northeast, they saw the area that would become Holyoke as their grandest opportunity. Here was an expanse of largely uncultivated land adjacent to a fall in the Connecticut River that dropped as much as sixty feet, potentially generating as much as 30,000 horsepower. With an average mill utilizing 100 horsepower, the river was capable of powering three hundred mills at this one spot, "the greatest potential mill development in New England." Lowell may have been the first industrially planned city in America, but Holyoke stood to become its most magnificent.

So taken with their extravagant vision were these Boston men that they failed to consider how long it might take to realize. Mills don't just spring up overnight; nor do markets. "With profits the dominant motif," observed the historian Constance Green, "it is noteworthy that none of the providers of capital investigated with any care the question of the probable lapse of time necessary to realize dividends." Ten years later only a fraction of the mill sites had been sold, and the Panic of 1857 killed any chance for selling more soon. The capitalists auctioned off their land and left. Their investments in the equally troubled town of Lawrence ("a six million dollar disaster") proved unsound as well, leaving Lawrence as beggared as Holyoke. And yet "[these] bankrupt cities did not dissolve into the dust from which they had come." Despite its inauspicious beginning, by 1874 Holyoke was on the verge of a real boom, thanks in part to its ingenious design.

As in Lowell and Lawrence, the city's mills were situated along a canal system that was fed by a powerful river—in this case, the Connecticut—but in Holyoke the system had been so well planned that the river's power was taken advantage of repeatedly. The water was not confined to one canal, as at Lawrence, or dissipated through a network of canals, as at Lowell. Instead the canals were arranged parallel to one another and staggered down a slope so that water from the river followed gravity down the incline, falling from one canal into another, the same water being used again and again. "In the construction of the canals," touted a circular in 1850, "it is so arranged that the whole Connecticut River can be used over *twice*." In fact it could be used over *three* times, since the original plan, which had called for two canals, was later altered to include three. Moreover factory sites were available on both sides of each canal, providing the city with a formidable foundation on which to capitalize and profit. "So admirable was the arrangement in all its technical details and so perfectly executed," wrote Green in 1939, "that no fundamental change or reconstruction has been necessary in eighty-eight years."

Following the Cotton Lords' failure, some local men, who organized under the name of the Holyoke Water Power Company, through a combination of shrewdness and patience, steadily realized Holyoke's potential. During the Civil War the company experimented with both financing and development, encouraging big business as a way to stabilize the town's economy even as they expanded it. Their efforts were also, fortuitously, supported by the war, which saw home manufactures protected by tariffs and the Union Army in need of supplies. The wool, cotton, wire, and paper industries in Holyoke all increased. And in 1864 Mother Nature gave the town its greatest promotion yet. The summer of that year "an unusual drought dried up many New England streams and shut down many water power mills. The Holyoke canals, however, continued to have water and local 'boosters' advertised the unfailing character of Holyoke's supply." Thereafter a thread company came to town, as well as seven new paper manufacturers in a period of two years. A later sketch of this time decreed, "The spirit of hustle and success pervaded the bustling town."

By the spring of 1874 the town had become home to more than twenty mills, which, though far from the three hundred once dreamed of, was by any reasonable standard impressive, and, as planned, many of the city's businesses were sizable. The Lyman cotton mills employed more than a thousand people, and the local brickyard employed a force of three hundred men who turned out 10 million bricks a season. Unlike its sister cities of Lowell and Lawrence, Holyoke was not a textile center; too many other industries had taken root. Nor was it a "company town" ruled by a set of stockholders. Holyoke was a uniquely diverse manufacturing center, with almost every business locally owned and run. Furthermore, with a population nearing sixteen thousand, it was no longer a township. In December 1873 it had become a bona fide city.

The day was rainy, the sky overcast. Skinner's head probably got wet as he looked around, and with so many half-built structures, mud-splattered laborers, dripping workhorses, and unpaved streets, there was nothing charming about Holyoke. Even that which had been built was ordinary, not extraordinary. Yet compared with what Skinner had observed elsewhere, the young city would have been amazing. Construction was everywhere, with buildings going up, bridges being built, mill sites being excavated, streets being graded and new ones being cleared. The sound of steam shovels rang in the air. Sand rose in piles toward the sky. Wherever one looked men were painting, graining, piping, laying brick, shingling, and whitewashing. Properties were for sale; rooms were for rent. Storeowners were petitioning the city council for awnings; deliverymen were demanding that the streets finally be numbered. The place was in perpetual motion, but it all seemed to be focused on building up the city, *creating* it, and each citizen, from the laborer to the landlord, was playing a part.

Skinner met with members of the Water Power Company, including the president, George Bartholomew, and the managing agent, William Chase. The contractors Daniel and John Newton, as well as their "brilliant" brother James, a visionary local manufacturer, probably appeared as well. None of these men needed to tell Skinner what he was up against in Skinnerville, but they may have anyway, reminding him of the exorbitant cost of building another reservoir, as well as the cumulative expenses of building another milldam, constructing a new facility, and restoring the boardinghouses and tenements of his workers. Holyoke, by contrast, as the *Holyoke Transcript* had advertised, had "ample room ready for occupancy," as well as empty lots awaiting development, and the ability to get him back in business *quickly*.

The city leaders knew full well that if they could convince Skinner and others from the Mill River Valley to reestablish in Holyoke, the city would gain tremendously. "We have been accused of coveting the establishment of the unfortunate Mill river valley," wrote the editors of the *Transcript*. "We frankly acknowledge that we can greatly benefit all these sufferers—employers and employees—and with that claim in our mouths, we don't hesitate to say, we should most cordially welcome them; although we are bound to pity the misfortunes of those who would be injured by the removal of these concerns, we can conscientiously advise the manufacturers to bring their works and employees to Holyoke, and that in time to get ready for the re-animation of business. However selfish it may be, to wish the removal [of] these heavy concerns to Holyoke, it certainly is no charity to advise their rebuilding upon a constantly lessening stream."

The men of the Water Power Company certainly told Skinner about their recent talks with Joel Hayden Jr., who suddenly wasn't nearly as committed to staying in Haydenville as he had originally expressed. Hayden continued to move forward with plans for rebuilding at home, but he was beginning to double back and engage in detailed discussions with Holyoke's men. No doubt Bartholomew and Chase pitched the possibility that these two firms, whose workforces were so intimately connected, might successfully relocate to Holyoke together. In fact Chase had picked out a lot on the third, or lowest canal, with a water connection that could accommodate Hayden's large brass works, Skinner's smaller silk mill, and even perhaps George Warner's button mill, saving everyone a lot of money in the rebuilding process.

Skinner was generally suspicious of anything that sounded too good to be true. Yet Holyoke had exceptional features to recommend it. Here was a city devoted to industrial pursuit, *planned* for industrial pursuit. Built entirely around canals, the place was a Venice for capitalistic endeavors and only beginning to be realized as such. Of greatest significance was its waterpower; the largest river in New England flowed into the canals every day of the year. Were he to rebuild in Holyoke, it was conceivable that Skinner would never want for waterpower again. Also, if the water were clean enough to produce the high-quality paper manufactured at the Whiting paper mill, then the water would absolutely be pure enough for dying his high-quality silk. Then there was the fact that the Holyoke and Westfield Railroad passed directly through the heart of the city, and at least one of the lots up for discussion could be equipped with a spur track leading directly to it. As if this weren't enough, there was no evidence of the recent Panic anywhere in the city: a few days after Skinner's visit the *Transcript* reported, "The last month's freights over the Holyoke and Westfield railroad exceed those of any month since its opening [in 1872]. Coal, cotton, rags and miscellaneous merchandise have poured in upon us in a way to remind one of anything rather than hard times."

That night, after Skinner returned home and told Will about his day, the boy recorded in his diary, "Father went to Holyoke and looked at the mills there and was very well satisfied with them." Indeed, continued Will, "[Father] now has Holyoke on the braine."

Will had been invited to go to Northampton that evening with Fred Warner, but he stayed home, perhaps on account of the rain, and Skinner, on his way home from Holyoke, may have decided against stopping at Northampton too. But there was a benefit this Saturday night, at Northampton's town hall, for which Skinner was primarily responsible. In a shrewd move that would have bolstered his reputation in this uncertain time, he had proposed giving some kind of "public testimonial" to George Cheney, Collins Graves, Jerome Hillman, and Myron Day for their life-saving efforts during the disaster, and the benefit was to raise money toward this end.

Within days of the flood the *Boston Daily Globe* had published a sensational piece entitled "A Blow to Their Worshippers—No Heroes at All—Cheney's Ride a Ride from Fright—Graves, a Terrified Milk Man, Fleeing for His Life—A Sorry Tale for the Poets." The article occasioned an outcry, and the *Globe* agreed to investigate the matter with an unbiased reporter. A lot of people, Skinner among them, didn't have time for this kind of thing. Skinner was then staring every day into the faces of hollow-eyed fathers and forlorn mill girls, talking to them about their future, his future, in the dirty, stained supply room at his house, as they filed in one after the other for some money and clothing. But the reporter got to him anyway and questioned him about what really happened on the morning of May 16. Skinner "enthusiastically confirmed" Graves's story, the same that Graves had recounted under oath at the inquest. There was no doubt in Skinner's mind that the man's warning had helped evacuate his mill. So what if Graves hadn't been aware of the fullness of the danger upon him as he drove down the valley? One might say he had acted foolishly. But his was a purely selfless act, and because of it, Graves had ridden into history, whether or not anybody liked it.

In the vein of his personal hero, William Cobbett, Skinner then sought to redress what many perceived to be an ignominious injustice with a calculating proposal. He made the suggestion, perhaps to his comembers on the finance committee, that each "hero" should be given a concrete award, something that no one would be able to take away from them. But it wouldn't have sat well with the public if money from the relief fund had gone toward buying gold medals, and Skinner evidently believed the men should have *gold* medals—hence the necessity of a benefit to cover the cost. In contrast to all the bad press about "the niggardliness of the men who paid for the dam," Skinner's gesture won accolades in the papers and was embraced by his colleagues, who no doubt wished to be seen as equally conscientious.

Headlining the evening was Henry Cornelius Hayden, a cousin of Joel Jr., who performed a series of dramatic readings. A sewing machine salesman by day, Henry Hayden thrived on a live audience after dark and threw in some of his own funny pieces along with ones by Tennyson, Mrs. Stowe, and others. He regaled the crowd with one of the more popular poems about Graves's ride, a twenty-five-stanza extravaganza written by a senior at Amherst College. And if anyone needed any more reminding about what had taken place in May or why they were participating in this benefit, Hayden recited a poem by Jean Ingelow from 1864 called "The High Tide," which brought everyone crashing back to the moment when the water was upon them and it was anyone's guess who would survive.

> *So far, so fast the eygre drave*
> *The heart had hardly time to beat,*
> *Before a shallow, seething wave*
> *Sobbed in the grasses at our feet*
> *The foot had hardly time to flee*

Before it brake against the knee
And all the world was in the sea.

Perhaps because of the rain, the audience was smaller than expected and the benefit not as big a success as had been hoped. It netted $100, which was to be handed over to Skinner to help pay for the medals. Skinner had commissioned his favorite jeweler, Tiffany & Co in New York City, perhaps while he was in the city the week before, to fashion the testimonials. Eventually there would be two designs, one featuring a rider on horseback for Cheney and Hillman, the other a rider with horse and wagon for Graves and Day. The front of each would be emblazoned with "Mill River Reservoir Disaster—May 16th 1874," and the back would be inscribed with the words "Humanity" and "Courage" surrounding the hero's name.

Profoundly embarrassed by his celebrity, Graves didn't want a medal (least of all a gold one), but the dairy farmer couldn't escape his notoriety, nor for that matter could Cheney escape his. Both men had been approached by showmen eager to hire them as spectacles, and Cheney, who was out of a job without the reservoir, had tentatively agreed to go on tour with his otherwise ruined horse. "L. J. Hobbs of Holyoke," reported the *Springfield Republican*, "has bought the horse and engaged the man, and proposes to exhibit them in a tent, beginning probably in Connecticut." Graves meanwhile had refused to be "exhibited," even though he had been offered as much as $50 to appear in Holyoke. It may have been coincidental that showmen in Holyoke were most eager to hire the heroes, but the fact remained, Holyoke's entrepreneurs had their eyes turned toward the valley and were offering no shortage of attention.

Chapter Thirteen

The following week, in an act approved by the governor, the Massachusetts State Legislature voted that Williamsburg would receive $100,000 from the state treasury to repair its roads and bridges—only a few thousand shy of what the town had finally requested. That Williamsburg stood to receive so much money was a decided boost to the morale of its citizens. What Skinner had originally argued, that recovery was impossible without aid from the state, had been answered with concrete dollars. Cash was coming in. Additionally the legislature voted to grant the town a tax abatement of $5,000, which would help ease some of the financial burdens on destitute landowners.

As Lizzie Skinner well knew, the legislature's ruling, though auspicious, was not enough to solve her husband's problems. Nor was it enough to stop him from contemplating moving. As a result, exactly one week after Skinner's visit, on June 13, an uncommonly cold June day, Lizzie joined her husband to see Holyoke for herself.

Naturally Lizzie was intensely interested in the debate over where to rebuild. Her life, and the lives of her children, would be profoundly affected by the outcome. More than at any other time in their marriage, she would have discussed with Skinner the merits of the opportunities before him, and one imagines they stayed up late many a night, talking in low tones before the fire so as not to wake the children, going over the myriad challenges that they were facing. From their earliest years together Skinner had "had the helping and counseling companionship of his wife," and he would have been leaning on Lizzie heavily during this time, eager for her appraisals and opinions.

Driving through Holyoke, Lizzie saw a city quite unlike the one her husband had seen. Certainly she understood the desirability of relocating to a place that had been praised as "among the most attractive manufacturing centers in New England." However, Holyoke was a city, and, like any city, it had filth, vulgarity, poverty, slums, and crime. There were sixteen thousand people living in Holyoke, and a lot of them were taking life out on each other. There was a police report in just about every edition of the *Holyoke Transcript* describing men breaking women's arms in domestic disputes, drunks falling asleep on the church steps, women cursing and fighting in public, boys stealing and throwing stones, people being arrested for lewd behavior. As if that weren't enough, "the most brutal and atrocious crime that [had] ever been known in Holyoke since the town has had a history" occurred just a month earlier, on May 6, when a seventy-nine-year-old man was murdered near a popular spot called Ashley Pond. First, he had been "kicked, beaten, [and] dragged through the water." Then his head had been crushed with a stone. His three attackers had been "much intoxicated." (They also happened to be Irish, which worsened existing prejudices.)

If this sort of horror could happen to an innocent old man by some roughs looking for trouble, what might happen to Lizzie's children were they to find themselves in the wrong place at the wrong time? Skinner had been careful to give his children an upbringing unlike his own, but now he ran the risk of putting them in a place as violent as his own childhood haunts. Lizzie had heard enough about Spitalfields to know she never wanted to go there; she certainly didn't want her family living anywhere remotely like it.

There was also the matter of the dam. Holyoke's waterpower was generated from a dam that stretched clear across the mighty Connecticut. The dam had been built at the crest of the sixty-foot falls, and it was huge. More than a thousand feet long, it was twice the length of the Williamsburg Reservoir dam. "This great structure, about one-fifth of a mile in length, is flanked by abutments of massive masonry, and may be described in detail as the dam and the apron which now appears in front of it," wrote an expert on the matter in the early 1870s. "The former has a base of ninety feet, and rises thirty feet above the original level of the river. It contains four million feet of sawed timber of large dimensions, all of which is submerged, and so insured against decay. A mass of concrete and gravel protects the foot of the dam and the upper portion is covered to the thickness of eighteen inches with solid timber, while the crest is protected its entire length with sheets of heavy boiler iron." There was a viewing platform at the western end of the dam, but even from this close vantage, Lizzie would have been unable to see the millions of feet of timber below the waterline, nor the masonry supporting it. She would simply have seen that this was an entirely different structure from the Williamsburg Reservoir dam. An awe-inspiring sight, this was a wall rising up against the greatest river in New England. Water cascaded over the top and crashed down to the channel below, with a deafening sound not a little alarming. For anyone who had just suffered from the collapse of a dam and barely escaped with her life, the idea of living anywhere near this structure would have been terrifying.

Nor was the dam without its own checkered past. When originally built, it had actually collapsed. On November 19, 1848, the dam's gates were closed for the first time, and crowds gathered on the river-banks in the morning "to see the show" of the water filling up behind it. What a show they got. By midday "leaks were appearing near the western bulkhead," and a short while thereafter the river had risen so high, so fast, that it was threatening to swamp the dam. The dam gave way before that could happen, however, and spectators watched the middle explode "with a thunderous roar" and "timbers, boiler plate and water swept downstream in one great flood." A series of telegraphs said to have been sent to the directors in Boston explain the scene with extraordinary understatement:

10 a.m.   Gates just closed, water filling behind dam.
12 m.   Dam leaking badly.
2 p.m.   Stones of bulkhead giving way to pressure.
3:20 p.m.   Your old dam's gone to hell by way of Wil-
            limansett.

After careful study of the catastrophe, engineers believed they knew what had gone wrong and how to fix the problem. They had completely underestimated the pressure of the river, and so they rebuilt the dam with extensive reinforcements. By the late 1860s, though, the base was becoming compromised "by the constant action of the falling sheet of water," and to remedy this, the Water Power Company invested in an "apron," finished in 1870, that created a protective covering for the entire face of the dam, from top to bottom and side to side. This apron alone cost $263,000, more than eight times what the Williamsburg Reservoir directors had spent on their entire dam. In the hope of quieting people's fears, the apron was reported to have solved once and for all any potential problems with the structure: "By rendering the further wearing of the foundations impossible, [the apron] establishes the durability and permanence of the dam beyond all future questions."

As Lizzie shivered on the viewing platform, wrapping herself up against the cold and the wind, looking distrustfully at the great monolith before her, the *Transcript* was trying its best to distinguish this dam from the one in Williamsburg. "How different has been the history of [our] own dam!" the paper exclaimed the day of her visit. The *Transcript* praised "the immensity of the enterprise and the triumphant success of the project," not to mention the perspicacity of its owners. These men had "watched and inspected" it over the years, and when chance arose that "some unknown and undiscoverable pressure was imparing the vast structure," they had embraced the repair work "irrespective of the cost." Alas, bemoaned the day's editorial, "how different had been the history of that thrifty valley, had a like care and vigilance been exercised, and the waters held in as complete subjection." Then, in a rare moment of shortsightedness, somehow forgetting that the owners of the Williamsburg dam were the same men that Holyoke was trying to impress, the essay glibly continued: "The responsible parties should be held to the most rigid accountability, for an irreparable and deep wrong has been done to the villagers which makes it imperative for the authority of the State to search out the criminality, fix it where it belongs, and bring condign punishment home to the culprits." The *Transcript* all but called Skinner a criminal on the day he brought his wife to see the city.

Lizzie did not like Holyoke. It lacked everything she cherished: decency, community, and safety. She was not about to leave the Mill River Valley—a place she had called home her entire life, where she had literally grown up with the local industry and striven to cultivate an educated, Christian family, where she had raised her children and, just as important, buried three of them—to move to a vulgar, self-indulgent, dangerous, and hostile city, simply because it had good waterpower. It was too high a price to pay. She and Skinner were not so desperate that they needed to sacrifice what they valued along with everything else they had lost. Without a doubt Lizzie's visit to Holyoke was the deciding factor in Skinner's turning, once again, to other localities. Will put it rather mildly in his diary that night: "Father and Mother went down to Holyoke to look at the place and see how they would like to live there. They do not think much of it." He then added, "Father has not yet made up his mind where he will go."

Back in Skinnerville, Ellen Littlefield received a letter from her younger sister Lovisa, who had been the first Littlefield sister to come to Skinnerville, back in 1866. She was married now and living closer to home in New York, but her attachment to Skinnerville was as strong as ever. She had spent much of her early twenties in the village, working at the silk mill, forging lifelong friendships, and experiencing the only independence she had ever really known. The notion that the village was gone was impossible for her to fathom and hard to stomach.

Lovisa didn't actually learn of the flood until a week after it happened. She was getting ready to go to church on Sunday, May 24, when a neighbor stopped her wagon and related the horrifying news. The neighbor, a woman named Ada, had seen an account of the disaster in the *New York Tribune,* which another neighbor subscribed to. Lovisa's first thoughts were of Ellen, but Ada had not seen Ellen's name on the list of the dead, and Lovisa soon reasoned that she surely would have heard by this time if anything had happened to her sister. Then Lovisa began to think anxiously about all the other people who might have died. She got her hands on that copy of the *Tribune,* as well as another paper, and devoured the stories. A few days later, tucked away in her farmhouse, in the isolated windswept country where she and her husband lived, she wrote Ellen, having heard by this time that Ellen had indeed survived. "I was much alarmed at first for fear you were among the lost," Lovisa told her. Then, after explaining why it had taken her so long to write, she peppered Ellen with questions: "Was Fred at Skinnerville? And were the Tower girls there? I conclude Relia's house was not taken. Did the water reach it? How did Mrs. Damon escape? Did Nettie Kendall lose her melodeon? Yours of course went, and Becca and Tom Skinner's girls organs, and a great many others, but that is not so bad as the lives lost." Then, clearly having spent a great deal of time thinking about it all, she added rather sadly, "I have thought I would like to go there sometime and see the place and people that I know but I think now I shall never want to go."

Lovisa wanted to remember the village as it had been, but Ellen, back at work for Skinner, did not have that luxury. Unlike her sister, she was not married, and her parents relied heavily on her income to subsidize their expenses back home. In years past, Ellen had helped her parents buy machinery and animals. That summer her mother hoped to redo the kitchen and was depending on Ellen to help cover the cost. Necessity fueled Ellen's labor, never more so than now, and since she had chosen to return to Skinnerville she was surrounded by its ugly reality. Yet she was just as unable as Lovisa to stop thinking about the Skinnerville that had been.

Ellen had so many memories of playing croquet across the river, making molasses in the boardinghouse kitchen, and working at the mill. One story she retold a lot was of an event that had taken place in the packing room. She and the other girls liked to wear modish hairpieces ("rats," they called them) such as faux curls, braids, and buns, and, to be more comfortable, they had sometimes taken their rats off while working, stowing them in the nearby drawers of silk. This was against packing room rules, since hairpieces were made from real hair and their natural oils could soil the silk. One day a new overseer came in and commanded, "Will every girl who has hair in her drawers stand up." There was a pause. The girls looked at each other, holding back their laughter, and the young man, realizing what he had just said, turned beet red and fled the room.

Ellen had made so many friends in the boardinghouse and at the mill; they understood her in ways that few others back home had been able to. Almost all were passionate about fashion and style. When the latest issues of magazines like *Demorest's* and *The Delineator* arrived in the mail, they had pored over the fashion plates, figuring out how to make the designs, or improve upon them if possible. "Gingham is all the rage here, now," Lovisa once wrote in a letter from Skinnerville, passing along the current trend. These young working women wanted to be at the forefront of fashion. They weren't on farms anymore, but working in a silk mill, helping to manufacture the most glamorous kind of thread in the world.

Of men at the mill, there hadn't been many, but enough for love to bloom on occasion. Ellen had watched handsome Tom Forsyth become sweet on Lovisa, and when Lovisa left the mill, Tom couldn't stop thinking about her. There were sad memories too, such as when beloved Mrs. Sears passed away from cancer. And, of course, there had been the bad times, such as that period when the quality of the board-inghouse fare plummeted, when Lovisa called the Skinners "the skin-flints." Even their mother had suggested Ellen look for other work at that time, perhaps in education again. "I think if I were you I should come away from that place, don't stay till you are nothing but a ma-chine." But Ellen hadn't wanted to leave. She had just wanted the situ-ation to improve, and in time it did.

Ellen genuinely liked her boss. Skinner knew she had once been a teacher, like his wife, and he encouraged her to continue her love of learning. "Mr. Skinner came around where I was [working] yesterday," Ellen wrote her mother one time, "and said that I could have any of Dickens' works to read that I liked; he has them all. He has a nice large library, he told me while ago to come over there and get any book to read that I would like to." Many of those books, of course, had been ruined forever, swept down into the basement when the library's floor collapsed. On more than one occasion, as she walked upstairs to the third floor to skein silk with Aurelia, Ellen would have stepped to the edge of that huge hole, rimmed with jagged edges of the broken parquet, and peered down into the dank cellar below, amazed at the work of the water.

Like everyone else, Ellen longed for the mill to be up and running again. Most of her dear friends were all over the map now, and the only way to resurrect their close-knit community was for Skinner to rebuild in Skinnerville. As sure as the flood had pushed everyone out, this would bring everyone back in.

On the evening of June 14, a day after Skinner returned from Holyoke with Lizzie, Jacob Hills walked up to the house and asked to speak with him. Originally from Württemberg, Germany, Hills had been in the United States for more than twenty years, the majority of them in

Skinnerville. Now his life was falling apart. His wife, Christina, had drowned in the flood, and there wasn't so much as a cellar hole remaining of his home. As an employee of Hayden, Gere & Co., he and his children were likely living in one of the cheap workers' houses that the company had quickly erected in Haydenville. Perhaps they were sharing part of a six-family barn. His land in Skinnerville—the only asset he now had—would be worthless if Skinner didn't rebuild. Worse, if Skinner chose to leave, that might influence Joel Hayden's decision. Hills needed both of them to stay. He couldn't have his wife back; she was gone. But he wanted his job back, and he wanted his home back. His children required no less.

Another person came to see Skinner that same evening. Driving down to the house from the other direction, Onslow Spelman came inside for what seems to have been a long and serious talk. Spelman also came to discuss, in part, Skinner's thoughts about the future of his silk mill, a discussion that invariably included the prospects of the town of Williamsburg as a whole. Spelman believed these prospects were bright if everyone stayed put, dug in their heels, and piled brick upon brick until the mills were restored. Any hesitation that Spelman himself had been feeling about rebuilding in Williamsburg had been put to rest. He was going to rebuild on his old site and hoped Skinner would do the same.

If Will wasn't in on the discussion, he certainly heard about it afterward from his father. Later that evening the teenager opened his small leather diary, turned to the page for June 14, and recorded the visits of both Hills and Spelman, noting what was arguably of most significance to his father: "O. G. Spelman . . . is going to build again."

By the start of the third week of June, Skinner had found no acceptable alternative to Skinnerville. Reported the *Hampshire Gazette,* with a dose of its own opinion on the matter:

> We are pleased to hear that Wm. Skinner, the silk manufacturer at Skinnerville, is strongly inclined to rebuild his

mill on the old site. He has examined several offers made to him by parties elsewhere, which at first looked tempting, but which do not prove to be so very much better than the old site, after all. . . . At Skinnerville he will always be at home, surrounded only by his friends, the father of his village, and will leave a name that will be worth more to his children than much money. Going away is like transplanting a large tree. You may think you can do it easily, but you must mangle the roots terribly to start with, and it will take long years to get the tree growing again—if indeed it ever grows at all. No, no, Mr. Skinner; your place is where the old mill stood, and in the long run it will prove so.

Apart from the legislature's ruling, however, Skinner had not received any financial incentive to rebuild in Skinnerville. He would still have to pay for rebuilding much of the village himself. As a result, he continued to entertain other offers, and on Tuesday, June 16, he took the train to Springfield presumably to meet with George C. Fisk, president of the Wason Car Works, on the outskirts of that city in a development called Brightwood. The area included a large, almost wholly undeveloped tract of land along the Connecticut River, through which passed the Connecticut River Railroad. On the same model as what had once been Skinnerville, Fisk wanted to develop Brightwood into a flourishing factory village.

He was halfway there. The Wason Car Works, itself, took up sixteen acres and had given Brightwood a promising start. Having supplied the Central Pacific Railroad, in 1869, with 75 coaches and 2,600 freight cars, Wason was partly responsible for linking the east and west coasts and was on its way to becoming "the largest car-works in New England." Fisk had also designed an orderly residential neighborhood for prospective manufacturers. He had originally been selling the house lots for $1,000 but, as he and Skinner proceeded down Riverside Road, their coats blowing in the breeze coming off the Connecticut, Fisk was probably willing to bargain. Wason may have been one of the most successful car shops in the country, but the Panic had wreaked havoc upon the railroad industry. With eighty-nine railroads going bankrupt since the previous September, production at Wason had come "to a grinding halt" and Fisk needed a business like Skinner's if Brightwood was to enjoy a bright future.

Unfortunately, despite its proximity to the river, Brightwood did not rely on waterpower. The Wason Car Works was run by steam, and Fisk, it seems, had not yet invested in establishing water privileges for water-powered mills. A huge operation like the Car Works could afford to run by steam, but Skinner simply could not. And even if he could have afforded a steam-powered mill, he would have still needed immense amounts of water to dye his silk. No matter how attractive the neighborhood Fisk had developed or how much capital he may have been willing to loan Skinner to rebuild, Brightwood ultimately held no potential for a silk mill.

Perhaps immediately following his trip to Springfield, Skinner visited Worcester, Massachusetts, partly inspired by the Reverend George Phillips, who himself had found a new life in the city. Equidistant from Boston, Springfield, and Providence, Rhode Island, Worcester was serviced by no fewer than five major railroads and strung with telegraph wires like a five-point star. Situated at the peak of the Blackstone River Valley, the place was also picturesque. "The city proper, with its vast mechanical establishments, its handsome stores, and its commodious private and public buildings, occupies in part a beautiful valley, environed by hills and gentle elevations rising toward the east and west," boasted the *Gazetteer of Massachusetts*. Small and large operations had found a ready home in the city. On a daily basis Worcester turned out an astonishing array of products: cotton, wool, boots, shoes, wire, knives, files, tools, ironware, brassware, brushes, ink, envelopes, soap, firearms, and a great deal more. The city's industrial landscape was well established, well financed, and well known to the rest of the country. But Worcester, alas, had no better access to waterpower than Brightwood.

The Blackstone River Valley may have become famous as the birthplace of the American Industrial Revolution (Samuel Slater built America's first cotton mill here in 1783), but the water that powered that revolution wasn't to be found in Worcester. The Blackstone River is a comparatively insignificant force there. In fact the river doesn't run through Worcester, or even alongside it, but rises south of the city. Worcester is veined with the headwaters of the Blackstone, small rivers and streams that, though initially beneficial to early enterprises, over time had proven unequal to the demands of the city's burgeoning industrial community. Reservoirs were built, and they had helped, but what ultimately solved the power problem for Worcester was steam. Years before the Civil War even, Worcester had joined a small legion of other cities and townships that, out of necessity, had embraced the steam engine "as the essential base for further growth."

In Worcester Skinner had two options: switch to steam, which he didn't want to do, or lease a water privilege on one of the small, outlying streams that was supplemented by a reservoir. The latter option would place him in a position similar to the one he had known in Skinnerville. But it would come with the singular advantage of placing his mill within reach of a major industrial center. Here was a chance to have the best of both worlds. Skinner was probably further encouraged knowing that Lizzie's reaction to this place would likely be positive. Although a large city with more than forty thousand people, Worcester was reportedly as clean and nonsuffering, as moral and upright as one could hope. "I have never seen, in a community of equal extent," said one man, "so few marks of poverty and human degradation as in this [place]."

All the same, Skinner was not entirely convinced, and so he continued to meet with more men in other locales, finishing out the third week in June with a trip to Connecticut's Naugatuck River Valley. But he was running out of time. While colleagues were filling orders for the coming season, he was walking around empty mill sites, wondering how to power them, and imagining potential returns as investors offered him possible loans. *He had to start rebuilding.* Once he made up his mind, though, Skinner knew, there would be no turning back. Nor would he get another chance after this one, not at his stage in life. He was almost fifty, "an age when some men feel the battle is lost or won." With everything on the line, he had to proceed with both caution and sagacity. He had to find the right mix of opportunity and security. "You stand either a success or a failure," he would tell his children, but his personal motto didn't even allow for the latter option: "There is no such word as fail." Where, then, would it be impossible for him *not* to succeed?

Down in Connecticut, at the confluence of the Housatonic and Naugatuck rivers, sat the factory town of Birmingham. "Behold her," wrote a native reporter, "at the confluence of two majestic rivers, seated like a queen, upon a commanding eminence." Founded in the 1830s, Birmingham was well situated for water-powered manufacturing and had developed into a bustling industrial and industrious community with small shops making hoopskirts and corsets and larger companies producing pins, axles, springs, organs, and pianos. Factories crowded the waterfront, and houses and churches the hills behind. When Skinner alighted from the train at Birmingham's depot, he may have noticed the deep ruts in Commerce Street out front, as well as delivery trucks in the rail yard. Those ruts in the road, created by the wheels of heavily laden trucks, gave some evidence of the amount of shipping coming and going from this place.

The Housatonic River was nearly as commanding a waterway as the Connecticut, and local capitalists had successfully built a dam across it just four years earlier. Built of solid masonry in a gentle arc, the dam provided some 2,500 horsepower a day. Canals off either end of the dam extended down into Birmingham on one side and the small town of Huntington on the other. An 1874 study of American dams concluded favorably on behalf of the Housatonic's, believing that it thoroughly enhanced the manufacturing capabilities of the region. "With the ample reservoir, extending back five miles and covering nearly one thousand acres, no apprehension can exist of a lack of water. . . . The almost unequalled extent of this water-power, combined with its close proximity to New York, with which it is in direct communication by water, in addition to ample railroad facilities in all directions, have given it wide celebrity, the advantages which it offers being apparent at a glance."

Skinner would have met with Edward N. Shelton, president of the Ousatonic Water Power Company that was responsible for building the dam, and Holyoke almost certainly came up in the conversation because Shelton and his colleagues had studied the work of the Boston Associates and wanted to transform their area "on the model of Lowell and Holyoke." As a result, Skinner found himself on the receiving end of a very ambitious sales pitch because, it became clear, Shelton had big dreams for both Birmingham and Huntington, and he was willing to use "every means at his disposal" to win over new business. Already he had "furnished capital to companies that would build there, offered favorable water power franchises, and even built factories." Here was a man who could—and would—give Skinner both money and water-power to rebuild.

A journalist in nearby Waterbury would report, promisingly, that Mr. William Skinner had visited Birmingham and "[was] likely to transfer his business there." Perhaps those in Waterbury knew of other incentives for transferring to the area. In nearby Watertown was the Heminway Silk factory, where so many of Skinner's operatives had found work after the flood. If Skinner moved downriver, he'd surely be able to lure back many of his old workers. But labor was not one of Skinner's primary concerns, and he rode home on the train knowing that in all probability Birmingham wasn't for him. Shelton's plans were ambitious but perhaps too raw. The dam had been built, and was a wonder, but the industrial community had a long way to go before it became fully realized. Huntington was still mostly farmland and Birmingham, while active with business, was no manufacturing center. It was, in truth, little more than a town with a dream. If Skinner was going to consider moving there, to a place that wanted to be like Holyoke, he might as well just go to Holyoke.

While Skinner was away that week, life had gone on without him. He missed his son's high school graduation. There had been some question as to whether Will's overall grades were high enough to earn a diploma, but Lizzie had taken care of the matter. ("Mother saw [teacher] Jo Sawyer and told him what she thought about it.") That Skinner would miss such a ceremony underscores the strain he was under. Since the day his son was born, Skinner had been hell-bent on the boy's going to school and then on to college. When Will floundered in his studies—having never had to work for anything in his life and not particularly caring about the worth of Virgil or mathematics—Skinner had strongly reprimanded him. Just a week before the disaster, as Will careened toward possible expulsion on account of his continued lack of effort, Skinner had told him, in no uncertain terms, "Improve your time and make a man of yourself. There are very few young men that have your chance."

More than anything, one would have thought, Skinner would have wanted to watch his son graduate from the prestigious Williston Seminary. What an extraordinary accomplishment that would have been for a member of the Skinner family, in which, it is safe to say, no man had ever received a diploma of any kind. And yet Skinner didn't hear the "soft strains of music" in the Payson Church, where the exercises took place, or the "eloquence of the graduates" in their varied speeches. Will, who was not eloquent, was not one of the chosen speakers, but his presence in that assembly of fine young men would have been just cause for pride. In years past Skinner had actually been the sponsor of the "speaking prize," donating a very generous $20 for the award. (Somewhat ruefully, Will had remarked in his diary, "It is a good thing Father did not give it this year.") When Skinner was a boy he had to forgo school in order to meet the demands of the hour. Once again demands of the hour had taken precedent, only now he had to forgo showing support for his child. Lizzie represented the home front on this special occasion, bringing one of her sisters, Will's Aunt Ruth, to see her oldest boy graduate. Will noted, "Mother enjoyed it very much."

Back home there was no excitement, apart from the nervous variety. "Nothing of any account has happened since the flood," wrote Will a few days later, "for it is all desolation." The same hulking carcasses of buildings leaned this way and that. Sand choked the fields. Stones and pieces of wood lay everywhere still, a nuisance to both pedestrian and rider. A depressing inertia pervaded the landscape, as if the horror of the flood hadn't simply swept through but settled here, and Skinner's uncertainty added significantly to his villagers' tension. People kept asking, "Well, is Skinner going to rebuild?"

As one man expressed it, "The facts are, that so soon as these men [Hayden and Skinner] decide to remove from here the real estate of this town sinks to one-half . . . and we receive a blow from which we shall not recover in the coming fifty years. We think we have suffered enough without having the last spark of life crushed out by those who have not suffered at all, and our last dollar taken to make Holyoke or some other place rich." But these townspeople had choices to make too: Were they going to wait and see what Skinner would do, or would they try to influence his decision?

Somewhere a private discussion was held, and Skinner's neighbors resolved that, while they couldn't woo him with canals or money, they could overwhelm him with an outpouring of neighborly generosity. Their time and their labor were their biggest assets, so they decided to come together one day to help restore Skinnerville. If they could erase the village's "dark look," they hoped Skinner might see the place and its potential in a new light. And so, on the morning of June 23, as Skinner was walking about downstairs with the day's correspondence on his mind, a crowd began to assemble in front of his house, and, stepping outside to see what was going on, he found seventy-five men at his door. He was completely stunned. John Belcher, the livery keeper, had brought six horse teams down from Williamsburg. Farmers had come down from the hills with eight teams of oxen. Shirtsleeves were rolled up, work boots were laced, and, with Skinner looking on, his neighbors and friends began to "set things to rights" in the village. They piled debris onto wagon beds, rolled boulders onto stone boats, drove off with loads and returned for more. They filled in ditches; they leveled the ground. Men came and went, heaving and sweating, right up until sundown. It generated quite a lot of talk. The *Northampton Free Press* observed, "The people . . . are bound [Mr. Skinner] shall not 'go back on them' and indeed it would be very foolish of him to do so."

More than anyone Skinner knew what rebuilding in Skinnerville would mean for some of these men, their wives, and their children. Jacob Hills remained as desperate as ever for him to stay, and others, like the Bartletts, had carved out a makeshift life for themselves in the ruins of their homes, hoping against hope for a miracle. (How the Bartletts managed to live in their house, pitched back on its side at an impossible angle, was anyone's guess, but it was all they had.) Skinner knew too that if he left, he would be abandoning these people to fend for themselves in a destitute environment. But he hadn't been aware of the lengths that they and others would go to voluntarily to stop that outcome.

He was filled with emotion. Reported the *Hampshire Gazette,* "Mr. Skinner was much affected by the kindness and sympathy thus shown by his townsmen." Unfortunately, while neighborly generosity could make a man feel special, it couldn't pay his bills or provide a future. No matter how much they cleaned up Skinnerville and imbued it with a life that it hadn't known in weeks, Skinner's neighbors couldn't erase the financial challenges of rebuilding in Skinnerville. There's a chance, too, that Skinner had already made up his mind and that when all those men showed up at his door, he was overcome with something that he didn't like to acknowledge: guilt.

Lizzie probably knew what was coming. For weeks now she had been following her husband's meetings closely and supporting his efforts to find opportunity within this disaster. They both wanted to move farther away from uncertainty, not closer into it, and they believed that there was, somewhere, a solution to their troubles. "They believed . . . in dreams and dreaming," young Will said of his parents, "even in the midst of turmoil." Although Skinnerville was certainly the favorite place in their hearts, Skinner couldn't see his way clear to rebuild in the village. Simply put, no one in the valley had made him an offer or provided him with an argument for staying that was as compelling as the dollars and waterpower being extended to him elsewhere. And of all the offers he received, none could beat the one that he finally accepted.

On Friday evening, June 26, Skinner walked up the steps of One Canal Street in Holyoke and stepped through the front door of the Holyoke Water Power Company. Inside he met with William Chase and George Bartholomew and at least two of the Newtons, James and John. They likely gathered in what would become known as the Directors Room, which, in later photographs, had blown-glass chandeliers, richly paneled walls, and a large rectangular table surrounded by leather-cushioned chairs. As wagons and trucks rattled by with their last deliveries of the day and workers emptied out of the neighborhood mills, soon to pass by on their way to the boardinghouses in an area called "the flats"—where Skinner was told he could rent cheap lodging for his workers—the Newtons, Bartholomew, and Chase formally presented Skinner with the offer he couldn't refuse.

The Newtons offered Skinner an empty lot on what was known as the Bigelow site, a parcel of land between Appleton and Cabot streets adjacent to and in the middle of the upper canal. Skinner would receive the northwest corner of the site, which was diagonally across the canal from the railroad station. The *Springfield Republican,* which was no fan of Holyoke, called the site "one of the finest locations for manufacturing in the city." The lot was worth $6,000, but the Newtons were willing to give it to Skinner rent-free for five years. They would also build him a new mill and have it finished by October—just four months away.

In addition they had worked out an arrangement with Bartholomew whereby the Holyoke Water Power Company would pay for the mill's construction. Skinner's only obligation would begin the following year. On January 1, 1875, Skinner would have to start paying the Holyoke Water Power Company an annual rate of 7 percent interest on its total investment in the mill—but that was it. Even better, Skinner had a full five years to get himself back on his feet, after which he could purchase both the site and the mill at their original costs.

Furthermore this offer included, for free, three acres on the hillside above the city on which to build a house. Three acres constituted a city block, and since much of the grid was still being laid down, Skinner would actually be able to choose which site he preferred. In other words, he would have his pick of the landscape for his home. Of added significance, this offer would have nothing to do with anyone else in the Mill River Valley. The "fine location" that Skinner would receive was actually quite far from the one on the lower, or third, canal that Chase had discussed earlier, which would have been for Skinner's silk mill, Hayden, Gere & Co., and perhaps others. Unlike that joint venture, this was a completely independent deal.

For a man in Skinner's position, this was his ticket back into the game. He signed the contract and began then and there on the table, with gaslight flickering on the walls, to lay out plans with John Newton for the mill. Newton had fifty men ready to begin excavating the very next day. Bartholomew meanwhile began to formulate the details of the indenture that Skinner would enter into on January 1. At a late hour they all shook hands and parted ways, and Skinner walked out of the building into the night, having resolved the biggest question of his career. A silk mill was about to be built in Holyoke.

Many years later a rumor would be passed down that within twenty-four hours of the disaster Skinner had known he wanted to go to Holyoke. "I've got my eye on a site that strikes me as much safer than the last one," he was reputed to have said in reference to the city. Of course, Skinner had no idea what he wanted to do so soon after the disaster, and there was no way he was going to make his decision quickly. But in just the same way that he had instantly known Lizzie was the woman he had to marry, he may have known right away that Holyoke was where he needed to be. The city held potential for him in ways that no other place did.

People would say too that Lizzie became instrumental in helping her husband ultimately decide in favor of Holyoke. What is certainly true is that she changed her tune about the place. When she visited Holyoke that first time, it had been so unlike any place she had ever lived or any city she had ever visited that she'd recoiled from it, and perhaps more than ever wished life could go back to the way it had been. Yet she was far too realistic to dwell on the past. Just as her husband's instinct was to trust his gut, Lizzie's instinct was to trust her husband. He had always come out ahead—why shouldn't he come out ahead again, in Holyoke? Her family's well-being depended on the success of her husband's mill, after all, wherever it was, and Holyoke had the waterpower, the infrastructure, and the financial resources to enable her husband, as a manufacturer, to give the future his very best shot. She may not have hated Holyoke the first time around. She may just have been shocked by it, a shock that faded in the weeks thereafter, when it became apparent that Holyoke wasn't so unfamiliar after all, not from an industrial standpoint. Moreover the city was not merely equal to other manufacturing centers; it was in truth a great deal more remarkable.

The day after he signed the contract, while crews began to excavate the proposed site, Skinner sat at his desk in Skinnerville and wrote an open letter to Samuel Bowles at the *Springfield Republican,* announcing his decision. The question of where he would rebuild had been so widely followed in the papers because more than a few people had a vested interest in the matter that its resolution demanded a public announcement. Such an announcement, however, also provided Skinner with a way to tell everybody at once what he had decided and probably enabled him to avoid some unpleasant personal confrontations. As ever, Skinner was clear, unapologetic, and straightforward.

> To the Editor of the Republican,
> I write to say I have fixed upon Holyoke as my future place of business. I have examined various places, and found none that offer such inducements as this place. Cheap and reliable water-power is to a manufacturer what good rich land is to a farmer. He can get good returns for his labor. And I take this means of expressing thanks to my friends in Worcester, Springfield and Northampton for the sympathy and interest they have expressed in my behalf and the desire they have evinced that I should, if forced to make a change, locate among them. I consider the competition is too great to allow me to run my business from steam. And to my dear old friends in Williamsburg: I leave you with a heavy heart, after spending so many happy and prosperous years among you, but my "poverty and not my will" compels me. And may the good old town soon recover from the sad calamity now resting upon it, is the desire of
> William Skinner

He laid his pen down, folded the letter, and placed it in an envelope. But if he thought the matter was settled, he was mistaken.

Chapter Fourteen

Word of Skinner's decision spread like wildfire—or, as a writer for the *Hampshire Gazette* put it, "like news of the flood"—and was a "severe blow" to those in Northampton and Williamsburg, with outside parties reporting that Skinner's definite removal was a "serious loss to the unfortunate Mill River Valley." The *Gazette's* correspondent, resigned to the dour outcome of Skinner's decision, or merely exhausted by the debate that had supposedly reached an end, went on to add, "All this of course means ruin to Skinnerville. In place of the once prosperous and beautiful little village, [skirting] the river banks for more than half a mile, there will be nothing left, except here and there a house, whose owner remains to gain a living by till[ing] the soil. Gone—all gone—swept away by the flood. Sadness again is in many households. Farewell to Skinnerville!"

Journalists recorded the "universal sorrow" and "deep and sincere regret" that Skinner's action had occasioned, but many in Skinnerville and Williamsburg were not nearly as sanguine as others. They were devastated and quite angry. Just three days after seventy-five men had showed up at Skinner's house to help him, he had turned his back on them all. What were they going to do? What would become of them? How could he do this? Even now, people were in disbelief that Skinner would ever consider leaving Skinnerville. Said some, "I thought he was going to stay. Won't he have to sacrifice more by going than he would to stay where he is?"

One man spoke for many when he implied, in an open letter to the *Gazette,* that Skinner needed to change his mind right away. He needed to shelve his pride and stalwart independence for the sake of his community, and if that meant accepting the generosity of his neighbors in any form to help him rebuild, he needed to do that, if not for himself, then for them. Yes, it was well known that Skinner did not wish to feel beholden to anyone, but there were times when it was appropriate to accept the outstretched hands of others. "Mr. Skinner has no occasion to sacrifice an ounce of manliness, but considering the true welfare of his fellow citizens, he can afford, and ought to be willing to crucify himself temporarily, for the public benefit." Like the valley's other manufacturers, Skinner "owed a duty at home." Did not the fact that his business and property had prospered in Williamsburg stand for something? Did not the fact that a village had "grown up under his protection" stand for something as well? Skinner was "abandoning" all those people who had depended on him, who in some cases had given their lives to his operation, and who were, to say the least, "anxiously awaiting further developments." There was no question but that, all things considered, Skinner should remain in Skinnerville. Said the objector, "No duty can be plainer."

Reverend Gleason, one of the most ardent campaigners for rebuilding in town, may have been this outspoken citizen who preached with his pen the direness of this new calamity—and who also had some choice words for the area's local capitalists. "Why hadn't anyone come forward," the writer lamented, "with the necessary capital to right this situation?" Like Skinner, the area's most prominent investors needed to make a course correction for the greater good. They could ill afford to ignore Skinner's potential, which stood to be their great loss. Already Skinner's locally made silks had turned the name of a little-known brook into a national brand, and with the prosperity of the silk industry Skinnerville could yet become so large that it might turn Williamsburg into one of the state's most promising towns. "When one reflects from what small sources Lowell, Fall River, Holyoke, and scores of other manufacturing places in this state have arisen," the writer remarked, "no one can foresee what more it means." He reminded readers that Skinner had publicly announced, "In ten years we shall be shipping silk to China!" And he urged people to think about the significance of that statement. If Skinner could be compelled to stay, silk made in their very own town might one day be known across the world. "We have hinted at what Mr. Skinner's remaining and rebuilding in Williamsburg meant, but it is less pleasant, to look into the future, immediate or distant, and see what his absence signifies. . . . Now, the question is, What is going to be done about it?"

On the evening of Wednesday, July 1, Governor Talbot and a committee from the state legislature left Boston for a three-day trip to the valley, during which time they planned to reexamine the flood's path in Williamsburg and review the town's plans for new roads and bridges as well as the county commissioners' proposed budget for the work. In light of Skinner's announcement the weekend before, the agenda for the meeting had swiftly expanded. When the governor and committee arrived in Williamsburg on Thursday, "all were much interested, not only in the rebuilding of the roads and bridges, but in the re-establishment of the manufactories, and disposed to do everything within their power to aid in the work."

The commissioners had been "willing, and even anxious to expend from $10,000 to $12,000 in restoring the damage done in Skinnerville, provided Mr. Skinner would rebuild his mill." They were apparently now willing to do more than that if Skinner would change his mind, but Skinner declined the overture. He had made his decision; he was not going to rebuild in Skinnerville. The commissioners, perhaps even the governor, may have reminded him that the legislature had "acted with great justice in giving Williamsburg $100,000" and that it had voted to do so "under the apprehension, that her factories, as well as her roads were to be rebuilt." As far as Skinner was concerned, the legislature had not asked him to agree to anything before bestowing its award, and he was not responsible for the legislature's action.

The result was that Skinnerville received yet another terrible setback: the commissioners decided that, under the circumstances, allocating money to restoring the damage in that village would be a waste of valuable resources. They agreed "to expend in that section only enough to put the road in good condition for travel." This meant, among other things, no building up of the riverbank, no protective wall to inhibit the river from flooding, no water privilege for another mill, and, of immediate consequence, no new bridges. Aurelia Damon, for one, would be stranded on the other side of the river without a safe way to get over to her house. She would have to make do with the temporary crossing now in existence, a "bridge" of narrow planking that had been swung across the river with rope, one portion of it resting on a sawhorse.

The governor's visit was not completely unsuccessful, however, for Joel Hayden and his partners were quite willing to bargain with the commissioners. Hayden had apparently received "even better" offers than Skinner to move to Holyoke but conveyed to the governor and the rest that what he really wanted to do was stay in Haydenville. Following the meeting the *Springfield Republican* announced, with some glee, "It appears that Holyoke is not sure of getting Hayden, Gere & Co. after all. The county commissioners granted all that the firm requested in relation to the change of highway and other minor interests in Haydenville, and it is announced with considerable positiveness that the firm have decided to rebuild in the village, and will commence at once to lay the foundations for their new building."

Joel Hayden Jr. had as much at stake as Skinner, but he was not in the same position as Skinner. Skinner had founded Skinnerville, whereas Hayden had inherited Haydenville. When Hayden had first entertained offers to relocate the brass works elsewhere, the *Hampshire Gazette* had sympathized with his difficult predicament but also noted, sharply, "Were Gov. Hayden living, there would probably be no doubt about the rebuilding. . . . With the present company, it is not so, to so large an extent. Though long identified with Haydenville, its members have not that local pride in the place which Gov. Hayden had." Indeed Joel didn't even live in Haydenville; he lived in Northampton. And for much of the past two years he hadn't even been in the valley, since he had been traveling to improve his health, which was quite poor. When his father died in November 1873, Joel had been convalescing in Europe. He arrived back in the States a month later and was immediately voted to the helm of his father's company and took over other leading positions his father had held, such as the presidency of the Haydenville Savings Bank, possibly even the presidency of the reservoir company. He was fully expected to take over his father's role in the community and, basically, become his father.

Governor Hayden, though, was a tough act to follow; his curriculum vitae included impressive runs as an inventor, manufacturer, reformer, politician, banker, Mason, and benefactor. In 1852, even before the war boom, he was already so successful that he had been included in a prestigious little volume with the very proud name *The Rich Men of Massachusetts: Containing a Statement of the Reputed Wealth of About Fifteen Hundred Persons with Brief Sketches of More Than One Thousand Characters.* Much like William Cobbett, the authors of this book wished to inspire young men to greatness, in this case through the example of prominent citizens and "from the contemplation of success resulting from a suitable combination of those sterling qualities, Perseverance, Energy, Carefulness, Economy, Integrity, Honesty." Governor Hayden was believed to have had all of these; he was considered a model citizen of the state. His biography read, in part, "Began poor . . . A very public-spirited and benevolent man. Gives much to poor people. A man of whom a town might well say, 'Wish we had *more* such.'"

Joel Jr. hadn't grown up poor at all. He had grown up in a Greek Revival mansion overlooking the village that bore his family's name and that supported his family's wealth and industry. He was akin to a prince in these parts. Nor did he feel any particular responsibility to the poor. As an adult he had thus far engaged in no social acts that merited any public recognition. In short, he was used to having a lot of money and very little responsibility. When he came of age, he assumed a financial interest in his father's companies and slid into positions of authority within the various enterprises, never having to step off the cushioned ground onto which he was born. In most, if not all, of his early endeavors, outsiders believed he was "helped" by his father. He eventually became a partner in the brass works and supposedly developed into a "sharp business man," capable of "feather[ing] his own nest"—yet he had to rely on his father to carry on the business while he took two years off for his health. Nevertheless, in 1874 he was as rich as he'd ever been. People estimated his worth to be "over $300,000," and because he had successfully and quietly diversified his investments, only a fraction of his wealth was in the brass works.

Before the flood, Joel Hayden Jr. was twice as rich as Skinner and ten years younger. He was also untested. He wasn't so much a businessman as a legatee, and a sick one at that. In this unenviable position he needed to figure out how to make a lot of money very fast and, like Skinner, was unsure that rebuilding on the old site was in his company's best interest—not when others elsewhere were willing to hand him just about anything he needed. He was further burdened with the pressure of having to prove himself and wanting desperately to do the right thing. Hayden saw opportunity in Holyoke, just as Skinner did, but he saw too what Skinner would be destroying by taking advantage of that opportunity. William Skinner was about to forsake the village he had raised. Did the son of Governor Hayden wish to be known as the Hayden who had forsaken Haydenville?

As Hayden looked around him, wondering what other manufacturers were going to do, it was clear as well that Skinner was the only one leaving. Henry L. James, who had been born in Williamsburg, was rebuilding in town. Onslow Spelman too. Spelman wasn't a native of Williamsburg, but he had been in town for more than thirty years and had known there a "very snug & good" life. Downriver George Warner was also staying put. He wasn't from the valley either, but his Warner ancestors—the same as Nellie and Nina Skinner's—had so thoroughly populated the area that he couldn't walk a half-mile in any direction without bumping into a cousin. His family was well rooted here. No, Skinner was the only one leaving, and he was the only Englishman— the sole foreigner—among them. Whose example would be better to follow: Skinner's? Or everyone else's?

Everyone longed for a jubilant Fourth of July, but as was so often happening in the valley these days, it rained on the Fourth, and no matter how far one seemed to get away from the despair of the past few weeks, it continued to pour back in. Four inches accumulated in Florence that night, and the roads were badly washed out. People just couldn't get a break. And a few days hence the *Holyoke Transcript* had to dump some buckets of its own onto everything, taking almost cruel pleasure in dousing the spirit of the festivities that those in the valley wished desperately to realize. "The Northampton papers are amusing themselves and their readers, by publishing items of news, to the effect that Mr. Skinner will not build in Holyoke but will rebuild in the 'valley of death,'" the paper taunted. "Go on, gentlemen, it's a pleasant sort of fiction—Mr. Skinner is coming to Holyoke and your almighty dollars can't help it."

Indeed, the same day Governor Talbot was riding in from Boston, some salvaged parts of Skinner's machinery were riding down to Holyoke. Skinner had also made at least one trip to the city himself to scout for "a favorable site on which to place his present house." He couldn't afford to build another $20,000 mansion or suffer the extreme financial loss that would come in trying to sell it, which would have been impossible. So he and Lizzie had embraced the drastic idea of attempting to move the old manse, which, fortunately, had been "so constructed as to admit of being taken to piece and transferred in section to any part of the world." The house wouldn't be dismantled till the last possible moment, however, because of the reeling and spinning going on inside. Additionally, though plans for the silk mill were "not fully matured" at this stage, Skinner and the Newtons had engaged the same architect that Joel Hayden had, Clarence Luce, and more formal plans were to be drawn up presently.

Then came other news. The inquest into the death of John Atkinson was over. After weeks of deliberation, the jury had reached a decision on July 3, and it was announced in the papers on the Fourth, lighting up that day in a most unexpected manner. The *Hampshire Gazette* noted wryly, "The verdict of the coroner's jury is like the sermons of the old-time divines—it covers many points and has many heads." The jury believed that everyone involved in the construction of the dam was partly responsible for its failure. Since the blame was so widespread, however, no one could be held accountable for the disaster that ensued. Everybody involved had successfully found shelter under someone else's wrongdoing.

The jury called the legislature "delinquent" for granting a charter to Skinner, Hayden, and Bodman for a reservoir "with no safeguard of guarantees for the security of life and property below [it]. . . . Indeed, our statute law, as it has stood for many years, has been calculated to repel rather than invite a careful scrutiny of works like the Williamsburg dam." After summarizing the ridiculous system that put the onus largely on citizens to call attention to defective structures, but then penalized those same citizens if their concerns proved invalid, the jury concluded, "In view of the utterly inadequate legislation on this subject, and the desolation and ruin in the case before us, it is to be hoped the Legislature, if it cannot provide indemnity for the past, will at least by prompt and stringent action insure security for the future."

Second, the jury felt the Williamsburg Reservoir Company as a whole had cared "far less" for the security and lives of those who lived below the reservoir than they did "for reducing the cost of construction to the minimum figure." But the jury then went a step further than probably anyone would have expected. "The building committee," they said, effectively singling out Lucius Dimock, William Clement, William Clark, and even Governor Hayden, "[was] especially responsible for the breaking away of the dam." They acted from the outset "from parsimony or some other unaccountable motive" that thoroughly jeopardized the integrity of the work. "Finally," said the jurors, "the recorded vote of the proprietors that counsel should be consulted and all necessary steps taken for relieving the owners from individual liability in case the dam should fail . . . is speaking evidence that self-interest, and not the welfare of the community, dictated the action of this company."

Third, in the judgment of the jurors there was no appreciable engineering connected with this dam. Julius Fenn had "[yielded] his own judgments" to those of the proprietors and done himself "discredit" as a result. The jurors considered his specifications "ambiguous in terms and defective in details." And Eugene Gardner, the architect expected to superintend once in a while, "had no experience or fitness as an engineer." From what the jury could deduce, "the entire active work on the dam, from the first breaking of ground for the foundation to the completion of the job, was without an hour's attendance of a competent and watchful engineer."

As for the contractors, their failings were so numerous, in the opinion of the jury, that they didn't have room to list them all (though they tried). The contractors were the only party in the judgment to which the jury applied the word *guilty*. The jury found them "guilty of great and manifest delinquency in executing the work required of them, even under the specifications as drafted." They "did not faithfully execute the work."

Finally, the county commissioners "shared not a little responsibility for this terrible disaster." The jury strongly believed that the commissioners had had "a duty and responsibility of the gravest character" that they had utterly failed to perform. "By the statutes of the commonwealth, the county commissioners have the fullest power to take all necessary steps for most thoroughly examining and testing a reservoir dam. . . . They have authority to call to their aid engineers and experts. . . . They have power to tear down, make alterations and make safe, or cause the same to be done by the owners thereof, and the statutes give to the supreme court full jurisdiction to compel the proprietors to comply with every requirement of the county commissioners." As a result, the jurors were "unable to view the action of the county commissioners in examining and accepting this reservoir dam in any other light than as a superficial discharge of a most important duty."

Every juror signed his name to the judgment that was published in the papers for all to read. The Williamsburg Reservoir dam, which Skinner and his colleagues had owned, had proven to be a spectacular failure on every level. Yet there would be no further legal proceedings. The verdict was in; the case was closed.

One imagines that as Skinner read the verdict, taking it in slowly, perhaps at his desk, a sense of exoneration washed over him even as he might have felt his blood begin to boil, thinking the contractors got off far too easily. No doubt he still wished them dead. Yet for Skinner, the verdict was something he could pick up and put down and be done with. He could have arisen from his desk, buttoned up his coat, and walked downstairs for a conversation with his wife about a new buggy, leaving the verdict in the trash. It didn't bear an ounce of influence on his life, other than confirming a sense of freedom to which he already felt entitled. For those in Skinnerville, however, or those who wished to live in Skinnerville again, one wonders if the verdict, being so open-ended, coming on top of Skinner's decision, which left their lives so open-ended, was akin to a one-two punch. They seemed to have no way to persuade Skinner to stay, and, as of July 4, they had no one to call to account for the injustice that had shattered their world.

"As far as penalty is concerned," concluded the *Boston Daily Globe*, "we suppose it ends here. There is no law that renders any one [involved with this disaster] responsible for [its] damages, a defect in our statute books to be deplored. It is well, however, to know what needs to be done, and one of the most important duties incumbent upon the next session of the legislature will be the enactment of laws covering all such possible contingencies and holding all officials, contractors, firms and individuals to a strict accountability in like cases."

One of the advantages of moving to Holyoke was that Skinner would no longer have to charter, build, invest in, or bear responsibility for a dam. Holyoke's waterpower was controlled entirely by the Holyoke Water Power Company. "Having entered into an indenture with the Company," wrote Judge J. P. Buckland, an expert on the city's infrastructure in the 1870s, the mill owner in Holyoke was "relieved of all anxiety or expense of maintaining the dam and canals, confident of the permanence and safety of the great hydraulic system and secure in the guarantees of the corporation which controls it." The freedom this system offered became even more apparent as the two reservoirs in Goshen and the smaller one in Searsville, all of which Skinner still co-owned, began arousing considerable concern, much to Skinner's frustration.

Following the disaster these remaining reservoirs had been inspected and each one found to be in need of repair, but as of July nothing had been done, and every time it rained, especially when it poured from a "very, very hard thunder storm," anxiety about the reservoirs increased. The summer was proving to be unusually wet. "Rain falls frequently and in profusion," reported the *Hampshire Gazette*. "The ground has seldom been so thoroughly soaked as this season."

On Sunday, July 12, Ellen Littlefield began a letter to her mother: "It is about 4 o'clock, the rain is pouring, it has rained hard most all day to day and yesterday and all night." The storm brought disaster in western Massachusetts. Between the towns of Middlefield and Becket in the Berkshires, two reservoirs were unleashed by the breaking away of a dam, and water inundated a lively factory village that suddenly mirrored hapless Skinnerville. "The damage done by the loosening of their hundred acres of waters was, first, to leave the industries of the little village of Bush Hollow without power; to utterly demolish an old woolen factory, destroy barns and out-buildings, wrench from their foundations and tear apart dwellings, strip the earth of rich gardens and orchards to the bare rocks and leave the roads impassably gullied; making, in fact, a second Skinnerville in its desolation of the bright little village." A few weeks earlier a reservoir dam in the upper reaches of Connecticut's Naugatuck Valley had washed away after a similar storm: "The result was, that when the heavy rain of Sunday night filled the pond, the solid stone-work was carried away from some thirty feet in width and four feet in height. The released water formed a new channel to Mad river, tearing up the door-yards and gardens in a way to remind one of Williamsburg, but doing comparatively little material damage."

Following the downpour in Massachusetts, the owners of the Goshen dams fell to infighting. Repairs cost money, after all, and no one could agree on a proper plan of action. Skinner, of course, usually left reservoir matters up to others, so it's unlikely he was involved in any of the heated discussions. Plus, he wasn't around much. Remarked one man, "I have scarcely seen Mr. Skinner in several weeks." But as a co-owner of the reservoirs, he was still culpable for any harm they might occasion. Furthermore, the owners were being held accountable for all the anxiety people were experiencing. A Northampton citizen, identified only as "L." in the *Hampshire Gazette,* accused Skinner and his colleagues of being "more prominent than any one else in creating a feeling of insecurity and unsafety among a class of the community they should have had an influence to quiet and calm." For the first time since the flood, neighbors openly lambasted the mill owners for incompetence.

In Holyoke not only would Skinner never again have to deal with the politics of owning a reservoir, but he would never be saddled with the impossible expectation that he should help allay the fears of a "class of the community," a burden that he would have resented. There were always going to be people afraid of reservoirs in the Mill River Valley, given the disaster that had occurred, and there was nothing anyone could do about that. Even "L" had to admit this in the end: "If the Goshen waters are finally held back by an adamantine wall as high as heaven and so thick and wide that no engineer can measure them, there will still be a class of the community who will fear to sleep under them."

By mid-July Skinner was making regular trips to Holyoke. Fred Warner often watched him drive away, and later recalled, "For many succeeding weeks and months the horse and buggy was brought to the door early in the morning and Mr. Skinner drove to Northampton, taking the train there for Holyoke where he spent each day superintending the building of the new mill, returning to Skinnerville at night. While the horse plodded along the road, Mr. Skinner could be seen loosely holding the lines, but always in deep study."

The excavations for his new factory were complete by now, and Coghlan & Mullen were well into installing the flume. Timbers were being put into the three wheel pits, bricks were being laid about the sides of the pits, and the raceways were being arched over. Derricks, wheelbarrows, wagons, teams, steam shovels, and all manner of (mostly Irish) laborers were in perpetual motion at the site, laying the foundation for the largest silk mill that Skinner had ever owned.

His former mill had been 130 by 60 feet. The Holyoke manufactory would be 180 by 43 feet. If Skinner was losing a bit in width, he was gaining fifty feet in length, which translated into about 40 percent more room for machinery along the longer shafting. The entire manufactory would be three stories tall and constructed of brick. It would have an ell at one end, measuring 24 by 34 feet, for office, storage, and finishing space, and a wheelhouse at the other end, measuring 12 by 16 feet. Separate from the main building would be a one-story dyehouse, about forty feet square. Just as Hayden, James, and Spelman had declared they would rebuild bigger and better, Skinner was emerging from this crisis as determined to conquer as before. Of singular significance, on the upper floor of the main building he planned eventually to install one hundred handlooms to be operated by skilled male weavers.

So much talk had been going on in the press about Skinner needing to honor the past and stay in Skinnerville with the people who had helped him become a success. But Holyoke was affording him opportunity to honor his past and build on it as never before. Skinner had spent the first part of his life sleeping under or beside a handloom. That mechanism had been the central component of his childhood, directing and defining it. After he escaped to America he probably hadn't seen another silk loom for fifteen years, since almost no one in the country had known how to make one or even how to weave fine silk. But all that was history now. Walking through the city of Paterson these days, with its population of English-born immigrants, one heard the time-honored *clack-clack-clack* (and the trilling of songbirds) emanating from the top floors of silk weavers' cottages. A number of weavers also worked in expansive new "weaving sheds"—mills with entire floors devoted to weaving, where looms lined the walls from end to end. Indeed the production of woven silks seemed destined to be the next great chapter for American silk. Encouraged by the Newtons and the Holyoke Water Power Company, Skinner was thus planning for the future, designing his mill to carry out the entire manufacturing process, from raw silk to finished thread to woven goods.

Specifically he planned on weaving narrow goods, or braids, for trimming. "The superiority of French silk braids for trimming ladies and gentlemen's garments has long been acknowledged," wrote one area reporter, "and silk braids of American manufacture have heretofore been looked upon as undesirable for the purpose of the better class of trade." But Skinner, "having a desire to excel in this as in other branches of silk manufacture," understood the inroads his peers were making and saw his new mill as a chance to take his business to a new level. He also aspired to begin weaving lightweight goods, such as linings for coats and jackets. Given the current unemployment rate in

Paterson, he quite possibly envisioned hiring some of its out-of-work weavers. That would certainly have brought his life full circle. Whereas once, long ago, he had been a slave to the loom, he was suddenly, as a result of the flood, in a position to be its master.

Skinner had begun buying impressive quantities of raw silk, even before all the flood-ravaged silk had been rewound. As a result of the Panic, prices of raw silk had been falling on the open market, and, not knowing how long this would last, Skinner couldn't let the opportunity slip by. "Good silk is always good property," he believed. And so, by mid-July, straw-colored bales of fleecy raw silk had begun arriving at the front door in Skinnerville and were being carried, probably on Fred Warner's and Will Skinner's shoulders, up the stairs for some of the girls to begin sorting. Of course, Skinner had no funds with which to buy the raw silk. He was purchasing everything on credit.

All of this meant progress for Skinner, but for his workers it meant no break, and Ellen was growing weary of the toil. Her summer thus far had been an endless stretch of laboring in a cooped-up environment with the occasional glance out a dormer window to the blighted ground below. She had written her mother on July 12, as rain fell outside, "We have not finished that old silk yet and Mr. S. keeps buying more. It is too bad. I thought I should get away from it this summer but I can't even get out of sight of it on Sunday. Mr. [S.] told us yesterday that we should be in Holyoke in Sept., they have a hundred men at work down there." She paused, thinking about when she could possibly leave. "I don't suppose Mr. S. will want me to go away before he moves nor very soon after, but I ought to stop a while—longer than a week—I am so tired of this."

She couldn't stop, though, and not just because Mr. S. wouldn't have wanted her to. Where there was work to be done there was money to be made, and Ellen, who rarely took time off even under normal circumstances (although she had never worked Sundays), wouldn't have passed up the opportunity to earn more cash. She had already managed to send some money home this summer, out of whatever she had received at the end of May. Her July 12 letter touched on this business. "I will inclose a note for you to sign for the last amount I lent you," she told her mother. And of the money that her father had thus far paid back: "Pa wanted for me to write a receipt for that which he paid me. . . . Could he not write one and send it here for me to sign?" Of the kitchen job she wrote, "I am glad you have got the kitchen begun and hope you will be finished soon. Shall you need any more money for it?"

Ellen had also resumed another old practice: buying finished thread from Mr. Skinner at wholesale, then sending assortments to her mother and sisters. Unlike before, though, the silk now seemed almost a novelty. "I got the silk," wrote her oldest sister, Mary. "Was it some that passed through the flood?"

A better response Skinner could hardly have anticipated. That Mary had to ask if the silk had gone through the flood demonstrates that she couldn't differentiate between the old silk and the new. The old silk was thus proving to be a rather incredible advertisement for quality and a desirable souvenir from the flood-ravaged region. With it, one could weave history into an article of clothing, actually enhancing the costume. The silk had been so well manufactured and revivified in the aftermath that it was as strong, clean, and colorful as before. For all the tremendous agitation that it had suffered in the great wash, Skinner's trademark black thread, for instance, hadn't lost an ounce of its richness. It wasn't spotted or streaky or faded; it wasn't brittle or loose. For all intents and purposes, it was as good as new. Mary was unable to tell if the water had touched it.

A degree of normalcy was beginning to return to the valley. Most people had returned to a certain routine, if possible, and many of the class distinctions that had been blurred in the aftermath of the disaster, when so many were working together for relief, had become clear again. Farmers were back in their fields. Carpenters were on their ladders. Fishermen were in their streams. Mill girls were spinning, mechanics were repairing, and teamsters were driving down the road. The proprietors, for their part, were walking about their sites, managing projects, and traveling, in many cases vacationing.

During July and August mill owners like Skinner often repaired to a resort for a spell, something that had become customary, even representative of an American state of mind. "It is the habit of Americans to go to some watering place every summer," noted Anthony Trollope, who found it amusing that well-to-do Americans showed off their privilege by leaving home and voluntarily living with others in a hotel. But families like the Skinners enjoyed the camaraderie and the benefits of breaking away from routine, and this year proved no exception. Nor did anyone seem to find this unusual. After they left for Hampton Beach, New Hampshire, on July 17 the *Springfield Republican* noted simply, "While the works are building, Mr. Skinner and his family are rusticating at the seaside." Even if his money was less liquid than most and contingent upon the kindness of his bank, Skinner remained among the ranks of the wealthy. Indeed for the first time all summer many would have considered him once again to be lucky: he had the resources to remove his wife and young children, the most susceptible to disease, from a fouled countryside that, as the heat of late summer set in, was expected to grow increasingly infectious.

Unlike in years past, the trip was not a full family affair, as the mansion could not be left unattended. The Van Vechtens were still living in the ell; employees were working between the first and third floors, running up and down the stairs; and Skinner's valuable silk lay everywhere about, in bales, in baskets, on tables, in drawers. Nellie and Nina stayed behind to keep the household running, and to manage the office and paperwork; Fred Warner apparently continued as Skinner's live-in secretary. But Fred couldn't have slept under the same roof as Skinner's two unmarried daughters without a male relative present—especially as a romance was blossoming between him and Nellie—so Will, who had just turned eighteen in June, stayed behind as well.

This was not the Skinners' first trip to Hampton Beach, a resort particularly favored by residents of Williamsburg. Joel Hayden Jr.,

Henry L. James, and Skinner even preferred the same hotel, the Ocean House, which sat atop a bluff at the southern end of the beach. Skinner's friend Hovey came here too. A typical day involved bathing in the ocean in the morning, going out for a drive in the afternoon, and then dancing in the evening. Skinner doesn't seem to have been much of a dancer, but Lizzie was known to do "several figures twice" with Mr. Hovey. Skinner loved to swim; it was his favorite summer activity. Joe loved swimming too and was well on his way to becoming a "splendid swimmer." Lizzie didn't know how to swim—swimming was not a decorous activity for ladies—but she enjoyed bathing, which more or less constituted walking along the water's edge in slippers and maybe wading out into the surf, in a woolen suit, up to her waist. She encouraged her girls to do the same, although they didn't always share her enthusiasm. One of the last times they were there she'd recorded, "Belle & May were frightened [of the water]." Little May had been alive then. Everything had been so different.

Lizzie believed salt air to be restorative. Of a later trip to Atlantic City she wrote, "[I] felt that every breath I drew of the salt air was doing me good so I slept with my window wide open to get it both night and day." Both she and Skinner were "invigorated" by the sea breeze then, and one can only imagine they hoped the air at Hampton Beach this summer would be a similar tonic, clearing their heads and relaxing their hearts, no matter how much they thought about all that was happening back home and in Holyoke. The hotels were all situated on a promontory and "surrounded by the sea except toward the west" so that there was "a constant breeze." Nor would they have had to contend with the mosquitoes and flies that often buzzed about one's head in July, since the hill was just high enough and breezy enough to avoid the intrusion and bother.

In the past absolutely nothing about this place would have reminded the Skinners of home. "It is in some respects, unlike any other upon our Eastern coast," wrote a visitor from Connecticut. "In the centre, a promontory known as Boar's Head, rises abruptly from the sea to the height of about seventy feet, while the beach sweeps off on either side in almost a semicircle." But this year, down along the coastline at least, the scene would have been evocative of the aftermath of the flood. Apart from a smooth sandy beach, the coast "present[ed] the variety of a rocky shore, composed of pebbles from the size of a pea to huge boulders." One of the prevailing questions after the flood was "Where did all of these rocks come from?" The boulders in particular that rumbled down the countryside and lodged like bullets in the ground were simply astonishing to residents of the valley. Some of these boulders had been quietly sleeping for thousands of years beneath vast layers of sediment that the floodwaters in a flash disrupted from their eternal sleep. Near the slaughterhouse of Gleason & Bisbee, upriver from Williamsburg, men had walked around one of these giants with the same degree of wonder as if it had been on display at a world's fair. The relocated boulder was perched atop a hemlock stump, "remote from and ten feet above the present stream," and so overshadowed its pedestal as to resemble an elephant on a toadstool. Fascinated, the men found it to be fifteen feet long, taking up nearly 530 cubic feet and weighing "not less than forty-eight tons." Looking at the giant breakers crashing against the boulders on the shore in New Hampshire would have impressed the Skinners again with the strength of the floodwaters. None of those boulders on the shore was moving an inch.

Skinner stayed at Hampton Beach for eleven days—this may have been a record for his being on vacation—and when he returned home in order to get back to business, Joe went with him. This surprised his older siblings. Nina thought Joe "had too much sense" to come home. Why return to such a dreary place when he could have stayed at the shore another month, exploring the beach for washed-up treasure and swimming for hours? While no answer is given, it's possible that Joe, having experienced the threat of eternal separation during the flood and the mortal danger of water, didn't want to play near the waves that summer and wanted simply to be home with his father.

The child was very likely suffering from what would now be called posttraumatic stress disorder. Following the Buffalo Creek Disaster a century later, in 1972, in which a dam that had impounded a reservoir of coal slurry gave way, precipitating an avalanche of waste that drowned a coal-mining valley in West Virginia, Dr. June Church "described children who refused to bathe for months after the flood, or who screamed if floods were shown on television." At the tender age of eleven going on twelve, Joe had witnessed a similarly horrifying, death-dealing flood—the worst industrial disaster in his country's history at the time, the likes of which not even his father, nearly fifty years old, had ever come close to experiencing. Joe had known so many people who had died in the flood that he couldn't count them on his two hands. He had witnessed people drowning, watched bodies appear and disappear in the water, and seen people screaming from portions of houses hurtling by in the current. In the hours that followed he had watched corpses being carried back and forth in front of his house, succeeded by coffins going by. He had seen grown men like Jerome Hillman prostrate with grief. He had seen mothers like Mrs. Hayden wild with anguish. He had seen grown-ups all around him completely undone, including his own powerful father, who had walked about as if in a daze. He had seen men digging for the dead and would have looked at every pile of debris with a fearful eye, especially near his own house, where people had said bodies were buried. He would have been afraid to breathe the air, even at home, out of fear that the malodorous environment might be infectious. And he heard many a tale about gruesome discoveries, of which there was no shortage and seemed no cessation.

Though most of the dead had been recovered by the end of May, more were found as summer progressed. In early June seven-year-old Rosa Wilson was recovered after the smell of her "much decomposed" body overpowered some passersby. They dug her body out from under a barn. In late June nine-year-old Julia Patrick was discovered in Leeds, "at a place not previously searched, hanging partly to a tree, and partly resting on a pile of rubbish lying against the tree." Images of the dead were also not unheard of; a particularly ghastly stereoview showed the body of a woman draped over a board, lying provocatively on her back with her right arm extending out toward the camera and her legs lying unnaturally beneath her wet dress. (They may have been broken.) These types of images could haunt a man; they certainly could haunt a boy. When Joe and his father returned from the shore they would have learned that another body had been found down in Leeds. There were now 139 confirmed disaster-related deaths. Fortunately this discovery would be the last, or the last one recorded, and the death toll from the flood would rise no higher.

Neither Skinner nor Lizzie nor any of the children who witnessed the flood would ever forget it. Some may have suffered nightmares, headaches, and neuroses. Some may have given in to fits of rage (like Skinner) and been uncharacteristically cross and short-tempered. Some, like Belle and Joe perhaps, may have been more frightened than usual by a storm, a wave, or an accident. With no such thing as therapy, Lizzie, for one, would have relied heavily on her faith. No one in the Skinner family recorded his or her feelings in the aftermath, but it's safe to say that the multitude of horrific memories occasioned by the flood haunted each of them throughout the summer, some more than others. The disaster was simply impossible to avoid, or escape. Fred Howard, a young man in Leeds who tried valiantly to record as much as he could, wrote his brother, "I have only to shut my eyes to see it all over again."

Chapter Fifteen

Coming home from New Hampshire on July 28, Skinner and Joe stopped in Boston for Skinner to attend to some business, and Joe got to see Bunker Hill for the first time. While Skinner read the paper, Joe climbed to the top of the granite monument there, one of the first in the United States, and imagined what it would be like to be staring at an advancing guard of British soldiers. A consummate history buff, Joe was filled with excitement, called out to his father from the top, and may well have recited every battle of the Revolution as they left "Bunk Hill" for the train station. He then slept all the way to Springfield, awakening in time to disembark at Holyoke, where history of another sort would unfold before his eyes.

Father and son had less than an hour to spend in Holyoke, but that was enough for Joe to take in a great deal. "As seen from the Connecticut River Railroad," wrote one journalist, "[Holyoke] is not of an attractive appearance, as the 'flats' lying along the road-bed are used mainly for manufacturing and the wholesale business, but upon reaching High street, the visitor has before him one of the busiest and most attractive localities to be found in any of the interior cities of New

England." High Street was so named because of its "sightly location" midway up the rise of the city. In truth the location wasn't exactly sightly, but the street was lined with great brownstone blocks of stores and shops, and partway down the east side, rising up imperiously, was the future city hall. Since Holyoke had only recently earned its status as a city, construction of the city hall was just beginning (and was already mired in politics), but the building promised to be spectacular. Determined that it should be "unsurpassed by [any other city hall] in the State west of Boston," Holyoke's city council had designed it to resemble nothing less than a cathedral.

On the day of Joe's visit, the dog days of summer had set in, and the city was hotter than ever. Watering carts were trying to keep up with the dust coming off the construction sites, but in some places the streets were still dustier than the poorest country roads. However, the city was effortless to navigate. Unlike much of New York, an incomprehensible maze of streets and alleys that one had either to master or accept getting lost in, Holyoke was a clean grid. A boy could learn his way around here very quickly. Standing on almost any corner, one was confronted with "straight, regular streets lined with the dwellings of laborers, merchants and manufacturers." But not all of the streets had been finished. Some of them ran up the hill north of High Street and then just stopped in the middle of nowhere. Cross-streets similarly vanished. This was a city in the making, its layout being completed as necessary.

Needless to say, uphill from the city center, there wasn't much for Joe to see in the Beech Street area, where, not so long from now, he would be living. Just a bunch of dirt and a lot of men at work, sweating under the implacable sun. And yet because it overlooked the city and was above all the fracas of downtown, this area promised to become the most coveted neighborhood in Holyoke. Already wealthier residents had begun gravitating to the "elevated tract of land beyond the present building limit." Joe wasn't going to have a lot of neighbors at first, but as one of the initial residents up this way, he was going to experience being a pioneer like his father.

Down near the mill, in the manufacturing sector of the city, there was more to see. For starters, there was the upper canal. Like its siblings, the upper canal was a hundred feet across—triple the width of the Mill River. On a day like this, when a boy was hot and sticky and covered in dust from passing teams, the canal must have been an extremely tempting expanse of water, its shimmering surface reflecting Joe's face as he peered over the railing of the bridge into its subtle current. Skinner would have told Joe not to get any ideas; swimming in the canals was dangerous. That said, boys often dipped into them to cool off—naked as jaybirds—much to the dismay of officials. It made the city look bad. When trains passed through, passengers often looked out the windows for the "great dam" that produced "the finest waterpower in the country," but their view could be indecorously compromised by "the spectacle . . . of groups of nude and very muddy boys sporting in the water near the brink."

The mill site was on the corner of Bigelow and Appleton streets, just off the Appleton Street bridge. Joe had seen houses built in Skinnerville. He had watched the new dyehouse go up the previous summer. And depending on the acuity of his memory, he may have recollected some of the construction of the main mill in Skinnerville, although he was a young child at the time. But the sight before him on this late July day was like nothing in his experience. Here was a huge pit, like some underground city, crawling with laborers. There were hundreds of men on the site, climbing ladders, crossing planks, rolling barrels, pushing wheelbarrows, wiping their brows, and engaged in hammering, sawing, framing, building, and shouting. An exciting development: the brickwork, led by L. P. Bosworth, had finally begun. Unlike the handmade bricks used in the old Skinnerville mill, Bosworth's were expertly manufactured with steam power into "superior pressed and sand brick" in his brickyard in South Holyoke. The mill would be rising at the rate of twenty thousand or more bricks per day.

If Joe didn't know already, he would have been told, watching the men tapping and sweeping with their trowels, "The walls of the basement will be 20 inches thick, those of the first story 16 inches and those of the second 12 inches thick." Skinner would also have told Joe, as the boy tried to envision the mill, how he would divide the various departments. The basement would be for sewing silk and machine twist; the first floor for organzine, tram, and cassimere silk; and the second floor for braids of all kinds, to be filled one day with beautiful handlooms imported from England. The basement was not going to be a dark, underground space; it would be sunk only two feet below street level so that it was in every other respect (height, width, fenestration) just like the other floors.

At the moment, the mill had no immediate neighbors on any side. However, to the south, one lot over, was the big new mill of the Farr Alpaca Company. Only a few months old, this mill, like Skinner's, was introducing another industry to town. The wool of the alpaca from the Peruvian Andes had achieved notoriety in England and Canada, and a Canadian manufacturer, Herbert Farr, seeing both a market for alpaca in America and more hospitable tariff laws, had brought his business south to Holyoke. Already, with the help of skilled English and Canadian operatives charged with training local workers, the company was producing twenty thousand yards of lustring a week.

Joe might have found it hard to imagine living here, after growing up in Skinnerville. Where would he go hunting? Would he be able to find arrowheads in the ground here? And what about his friends? But he would be able to make new ones at school and at church and do a lot of the same things he'd always done. There was dancing and ice skating, just as at home, and baseball and swimming in the summer in the parks and ponds around the city. Yes, it might take some adjustment, but Holyoke was brimming with activity, inside and out, and right up to the end of his visit Joe witnessed how alive and unexpected the place was.

At the depot, waiting for the next Northampton-bound train with his father, Joe saw a horse go wild and heard a lot of screaming. In a split second his father grabbed the horse's halter and stopped the horse in the street before anyone could be thrown from the carriage.

"I caught a run away horse," Skinner later told Lizzie, with remarkable aplomb, "and prevented a great smash up." Unfortunately that wasn't the last of the excitement. No more than an hour after this episode, after Will had picked them up at the Skinnerville depot, they were just coming down the hill when the buggy fell apart (again), the king bolt breaking and everyone being thrown over the dashboard as the horse took off without them. No one was hurt, thankfully, but still, that made two near-fatal accidents in a single day. "It is wonderful how we escaped," wrote Skinner. "We all rolled in the dirt & poor Joe did not know if he should cry or not—but thank God we all escaped."

It must have been a relief for Joe when they finally arrived back home. He could fall into the arms of his sisters, then run upstairs and plop down on his own bed, so glad to be in his room again. That night around the dinner table, in the familiar old dining room with its large fireplace and gas-lit sconces, and with its large bay window looking out onto the blackness of a quiet country night, Holyoke may have seemed a world away, but it was all anyone could talk about. Will had been to Holyoke himself just the week before, checking out the place with some friends and, after looking at where the mill and house were to be and having dinner at one of the city's restaurants, found that he "liked the place very much." In fact, second to his father, he may have been the most enthusiastic about it.

At eighteen, Will was enthralled with city life in general and, even without the flood, may have been ready to leave his small-town existence behind. But the teenager also closely followed the vicissitudes of his father's operation. Despite his indifference to school, Will was intensely interested in the business of making money. When he was thirteen he had raised a calf and sold it for $50, then opened his own savings account to earn interest on the amount. Within a year, after other small ventures, he was a rich young man with $100 in savings. He had a genuine aptitude for making decisions that generated income, and he had inherited his father's desire to rise in the world. More than his younger brother, who loved nature and history and science, Will loved finance and trade. He seems to have understood what Holyoke could offer his father and his family, recognizing the city as a passport out of disaster.

On July 28, the day Skinner arrived home, he might have read with interest that the Holyoke firm of Delaney & Sons had been awarded a $50,000 to $60,000 contract for rebuilding all the bridge abutments and retaining walls in the town of Williamsburg, as well as most of the town's roads affected by the flood. While the award of the contract was understandable—they were expert contractors, consistently employed throughout the region—the fact that Holyoke men were going to be the ones rebuilding the infrastructure of Williamsburg was uncomfortably ironic. Several villagers must have been disgusted that even more Holyokers were going to profit from their disaster. But some solid reconstruction work was about to commence, and that, at least, was a good thing.

Skinner would have been pleased to hear that the road through Skinnerville was going to be repaired at last, and the river confined to its course once again. Since the departure of his business would render the area vacant of enterprise, all his land here was about to be worthless, and he was personally facing thousands of dollars in loss in real estate. Anything that could be done to salvage a sense of opportunity here, he welcomed tremendously. Upon returning from vacation he even met with the county commissioners about how best to restore the area. He looked at surveys and helped lay out the new highway. He shared some of his earlier plans— he would have rebuilt his mill across the street, at a safer distance from the river—and he apparently suggested that a lumber mill go up in that location. A lumber mill wouldn't require anyone to build boardinghouses, tenements, or a school, but it would provide the impetus for restoring the water privilege at this spot and give rise to some much needed activity.

Unfortunately, Skinner's involvement in these discussions gave him one more headache that he didn't need. Some nosy reporter completely misconstrued the details of his meeting with the commissioners, and one of the very first news items that splashed across the page in August's papers announced that William Skinner was going to rebuild in Skinnerville. Such was the interest that this generated that Skinner had to take time out from his more important business in Holyoke to set the record straight back home. "All talk," he said, of his rebuilding a mill at Skinnerville, "was simply gammon." A new mill dam was going to be built and a lumber mill put up nearby, "but no silk mill."

Life was moving on. Mrs. Van Vechten gave birth on August 3 to a little girl named Flossie, the last baby to be born in the mansion in Skinnerville. Another guest arrived at this time as well: eighteen-year-old Isabel "Izzy" Skinner, George's eldest child. Izzy arrived with a healthy dose of tales from her past year in an upstate New York seminary where they spoke nothing but French. (Upon hearing that his daughter was going to a school where they spoke French "all the time," George had mildly protested, "Speak French—I want to have her *speak English correctly*.") In concert with their cousin's arrival, the Skinner children threw a "sheet and pillow party" for thirty friends, with refreshments in the sitting room and music by a local string band. Socials, in other words, were back in swing, as were other summer activities: picking berries, making jam, playing ball. The *Hampshire Gazette* reported, "This is the season for cross babies, scolding housewives, mad dogs, crickets, green apples and bowel complaints." Little else was of note, the lack of eventfulness a blessing to all.

Ellen Littlefield, exhausted, left Skinnerville to visit with family for a few weeks. Perhaps unrealistically she and the other girls had expected Skinner to pay them as he always had, on the third Saturday of each month, for the previous month's work. Consequently she had fully expected to receive a pay envelope in July for her work during June, but Skinner had gone away on vacation without paying anyone anything. On July 23, in the last throes of daylight, Ellen had written her mother, "It is getting to be quite dusky. . . . It is 8 weeks to night since I came back and Mr. Skinner has not paid me nor any of the girls for our work since the flood. I thought he would certainly pay last Saturday but he went away last Friday and there was nothing said about it, therefore I don't know when I can send any [money] to you. I have not paid any board yet. I think he must pay us before long." Nothing Skinner was doing was predictable. Then again, neither was his income. He was dependent on lines of credit and whatever sales he could make in the city from salvaged silk. When he finally paid Ellen in August, he paid her in full for all of her work in May, June, and July, a total of $89.99, the fattest pay envelope she had ever received.

Skinner spent the end of the summer in perpetual motion, bouncing between Northampton, Holyoke, New York City, and Paterson. With Luther Bodman he closed his account with the finance committee, having dispensed a total of $12,000 to his villagers. While the relief fund had never reached $100,000, the $75,683 that was received was nevertheless remarkable, given that it had come almost entirely from individual donations, some as small as 50 cents. In Holyoke Skinner finished plans for the dyehouse and machine shops with the architect Luce. He oversaw the mill reaching its third story, the cornices being put on, and the roofers arriving to finish the building. Around August 12 he headed down to New York City for the third quarterly meeting of the Silk Association. His colleagues found him in much better shape than in June, and a few of them might have been jealous of the state-of-the-art mill he was about to have, complete with the latest kinds of machinery he was ordering from Paterson.

By mid-August Joel Hayden Jr. was back in Holyoke. "The projected new brass works is a sure thing," declared the *Springfield Union* on August 18, explaining that in Holyoke "enough money ha[d] been secured already to guarantee their erection." A few days later the paper reported, "Joel Hayden was in town, in consultation with businessmen all Saturday. What was up, does not transpire, but rumor has started."

Hayden's somewhat exasperating lack of resolve unfortunately encouraged other cities to keep campaigning for his business. Norwich, Connecticut, sent a delegation to present Hayden with the offer of a $50,000 brick factory—which the citizens of Norwich themselves would pay for—if he moved to their city. This was an incredible offer, and the citizens of Norwich, fully expecting Hayden to be on the return train with their delegates to tour the town, "assembled in crowds at the depot with two bands of music" to greet him. But Hayden rejected that offer—flat out rejected a free, $50,000 brick factory—without so much as discussing it, telegraphing the fact that, behind closed doors, talks were indeed advancing with Holyoke.

"Business is looking up in the village," the *Hampshire Gazette* reported on Haydenville, "and at no distant day the devastated portion will show few traces of the great disaster. Building has already commenced and transactions in real estate are lively." The hotel had been rebuilt. Individual shop owners were repairing, rebuilding, and improving their properties. Others were buying flood-destroyed lots to put up new homes and businesses. For once the brass works wasn't the news here. The news was the *life* that was in this village and the willingness of its residents—a clear sign to Hayden—to reinvest in it.

Skinnerville bore no such signs of reconstruction and, apart from one road crew, had little activity. Houses remained gaping wrecks, and some still stood at impossible angles. Grass poked up here and there, undaunted, but sand and rocks still suffocated most of the fields. Some trees had branched out into flower, and stacks of firewood met the eye in places, small signs of domesticity, but nothing even remotely resembling the village of yore was evident. Certainly no one was rebuilding anything. Consequently, despite the routines that had developed and the stopping in on neighbors to say hello, as people used to do, there remained a deep and irreversible foreboding about the place. At some point soon Skinner would be taking his family and his business away forever. More symbolic yet, he would be taking his house with him too.

In late August Lizzie returned from the shore with her young girls, refreshed and relaxed, in stark contrast to everyone else, and began to prepare for the big move. It was time to begin organizing the contents of her house and making the endless decisions of what to keep, give away, or throw out. It was time to find a house in Holyoke to rent as the family's own was being rebuilt, and it was also time to meet with the architect about updating the mansion during the rebuilding process. The Skinners were moving to a city, away from a troubled past and into what they hoped would be a bright future, and Lizzie wanted her home to reflect this change, both inside and out.

While the family was on holiday, Clarence Luce had drawn up some plans for the house, perhaps on Skinner's request, but Lizzie had little desire to work with a young man, not yet twenty-three, whose primary interest was designing industrial buildings. William Fenno Pratt, the home's original architect, was rehired. Besides, Pratt had a personal connection to Lizzie's family that involved a historical understanding of the silk industry, since he had shared the extraordinary experience of trying to raise silkworms in Jamaica. More than most folks, he appreciated how far the American silk trade had evolved from its agrarian days, and he understood Lizzie's desire for her home to stand out as the residence of a promising silk manufacturer and his family.

Significant changes would be made to the exterior to capture the full essence of its Second Empire style, the preeminent architectural mode in America at this time. This style was based on Parisian architecture and was notable for its effusive ornamentation and grand proportions. The mansion was already rich in both, boasting pedimented dormers, large bay windows, decorative finials, bold cornices, and a great deal more. But the most notable feature of the mansion was its mansard roof, modeled on the roof of the Louvre, and in no small part because of its prominence would play a key role in the redesign. Where in Skinnerville the base of the roof flared out, the new base would be straightened to yield a more dignified effect. In addition, decorative iron casting would be added to the roof's perimeter, effectively crowning the house. Most significantly, a tower would be added to the façade, its cupola rising fully six feet above the roofline. This tower would announce, like nothing else, that the house represented a different chapter in the lives of its occupants. The mansion would still be an ambassador of the Second Empire style, just as the Skinners were still the family they had always been, but in Holyoke neither would be the same. They would both be more ambitious.

While the mill was being roofed and slated, grading had commenced on the lot for the house. This acre of land was not simply removed from the activity of downtown but spectacularly situated with a commanding view of the city. The *Holyoke Transcript* would one day describe its lordly eminence thus: "In its original location the house faced west; now it looks towards the east; originally it stood upon the border of a valley with high land rising up in the rear; here it occupies a conspicuous eminence and from its front piazza can be seen almost the entire city, the Hadleys and other towns beyond the river, while from the cupola are visible the city of Springfield, and this entire region." At least as satisfactory to the Skinner family, the property was nowhere near a river or canal and was in no danger of ever being flooded. Indeed there was hardly any water in the area at all, which is why the city had to extend sewer and water lines to the plot this month. So undeveloped was the area that directly behind the house's future site contractors were still excavating the landscape.

No description exists of the interior of the house prior to the flood, but much is known of its plan afterward. The parlor, library, and sitting room would be frescoed. Several of the upstairs rooms would be "beautifully painted in party colors," meaning multiple colors. Skinner's bedroom, by contrast, would be white. None of the layout would change. Skinner's bedroom would remain on the first floor, second door on the right off the front hall. However, his large bay window would face north now, instead of south, and, as opposed to looking out at the pig in John Coogan's backyard (as it did in Skinnerville), Skinner would "[command] a view of his own mill and nearly the entire city north of it." His bedroom would also have "every necessary furnishing, a spacious wardrobe, closet, and a bath room." As in Skinnerville, the whole house would be fitted with speaking tubes, so that Skinner could communicate with Will and Joe on the third floor, telling them to get up out of bed, without leaving his own. Eleven of the mansion's fourteen rooms would be serviced with electric bells that communicated directly with the kitchen. The house would be equipped with a state-of-the-art "steam heating apparatus" in the basement that would supply heat to the north side of the house (including Skinner's bedroom); the other half of the house would rely on chimneys that had been so improved that "fires [could] be run six months without clearing." The house would have indoor plumbing, of course, and the washroom would be outfitted with several soapstone sinks and its own boiler. Even the two coal rooms in the basement (next to the remodeled wine cellar) were going to be "furnished with every convenience."

But before any transformation could take place, Lizzie had to pack up all those fourteen rooms, plus the kitchen and cellar. "The most important thing to remember when you move from one house to another is not to lose your head," advised a contemporary *Scribner's Monthly*. "This being well secured, you may verify the adage and find the ordeal not worse than three fires." As summer came to an end, the hallways became cluttered with washtubs, bins, barrels, and boxes filled with china, utensils, boots, frying pans, dolls, needlework, samplers, pillows, linens, towels, books, and more. All of this required Lizzie to do a great deal of labeling and organizing so as to lose neither her mind nor her temper, and her handwriting would have raced across boxes with inscriptions such as "China Closet—breakfast cups and saucers" or "Nursery—blankets and extra rattles." Yet having already spent the summer in a house turned upside down from ruin, with everything in disarray, she may have found it more of a relief than a disruption to get things organized and moving at last. She had precisely a month to get everything ready. With the mill projected to open in mid-October, the family planned to move to Holyoke around October 1.

Chapter Sixteen

At the beginning of September shipments of silk machinery began to arrive in Holyoke from the machine shops in Paterson. These giant crates were hauled over the Appleton Street bridge to the mill, where they were left to be opened on Skinner's authority. There were *a lot* of crates.

Skinner had had to go looking for every kind of machinery he had previously used. The process whereby raw silk is turned into thread, preparatory to being dyed and packaged for market, is loosely termed *throwing,* from the Saxon *thrawan,* meaning "to twist." A mill like Skinner's needed winding, cleaning, doubling, spinning, reeling, and stretching machines, and sometimes more than one type of each, since different models produced different threads. In all, Skinner purchased seventy-one throwing machines at this time, nearly all of them exhibiting the very latest in technology. None of these machines even remotely resembled the machinery he had first seen in Vallentine's silk mill. Back then, in the 1840s, one of the more exciting advancements had been a silk spinner invented by Harvey Holland's father, Harrison Holland. It was a wooden, manually operated machine, patented with six spindles.

The current models that Skinner was buying were vibration-resistant, iron-framed apparatuses with hundreds of spindles. Current models were also notable for their speed and sophistication, which enabled "the employment of cheaper, less skilled workers." In Holyoke, Skinner would not have to rely on his workers skillfully manipulating the thread as much as he would need them simply to operate the new machinery. He wouldn't need to find girls who were smarter than average and required higher pay, just those who were nice, reliable, and trainable.

Because the silk industry was one of the few growing industries in the United States at that time, machine shops that had never before produced silk machinery were now trying their hand at doing so and designing some of the most exciting silk machinery to date. In Paterson, the Danforth Locomotive & Machine Company, which had previously serviced the railroad industry, was perfecting a double-decker silk spinner that would be twice as fast as its European and American counterparts. Whereas the spindles on other machines rotated at 3,500 revolutions per minute, beyond which the machines lost their stability and reliability, the spindles on the Danforth frame would revolve "with ease 7,000 or 8,000 revolutions." To compare such machinery with Holland's spinning frame, from the days of the *Morus multicaulis* mania, was to grasp how far American silk machinery had advanced. One expert, Linus Brockett, declared, "Our American silk manufacturers . . . have long enjoyed the reputation of having improved materially on the European machinery . . . but the throwing machines built by the Danforth Locomotive & Machine Co. at Paterson, are greatly in advance of any other produced in Europe or America." When considering the changes that had taken place, Skinner himself once expressed "a feeling of surprise much akin to awe." To have a new mill with the most modern machinery would have been thrilling.

Skinner must have been one of the biggest customers in Paterson that season. At least thirteen other silk mills went up that year, but they were not all on the same scale as Skinner's. In Maine, a new concern called the Haskell Silk Company was going up along the Presumpscot River, but to hedge its bets, the company was starting small, building a mill just fifty feet square and spending $12,000 on machinery and supplies. More than three times the size of the Haskell mill, Skinner's new manufactory required not only more machines and materials but also greater variety, thus necessitating, one can reasonably assume, a budget three times the size, or about $36,000.

As for the structural components of the mill, the Holyoke Machine Company was supplying all the gearing, shafting, gas fitting, and plumbing, as well as the all-important turbine, or water wheel. Being responsible for all the motive power in the mill, the turbine was the single most critical component of the entire operation. The success of its design was paramount to productivity. Every angle of every blade, every inch of its curb, every subtlety imaginable affected the turbine's horsepower and ability to translate power. Skinner was as well versed as any manufacturer in the advantages of various turbines, but deciding on one had always included a lot of guesswork because there was no way to know how a model would function before it was installed, at which point the manufacturer had already purchased it and was stuck with it. But in the previous four years another type of revolutionary advance had taken place. A man named Emerson had devised a "testing flume" that scientifically determined the efficiency of each model on the market, and his facilities, which received turbines from all over the country, were in none other than downtown Holyoke, providing an invaluable resource especially for local machinists. Rather than purchase a turbine in the dark, Skinner could now look through Emerson's catalogue of data, choose a model that would best fit the needs of his mill (he wanted a fifty-inch Risdon wheel), and commission a replica from the Holyoke Machine Company. The latter was currently at work on that very wheel.

As often happens, the original estimate for the cost of the mill ($32,000) was turning out to be unrealistic, but not by much. In round figures the shafting and gearing was costing $3,500, the water connection $7,000, and the buildings themselves $26,000. The mill site was worth an additional $6,000, which made the total value of the new silk mill property about $44,000. Incredibly, Skinner wouldn't have to pay a penny until his interest payments commenced the following year.

Factoring in machinery, the cost of the new enterprise soared to a minimum of $80,000 (in modern figures at least $14 million), and Skinner was getting virtually all of it on credit. When the Mercantile Agency came around again in early September to follow up on the valley's businessmen and assess their efforts to reestablish themselves, the reporter who took Skinner's case seems to have been at a loss for encouraging words. All he could summon for present and future creditors was the tepid comfort: "He . . . has been successful in business."

George Skinner returned to Skinnerville on September 2. This successful man had a way of showing up at just the right time, and he couldn't have been in Skinnerville more than a few hours when he joined his brother for a ride in a palace car down to Holyoke with the directors of the railroad. The purpose of the excursion was ostensibly to inspect a portion of the track in Holyoke, but that doesn't explain why a palace car would have been needed or why so much reveling ensued within that plush, wood-paneled interior. Young Will noted in his diary that night, "They had plenty of champagne."

The Skinner brothers liked their liquor—so much so in George's case that he would eventually die from too much of it—but future concerns were far away, and they had cause to celebrate just now. William's mill was nearly finished; the machinery was on its way. And if Skinner needed any more confirmation that he had made the right decision, the Mill River was once again so dry it was making the news, the plentiful rains of June and July having entirely disappeared during sweltering August. On September 1 the river was so low that "it ha[d] not furnished enough water to keep the Florence Mills running full force." The drought would continue for several more weeks, during which time those relying on the river for power would have to fire up their steam engines. Even later in the fall a correspondent would report, "Williamsburg wants water. One would suppose after the experience of last May that this would be the last thing she would sigh for. But she needs it . . . for her mills."

Despite all that Skinner had accomplished thus far, there was still much to be done, and the day after their escapade the brothers reviewed a great many particulars. They returned to Holyoke by themselves. On the agenda at the moment was a tenement block for some of Skinner's workers. The Water Power Company had provided land west of the mill for workers' housing, and Luce had designed a ten-house tenement block for Skinner, modeled on others in the neighborhood. Each house was to be a three-story brick row house with a small yard out back. Fifty teams were already grading the site, and based on the appearance of so many men and horses working the ground, all would have seemed to be moving ahead. However, Skinner had finally come up against a wall in the form of a shortage of funds. He wanted to build the block for $12,000, but no contractor would agree to so cheap a price and Skinner was unwilling—or unable—to offer more. He had a lot of expenses piling up suddenly, the kind he couldn't pay on credit. He had to pay for the removal of his house to Holyoke, purchase a boardinghouse for his single female operatives, and lease a cottage for his family. He had had an estimated $14,000 in cash, stocks, and bonds at the time of the flood, but he had already used up most of the cash paying his workers back in May, and he was looking at housing and moving expenses of well over $20,000.

Enter George.

Worth over a quarter of a million, George may have had more than just a filial interest in his older brother's rebuilding efforts. He had been one of the first to put cash in William's hands after the disaster and may well have acted as a financial backer as William moved forward. Rumor had it the following year that Skinner was "supposed to be assisted by his bro. Geo. B. Skinner [of] New York & Yonkers." If so, that must have been an extremely uncomfortable turn of events for William, who hated accepting money from anyone (least of all his own brother). Was the rumor true? Did William accept the assistance that George surely offered? William would staunchly declare of this period, "I never asked a man to indorse a note or me," and that as a result he did not owe any man a dollar—including, presumably, George.

How William covered all of his expenses in the fall of 1874 is impossible to know, but two things are certain: first, he figured out a way, and second, George was in on the plan. Later, in the 1880s, the tide would turn and William would be in a position to bail out George in a significant fashion. Sadly, by that time George had wasted all of his own opportunities. His luck had run out and his money too. William's action looked more like a big brother coming to the rescue. But it may have been something of a payback.

Looking ahead, Skinner's workforce was about to change considerably, but he was fortunate that several of his former operatives were following him to Holyoke. About a dozen men would be going back on the payroll, or more than half his male workforce. All of his dyers would be working at the new mill, as well as his mechanic, superintendent, bookkeeper, at least one of his overseers, and a handful of others. These men were Skinner's highest-paid, highest-ranking employees. Most of them had families, and it was for them that Skinner needed to build that tenement block. As for his female operatives, about a dozen of them would be moving to Holyoke as well, but considering that he had employed more than forty women the year before, he would be moving to Holyoke with a very small number of his former female hands. In fact he would be starting up with fewer women and girls than he had in his very first mill, back in 1854. The *Springfield Union* reported enthusiastically, and erroneously, "[The new silk mill] will give employment to about 200 hands, most of whom were employees of Mr. Skinner at Skinnerville." In reality "only a few employees moved to Holyoke from

Skinnerville and the rest [of those eventually employed in the mill] were Irish and American men and women trained to their jobs here [in Holyoke]."

Some of the workers who had found temporary work in other mills during the summer, intending to move with Skinner, changed their minds and stayed where they were. Ed Bartlett, for instance, had decided to remain with the Heminway Silk Company in Watertown, Connecticut. Others, such as Fred and Jerome Hillman, would simply remain in the Skinnerville area. Some girls who had found employment in a silk mill at Warehouse Point, Connecticut, had also decided not to return to Skinner's employ—until their new mill suffered a terrible fire in December that left them out of work once more. At that point they all started toward Holyoke, sending a telegram to Skinner informing him of the fire and "asking him not to disappoint them." Skinner hired them all back.

One might have expected Aurelia Damon to stay in Skinnerville, given her cozy home on the opposite side of the river, but she needed a job, not least as she had sole responsibility for her aged mother, and as September advanced she began making preparations to move. Like Ellen Littlefield, Aurelia was going to Holyoke, and she would be moving into the boardinghouse that Skinner soon purchased down by the canals. A large brick building that Skinner bought fully furnished for $7,500, the boardinghouse was not far from the Holyoke Water Power Company, but although it had acquaintance with that powerful headquarters, it was on Mosher Hill, a decidedly shady part of town. On August 15 the *Holyoke Transcript* had this to report: "Some of the residents of Mosher Hill say they can hardly realize that they live in one of the most enterprising cities in the world when they try to grope their way home on a dark night and find the hill lit up with one solitary glimmer. They hope the day is not far off when the city will give them some lamp-posts and shed a little more light on their dark ways. And the same parties suggest that they need more hydrants to protect that section in case of fire. The locality is building up rapidly and the houses fill with tenants as fast as they can be completed, and its interest should be cared for."

It was one thing to walk along a country road at night in the dark, but something else entirely to walk along a city street under those conditions. In August Holyoke's police "brought eighty-four cases into the police court, the largest number of arrests [in the city] they ha[d] ever made in one month." Apart from drunkenness, the police arrested men and women "for assault, malicious mischief, fornication, larceny, and trespass." This was what Aurelia and Ellen, whose greatest worry had hitherto been bedbugs, had to look forward to in their new surroundings. Mosher Hill was poor, crowded, dangerous after dusk, and largely neglected by city hall. Still, it was elevated. Of a street down by the water, Aurelia later told Ellen, "I could never think for a moment of going into a house on that street. I could never live in a house below high water mark, and it is so near the canal that the air would be bad." Nor was Mosher Hill as awful as "the Patch," where the Irish lived in shanties, or "Frenchville," where the French Canadians lived in equally abysmal conditions, but combined, these poverty-stricken neighborhoods revealed a vastly different city from the "land of golden opportunity" that the Holyoke Water Power Company conveyed to prospective manufacturers. Within a year state agents for the Bureau of Statistics of Labor would report:

> Holyoke has more and worse large tenement houses than any manufacturing town of textile fabrics in the state, and built in such a manner that there is very little means of escape in case of fire. The sanitary arrangements are very imperfect. . . . Portions of yards are covered with filth and green slime. . . . [One block] has eighteen tenements, with ninety rooms, occupied by nearly two hundred people; and yet there are only two three-feet doorways on the front. . . . Our agents visited some tenements having bedrooms into which neither air nor light could penetrate, as there were no windows and no means

of ventilation, and some of them were actually filthy. It is no wonder that the death-rate in 1872 was greater in Holyoke than in any large town in Massachusetts, excepting Fall River, and if an epidemic should visit them now, in the state they are in, its ravages would be great.

In late September 1874 a story was making the rounds that a conductor on the Connecticut River Railroad asked one of his passengers where he was going. The man replied, "Going to hell," after which "the conductor opened the door and said to the brakeman: 'See that that man gets out at Holyoke.'"

In the end, the boardinghouse on Mosher Hill, run by the previous owner, Mrs. Wait, was the only housing Skinner contracted for in Holyoke. His brother Thomas, Nash Hubbard, John Ellsworth, James Hibbert (who returned from England), and others with families found their own housing when they arrived in the city that month and, for the first time in their careers as Skinner employees, began paying rent to someone other than Skinner. Many chose to live across the river in the town of South Hadley, which might have been cheaper. It was certainly less congested.

Gone, then, was the old-fashioned, tight-knit silk mill community that everyone had known in Skinnerville. In Holyoke it became clear right away that they would all be leading lives independent of one another. The only geographical space that Skinner and his workers would share was the block off Appleton Street where, on October 15, at 7 a.m., they would all begin working again.

Back in June, Skinner's decision to move to Holyoke had upset people, but at least he had made up his mind. As of mid-September Hayden still hadn't made up his. He just couldn't say no to Holyoke. Even Jacob Hills began talking about moving to the city, because the relocation of the brass works seemed inevitable and he wanted to keep his job. Hayden's negotiations with the Holyoke Water Power Company continued, and the Newtons had begun making water connections to an agreed upon site. Throughout the city businessmen were beginning to bank on the deal. An advertisement for a shoe shop exclaimed, as if the brass works was already halfway in town:

HAYDEN, GE—!
Buy Your
Boots and Shoes
Of
!!! CORSER !!!

But then, out of nowhere, "the negotiations were suddenly suspended," and Hayden walked away from the table for good.

No matter how much he stood to gain by moving to Holyoke, he finally decided to rebuild on the original site "to avoid total loss of value in [his company's] connecting property, . . . water privilege, Tenement houses, etc." He didn't want to lose more money than he already had and felt that the safest way to preserve capital was to stick with the tried and true. He decided to invest in the future of Haydenville, a village that had made his father one of the richest men in the state. Right there at home he resolved to make the brass works bigger and better than ever and continue with business as usual. His men had been working nonstop in their makeshift quarters since just after the flood. If being in Haydenville hadn't slowed down their work this summer, why should it ever?

Hayden's partners, Sereno Kingsley and Collins Gere, must have been involved in the decision-making process, but their input is less than clear. For some time now Collins Gere hadn't even been on the east coast. At the beginning of September he returned from a trip to Ohio. Exactly why he was in Ohio, and how long he had been there, is unknown. It's possible he was investigating other opportunities for the company. Regardless, he didn't remain long in Haydenville after coming back, immediately leaving for some trout fishing on the Androscoggin River in Maine. Hayden may have wished he could do the same, but for the first time in years he wasn't going anywhere. And Jacob Hills, like countless others, would have been overjoyed at that fact. Hayden was digging in his heels for the long term, and the Hills family could settle down for good in Haydenville, saying good-bye to Skinnerville but embracing a new chapter in their lives, right next door.

On October 1 the last brick was placed in the chimney at Skinner's Holyoke mill. The outside work was nearly complete, almost all of the windows had been installed, and the last slates had been put on the roof. Inside, work continued at a furious pace. The floors were being laid, the water pipes were being put into position, and the walls were being plastered. All of the silk that the girls up at the mansion had been working on had been shipped down to Holyoke. The first carloads of furniture from the mansion had also been shipped down and placed in the "very pretty" cottage that Skinner had rented on Chestnut Street. Nina had left for her junior year at Vassar, accompanied by Libbie, who was entering the college's preparatory program. The Van Vechtens had moved out. The great move was set to begin.

On Friday October 2, Lizzie dressed the younger children in their traveling clothes and walked around her house one last time. With the baby perhaps in her arms, she ran her hands absently along sills and doorframes and went over last-minute details with the movers, who would send a final carload in another few days. Finally, she ushered the family outside so that they wouldn't miss their train. Will drove everyone to the depot in their brand-new buggy, which Skinner had purchased in preparation for the move, and, at the appointed hour, the Skinners rode out of town, with a small window—maybe two minutes—to linger on the landscape one final moment before the train puffed south beyond Skinnerville and they were on their way to Holyoke. After watching them leave, Will turned the buggy around and began driving to Holyoke, passing the now emptied house as he did so, the last Skinner to see it standing there. That evening he recorded in his diary, "Pulled up stakes and left Haydenville."

One wonders if any neighbors came to say good-bye, and if so, how many. There weren't many left in the village at this point. Among others, the Kaplingers had gone. The Bartletts had finally left. The Hubbards had long since gone (but would be moving on to Holyoke). Captain Hayden and his wife had found a home elsewhere. Thomas Skinner and his family were probably in Florence with Rosamond's family, awaiting the start-up of the new mill. The Hibberts were in England. The Hillses were in Haydenville. Those who had been living in tents had surely dispersed by now, and the tents taken down and returned. Out of two hundred people who had started the year together in Skinnerville, only about fifty adults and children remained as autumn began.

Directly after the family left, a team of six men showed up at the house and began taking it apart, which occasioned "no small share of public interest." This was, after all, a three-story, five-chimney, 12,000-square-foot house. Lizzie would later claim that "superstition" had persuaded her husband against building a brand-new home because "there was a saying that if you built a house after you were fifty, you would not live to move into it." Perhaps, but it was also a lot cheaper to save the old one, rather than invest in building a new one, especially after Skinner had found a contractor in Holyoke, William C. Walton, who agreed to move the house and resurrect it "in exactly its present condition, besides improvements," for just $7,000. Apart from Walton and the Skinners, however, few realistically believed this building could just be upped and moved away, and definitely not for so paltry a sum. The house's original contractor flatly declared the project "could not be done." Even as the dismantling got under way, "there rose up a race of prophets . . . who predicted, if not the failure of the enterprise, at least the failure of the rash contractor who had engaged, for a consideration of $7,000[,] to place the huge structure upon its destined site." One didn't need to be a carpenter to appreciate the challenge.

Walton walked through every room in the house and "carefully calculated" the entire job. He marked the first floor A, the second floor B, and the third floor C. Then he gave each room a name and labeled each object in each room "with reference to a certain corner." The *Holyoke Transcript* was hugely impressed by all of this. "This numbering, including the windows and cases, and boards and joists and flooring, was carefully transcribed in a book which doubtless constituted the strangest and most nearly perfect plan from which a builder has ever before erected a residence." All the woodwork in the house was "of black walnut, oak and butternut, highly finished and filled," and in order to preserve this woodwork, the doorframes and window casings were going to be "carefully removed, by tearing off the lath, and sawing off the studs, [and taken] down entire." The marble mantels, extraordinary showpieces throughout the house of Italian and Tennessee colored marbles, also were going to be removed whole and shipped in one piece. Walton would need twenty-five railroad cars to transfer the bulk of the materials. The mansion's bay windows posed one of the bigger challenges, since they were too large to fit on the train. They were going to demand "careful loading" onto wagons drawn by teams, with every bridge along the way being measured beforehand to ensure the load would fit across. Once the inside work was done, men would scale the roof and begin to take that apart. Then the walls would come down, the frame would be dismantled, and finally the cellar would be gutted.

Everyone knew that once the mansion was gone, Skinnerville itself would be gone. Watching the mansion come apart was like witnessing a death, and as parts of the house began actually to be taken away, those outside the village began to experience the loss as well—and they didn't like it. One of the first spectacles people saw was Skinner's bay windows going by. The parade of wagons wound slowly down the valley, all the way to Northampton, and then turned south onto the highway for

Holyoke. Proclaimed Northampton's *Free Press,* "Mr. Skinner is indeed leaving us with a vengeance."

October 15, the day the mill was supposed to open in Holyoke, proved to be just another day of construction. Despite the blistering pace at which the suppliers and laborers were proceeding, things had simply taken longer than expected, as was normal for any big construction job (except the removal of the house, which was proceeding like clockwork). Skinner was personally superintending the installation of the machinery, while the Holyoke Machine Company had placed the turbine in position and was now working on the shafting. The wheelhouse had been roofed, the steam piping had been installed, and the floors were nearly finished. Out on Bigelow Street men were "laying 600 feet of 4 inch gas pipe" to supply the mill with illumination.

Skinner was also keeping an agitated eye on the completion of the office wing, the basement of which was being made into a "fire and burglar proof vault" for storing silk. When questioned about the necessity of the vault, Skinner told the *Springfield Union,* "[I have] more fear of burglars than of fire, and with good reason." Although the *Union* didn't go on to say what Skinner's rationale was, one supposes that the activity in Holyoke's police court was evidence enough. Skinner also told the *Union* that some of his mill girls had already arrived at Mrs. Waits's boardinghouse. Only a few days more and he'd be manufacturing again.

Up the hill on Chestnut Street, Lizzie and the children were settling into their temporary home, back in an environment full of life and surrounded by lovely, stylish houses. The Chestnut Street neighborhood was where the city's proprietors lived, where women such as Mrs. Newton talked of installing fountains with bronze statues in their yards. Here women walked the sidewalks in the latest fashions, made by one of the nineteen dressmakers right there in Holyoke. Nina, far off at Vassar, wrote to Nellie, "You have all written such glowing accounts of Holyoke and the home that I am indeed anxious to have xmas vacation come." The college junior may have grown even more excited by the "rumors [about] a big masquerade ball . . . during the coming season." As with any city of sufficient scale, Holyoke had its wealthier residents, who lived well and enjoyed their prosperity.

Lizzie soon began to receive callers, and after the family made their presence known at the Second Congregational Church, the minister, Reverend Trask, paid a social call as well. Church introduced them to all the influential people, those who went on summer vacations, sent their children away to schools, and could afford to go to Springfield to buy the best attire. A few of these people were already familiar faces. Mrs. Whiting, the wife of the well-established paper manufacturer William Whiting, had gone to Williston Seminary in Lizzie's time, before the Civil War, and Will knew one of the Whiting boys who had attended Williston with him. Skinner made a point of renting the pew behind the Whitings, beginning a lifelong friendship between the families. Joe and Belle started attending school, while Nellie helped Lizzie with the household, and Fred Warner continued his secretarial duties for Skinner. As for Will, whose grades had not been sufficient to earn him a place at Yale, he began (upon order from his father) to take the 8:22 a.m. train on a daily basis to the facility of a Dr. Hall outside the city, whom Skinner had hired "to improve in manliness and mental discipline" the abilities of the young man and in all other ways prepare him for college. Hall found that Will "required a great deal of time."

In this time of transition, as might be expected, the family stayed close to their former ties, trusting those they knew over those they didn't and wishing to maintain old friendships. The family may have been in their honeymoon phase in Holyoke, but the Mill River Valley, at least in their hearts, remained home. Lizzie returned regularly to visit her father and other relatives. The children attended parties in Northampton, visited the Hill boys and other friends, and wouldn't have missed the Cattle Show, the valley's biggest fall festival, for anything. When Joe had to have some teeth filled and others pulled, Skinner took him to their old dentist in Northampton. For all his activity in Holyoke, Skinner made several trips up to the valley, one of them to pick up Little May's picture. After the family moved out of their house, the picture of Little May remained one of the few articles left behind. Lizzie apparently didn't trust the movers with this precious portrait of her lost daughter, so Skinner and Will transported it down to the cottage themselves.

On Tuesday, November 3, Election Day, the Newtons' job was finished, and as other men were casting their ballots for state and local officials, Skinner formally took possession of his new factory, described as a "splendid mill."

The superstructure had ultimately called for 550,000 bricks. The foundation used 4,450 feet of flagstone, quarried from nearby Ashley Pond. Large, nine-over-nine sash windows lined the walls on each side, providing dignity to the exterior with their orderly, uniform arrangement, their rhythm only slightly interrupted by symmetrically placed hoistway doors in the southern and eastern walls for the loading and unloading of machinery and materials. The mill was L-shaped, with the office wing at a right angle to the front of the main building. The whole complex was three stories high, its architectural lines in complete balance. The roof, punctuated by skylights, was tiled in unfading green slate, purchased by the Newtons in Castleton, Vermont, and it contrasted beautifully with the red bricks of the structure below. Nor was any of this accidental. Industrialists like Skinner "had a real interest in the appearance of their works, which represented considerable financial investment and hopes for continued economic success. . . . Works that appeared substantial and commodious also implied technological and organizational mastery. Interest in an attractive factory was coupled with pride in ownership and the desire for a prominent position in the community." That Skinner wished for a prominent position some day in Holyoke was evident by the carefully appointed aesthetics of his brand-new silk mill.

The entrance to the mill was on Appleton Street, as was the entrance to the office building, both up short flights of steps. In the office building Skinner's office was immediately to the right. This generous apartment took up half the first floor and sported windows on three sides. From his desk Skinner would be able to look north onto the street, west across the canal, or south into his mill yard. He had never actually been able to see his factory from his office before, as in Skinnerville the office building had been in line with the factory. Now, attending business in a wing perpendicular to the rest of the complex, he would be able to lean back in his swivel chair, glance out a window, and take in his manufactory, dyehouse, coal shed, and chimney tower all at once. By this time gas lamps with decorative globes would have been installed, and, according to a later photograph, the walls were covered floor to ceiling in bead-board paneling. There was no carpet, nor any paintings, but in time there would be railroad schedules and silk samples tacked to the walls. The centerpiece was Skinner's rolltop desk, flanked by a wastebasket. He didn't bother with finery at the office.

Across the hall was the packing room, where Ellen Littlefield and the other packers would soon set to work (minus their rats), packaging up shipments for the New York store, and in the rear of the building was a "neatly furnished closet" (water closet, that is), where one could attend to appointments of a more personal nature. Downstairs was the fireproof stockroom that would double as a sorting room. Skinner's raw silk was already piled up against the walls in large woven sacks shipped from Hong Kong. The room would have been slightly damp, being in the basement, which would have been to Skinner's liking; this was good for the fiber. It would also have been furnished with long wooden tables, on top of which were dividers, or bins, for organizing the silk and small scales for weighing the myriad selections. To the unsuspecting eye the significance of this room would not have been apparent, but Skinner's entire operation depended on the quality of the work that took place here since all of his silk had to start out "as even as possible." The skeining department, where Aurelia Damon would work, was two flights up, on the second floor of the ell. Like the sorting and packing departments, the skeining department didn't require motive power. This room was bright and airy.

The ell shared one structural wall with the main building, and on the other side of this, on the first story, was the spooling department. A hallway leading from the ell into the main building brought one directly to the spooling room, before heading into the other departments where all the manufacturing took place. The smallest department in the main mill, the spooling room was furnished with several chairs and a cluster of tables, specially fabricated with pedal-operated machines on top of them. There was a girl once "who worked at [spooling] three months and could not make a perfect spool." It was hard work, but expert spoolers—Ellen's sister Lovisa had been one—could finish a hundred spools in a day, five hundred yards of silk to a spool. The rest of the mill was composed of wide-open lofts that stretched from one end of the building to the other. The throwing departments were on the lower and first stories, with columns of chestnut pillars running through them and thick ceiling beams of strong southern pine. The brand-new floors, as yet unscratched, were Vermont spruce, supplied by the Newtons' lumber mills in Newport, Vermont. Everything smelled exceedingly fresh.

Along the east side of each manufacturing floor were the spinning frames; down the west, the winding frames. There were also reeling and doubling apparatuses, arranged in allotted bays. With most of the machinery in position, each floor was a forest of steel frames and spindles. But the Holyoke Machine Company had not yet finished making all of the necessary connections. Skinner could only look at the potential of what lay before him and imagine how it would all work.

Once water was let in, the turbine in the wheelhouse would transmit power to two seven-foot pulleys in the pulley room at the southern end of the mill, which in turn, through twelve-inch belts, would transfer energy to the power shafts suspended from the ceilings. A power shaft ran down each side of the throwing floors, and every frame would draw power from a shaft. Skinner had approved the use of "Volney Mason's patent friction coupling" on the spinning frame connectors. This particular part would enable an overseer to start the machines gradually and safely, even when the power shaft was turning at maximum velocity. In another month the *Holyoke Transcript* would proclaim the motive machinery in Skinner's mill to be "of the best improved kinds throughout."

The second floor of the main building—an enormous expanse of virgin space, the kind that could make one take several deep breaths because there was so much air—would remain vacant for the time being, but here is where Skinner envisioned his braiding and weaving department. And, like the garrets of old, the "commodious attic" above, an equally finished but empty space, was destined to house even more looms, if all went according to plan.

In the basement, two doors led out to the mill yard, from which one could walk over to the dyehouse, passing under the wire pulleys that extended power to the outbuilding. Compared to the hovels that Skinner and his brothers knew in their younger days, this dyehouse would have been a veritable palace. It was about twice the size of the dyehouse in Skinnerville and, rather than looking like an afterthought or obligatory appendage, commanded a certain dignified presence, attracting attention from those who passed by over the Appleton Street bridge. Doing credit to its owner, it looked like an extremely well-appointed workshop, with even more generous fenestration than the mill and a stylish but practical monitor roof that would prove of incalculable value to Thomas Skinner and the boys. Such roofs, defined by a raised center span of ventilating windows, were uniquely suited to one-story spaces like dyehouses that required a great deal of both light and ventilation. Monitor roofs "drew hot air currents upward and allowed them to escape" and didn't leak or drip like skylights. The only negative aspect of the dyehouse was its close proximity to the fetid air off the upper canal—the shop was only a few yards from the canal and faced it directly—but then Thomas probably wouldn't notice the outside air much, surrounded as he would be by simmering vats filled with ammonia, blue vitriol, copperas, logwood, and countless other chemicals and dyes.

The new Skinner silk mill was exemplary of the changes under way in the industrial zeitgeist. Gone were the days of the small clapboard mill that had once served as a school or blacksmith shop. Gone were the days of having to convince an agricultural society that textile factories could fit into a decent, moral landscape. Mill buildings had become an integral, defining component of the country, of an industrial society that was growing bigger, bolder, and more systematic every day. Mill buildings were no longer fitting into the landscape; they were the landscape. And the larger they became, the more accurately they reflected the ambition driving the country's devout capitalism. Yet they continued to convey in their aesthetics the old-fashioned ideals of Protestantism: uniformity, order, industriousness, and faith. Indeed, if one looked closely at Skinner's new complex—or, rather, tilted one's head and looked up at it—one saw that the mill was graced, churchlike, with ornamental spires. Skinner might have moved his mill to an urban center, but he still intended it to be a wholesome atmosphere, where God-fearing Christian women would find like-minded souls and good, honest work.

Chapter Seventeen

Three days after the mill was accepted from the builders, Baby Katharine turned a year old. The family celebrated her first birthday in the house on Chestnut Street. Unlike the rest of her siblings, Katharine Skinner would grow up without any memory of the Mill River disaster. Nor would she know any home other than Holyoke.

Four days later, on Tuesday, November 10, exactly a week after the mill was accepted, another celebration took place, this one in Florence, where "the largest crowd ever convened in Cosmian Hall, gathered . . . to witness the presentation of gold medals to the four men, who worked so nobly in warning the inhabitants of Mill River Valley of impending peril." By 7 p.m. it was standing room only, with George Cheney, Collins Graves, Jerome Hillman, and Myron Day seated in chairs of honor on the stage, facing an audience of about seven hundred.

The fund-raiser that Henry C. Hayden had headlined back in June, to raise money for the heroes' medals, had contributed less than a third of the $325 needed to cover the cost. Skinner, Hayden, James, Spelman, and a handful of others had pitched in to cover the rest. In September the heroes' medals had been placed on display at the

Tiffany emporium in New York City. Not only fine samples of gold-smithing, their heroes emblazoned in frantic charge in great detail, these memorials also served as a reminder of what had only recently been national news. Not a few young ladies might have exclaimed, pointing a gloved finger at the medals, *There are those heroes of that Massachusetts flood.*

Before presenting the medals, the Reverend E. G. Cobb of the Congregational church in Florence took everyone back to that fateful Saturday, recalling the appalling force of the water, the breathtaking escapes and heartbreaking losses, the crippling of so many businesses, and the strength of spirit that had been required in the aftermath. As his words spilled forth, people looked around the hall, remembering who had died and reflecting on how far they'd all come since May 16. No longer was anyone wandering over fields of destruction. Here they were, side by side in a warm, beautiful theater, listening to music and feeling the pleasant stirrings of a ceremonial occasion. Finally Cobb introduced the honorees, who "stood up amid deafening cheers," and as he called each man forward, handed him a black jewelry box, inside of which was a gold medallion on a bed of green velvet. He also took a moment to reflect on each man's story, reminding the audience of the significance of this evening: these were ordinary citizens who had simply, and bravely, fulfilled the duty of an extraordinary moment.

No one begrudged these courageous men their honors this time. "It was eminently proper and appropriate that their heroic services, in behalf of humanity on that terrible Saturday morning, should be recognized in some specific and tangible manner, expressive of the gratitude of the public," concluded the *Hampshire Gazette,* "and the large gathering at Cosmian Hall . . . was a legitimate public expression of that gratitude."

Ironically, although responsible for the medals, Skinner does not seem to have been part of their presentation. A reporter for the *Springfield Republican* learned midweek that he was in New York buying more raw silk. It's somewhat remarkable that he wouldn't have been in attendance for the presentation of the medals that he had taken such pains to commission. Then again, business always came first for Skinner, overriding personal obligations. Nor is it surprising, really, that he'd be absent from a community affair so directly connected with the disaster. One can imagine that there would have been nothing less pleasurable to Skinner at this moment then being taken on a trip through the past, just as he was trying to move forward. Moreover, he was the sheep who had left the flock, and attending this event might have been politically unwise. For the time being at least, he represented the anti-hero to many people. This wasn't the time for public appearances in the valley.

Skinner may not have been inclined to reflect, but a great many others felt it not only appropriate but newsworthy to do so six months after the flood. In the days leading up to the tribute, Samuel Bowles at the *Springfield Republican* sent one of his correspondents to the affected region to report on its current condition. The reporter was taken aback by the enduring scarring, for despite all the efforts to rebuild and restore, "the Valley and its villages . . . put on no semblance yet of their former cheerfulness and prosperity, and almost seem[ed] in one sense more dreary than on the dread days when their calamity was new." Perhaps the future held greater promise. But the damage would take more than a matter of months to overcome; it would, said another journalist, "take years to replace what has been lost."

Bowles's reporter canvassed the valley from top to bottom. The infamous reservoir, he found, looked nothing like a reservoir anymore. Its bed was filling in with grass, wildflowers, and weeds and would soon appear to the unsuspecting eye to have never been more than a meadow. The surviving parts of the dam were still there, eerie stone buttresses in the hillside, the only change being that the top, finger-like projection of the west wall had been knocked over for safety reasons. The Mill River, unstoppable as ever, meandered through the scenery, but it was quite unimpressive at present, and the reporter found "a rill so tiny that one can hardly believe that it is all that represents the springs which fed such a volume of waters."

Spelman hadn't yet laid a single stone for a new mill, but he told Bowles's reporter "that he will probably ere long rebuild his button factory." Down the road Henry L. James, whose woolen mill had fared better than most, had repaired most of the damage and was back in business, restoring liveliness to that part of town. In Hayden-ville construction of the magnificent new brass works wouldn't start until the spring, but smaller buildings were going up and "the village [appeared] neat and trim." Farther south, in Leeds, George Warner had secured all the financing he needed for starting over, and his button mill, nearing completion, would give "new life" to its sur-roundings. Finally, in Florence, the visitor noted happily, "The im-mense 'drives' that buttressed the trunks of stalwart trees or lodged against projecting points of land, are utterly gone." No more could the passerby expect to find such unnatural curiosities as piano keys in the bushes or buttons by the handful in a scoop of dirt. The Florence meadows were once again filled with wildlife and growing grass, as nature intended.

Yet scars surfaced meanly, everywhere. Some were small, like the marks on a tree in Williamsburg that spoke of its trial as a bulwark, and some were large, such as the windowless tenement in Haydenville that was about to fall into the river. In Leeds, sighed this correspondent, "The road is renewed, the bowlders[*sic*] removed, but the houses rest in the middle of dreary sand. . . . Nothing yet reminds one of the street as it was; and the romantic rocky gorge below the village is sadly stripped of its beauties."

As one might expect, the legacy of the flood was most astonishing in Skinnerville, which the visitor described as "lonely Skinnerville" and "the only utterly hopeless spot in all his survey." The correspondent knew what the place had been like, his imagination easily able to re-create pleasanter days, and as he stood in the road, recalling what it had been, he had a tough time reconciling the fact that Skinner had walked away: "The street of pretty houses, with Mr. Skinner's mansion standing foremost among them, like a castle among the houses of vassals, facing the brawling stream and the wooded hill beyond, backed by quiet meadows reaching to the railroad and with the thrifty factory for a center—it was a proud demesne for any man to be the patriarch of, as Mr. Skinner was."

Unlike elsewhere, the laborers in this village weren't busy building houses; they were taking Skinner's apart, the demolition of which stung the reporter. The stripping away of that mansion, "the pride of Skinnerville," "renders the locality almost as unattractive as at any time since the flood." Furthermore, Skinner had decided to leave behind his damaged turbine. It was worthless, and he had no need for it in Holyoke, so he was apparently abandoning it in Skinnerville for the meantime. But this hollow turbine, rusting in the open air, was like a carcass on the side of the road, and symbolic of the end of industry here. Unable to produce waterpower ever again, the damaged wheel was quietly, and eerily, "rest[ing] from its labors beside the river."

The county commissioners had done more than they said they would. They had replaced the bridge, enabling Aurelia Damon and her mother, among others, to cross the water safely. The road had been improved with a "substantial" new board fence along the water's edge, to protect travelers from accidentally plunging down the embankment, and near the old factory site the road had been "carried 44 feet to the east for the purpose of furnishing a large mill privilege." But as the correspondent noted, "This mill site will, however, probably be long unoccupied."

Samuel Bowles didn't see things as pessimistically as his correspondent. "Of the four villages on which the flood spent its fury," he opined, "Williamsburg, Haydenville, and Leeds have made substantial progress on the road to reconstruction, and it seems quite reasonable to an-

ticipate a return of their old prosperity in the not remote future. Skinnerville alone, the smallest of the four, is not likely ever to be rebuilt.
In some respects, indeed, as in the matter of roads and bridges, the
ill-fated valley is really better equipped than it was before the flood. All
this affords new proof of the energy and hopefulness of our people, and
is a pleasant contrast to that horrible picture which was thrust upon the
public mind, half a year ago." Bowles then sought to bring this chapter
to a close: "The presentation of deserved testimonials to the heroes
of the flood is a fitting finale to the public history of the 'Mill River
disaster.' For six months is quite as long as the busy, restless American
public can be expected to concern itself with even so terrible a calamity as that of last May—however long its individual losses may cast a
gloom over the lives of persons and families." It was, Bowles believed,
time for everyone to move on.

The following Saturday, November 14, Skinner turned fifty. He probably spent most of the day at the mill, where the machinists had run
into some problems due to mistakes in designing the shafting. This
would unfortunately impact the start-up of most of the departments.
The mill would not be fully operational until December, but some
manufacturing could yet get under way before that. In the evening
he celebrated the day with Lizzie and the children at the house on
Chestnut Street.

The year before, his family had honored him in Skinnerville, as
they had done for twenty years, and the biggest present at that time had
been the one his wife had just given him: Baby Katharine. This year the
greatest gift he received was the health of his wife and children; none
had perished in the disaster or showed any signs of physical illness in
the aftermath. Now they were in Holyoke, and he was about to begin
anew. Indeed, of the four manufacturers who had lost every vestige of
their factories in the flood—Spelman, Skinner, Hayden, and Warner—
only Skinner had a fully rebuilt mill.

On Monday November 16, six months exactly from the day of the flood, Will recorded some of the biggest news in his father's life: "They began to make silk in Holyoke." Skinner's new mill started up around 7 a.m. with about a dozen girls at the winding frames. With such a small number of workers, the building seemed cavernous and empty, but it wouldn't be for long.

The first snowfall of the year had occurred the day before, and a light snow covered the ground, the new front steps, the eaves, the fresh windowsills. Wagons rattled by on Appleton Street. Vendors pulled their fruit carts to nearby corners. Teams came and went across the bridge over the canal. The sidewalks were thronged with people. In his office Skinner placed an inkstand and paperweight on his desk—birthday gifts from Fred—and began to think about everything yet to be done. He had to pay Luce for the designs of the mill and get the entire property properly enclosed for safety reasons. He had to sort through hundreds of applications for employment and fill at least forty positions by December. And he needed to begin plans for another wholesale store, as he wanted one in Boston to expand his reach in the New England market.

There was no guarantee that Skinner would make it in Holyoke. He'd rolled the dice in moving to this city, and he would be facing the new year of 1875 with a mountain of debt at a time when the country was laboring through a national depression. In one of the toughest economic environments of the century, he had a business to rebuild, a reputation to re-create, and a life to reestablish. But he knew his trade, and he had negotiated the deal of a lifetime in one of the greatest waterpowers in the nation. On the morning of November 16, 1874, when Skinner unlocked his mill for those twelve girls, he stepped into a new era, certain of only one thing: he had another chance.

Epilogue

What Makes Private Murphy Such a Well Dressed Man?
— William Skinner & Sons, advertisement, 1943

William Skinner used disadvantage to his favor. Throughout his life he relied on what the poverty of his childhood had taught him: that to survive one must persevere, to rise in the world one must seize opportunities, and to succeed one must make sacrifices. Regardless of what others thought, he gave his imagination free rein, listened to his own instincts, and did not let circumstance define him—he defined himself. His early years also taught him the difficult truth that he alone knew what was best for him to do. Loyalty to others was important, but loyalty to himself was essential, as well as respect for the brevity of life. He repeatedly told himself, and his children, "Time lost can never be regained." This fostered an intense but highly motivating restlessness. To friends and neighbors he'd also say, "The smartest horse jumps the ditch," believing one must never back away from an obstacle but take a leap of faith—and have confidence.

Skinner would later say of those first years in Holyoke, "It was an up-hill fight, with everything against [me]." Although the silk trade had weathered the Panic of 1873, it was not immune to the depression that followed. Pinched for resources, dressmakers and tailors began to prefer spooled silk to silk in the skein, forcing manufacturers like Skinner to adapt quickly. Within eight months of opening the mill in Holyoke, Skinner had all but shut down his skeining department. Out of a job, Aurelia Damon returned to Skinnerville, and her ensuing letters to Ellen Littlefield reflect both the difficulties of the time and the changes on the horizon. Aurelia was depressed to be back home, with no future prospects at the new silk mill in Holyoke. "It will be an act of charity to write me a long letter," she wrote in May 1875, "for I do get pretty blue some times." News that the silk mill was doing poorly and that Skinner was "not making any sewing silk to speak of" was disheartening on several levels. Having worked for Skinner all of her adult life, Aurelia was genuinely attached to his progress. "I am sorry [to hear of such things]," she wrote Ellen. "Mr. Skinner has a great deal to bother him."

For a long time productivity at the mill remained low. In 1877 another employee wrote, "Mr. Skinner complains bitterly of dull times," and "Mr. Peck was here [from the New York store] but brought no orders." Rumors swirled about Skinner's demise. One particularly slanderous and ridiculous story was that Skinner "had failed, gone insane and was in the Northampton insane asylum." Will Skinner recorded in his diary, "The story about Father has had this much added to it, that he beats his wife, locks her up in a room, and that it took six men to take him to Northampton."

Malicious remarks are perhaps not surprising. Following his move to Holyoke, Skinner's name became a target for ill feeling in some circles. But any talk of the silk mill failing was, as Skinner might have said, "pure gammon." For while his sewing silk and twist departments suffered mightily in the difficult economy, his new braid department began to thrive. Indeed Skinner's bold decision to expand his operation right when he was starting over proved a critical factor in the survival of his business. He'd built a mill that could accommodate not only his previous product lines but also an array of new ones, providing him with versatility and flexibility in the marketplace. Woven silk braids were, one creditor noted, "a class of goods that [would] promise good returns." They were becoming enormously popular, especially in men's clothing to which they added style while covering up loose seams. Despite the prevailing dullness in the market, young Will remarked, almost two years after the disaster, "Father's braid business was never better and the only trouble is he cannot get them out fast enough."

Weaving braids—when weaving *anything* was still rare in the American silk trade—put Skinner at the forefront of the next great advancement in his trade. And in 1879 he made the leap to weaving fabric, specifically satin linings for menswear, realizing his vision of housing the entire silk production process under one roof, from thread to finished cloth. His timing, again, was impeccable. American-made silk linings were on the cusp of sparking a "revival in confidence" among consumers who were becoming increasingly frustrated with the products from Europe. The age-old trickery of weighting silk in the dyehouse with substandard additives was in full swing abroad, and it was becoming common to hear at the local sales counter, "Buying an imported silk is like purchasing a ticket in the lottery." One could not depend on its quality. "The chief point," said an official at the Silk Association, "is that American linings wear longer, because they are of purer silk." Skinner even embraced the old-fashioned way of making cloth. Instead of dyeing pieces of satin after they were woven, he dyed the thread first, before it was woven into cloth. This approach contributed "greatly to [the silk's] strength, durability and luster" and gave his satins "an enviable reputation for their high quality."

The Mercantile Agency predicted that Skinner's long-awaited production of silk cloth would become "the most profitable part of his business." It did. Within six months of starting to manufacture linings, Skinner received his first promising report from the Agency since the disaster. He was regarded as "doing as well if not better than ever," and by January 1880 his business had swelled to a value "not less than $100,000"—almost back to where it had been at the time of the flood. Of this period Skinner would say, "The sun finally burst through the dark clouds which had hovered around, and success crowned my efforts."

Of incalculable significance to his growth was the city of Holyoke. Regardless of the season, Holyoke's canal system provided safe, dependable waterpower to his mill, offering Skinner a peace of mind and a level of productivity he'd never known. It also saved him a lot of money, since he never had to rely on a steam engine. In Holyoke, too, he had access to a steady stream of labor, given the number of people, both native and foreign-born, looking for work in the city. With the depot less than a block away, he could ship his goods anywhere in the country with remarkable ease. And since he had negotiated a deal with the Newtons that gave him years to get back on his feet before having to buy his mill, he had a providential grace period after the flood. From the start he was able to concentrate fully on growing his business rather than paying off debt. He knew too that he had the unequivocal support of Holyoke's leaders, who would help him in any way possible. Skinner's decision to move to Holyoke had been so well publicized in the aftermath of the disaster that his prosperity, if fate allowed, would be a shining reflection on the city.

Before Skinner moved to town, the *Holyoke Transcript* rarely published items about the silk industry. But after his arrival the latest doings in the trade were considered newsworthy. The success of the silk market meant more business and jobs at Skinner's mill, which meant more money flowing into the local economy. Although one of the world's most ancient textiles, silk represented the future among American textile manufacturing and was seen as vital to the city's growth and national reputation. It was something Holyokers wanted to trumpet as the silk industry became steadily more powerful and glamorous. The *Transcript* crowed that the American silk industry was in a position to claim "as proud a position, relatively, as the paper, cotton, the woolen and the numerous other trades." At the Centennial Exhibition in Philadelphia in 1876 American silk products were going to be a "wonder" to sightseers. "Those who visit the Yankee World's Fair," declared the paper, "will have an opportunity to see specimens . . . of all these cunningly wrought silk fabrics [that are] made, not in Lyons, nor even in the famed silk producing district of St. Etienne, but in some Yankee Holyoke or Paterson."

American silk became big business, something that Skinner had known in his blood was inevitable. The early Industrial Revolution had established a burgeoning middle class with money to spend and aspirations to realize at a time when fabric was fashion. As the middle class grew, veritably exploding in the last quarter of the nineteenth century, the demand for silk rose exponentially. Everyone wanted to wear silk; it made them feel rich. Once silk had been the exclusive property of kings and queens, lords and ladies, but now it was obtainable by everyone, and America, assuming its stature as an industrial superpower toward the end of the century, became "the world's largest single consumer of silk goods." In the 1880s, for the first time, raw silk imports for home manufacture equaled the amount of imported silk goods. Foreign silk remained popular but insufficient to meet the demands of the growing marketplace, and the result was the heyday that Skinner and his colleagues had dreamed of through the long dark years of the past. By 1900 more than 70 percent of the silk that was purchased in America was made in America—in places like Holyoke, by manufacturers like Skinner.

"This is a prosperous firm," wrote an agent enthusiastically about Skinner's company in the fall of 1883. "In excellent standing & credit. Now doing a successful business. Estimated Worth $250,000–$300,000." Will dropped out of college to become a salesman for his father in New York. The store needed help, and the teenager successfully talked his father into letting him leave school and work the counter. On July 10, 1876, he recorded his triumph: "It is seriously considered about my going to work in N.Y. as I am now about as [old as] Father was when he came to America." Will was a born salesman, and in almost no time at all had taken charge of the store. Then, in 1881, on the cusp of the mill's real success, Skinner made young Will a partner. Two years later Joe joined the firm after graduating from Yale (and doing his father much honor). Unlike his wild and winning brother, Joe was quiet and studious, with a natural aptitude for science and mechanics, and took more to the operational side of the business, beginning a hands-on tutorial of the entire process of production under his father's care. Not long afterward Joe became a partner as well.

The firm became known as William Skinner & Sons, was incorporated as the William Skinner Manufacturing Company in 1889, and by the early 1890s was manufacturing a full line of satin sleeve linings, braids, and serges, as well as machine twist, buttonhole twist, and sewing silks. Thomas Skinner remained in charge of the dyehouse, and the quality of the satin that the mill produced was in large part due to his expertise. William Skinner also explored ways to lower the cost of his linings without compromising on quality, in order to appeal to a wider market. Historically satin linings had been backed with linen, but Skinner started using cotton instead, taking advantage of local cotton mills that were "spinning better and better cotton yarns at far less than the cost of linen." His market share soared.

As Skinner's sons added their own touches to their father's brand, they too thought of ways to stay on top of the competition, carrying on their father's forward-thinking style. Joe, for instance, invented a way to weave the name "Skinner's" into the edge, or selvage, of every bolt of company fabric. The idea was completely novel. Customers could now recognize Skinner's satin without the aid of a clerk and see for themselves how it differed from the competition. Distinguishing itself further, the company then began guaranteeing that its products would last two full seasons, and if not, the company would replace them free of charge. At a time when so many clothes were handmade and so much effort went into making one or two outfits that would be worn all year, this kind of guarantee was hugely appealing. Proclaimed one advertisement, "You can buy Skinner's Satin for waists and gowns with the assurance that none of the labor of making will be lost through poor service on the part of the material."

As the company's popularity grew, it won the acclaim of large-scale ready-made clothiers. The National Cloak & Suit Company, one of

Skinner & Sons' biggest clients at the turn of the century, proclaimed to its thousands of customers, "Our Best Satin is SKINNER'S GUARANTEED SATIN LINING, which is fully worth the small difference it costs." Thereafter the company instituted yet another innovation: a marketing campaign. Skinner's began telling customers through promotional booklets and advertisements that they should "Look for the name in the selvage." This slogan proved so successful it remained in effect for half a century.

When Skinner opened his new mill in November 1874, only twelve girls stood at the winding frames. The following summer he had about seventy-five employees. Ten years later he had about three hundred. Two more floors were added to the mill, making it a five-story factory. Then an entirely new factory was built adjacent to the original one. By 1902, with another expansion on the horizon, his mill employed roughly a thousand workers and produced $2.5 million worth of silk goods annually. Skinner's silk company was one of the largest in the nation, and he, at the age of seventy-seven, was at the top of the healthiest silk industry in the world.

Skinner's meteoric success would have been impossible in Skinnerville, in the land-rich but water-poor and, in the wake of the flood, financially destitute town of Williamsburg. In 1882 young Will made a telling statement to one of his sisters: "I am glad Father is going to build an addition as I certainly hope & expect that we shall be a big concern before long—What a good thing it is that Father moved to Holyoke where he can do these things."

Had Skinner stayed in Skinnerville he would have been severely limited in his ability to grow his business. Fields for farming abounded, but the water privilege was modest at best, and the Mill River could never have generated enough power for continual expansion on a large scale. The river needed significant supplementation from reservoirs, and owing to fears from the disaster, reservoirs were never again going to be a solution for manufacturers in the valley. Instead, steam power became the reliable source for production. The repaired Goshen reservoirs remained in use, but the Williamsburg Reservoir was not rebuilt. Nor were any additional reservoirs built, despite the fact that the legislature remained sympathetic to dam owners and reluctant to institute stringent reform. (In 1875, the legislature instituted "subtle changes" in the laws regarding reservoirs, namely requiring that dams be officially inspected while being constructed. More substantive change, however, "would take generations to complete.") Furthermore Skinnerville was too small to accommodate hundreds of workers and their families, and Skinner could never have afforded tenements and boardinghouses for so many people. Short on room, power, and labor, the old factory village was no place for a "big concern."

Whether Skinner could have survived those early, difficult years after the flood in Skinnerville is doubtful, but the absence of his business contributed to the valley's industrial demise. As Skinner became successful in Holyoke and his satin became a staple in people's wardrobes, men like Reverend Gleason must have been thinking that Skinner's silk mill was one of the greatest losses occasioned by the flood.

On May 16, 1876, Will noted, "Today is the 2nd Anniversary of the Mill River Disaster. Nearly all the mills in Berkshire County have failed." Most likely he meant Hampshire County instead of Berkshire County, but mistake or no, manufacturers in the valley experienced extremely hard times as they tried to recover. "In the place of wealth there came to many poverty. In the place of business activity came stagnation, paralysis," wrote the historian Louis Everts. "With a third of the business and wealth of the town swept away, and much of it irretrievably lost, merchants could no longer make extensive sales. Men of abundant means who seemed to stand the first shock of the disaster proved to be more embarrassed than was expected, and some went down in the storm of commercial distress that followed the flood."

Hayden, Gere & Co. dissolved in October 1877, awash in debt. The Mercantile Agency openly denounced Hayden's decision to rebuild in Haydenville: "Rebuilding on such a large scale in the little village of Haydenville is criticized as poor investment of money." Spending hundreds of thousands of dollars to build a large manufacturing facility in a devastated, remote, rural community was considered to have been financially reckless. The brass works passed into the hands of trustees, and then from one group of capitalists to another—including, finally, three sons and a grandson of Jacob Hills—but Hayden had nothing to do with its survival. He left town and never returned.

Onslow Spelman rebuilt his button mill in Williamsburg, but the mill went out of business at about the same time that Hayden, Gere & Co. did. He regrouped, but ultimately quit manufacturing in Williamsburg altogether since it was no longer profitable. Henry L. James made a show of prosperity for a while, but it was short-lived. After years of struggle his woolen mill went out of business in 1891, and shortly thereafter all of his property was sold at auction to pay off creditors. Down in Leeds, George Warner's button mill went out of business also. He proved another poor financier and was "criticized quite severely & accused of disloyalty to friends, who [had] assisted him in time of need [after the flood]." With the loss of these establishments, combined with the departure of Skinner's silk mill, the northern portion of the valley lost its industrial pulse forever.

While Williamsburg staggered in the wake of the disaster, Northampton quietly became identified again with the silk industry. Of all the industries the town had seen, silk "establish[ed] the region in its position as a manufacturing center." In addition to the Nonotuck, the Belding Brothers Silk Company, a Connecticut firm, opened a branch plant in Northampton in 1877. There was also Joseph Warner's silk mill, which marched along for a while like an old reliable workhorse. And in 1899 another silk company came to town, McCallum Hosiery, "America's first silk stocking mill." As the nineteenth century gave way to the twentieth, Northampton was producing $2.4 million worth of silk goods, and in 1902, $3.2 million—only 22 percent more than Skinner's one silk mill.

• • •

When Skinner moved to Holyoke he and his family were the subject of much comment. Completed in the summer of 1875, their mansion was considered "the finest residence in the city." Even its new barn was "a handsome article, nice enough to live in." In an age before celebrity, the wealthier set was regularly followed in local news sections, but as a result of the disaster the Skinners experienced a new level of notoriety. An event as minor as Joe Skinner's winning a wordsmith contest was published in the paper, and when Nellie was married to Fred Warner in the double parlor that September, the *Holyoke Transcript* reported on the wedding for all those who were not invited. The bride was "beauti-fully dressed in white silk" and received "costly" and "beautiful" gifts. Names from the guest list were also published, including at least one congressman's, implying that the Skinners had friends in high places.

Just as in Williamsburg, almost everyone eventually knew who William Skinner was. Said one, "His close attention to business affairs often excited comment as he was seen early in the morning on his way to the mills." He had successfully cultivated the characteristics he had yearned for as a youth, watching Macready play Othello. Tall, dark, and kinetic at that time, he had since matured into "a huge man." Among his friends he was known as "the old Roman" for his commanding pres-ence. His hair and beard turned "white as snow" and he gained more weight and became quite portly. If not known by his looks, he was known to all by his reputation. "I never saw anyone carry money in a great roll as Grandfather did," remarked his oldest grandchild.

In Holyoke, Skinner quickly earned respect for being a "very good manager and financier." Within months of his arrival parish members of the Second Congregational Church nominated him to be on the church's governing committee, but he declined on account of "new-ness." After only two years in the city the Democratic Party asked him to run for mayor. This too he declined. He did accept a directorship at the Holyoke Savings Bank, however, as well as at the Hadley Falls

National Bank, and he remained on the board of the Northampton National Bank.

In the wake of the disaster many in the Williamsburg community wondered why Skinner would settle for being one among many manufacturers in Holyoke when he could have remained the leader of his own manufacturing village. In fact, moving to Holyoke enabled him to become an even greater leader and focus on what meant most to him: business, banking, and eventually philanthropy. He sacrificed not an ounce of authority by moving, especially as his silk mill grew to be one of the city's largest and healthiest places for employment, as well as one of its most popular among laborers, since working with silk was cleaner and considered more prestigious than working with other textiles. As a result of the mill supporting close to a thousand workers and their families, his company contributed substantially to the local economy and became far more influential than anyone could have predicted when he first moved to town. In Holyoke Skinner was no longer the patriarch of a village; he was one of the most prosperous men in a modern industrial city.

His relocation to Holyoke was also strikingly prescient. The *Holyoke Transcript* was not being overly sensational when it foretold in the days following the flood the demise of the advantages of rural manufacturing. This was an effort to play on the psychological weakness of Mill River Valley proprietors who were looking for an exit from their misery, but the prediction was accurate. The year 1874 would prove to be right on the cusp between America's first industrial revolution and its second, the latter marked in part by a centralization of industry in city centers, which led to extraordinary growth and innovation for urban manufacturers. Holyoke offered not only salvation from ruin but also the landscape of the future, and Skinner chose to leave behind the pre–Civil War paradigm to embrace the untold but certain potential in "a live manufacturing place like this."

In October 1898 Skinner told a crowd of Holyokers, "Fellow citizens—It is twenty-[four] years this month since I came to Holyoke, after the Mill River disaster, and I have never regretted coming. I have seen the city grow and prosper, and I have prospered with it." For the rest of his life he felt deeply indebted to the city that gave him another chance, and, like many industrialists of his era, he believed it was his duty to give back to the community that had supported his growth. At home he had a policy that "no hungry man should be sent from his door," so that for years there was often one or more "eating out back of the kitchen." (Lizzie put a stop to the policy after some miscreants stole into the house during mealtime and made off with a bundle of jewelry.) People remembered that he "seemed to closely follow the Biblical admonition, 'let not thy left hand know what thy right hand doeth; that thy alms may be in secret.'" Said one, "His gifts in a private way to relieve need and destitution exceed the charities of any other man in Holyoke." But Skinner was as particular with his generosity as he was with his silk. There was nothing indiscriminate about his assistance. Someone once approached him about establishing an art gallery in Holyoke, and Skinner replied bluntly, "What Holyoke needs is soap." In his mind, money would be better spent providing people in rough conditions with "clean homes, clean bodies, clean lives."

Over the years Skinner became an impressive local philanthropist, most notably cofounding the city's first hospital, which, as president of the board, he delivered to the public free of debt. He pledged $10,000 for the erection of a public library downtown. He "gave without reservation a complete site for a Young Men's Christian Association building" and then gave more to help build the building. He donated substantially to Smith College in Northampton, Mount Holyoke College in South Hadley, and Vassar College in Poughkeepsie, New York, continuing to support higher education for women. (Three of his daughters graduated from Vassar: Nina, class of 1875; Libbie, class of 1880; and Belle, class of 1887.) To the Northfield Seminary for girls in Northfield, Massachusetts, he gave a gymnasium building and "usually had several wards at school there and at other institutions."

True to form, he never let up. When probably in his seventies, Skinner wrote to Will, "I am feeling good, full of ambition." He remained "the typical Englishman," always "firm in his opinions" and "difficult to win from them except by the most convincing argument." He also remained "bitterly opposed . . . to trusts of all kinds," such as any organization of labor. In 1886, during the first and most famous strike at his mill, Skinner refused to negotiate with his striking employees, members of the weaving department who wanted an abusive foreman fired. These men were supported in their plight by the powerful Knights of Labor, who, in an effort to bring Skinner to terms, put a stranglehold on much of his business in New York City. The Knights of Labor convinced city tailors to boycott Skinner's satins until Skinner agreed to fire the foreman. Unable to weave his own silks, Skinner "simply sent his sons to France to buy manufactured goods in the market there," and then, for a short while, sold foreign goods instead of his own. Incredibly Skinner actually profited from a strike that had been meant to cripple him into submission. By this point, though, that kind of flipping the ending was hardly unusual for him. He was never going to be told what to do and, when pressured, instinctively became more creative, whatever the cost to others.

Yet his ego continued to be subject to flattery, and as a result he flirted with politics twice more. In 1888 he was "unanimously nominated for Congress" and became the democratic candidate for the state's eleventh district, a district that included Hampshire County—included, in other words, the votes of citizens in the Mill River Valley. If Skinner's reputation had been at all soiled by his departure, the ballot box showed none of this; he handily won the vote of his former county. But he lost the election owing to his handling of the 1886 strike, because the Knights of Labor rose up against him and swung the winning votes to the competition. Ten years later Holyokers wanted Skinner to run for mayor again. Commented a local lawyer, "Some men complain that [Skinner] is impulsive. I heard one man say to-day that if Skinner came down to city hall and found the light coming in from the wrong direction, he would order the building turned about so as to face west." However, Holyoke's government had become the stronghold of a few, and many thought Skinner was exactly the sort "to shake things up there." The Democrats already had a nominee, though, and finally Skinner decided that running as an independent would be a losing proposition, and he was tired of losing at politics. "My observation," he told a reporter, "has been that in few cases, if any, have candidates on citizens' tickets been elected." He then added that "he appreciated the handsome way in which the press had treated him and jokingly remarked that he had a chance to read his own obituary sooner than most people."

Skinner may secretly have known that he no longer had the stamina for the grueling job of mayor. His health was failing, and over the next few years he resigned from most of his obligations. At times he would remark that he still "felt like a boy," but the wearying effects of Bright's disease, a nineteenth-century term that broadly signified kidney disease, began to take their toll on his body. He felt a great deal of physical pain, mostly localized in his lower back, which limited his mobility severely, and may have suffered from fevers and swelling too. He remained thoroughly involved in operations at the mill, but after "a severe attack of his malady" in the summer of 1901, he finally "yielded [the company's] active management to his sons." Thereafter he was confined mostly to his bedroom, his health gradually slipping away until, in the last days of February 1902, he began to lose consciousness. His children came home immediately and, with Lizzie, sat vigil at their father's bedside. Surrounded by family, Skinner died on February 28, "just as the clock was striking 3 o'clock in the afternoon."

During a private funeral service at the house, Dr. Reed, pastor of the Second Congregational Church, recited several lines of poetry that Skinner had chosen. The lines were by an eighteenth-century British poet and essayist known formally as Mrs. Barbauld. (Her full name was Anna Laetitia Barbauld.) She had once written such "exquisite" lines of verse about life that Wordsworth himself apparently said he "would rather have written [them] than any lines of his own." But Mrs. Barbauld was vilified in the British press, as Cobbett had been, when she spoke out against the British government. In a poem published in 1812 she predicted that Britain's reign was coming to an end and that the young country of America would be stealing its crown. Although Mrs. Barbauld was largely neglected in literary circles as the century wore on, some, like Skinner, did not forget her. Much of her verse was sentimental, in keeping with the fashion of her time, and thus it is somewhat unusual that Skinner chose her verse to be read at his private funeral. But it is absolutely fitting that he chose lines written by a rebel, a Briton, and a woman to voice what he could not say:

> *Life! We've been long together*
> *Through pleasant and through cloudy weather;*
> *'Tis hard to part when friends are dear;*
> *Perhaps 't will cost a sigh, a tear;*
> *Then steal away, give little warning,*
> *   Choose thine own time;*
> *Say not Good Night, but in some brighter clime*
> *   Bid me Good Morning.*

"The shock now that he is gone is severe," reported the *Springfield Union*, and the *Holyoke Transcript* quickly mourned the loss of his presence: "William Skinner stood with Holyoke's first men as he stood in the first rank of America's silk manufacturers." Within days the Silk Association publicly announced, "*Resolved:* That by the death of William Skinner on February 28, 1902, at Holyoke, Mass., the Silk Association of America has lost one of its most distinguished members and the silk industry, one of its foremost representatives."

When William Skinner died, he owned what some said was "the biggest [silk plant] in the country," and his achievements seemed exemplary of the impact that skilled immigrants had made on American industry. "His career," wrote an official at the Silk Association, "furnishes another illustration of the decided tendency by the United States in recent years of transplanting the art and skill of the foreign born to this side of the Atlantic in the upbuilding of our domestic industries." After Skinner's will was read and some of the bequests made public, it also became clear just how wealthy he had become, which only further reinforced the stature he had attained. Reported the *Transcript*, "It is known that he was a millionaire, but the indications are from the bequests that he was one at least three times over." Indeed, when factoring in profits from his mill, he would have been worth about $3 million, having an economic status equivalent to someone worth $475 million today. The paper then made a point of adding that the bulk of this wealth had come after he moved to Holyoke. "The property has practically all been accumulated since his coming to Holyoke early in the seventies and speaks volumes for the ability and push of Mr. Skinner."

A public funeral took place on March 3, 1902, in the Second Congregational Church. Observed one Springfield man, it passed "with impressive ceremony." Among the delegations present were those from the Silk Association of America, the Paterson Silk Association, and the China Japan Trading Company. By this time the American silk trade was doing a booming business with Japan, and Skinner had had one of the longest relationships with Japanese silk exporters. Arai Riochiro, a young Japanese who had been instrumental in winning over American manufacturers to Japanese silk, credited Skinner with being brutally honest with him on his first visit to the United States in 1876 and inspiring him to increase the quality of his country's exports. When Arai walked into Skinner's store that year, Skinner took him to the back, pointed to some adulterated silk that he had recently received from a dishonest Japanese merchant, and told Arai in no uncertain terms that he was through with the Japanese. "See here, I don't want this kind of stuff. Young man, you get out!" Ironically that was the start of a beautiful friendship, because Arai learned exactly what had to be overcome for his country's silk to make it in America. Almost thirty years later Japan was one of the biggest suppliers of raw silk to the United States, and Skinner's mill, by virtue of its size, was one of the largest American consumers of Japanese raw silk.

Skinner's pallbearers were all superintendents from his mill, including an employee who had been with him since Skinnerville, Edward Welch, whose wife had given birth to a son two days before the flood. In addition to Welch and the other pallbearers, a great many from the mill attended Skinner's funeral, forming a procession through the streets to the church. "A large delegation of the mill operatives formed in line at the mills of the Skinner manufacturing company, and marched to the church," reported the *Springfield Republican*. "This unsolicited tribute of affection was in a way a measure of the sorrow of the men and women of the mills."

One wonders if Ellen Littlefield attended. She had long since left Skinner's employ, but she hadn't left the area. In 1877 she had married Skinner's bookkeeper, Moses Nash Hubbard ("the widower," as he was known in Skinnerville). At about this time, if not before, Nash had started his own silk braid company in Springfield, where he and Ellen raised a family and lived the rest of their lives. Nash died in 1917, and Ellen in 1936. As for Ellen's close friend Aurelia, she too might have attended Skinner's funeral, though it's more likely she read about it in the papers. Aurelia continued to live in the Hampshire hills, ultimately moving back to the town in which she was born, Chesterfield, the town from which so many of Skinner's early operatives, such as the Tower sisters, had come. Aurelia remained unmarried, supporting herself to the end. She died in 1916.

After Skinner's death Will and Joe took over the business. They made a formidable team, their different talents suiting the company perfectly, with Will running the stores and Joe, the mill. By 1912 they had masterminded the completion of the largest silk mill under one roof in the world. A thousand feet long, it stretched over three city blocks, contained more than five acres of floor space, and required "a walk of several miles" in order to tour the whole operation. Although Holyoke would gain industrial fame as America's "paper city," given the number of paper mills it had, Skinner's silk mill turned out to be "the single corporate symbol of Holyoke," best representing the city's success, growth, ambition, quality, and prosperity.

Perpetuating their father's nineteenth-century paternalistic style of management, Will and Joe opened a dispensary at the mill for free, on-site medical care. They provided employees with home mortgages, subsistence allowances in times of financial distress, educational support, and other means of assistance. While unions continued to gain momentum as the years went by, answering a real need for labor reform, many at Skinner's were initially uninterested in joining them. "Twenty-three years or more I was in Skinners," said Catherine Hart, who worked at the mill from 1904 to 1928. "We didn't have a union. We didn't think it was good. We had a nice time [at Skinner's]. Mr. Skinner was a nice man."

Catherine Hart was probably referring to Joe when she spoke of Mr. Skinner, since Will was in New York most of the time, but the brothers were equal partners in the company and ran their respective sides of the business, operations and merchandising, with astonishing success. The next generation of Skinners entered the family business, and for nearly another half century William Skinner & Sons in Holyoke remained one of the nation's leading textile manufacturers, despite the radical changes that began taking place in manufacturing in the Northeast,

New England's wondrous Industrial Revolution, with its great technological and sociological advances, its masterful utilization of the region's natural watershed, and its extraordinary manipulation of capitalism, came to a close in the twentieth century. The success of industrialization in the North had inspired stiff competition in the South, and a surge of new southern mills, with more modern equipment, changed the game forever. The North became a region of inefficient industrial excess, with large, bloated mills, antiquated machinery, and an over-population of skilled labor too expensive to employ under union control. Some northern manufacturers, wishing to lower production costs, began to move south to take advantage of southern tax breaks and the absence of labor unions. Smaller manufacturers acquiesced to takeovers by larger ones, and still others resorted to dissolution in order to preserve what capital was left, unwilling (or unable) to invest in innovative techniques to remain competitive.

The Nonotuck Silk Company, for instance, ultimately went out of business for lack of innovation. The company never graduated to making products other than silk thread, and once mercerized cotton thread gained popularity in the 1890s, proving cost effective in boots, shoes, and ready-made clothing, the trend never reversed. Silk thread remained preferred by women who did their own sewing, but customers who wanted ready-made apparel were not nearly as discerning. To stay afloat in the 1920s, the Nonotuck merged with another concern and was renamed the Corticelli Silk Company, but this didn't save its bottom line. By 1929, quite apart from the Crash, stock in American silk thread was plummeting, and its manufacturers were, somewhat remarkably, totally confounded by the retail market. "We still fail to see," wrote Corticelli's president that year, "why [women] are willing to accept ready made silk dresses sewed with cotton when they know that only silk sewed seams will give the desired finished appearance." Silk remained the "queen of fabrics," but suddenly her reign was being challenged by inventions that mimicked her strength and durability and provided the consumer with cheaper alternatives without sacrificing quality. Changing fashions (shorter skirts, sleeveless dresses) compounded the situation by requiring less fabric—and therefore less thread. Three years after Corticelli's president expressed his astonishment, the last spools of Corticelli thread left the company's warehouse and what remained of its property was liquidated. Much of its machinery had already been sold as scrap.

In sharp contrast to that end, in 1931 Will Skinner wrote to his family's old friend Arai Riochiro with a sense of exuberance about the future: "Yesterday, I read in the Japanese American, with great interest the account of what you had accomplished in introducing Japanese Raw Silk to the United States. Just think, 108 bales in 1876 and over 532,000 in 1929. It seems incredible." Countless silk manufacturers went out of business in the 1920s, unable to adapt to the changing landscape of fashion and unable to afford the expenses of manufacturing in the North. The Nonotuck's fate was hardly unusual. But Skinner & Sons continued to experience growth. The company took full advantage of Holyoke's brilliant engineering, held off the unions for decades through paternalistic management, and constantly diversified its product base. Will, Joe, and later Skinner's grandsons fully embraced Skinner's philosophy of adaptation and expansion within the context of the times and the demands of the market. "Today, as always, the search for new fabrics and better ways to make them goes on," proclaimed the company on its hundredth anniversary in 1948.

Unlike other second- and third-generation mill owners "[who] had little interest in their inherited factories" and "[who] had lost their nerve for initiative," the Skinners were among the few who embraced "radical modernization" in both equipment and management. They installed faster machinery, then automated machinery, and in each case reduced the number of hands they needed. The old paternalism eventually fell away, but the company's commitment to Holyoke never wavered. The firm also capitalized on advances in other industries. One of Skinner's grandsons saw the burgeoning field of aviation offering unlimited possibilities in shipping merchandise and, in 1928, with his own pilot's license, flew a collection of silk goods from the New York store to a retailer in Troy, New York, making one of the Northeast's "first shipment[s] of merchandise by airplane."

At the beginning of the twentieth century, William Skinner & Sons was weaving silks, satins, and taffetas "in a wide range of fashionable shades" for use in linings, dresses, petticoats, lingerie, blouses, and even bathing suits. (Skinner's "bathing satin," as developed in the mill's lab, was specially treated to withstand the fading effects of sun and water and helped inspire the vogue for satin suits, thus replacing woolen bathing apparel.) During the 1920s the company added stylish shoe satin as well as graceful silk crepes to its product line, responding to the latest trends from Europe, so that, as one of its ads read, "When Paris says 'Crepe Satin,' America answers 'Skinner's.'" In the 1930s the company boldly reduced its production of silk linings, for decades the backbone of its business, and experimented with synthetic linings using rayon, the new "artificial silk." The growing popularity of rayon—it wore well, washed easily, wrinkled less—made certain that the use of pure silk in manufacturing, for the volume market at least, was "on the way out." From this point on, the company "moved over into synthetics in a big way."

In the late thirties Skinner & Sons invented Tackle Twill, a predecessor to Lycra, that became famously sought after in sportswear, rainwear, and children's wear. (It remains a staple in sportswear manufacturing to this day.) By the 1940s the company was developing synthetic fabrics with DuPont, supplying nylon parachute cloth for the war effort and creating all-nylon Combat Cloth for casualty blankets. It worked with General Electric to create F-2 flying suits for the U.S. Air Force, while the Brooklyn Dodgers wore Skinner's rayon-faced, cotton-back satin uniforms during night games. In the late 1940s, when so many returning soldiers were marrying their sweethearts, Skinner's bridal satin catapulted the company to a new level of success. The company had long before claimed "the most famous name in silks" but its supple, luxurious bridal satin, observed industry experts, "made Skinner a household word in the United States."

By the 1950s, William Skinner's company had been around for so long that few could remember a time when the company hadn't existed. It was one of the first textile houses to branch into consumer advertising, placing an ad in *Ladies' Home Journal* in 1903. Six years later it began a run in the *Saturday Evening Post*. Thereafter Will, who was in charge of marketing, saw to it that advertisements for Skinner's appeared in every major American magazine: *Bride's, Esquire, Fortune, Glamour, Good Housekeeping, Harper's Bazaar, Life, Mademoiselle,* the *New Yorker, Photoplay, Time, Town & Country, Vogue, Vanity Fair,* and more. As cinema began its ascent, Will wooed Hollywood, and the company became a darling of Hollywood costume designers. Skinner's silks and satins appeared all over the screen, and, at a time when "the costume designer was king," Skinner's gained the favor of the greatest costume designer in Hollywood: Adrian. Head designer for MGM, Adrian draped his famous stars—Joan Crawford, Greta Garbo, Norma Shearer, and the like—in lavish, shimmering gowns of Skinner's satin that made audiences swoon not only for the star, but for the silk fantasies in which she appeared. Adrian went so far as to participate in an advertising campaign for Skinner's in 1931 in which he applauded the "perfect texture and draping qualities" of Skinner's silks. For an ordinary woman to achieve the glamour of Hollywood, this campaign implied, Skinner's silk was the place to start.

Apart from its executive offices in New York, Skinner & Sons maintained sales offices in Atlanta, Baltimore, Boston, Cincinnati, Cleveland, Chicago, Dallas, Detroit, Los Angeles, Philadelphia, Rochester, San Francisco, and St. Louis. During the 1950s the company had representatives in Latin America, Australia, New Zealand, and South Africa. By this time, however, it had all but ceased manufacturing silk, so unprofitable had that become with the advent of synthetics. (The last piece of "perfectly woven" satin was apparently made in 1948 for a wedding dress worn by one of Skinner's great-granddaughters.) Moreover, not even a company as ambitious as Skinner's could expect to survive much longer as a U.S. silk manufacturer. The fact that the mills were still around was remarkable; the silk industry had all but vanished in the United States by this point, a victim of, among other things, cheap imports from overseas manufactured for a fraction of the cost. In a repeat of history, foreign competition had again become the bane of the American silk manufacturer. But whereas foreign silks had long ago cornered the market because of their luxuriousness, they now cornered it because of their affordability.

The company began purchasing silks abroad and "finishing" them or re-branding them with the Skinner name, but it eventually could no longer capitalize upon its name, because textile manufacturers had lost their influence over the retail market. What consumers wanted in the post–World War II era were designer labels. It didn't matter anymore what a dress was made of, but rather who had made it and where it came from. In its heyday Skinner & Sons had driven trends and reaped the rewards, but as fabric lost its influence on consumers, the company lost its historical advantage. A seismic shift was taking place in the fashion world, one that Skinner's ultimately found unconquerable.

Accepting the inevitable on the books, but also, to its detriment, suffering from a loyalty to Holyoke and an unwillingness to downsize or leave the city in an attempt to somehow survive, Skinner's board of directors reluctantly sold William Skinner & Sons in February 1961 to the Indian Head Mills, a New York–based firm that viewed mills like Skinner's as opportunities to make money. The opportunity lay not in manufacturing in this case, but in profit from liquidation. That the mills would be liquidated by an outfit using for its name what had once been the Skinner company logo was an arresting irony. The logo had evolved many times over the years; this would be its last incarnation.

As unfortunate as the end may have been, however, this "giant textile house" had survived longer than anyone could have foretold. William Skinner & Sons had risen to become one of the longest family-owned textile companies in American history and, as an independent concern, outlasted all of its original competitors. It had even outlasted the American silk trade itself. When the mills closed in 1961, almost eighty-seven years after the disaster, the company had been in business for more than a century—113 years.

What's perhaps more surprising is the legacy left by Skinner's original thread. More than a quarter century after the Mill River disaster, people found spools of silk thread that had been swept away with Skinner's old mill. They surfaced when a farmer turned the soil for planting or when construction workers excavated land for a foundation. While the spools had mostly rotted, the thread, once cleaned, was as bright, colorful, and strong as the day it had been manufactured back in 1874. That Skinner's silk could survive buried in the ground for more than twenty-five years and still be as good as new demonstrated, as little else could, the quality of his products.

"Talk of giving up . . . *NEVER*," Skinner once wrote, and whenever articles were written about him or his company, his unwillingness to face defeat after the Mill River flood proved central to the narrative. "What seemed to be an irreparable disaster," wrote the *Holyoke Telegram* in 1902, "was quickly turned by Mr. Skinner into a better fortune." That the disaster had occurred in his fiftieth year and his real success didn't arrive until his sixties gained him tremendous admiration for his perseverance. Another paper noted that the obstacles he faced "to a lesser man would have proven a stepping stone to defeat." His choices following the flood remained exemplary of the courage and integrity one can summon in a crisis. He did not act hastily; he did what he felt was right, and he bravely went forward in a direction where no one else was willing to go, all the while imagining his future and what that could still be.

Long after his passing Skinner's personal and professional triumph remained inspirational. In 1929 the *Boston Sunday Post* called his turnaround after the flood "one of the greatest comebacks in the annals of American industry," and his sons retold the story of the flood in several of the firm's promotional booklets and advertisements. If an item was made with Skinner's satin, the story implied, it was something to admire not just for its quality, but also for its history.

Given the extraordinary impact of Skinner's company in the twentieth century, *Reader's Digest,* which had the largest readership in America in the 1950s, highlighted Skinner as one of the most influential Englishmen to land on American soil. Skinner had "struck out on his own," arriving by himself in the United States at the young age of twenty with just one skill—how to dye silk—that he parlayed into one opportunity after another. In the process he helped build a new American industry, one that clothed millions of Americans in the most glamorous fabric the world has to offer. And he built a company—not once, but twice—that manufactured American silk in all its brilliance from the eve of the Civil War to after World War II.

The Mill River Disaster altered Skinner's life forever and, apart from his company, defined him as little else would. The effects of the flood also reverberated through his family for years, sometimes with dramatic consequence. When the Massachusetts towns of Dana, Enfield, Greenwich, and Prescott were purposefully flooded in the 1930s, to create the Quabbin Reservoir for fresh water for Boston, Joe Skinner purchased and saved Prescott's First Congregational Church. He moved the building to South Hadley, where he was then living, and turned it into a museum of Americana and curios, featuring, among other things, his boyhood collection from the Hampshire valley of rocks and arrowheads. He also saved the Paige house in Prescott and moved it adjacent to the church. The Paige house was initially "reconstructed to resemble an early schoolhouse" but eventually housed a collection of birds, including, of no small importance, a selection of songbirds. Joe, Will, Belle, and Katharine Skinner all became noted philanthropists, but Belle left the most permanent mark of them all. After volunteering in the relief effort during World War I, both at home and abroad, she legally adopted a war-torn village in France that the government had decided to abandon. With stock from her father's silk company, she rebuilt the village of Hattonchâtel, thoroughly modernized it, and enabled its inhabitants, who had been dispersed during the war, to come home again. As a result, with money that had been made in American silk in Holyoke, a community in France that faced total abandonment was saved. Thanks to Belle Skinner, the village of Hattonchâtel exists to this day.

Skinnerville does not, except in the minds of the locals, who refer to a small stretch of Route 9 in Williamsburg as Skinnerville. There is no village there, just a few houses, an old bar, a plant nursery, and an ice cream stand in the summer. You can find the place where Skinner's mansion used to be only because a small electric plant is hidden in some trees there, and those who know the history will say that is the spot. The mansion itself is still in Holyoke, where Skinner rebuilt it, and is now a museum on the National Register of Historic Places. You can tour the grounds and look up at this great building that saw so much so many years ago. You can walk around the double parlor where the floor once caved in, and you can stand on the front veranda that was half torn off. You can even imagine Skinner running out there on that fateful morning, having just heard the shout, "The reservoir has given way and is right here! . . . Get out of the way!" You can imagine him at that unexpected hour, when he lost everything in an instant to the water. But if Skinner were standing beside you as you looked out from the veranda and envisioned that moment of defeat, he might tell you, in that accent that never entirely left Spitalfields, what he used to tell his children: "Energy and pluck will win."

Notes

Abbreviations Used
BDG *Boston Daily Globe*
RGD *R. G. Dun & Company Collection, Baker Library Historical Collections, Harvard Business School*
ESH *Elizabeth Skinner Hubbard*
HG *Hampshire Gazette*
HT *Holyoke Transcript*
NFP *Northampton Free Press*
NYT *New York Times*
PDP *Paterson Daily Press*
RCHS *Rensselaer County Historical Society*
SAS *Sarah (Elizabeth) Allen Skinner*
SDR *Springfield Daily Republican*
SDU *Springfield Daily Union*
SFP *Skinner Family Papers, Wistariahurst Museum*
WCS *William Cobbett Skinner*
WHS *Williamsburg Historical Society*
WS *William Skinner*

Chapter 1
4 "without the thought": Silk Association of America, *Annual Report of the Silk Association of America, 1874* (New York: Silk Association of America, 1874), 64.

Notes

4 "to lunch, dine or sip": *New York World,* quoted in Lately Thomas, *Delmonico's: A Century of Splendor* (Boston: Houghton, Mifflin, 1967), 121.

4 "the most luxurious restaurant": www.steakperfection.com/delmonico/History.html, accessed Jun. 5, 2006.

4 "the American silk industry is": *New York Commercial Advertiser,* May 16, 1874.

5 "all this of course": Thomas, *Delmonico's,* 102–3.

6 "to compel [the colonists] to supply": Linus P. Brockett, *The Silk Industry in America: A History. Prepared for the Centennial Exposition* (New York: Silk Association of America, 1876), 26.

8 "the most eminent silk manufacturer": Ibid., 29.

9 "was pronounced in England": Ibid., 30.

9 "a silk waistcoat": Ibid., 28.

10 "seems . . . to have been": Alfred T. Lilly, *The Silk Industry in the United States, from 1766–1874* (Boston: John Wilson and Son, 1875), 2.

10 "I find men and manners": David McCullough, *John Adams* (New York: Simon & Schuster, 2001), 398.

10 "Gentlemen, you have in your hands": Brockett, *The Silk Industry in America,* 36.

11 "To do this would necessitate": Ibid., 42.

11 "one after another of the experimenters": Ibid., 38

12 "the extravagant prices": Ibid., 44.

12 "Plant mulberries": Samuel Whitmarsh, *Eight Years Experience and Observation in the Culture of the Mulberry Tree, and in the Care of the Silk Worm* (Northampton, MA: J. H. Butler, 1839), 11.

12 "from different parts of the country": Lilly, *The Silk Industry in the United States,* 7.

13 "Our Connecticut women": Brockett, *The Silk Industry in America,* 32.

13 "operations begun": Victor S. Clark, *History of Manufactures in the United States, 1607–1860* (Washington, DC: The Carnegie Institute of Washington, 1916), 580.

13 "There is not, positively": "Christopher Crowfield" (pseudonym for Harriet Beecher Stowe), "House and Home Papers," *Atlantic Monthly* 14, no. 18 (1864): 94–95.

14 "expressed the belief": Agnes Hannay, "A Chronicle of Industry on the Mill River," *Smith College Studies in History* 21, nos. 1–4 (1935–1936): 61.

14 "to be a very excellent article": HG, February 1, 1837.

14 "*Resolved*": Silk Association of America, *Annual Report* (1874), 52.

15 "the times which tried the souls": Brockett, *The Silk Industry in America,* 67.

15 "almost annihilated": Ibid., 79.

16 "The war . . . compelled": Ibid., 61.

17 "forty-four firms and companies": Ibid., 84.

17 One congressman: Silk Association of America, *Annual Report* (1874), 55.

Notes

17 "I do not know why": Silk Association of America, *Annual Report of the Silk Association of America, 1873* (New York: Silk Association of America, 1873), 29–30.

18 "People do not realize it": Ibid., 33,

18 "No one need be ashamed": Ibid., 31.

19 "anti-inflationists": PDP, May 14, 1874.

19 "Tonight, gentlemen": Silk Association of America, *Annual Report* (1874), 55.

20 "While many trades are languishing": Ibid., 17.

20 "In times past": Ibid., 56.

21 "exceedingly anxious": Ibid., 65.

22 "It gave me great pleasure": Ibid., 32.

22 "[saying] something so original": James Cowan, *Twelve Years of The Club* (Holyoke, MA: The Club, 1902), 14.

23 "If we progress": Silk Association of America, *Annual Report* (1874), 64.

24 "loved giving things": Florence W. Gibson, "Recollection of Grandfather Skinner," December 1969. Author's collection.

25 "amazing genius": Recollection of Belle Skinner, in Helen Burt Clark, *Skinner Family Reunion* (New Rochelle, NY: The Knickerbocker Press, 1927), 37.

26 "a little one-car special": Author email correspondence with Gregg M. Turner, former director and curator of the Railway & Locomotive Historical Society, Harvard Business School, October 3, 2006.

26 "a very expert player": WCS, 1890 Diary, entry for May 26. Author's Collection.

Chapter 2

28 "very pretty cottage": Ellen Littlefield to Elizabeth Littlefield, May 9, 1872, Huntley/Littlefield Collection, RCHS.

29 "seeking employment": Thomas Dublin, *Women at Work: The Transformation of Work and Community in Lowell, Massachusetts, 1826–1860*, 2nd ed. (New York: Columbia University Press, 1993), 31.

30 "on account of": SDR, May 18, 1874.

30 "Seldom is there a river": NFP, May 9, 1874.

30 "Have you any fear": Chloe Littlefield to Ellen Littlefield, February 30, 1873, Huntley/Littlefield Collection, RCHS.

31 "What do you have for excitement": *New York Tribune*, May 19, 1874.

32 "wired so the backs stood up": Elizabeth Hubbard Jennings, "The Williamsburg Flood," 1933, Private Collection, Peabody, MA.

33 "The first process": *Manufacturer and Builder* 2, no. 3 (Mar. 1870): 82.

36 "The reservoir has given way": NFP, May 30, 1874.

37 "he didn't drive any faster": Jennings, 1933.

37 "With great presence of mind": *New York Tribune*, May 20, 1874.

37 "all the machinery stopped": Jennings, 1933.

Notes

38   "something was wrong": Ibid.

38   "They're all burning out up there," Louis H. Everts, *History of the Connecticut Valley in Massachusetts*, Vol. I (Philadelphia: privately printed, 1879), 421.

39   "commanded him": Recollection of Fred Warner, in Martha Skinner Hubbard, *Skinner Family Reunion* (New York: Knickerbocker Press, 1922), 19.

39   "one of the young men": Jennings, 1933.

39   "men & boys were running": Ellen Littlefield to Elizabeth Littlefield, October 10, 1869, Littlefield Letters, SFP.

39   "happened to look out his door": NFP, Jun. 6, 1874.

39   "It seemed to stop": SDU, May 21, 1874.

40   "terror-stricken": Recollection of Fred Warner, in Hubbard, *Skinner Family Reunion*, 19.

41   "fly to the hill!": *The Daily Graphic* (New York, NY), May 19, 1874.

41   "At one time": ESH, "The Haydenville Flood," Private Collection, Essex, CT.

42   "rolled on in its appalling force": SDR, May 18, 1874.

Chapter 3

43   "For God's sake, George": SDR, May 18, 1874.

43   "small, dismal-looking dwelling": Ibid.

44   "pretty well frightened": NFP, May 30, 1874.

45   "Keep off the dam!": SDU, Sep. 30, 1894.

45   "looked white": NFP, May 30, 1874.

45   "panting terribly": BDG, May 26, 1874.

45   "What's the matter?": Dialogue drawn from testimony in SDR, May 18 and 26, 1874; BDG, May 26, 1874; HG, May 26, 1874; NFP, and May 30, 1874; as well as from recollections in *Boston Sunday Globe*, Dec 21, 1902.

45   "of little education": SDR, May 18, 1874.

46   "considerable excitement": HG, May 26, 1874.

46   "a load or two": NFP, May 30, 1874.

46   "The dam is breaking away!": Dialogue drawn from testimony in SDR, May 26, 1874; HG, May 26, 1874; BDG May 26, 1874; and NFP May 30, 1874.

47   "wasn't possible": BDG, May 26, 1874.

47   "one of the best barns in town": HG, Jun. 11, 1872.

47   "George, what's the matter?": Dialogue drawn from testimony in BDG, May 26, 1874.

48   "'keeping his head' under excitement": NFP May 30, 1874.

49   "there was not a minute to lose": *Boston Sunday Globe*, Dec 21, 1902.

50   "the noise and din": HG, May 26, 1874.

50   "great danger . . . so close": *Boston Sunday Globe*, Dec. 21, 1902.

50   "somewhat known for chaffing": BDG, May 27, 1874.

51   "thousands of water and steam valves": NFP, Jul. 14, 1871.

Notes

51 "It won't be down here for four days": *Boston Sunday Globe,* Dec. 21, 1902.

52 "looks down on the overseers": "Letter to Brother Dean," May 3, 1856, WHS.

52 "[Cheney] is as 'smart'": BDG, May 27, 1874.

52 "If what [Wentworth] said is true": *Boston Sunday Globe,* Dec. 21, 1902.

53 "roaring [like] rolling thunder": HG, May 26, 1874.

53 "shouted and gesticulated": BDG, May 27, 1874.

53 "I had to wade": SDU, Sep. 30, 1894.

54 "like a pyramid of sugar in hot water": HG, May 18, 1874.

55 "the very turf torn off": SDU, Sep. 30, 1894.

56 "I question if the noon": "John Paul" in *Full and Graphic Account of the Terrible Mill River Disaster* (Springfield, MA: Weaver, Shipman & Co., 1874), 37.

Chapter 4

59 "in which Lord Byron died": HT, Dec. 12, 1874.

60 "Nature cast my lot": WS, "A Silk Dress." Paper delivered at The Club, Holyoke, MA, January 21, 1893, Gibson Family Papers, The Vaughan Homestead Foundation, Hallowell, ME.

60 "not very strong": WCS, "The Skinners," n.d., SFP.

60 "from generation to generation": HT, Dec. 12, 1874.

60 "attributed his success": Belle Skinner, Skinner Coffee House Founder's Day Speech, November 1920, SFP.

60 "The boys and girls of weavers": Thomas Archer, *The Pauper, The Thief and The Convict: Sketches of Some of Their Homes, Haunts and Habits* (London: Groombridge and Sons, 1865), II: 17. Courtesy of Lee Jackson, www.victorianlondon .org/publications3/pauper-2.htm.

61 "all the household was obliged to assist": WS, "A Silk Dress."

62 "the blackened forest of chimneys": Charles Dickens, *Little Dorrit,* 1857 (Reprint, New York: Penguin Books, 2003), 56.

62 "the delicate fabric": Archer, *The Pauper,* II:19.

62 "and perhaps a red herring, or a piece of cheese": Margaret Cox, *Life and Death in Spitalfields, 1700–1850* (York, England: Council for British Archeology, 1996), 23. For the rest of his life, Skinner considered herring to be a delicacy, and he believed, to the amusement of his friends, that people who ate cheese were more culturally advanced than those who didn't.

62 "eating in one corner": HT, Dec. 12, 1874.

63 "House after house presents": Charles Knight, *Knight's Cyclopaedia of London, 1851,* Vol. II (London: C. Knight, 1851), 386.

63 "a lecture on the wrongness of shooting songbirds": Gibson, "Recollection of Grandfather Skinner."

63 "more sheets of paper": Sir Frank Warner, *The Silk Industry of the United Kingdom: Its Origin and Development* (London: Drane's Danegeld House, 1921), 60.

379

Notes

63 "walls and ceiling[s]": George Godwin, *London Shadows* (London: George Routledge & Co., 1854), III: 17. Courtesy of Lee Jackson, http://www.victorianlondon.org/publications4/shadows-03.htm.

63 "The water runs off": Alan Palmer, *The East End: Four Centuries of London Life* (New Brunswick, NJ: Rutgers University Press, 2000), 57.

63 "[argued] that it would cost less": Ibid.

64 "more machines than active livers": James Cantlie, *Degeneration Amongst Londoners* (London: Field & Tuer, 1885), 39. Courtesy of Lee Jackson. http://www.victorianlondon.org/publications/degeneration.htm.

64 "miserable objects of charity": William Hale, *A Letter to Samuel Whitbread, Esq. M.P. Containing Observations on the Distresses Peculiar to the Poor of Spitalfields, Arising from Their Local Situation* (London: Williams and Smith, 1807).

64 "ashamed to appear in the streets": Sir Thomas Fowell Buxton, *The Speech of Thomas Fowell Buxton, Esq. at the Egyptian Hall, on the 26th of November, 1816, on the subject of The Distress in Spitalfields: to which is added The Report of the Spitalfields Association, read at the meeting* (London: W. Phillips, 1816).

64 "a stunted, puny race": Cantlie, *Degeneration Amongst Londoners*, 39.

64 "It is not that some starve": Sir Thomas Fowell Buxton, *The Speech of Thomas Fowell Buxton.*

66 "more to France than": Jeanne-Baptiste Colbert, as quoted in Warner, *The Silk Industry,* 41.

66 "nearly annihilated": Brockett, *The Silk Industry in America,* 24.

67 "whose head [was] well turned": Warner, *The Silk Industry,* 199.

67 "so incensed": Ibid., 200.

69 "the religious fervor": Samuel Smiles. *The Huguenots: Their Settlements, Churches, & Industries in England and Ireland* (London: John Murray, 1867), 426.

69 "This is the only district": Hale, *A Letter to Samuel Whitbread.*

69 "not a piece of fine feminine Spitalfields silk": Herman Melville, *Moby-Dick: or, The Whale: The Writings of Herman Melville* (Evanston and Chicago: Northwestern University Press and the Newberry Library, 1988), 686.

70 "exotic": J. L. Hammond and Barbara Hammond, *The Skilled Labourer, 1760–1832,* Reprint (New York: A. M. Kelley, 1967), 205.

70 "in a single stroke": Steve Dunwell, *The Run of the Mill* (Boston: David R. Godine, 1978), 9.

70 "Slater the Traitor": Griff Everett and the Slater Study Group, *Samuel Slater—Hero or Traitor? The Story of an American Millionaire's Youth and Apprenticeship in England* (Milford, Derbyshire, England: Maypole Promotions, 2006), preface.

70 "it was inexpedient": Harriet Martineau, *History of the Peace: Being a History of England from 1816–1854,* Vol. II (Boston: Walker, Wise & Co., 1865), 395.

71 "never doing anything": WCS, "The Skinners."

Notes

72   "the curriculum is thorough": "John Paul" in *Full and Graphic Account,* 37.

72   "It is my strong hope": WS to WCS, Nov. 19, 1875, SFP.

72   "vividly": HT, Nov. 14, 1924.

73   "a friend": ESH, Skinner Coffee House Founder's Day Speech, pre-1920, SFP.

74   "drunkenness . . . [was] the regular and normal state of affairs": Glinert, *East End Chronicles,* 162.

74   "highly-coloured deposits": Palmer, *The East End,* 60.

74   "At this time": Quoted in Briton Richardson, *An Address Upon the Silk Industry of the United States Delivered in the* SDU *of New York, October 28, 1869* (New York: S. W. Green, 1869), 8.

74   "Fancy yourself": Charles Dickens, with W. H. Wills, "Spitalfields," *Household Words,* 5 April 1851, reprinted in *Selected Journalism 1850–1870* (New York: Penguin Books, 1997), 298.

75   "[merge] intellect and passion": Virginia Mason Vaughan, *Othello: A Contextual History* (Cambridge: Cambridge University Press, 1994), 140.

75   "much of his early education": Cowan, *Twelve Years of the Club,* 14.

75   "Shall we ever forget": Ibid.

75   "strong and implacable hatred": William Cobbett, *The Progress of a Plough-Boy to a Seat in Parliament, as Exemplified in the History of the Life of William Cobbett, Member for Oldham.* Edited by William Reitzel (London: Faber and Faber, 1933), 275.

76   "prodigious band of spungers": Ibid., 274.

76   "a mass of blunders": Ibid., 245.

76   "until the last hour of [his] life": Ibid., 275.

76   "I know just who you are": Author interview with Jonathan Logan, descendant of William Skinner, Jul. 14, 2008.

77   "I hate the United States": Cobbett, *Progress of a Plough-Boy,* 84.

77   "suffered from a death rate": Ed Glinert, *East End Chronicles* (New York: Allen Lane, 2005), 158.

77   "the evil quarter-mile": Ibid., 162.

78   "greatly attached to their neighborhood": Godwin, *London Shadows,* VI, 34.

78   "virtual death": Nancy L. Green, "The Politics of Exile: Reversing the Immigration Paradigm," *Journal of Modern History* 77 (June 2005): 267.

78   "There was something so powerful": Cobbett, *Progress of a Plough-Boy,* 173.

79   "garden suburb": Warner, *The Silk Industry,* 56.

79   "he had some French blood in his veins": Belle Skinner, Skinner Coffee House Founder's Day Remarks, HT, Nov. 15, 1922.

80   "fast becoming the focus": Brockett, *The Silk Industry in America,* 134.

80   "William came to the United States": *Dictionary of American Biography* (New York: Charles Scribner's Sons, 1935), 202.

Notes

80 "was noted for having": Interview #13A with Elizabeth Kilborne Hudnut. Private Collection, New York, NY.

80 "Every time he had a chance": Ibid.

82 "but enough—": WS to Eleanor Skinner, Sep. 16, 1892, SFP.

82 "take a bath": Interview #13A with Elizabeth Kilborne Hudnut. Private Collection, New York, NY.

82 "the hardest kind of men": Charles Porter Low, *Some Recollections by Captain Charles P. Low* (Boston: George H. Ellis Co., 1906), 34.

Chapter 5

83 "fought their way": Robert C. Leslie, *Old Sea Wings, Ways and Words, In the Days of Oak and Hemp* (London: Chapman and Hall, Ltd., 1890), 217.

83 "The air is so bad": WS to SAS, Jun. 18, 1860, SFP.

83 "the only regular line of packets": Leslie, *Old Sea Wings,* 216.

84 "struck upon the ice": Charles Dickens, *American Notes* (New York: Modern Library, 1996), 292.

84 "a deep ship, will, very probably": Evidence of Captain Schomberg, R. N., emigration officer, in *Second Report from the Select Committee on Emigrant Ships,* Vol. 13 (House of Commons, 1854), 19.

84 "gloomy place": Leslie, *Old Sea Wings,* 228.

85 "a dip-candle hanging": Ibid.

85 "supplied uncooked": Terry Coleman, *Going to America* (New York: Pantheon Books, 1972), 288.

85 "[such] a rancid smell": William Bell, *Hints to Emigrants, in a Series of Letters from Upper Canada* (Edinburgh: Printed for Waugh and Innes, 1824), Letter IV.

86 "uneasy" and "as nervous as can be": WS to SAS, Jun. 18, 1860, SFP.

86 "Glorious morning!": Coleman, *Going to America,* 169.

86 "rarely seen lightning": George Templeton Strong, *Diary, 1835–1875* (New York: 1835–75), entry Jul. 22, 1845.

87 "tremendous" : Cobbett, *Progress of a Plough-Boy,* 62.

87 "beautiful sight": WS to SAS, Jun. 18, 1860, SFP.

88 "notions of wealth": Brockett, *The Silk Industry in America,* 112.

88 "the biters were bitten": WS, *A Silk Dress.*

89 "dear bought and far-fetched": Richardson, *An Address Upon the Silk Industry,* 12.

89 "I have been . . .": Captain Conant to Orwell Chaffee, Jun. 6, 1846, Orwell S. Chaffee Papers, Thomas J. Dodd Research Center, University of Connecticut.

90 "Don't laugh": Almira Stetson to James A. Stetson, n.d., letter no. 40, Christopher Clark and Kerry W. Buckley, eds. *Letters from an American Utopia: The Stetson Family and the Northampton Association, 1843–1847* (Amherst, MA: University of Massachusetts Press, 2004), 89.

90 "had no dyeing facilities": Albert H. Heusser, *The History of the Silk Dyeing Indus-*

try in the United States (Paterson, NJ: Silk Dyers' Association of America, 1927), 134.

90 "The only reason": Amy Butler Greenfield, *A Perfect Red* (New York: Harper Perennial, 2005), 14.

91 "all the information": Records of the Northampton Association of Education and Industry, American Antiquarian Society, vol. 2, p. 34.

91 "followed up this entering wedge": Brockett, *The Silk Industry in America,* 134.

92 "also dealt extensively in real estate": *Commemorative Biographical Record of Tolland and Windham Counties, Connecticut* (Chicago: J. H. Beers & Co., 1903). http://www.rootsweb.ancestry.com/~cttollan/records/vitalrecords/biographies/olonschaffeeandjosephconant.html. Sep. 25, 2008.

93 "It is natural for persons": Coleman, *Going to America,* 41.

93 "making silk was not": Charles A. Sheffield, ed. *The History of Florence, Massachusetts* (Florence, MA: Charles A. Sheffield, 1895), 61.

94 "robust constitution": Lilly, *The Silk Industry in the United States,* 11.

94 "an emigrant might do well": Coleman, *Going to America,* 41.

94 "Succeed . . . you cannot afford": WS to WCS, Oct. 27, 1875, SFP.

94 "[undergoing] frequent changes": RGD, Massachusetts, vol. 46, p. 107

95 "A good dyer": Rita J. Adrosko, *Natural Dyes and Home Dyeing,* Reprint (Mineola, NY: Dover Publications, 1971), 3.

96 "mordants, while necessary": Greenfield, *A Perfect Red,* 12.

96 "with alum a primrose-yellow": Dr. John Feltwell, *The Story of Silk* (New York: St. Martin's Press, 1990), 120.

96 "had to become adept": Ian Holme (2006), "Sir William Henry Perkin: A Review of His Life, Work and Legacy," Coloration Technology, 122: 235–251. doi: 10.1111/j.1478–4408.2006.00041.x. February 11, 2008.

96 "eternal vigilance": Heusser, *History of the Silk Dyeing Industry,* 503.

97 Take four pounds of good logwood: *The Domestic Dyer: being receipts for dying cotton and linen, hot and cold* (New England: Printed for Domestic Uses, 1811). http://www.elizabethancostume.net/dyes/domesticdyer.html#12. December 8, 2008.

97 "the only material": Richard Gibson, *The Art of Dyeing All Colors of Raw Cotton or Cotton Waste, For the Purpose of Working with Raw Wool: Also the Methods of Dyeing All Colors in the Piece* (Willimantic, CT: Joseph Rollinson, agent, 1861), 393.

97 "the dyer, in effect, had to act": Sidney Edelstein, "Coppers, Kettles and Vats: Equipment in Early Dyehouses," from *The American Dyestuff Reporter* 44 (April 1955). http://www.elizabethancostume.net/dyes/vats.html. May 14, 2008.

98 "would have been broadly familiar": Holme, "Sir William Henry Perkin."

98 "the age-honored long vat": Heusser, *History of the Silk Dyeing Industry,* 498.

98 "not fit for either man or beast": Gibson, *The Art of Dyeing,* 14.

Notes

99   "As everybody knows": Steve Golin, *The Fragile Bridge: Paterson Silk Strike, 1913* (Philadelphia: Temple University Press, 1922), 24.

99   "Shoes up!": Heusser, *History of the Silk Dyeing Industry,* 496.

99   "A few moments": Ibid., 503.

100 "the cloth when first taken": Edelstein, "Coppers, Kettles and Vats: Equipment in Early Dyehouses."

100 "relief and increased power": J. J. Hummel, F. C. S, *The Dyeing of Textile Fabrics* (London: Cassell & Company, Ltd., 1890), 292–93.

100 "appear more solid, and thicker": Brockett, *The Silk Industry in America,* 93.

100 "[took advantage] of this operation": Alfred Barlow, *The History and Principles of Weaving by Hand and by Power,* 2nd ed (London: Sampson, Low, Marston, Searle & Rivington, 1879), 394.

101 "to deceive": Greenfield, *A Perfect Red,* 13.

102 "the better known": Rev. Solomon Clark, *Antiquities, Historicals and Graduates of Northampton* (Northampton, MA: Stearn Press, Gazette Printing Co., 1882), 157.

103 "I don't mean to stay": Mary Warner to Joseph Warner, Jun. 28, 1839. Letters of the Warner Family, Historic Northampton Archives and Manuscripts Collection.

103 "the smartest in [the] family": Mary Warner to Joseph Warner, Aug. 10, 1839. Letters of the Warner Family, Historic Northampton Archives and Manuscripts Collection.

104 "I'm miserable": Thomas Haynes Bayly, *The Spitalfields Weaver: A Comic Drama* (London: Thomas Hailes Lacy, n.d), 6.

104 "more than the ordinary degree": RGD, Massachusetts, vol. 46, p. 107.

104 "a close observer": Cowan, *Twelve Years of the Club,* 13.

104 "rugged, forceful personality": SDR, Nov. 17, 1898.

105 "I heard that [Joseph]": Eliza Warner Strong to Nancy Warner, Jan. 2, 185[2], Letters of the Warner Family, Historic Northampton Archives and Manuscripts Collection.

105 "authorized to settle": HG, Jan. 6, 1852.

105 "Get all luck notions out": WS to WCS, Sep. 30, 1875, SFP.

106 "the thread snapped": Frank P. Bachman, *Great Inventors and Their Inventions* (New York, Cincinnati, and Chicago: American Book Co., 1918), 138.

106 "great difficulty": *Scientific American* 5 (April 6, 1850), 228.

107 "entirely free from slugs": Francis A. Walker, ed., *United States Centennial Exhibition 1876, Reports and Awards, Group IX* (Philadelphia: J. B. Lippincott & Co., 1877), 97.

107 "The silk was handed": Ibid., 96–97.

107 "[made] the manufacture of sewing-silks": Brockett, *The Silk Industry in America,* 72.

107 "bashfulness": Joseph Warner, Sr., to Joseph Warner, Jun. 1838, Letters of the Warner Family, Historic Northampton Archives and Manuscripts Collection.

107 "safe": RGD, Massachusetts, vol. 46, p. 131.

108 "one of those go-ahead men": HG, Jul. 17, 1860.

108 "Warner hypo": WS to Fred Warner, Dec. 28, 1899, SFP.

108 "a man of action": Remembrance of Dr. E. A. Reed, SDR, May 18, 1903.

Chapter 6

110 "The effects of trade and manufacturing": Henry S. Gere, ed., *An Historical Sketch of Haydenville and Williamsburg,* typescript prepared from the *Hampshire Gazette* 1860–61 (Reproduced for the Town of Williamsburg by Ralmon Jon Black, 1999), 23.

113 "always neatly dressed": Gibson, "Recollection of Grandfather Skinner."

113 "He would never have bought": HT, Nov. 16, 1908.

113 "the mill simply continued": Dunwell, *Run of the Mill,* 14.

115 "a manufacturer [could] start": Shichiro Matsui, *History of the Silk Industry in the United States* (New York: Howes Publishing Co., 1930), 177.

115 "received the silk that Europe rejected": Ibid., 60.

116 "a good assortment of all kinds": HG, Dec. 12, 1854.

116 "had more than an ordinary understanding": *Boston Sunday Post,* Jul. 7, 1929.

116 "an honest, upright, straight forward man": RGD, Massachusetts, vol. 46, p. 127.

116 "doing a good business": Ibid.

116 "suddenly stopped": Betsy Cantwell, "Courage and Quality: The Story of William Skinner and Sons" (1955), Robert Cantwell Papers, Division of Special Collections & University Archives, University of Oregon Libraries.

117 "one of the country's prominent woolen concerns": Hannay, "Chronicle of Industry on the Mill River," 9.

117 "presented with [a] roll of broadcloth": Robert P Emrick, comp., *Leeds: A Village Within the City of Northampton, Massachusetts,* James Parsons, ed. (Northampton, MA, 1999), 21.

118 "chief aim": SAS to Belle Skinner, May 3, 1882, SFP.

118 "had never heard of God": Godwin, *London Shadows,* vol. 8, 47.

119 "pure American ancestry": *Boston Sunday Post,* Jul. 7, 1929.

119 "the first woman in Massachusetts": Heusser, *History of the Silk Dyeing Industry,* 144.

120 "good character and habits": RGD, Massachusetts, vol. 46, p. 127.

120 "keep his head above water": Matsui, *History of the Silk Industry in the United States,* 173.

120 "was always complaining": *Boston Sunday Post,* Jul. 7, 1929.

121 "not so imperative": Matsui, *History of the Silk Industry in the United States,* 193.

122 "prominent stocks fell": *Harper's Weekly,* Sep. 12, 1857. http://memory.loc.gov/ammem/today/aug24.html. Mar. 11, 2009.

123 "[Skinner] has just put up": RGD, Massachusetts, vol. 46, p. 127.

Notes

123 "but neither, we believe": HG, Jan 5, 1858.

123 "would not extend his paper": RGD, Massachusetts, vol. 46, p. 127.

123 "My advice to you": WS to Dr. Worthington Miner, Aug. 6, 1868. Charles E. Garman and Eliza Miner Garman Family Papers, Archives and Special Collections, Amherst College Library.

124 "fine mill": RGD, Massachusetts, vol. 46, p. 127.

124 "safe": Ibid.

125 "meticulously honest": *Boston Sunday Post,* Jul. 7, 1929.

125 "sincere in purpose" and "untiring": *Holyoke Evening Telegram,* Mar. 1, 1902.

125 "fair business": RGD, Massachusetts, vol. 46, p. 127.

125 "How pleased I was": SAS to WCS, Jun. 11, 1876, SFP.

126 "doing well": RGD, Massachusetts, vol. 46, p. 127.

126 "His silks are noted for their excellence": HG, Jul. 17, 1860.

126 "Mr. Skinner [knows] no such word as fail": Ibid.

127 "should have more capital": RGD, Massachusetts, vol. 46, p. 127.

Chapter 7

129 "If it was any place": Kerby A. Miller, *Emigrants and Exiles: Ireland and the Irish Exodus to North America* (New York: Oxford University Press, 1988), 252.

130 "I am mighty nervous": WS to SAS, Jun. 13, 1860, SFP.

130 "all the silk dyers and manufactures": WS to SAS, Jun. 18, 1860, SFP.

130 "[write] down all the facts": WS to SAS, Jun. 14, 1860, SFP.

130 "What a wonderful thing steam is": WS to SAS, Jun. 18, 1860, SFP.

131 "You cannot think": Ibid.

131 "Absence will make my heart grow fonder": Ibid.

131 "with all [his] soul": WS to SAS, Jun. 14, 1860, SFP.

131 "I often shut my eyes": WS to SAS, Jun. 29, 1860, SFP.

132 "have things done up in shape": WS to SAS, Jun. 18, 1860, SFP.

132 "I must now say my darling": Ibid.

132 "all the poetry of fair weather [was] gone": WS to SAS, Jun. 22, 1860, SFP.

132 "A week has nearly passed": WS to SAS, Jun. 29, 1860, SFP.

132 "[suffering] every day with cold": Ibid.

133 "struck with the general improvement": Ibid.

133 "There has been quite a change": WS to SAS, Jul. 7, 1860, SFP.

134 "Jim Keith thinks well of it": WS to SAS, Jun. 29, 1860, SFP.

134 "[Parties] that have seen it work": WS to SAS, Jul. 7, 1860, SFP.

135 "I must make the thing go": WS to SAS, Jun. 29, 1860, SFP.

135 "Again I am about to address you": SAS to WS, Jun. 28, 1860, SFP.

135 "Everything is working like a charm": George McFarlane to WS, Jun. 28, 1860, SFP.

136 "the silk trade is very dull": WS to SAS, Jun. 29, 1860, SFP.

136 "the silk trade is very dull in all its branches": WS to SAS, Jul. 7, 1860, SFP.

Notes

136 "I felt such a contempt for her": Ibid.

137 "I have seen nothing here": WS to SAS, Jun. 29, 1860, SFP.

137 "Williamsburg was too far north": Phyllis Baker Deming, *A History of Williamsburg in Massachusetts* (Northampton, MA: Hampshire Bookshop, 1946), 355.

137 "the largest and most enthusiastic meeting": HG, Jul. 15, 1862

138 "Occasionally the pulse of patriotism": HG, Mar. 28, 1865.

138 "one of the ways": Matsui, *History of the Silk Industry,* 30.

139 "We must have a high tariff": WS to SAS, Jul. 7, 1860, SFP.

139 "It is an undeniable fact": Matsui, *History of the Silk Industry,* 32.

139 "Wm Skinner [of] Haydenville . . . ": RGD, Massachusetts, vol. 46, p. 127.

139 "very good": Ibid.

139 "We notice that Wm. Skinner, Esq": HG, Jan. 9, 1866.

141 "much excitement": HG, Aug. 1, 1865.

141 "sensitive disposition": HG, Aug. 12, 1865.

142 "Many of the circumstances": Dickens, *American Notes,* 91.

142 "healthy in appearance": Ibid., 89.

142 "The owners of the mills are particularly careful": Ibid., 88.

143 "Employment in a factory": Anthony Trollope, *North America,* Donald Smalley and Bradford Allen Booth, eds. (New York: Alfred A. Knopf, 1951), 253.

145 "Such a man I have no use for": HT, Feb 9, 1886.

145 "he was straight-forward": *Boston Sunday Post,* Jul. 7, 1929.

145 "At times he was not diplomatic": Ibid.

145 "There are just as intelligent Irishmen": HT, Nov. 16, 1898.

145 "As an employer": HG, Mar. 5, 1902.

146 "a girl from Vermont": Lovisa Littlfield to Ellen Littlefield, Dec. 16, 1866, Huntley/Littlefield Collection, RCHS.

146 "a very good boarding house": Frances Littlefield to Ellen Littlefield, Jan 9, 1867, Huntley/Littlefield Collection, RCHS.

146 "a white hat": Ellen Littlefield to Elizabeth Littlefield, May 24, 1868, Huntley/Littlefield Collection, RCHS.

146 "teaching the young idea to shoot": HG, May 26, 1868.

146 "always had a pleasant smile"; Thomas Skinner obituary, HT, Dec 18, 1922.

147 "By comparing the past": HG, Mar. 28, 1865.

147 "Nature affords us many a contrast": HG, Jan. 22, 1867.

148 "Wm. Skinner . . . is building": HG, Jul. 28, 1868.

148 "Mr. Skinner's residence": NFP, Mar. 1, 1870.

149 "for the extinguishment of fires": HG, Nov. 26, 1872.

149 "independent character": SDR, Nov. 15, 1898.

149 "an argument against him": SDR, Nov. 17, 1898.

149 "Mr. Skinner is a blunt, plain man"; Reprint from HT in SDR, Nov. 17, 1898.

149 "original, forceful, masterful": Dr. E. A. Reed, SDU, Feb. 14, 1912.

149 "breaking down sales resistance": *Boston Sunday Post,* Jul. 7, 1929.

149 "merchandising genius": Ibid.

150 "I saw only one thing that I did not like": HG, Aug. 21, 1866.

151 "a man of striking appearance": HT, Feb. 28, 1902.

151 "superb strength": Remembrance of Mrs. W. G. Dwight, HT, Nov 15, 1917,

151 "of great value": Charles Carroll Dawson, *Saratoga: Its Mineral Waters and Their Use In Preventing and Eradicating Disease and as a Refreshing Beverage* (New York: Russell Brothers, 1874), 40.

151 "never saw such a change": WS to SAS, Sep. 6, 1866, SFP.

151 "Saratoga agrees with me": Ibid.

152 "Mind is the standard of the man": WS to WCS, May 5, 1874, SFP.

152 "Actions is eloquence": SDR, Oct. 10, 1888.

152 "At his office": HT, Nov. 16, 1908.

152 "It would, in my judgment": Dr. E. A. Reed, SDU, Feb. 14, 1912.

152 "expected obedience": Recollection of ESH, in Hubbard, *Skinner Family Reunion,* 39.

153 "The board would be called": Ellen Littlefield to Elizabeth Littlefield, Mar. 27, 1870, Huntley/Littlefield Collection, RCHS.

153 "bread and butter is": Ellen Littlefield to Elizabeth Littlefield, May 29, 1870, Littlefield Letters, SFP.

153 "To live a day without meat": Trollope, *North America,* 250.

153 "I have been so 'riled up'": Ellen Littlefield to Elizabeth Littlefield, May 29, 1870, Littlefield Letters, SFP.

153 We have been used most awful mean: Ibid.

153 "I should be very much pleased": Ibid.

154 "Sometimes we have": Ibid.

154 "Well": Ibid.

156 "inflammation of the bowels": SAS, 1870–1877 Diary, "Items Worth Remembering," entry for Mar. 30, 1872, Author's Collection.

156 "Oh the sweet little child": Ibid.

157 "Isn't it splendid": ESH to WCS, Nov. 16, 1873, SFP.

158 "This is a country": Silk Association of America, *Annual Report* (1873), 30.

158 "I am afraid": Nina Skinner to WCS, Nov. 9, 1873, SFP.

159 "William Skinner . . . is running": HG, Dec. 16, 1873.

Chapter 8

163 "No marked increase": SDR, May 15, 1874.

163 "The Williamsburg Reservoir gave way": NYT May 17, 1874.

163 "noticed that the men": WCS, 1874 Diary, entry for May 16, WHS.

164 "especially as the headmaster": HT, Jul. 17, 1937.

164 "was reported to be lost": Ibid.

Notes

164 "very anxious": Ibid.

165 "very nearly the only one standing": WCS, 1874 Diary, entry for May 17, WHS.

165 "confusedly resolved": Cantwell, "Courage and Quality" (1955).

165 "away from home at play": *New Haven Register,* May 18, 1874.

166 "potatoes and pianos": *The Daily Graphic* (New York, NY), May 18, 1874.

166 "All day": ESH, "The Haydenville Flood."

166 "buried in mud": Ibid.

167 "sat upon the tracks and knolls": NYT, May 18, 1874.

167 "escaped from the [boarding]house": HT, Dec 8, 1875.

167 "Well do I remember": HG, May 16, 1924.

167 "I worked for what I had": *New York Herald,* May 18, 1874

168 "great disaster": Eliza Miner, 1874 Diary, entry for May 16, Charles E. Garman and Eliza Miner Garman Family Papers, Archives and Special Collections, Amherst College Library.

168 "My Head": Recollection of Fred Warner, in Hubbard, *Skinner Family Reunion,* 20.

168 "as rapid a general view": NFP, May 16, 1874.

168 "gathering every detail": SDR, May 18, 1874.

168 "Reporters from New York": *New Haven Register,* May 16, 1874.

169 "with great difficulty": HG, May 19, 1874.

169 "I was just sitting down to breakfast": *The Daily Graphic,* May 18, 1874.

170 "the heaviest loser": *New York Sun,* May 18, 1874.

170 "a single brick left": *The Daily Graphic,* May 18, 1874.

170 "The ruin of Mr. Skinner's property": SDR, May 18, 1874.

172 "It was at Skinnerville": SDU, May 13, 1923.

172 "a perfect picture of devastation": "John Paul" in *Full and Graphic Account,* 37.

172 "The village of Skinnerville": SDU, May 18, 1874.

172 "appalling loss of life": SDR, May 18, 1874.

172 "In the United States": PDP, May 18, 1874.

172 "It begins to be understood": *New Haven Register,* May 16, 1874.

172 *Over the course:* The number of deaths ultimately tallied for each village is as follows: Williamsburg, 57; Skinnerville, 4; Haydenville, 27; and Leeds, 51. See Elizabeth M. Sharpe, *In the Shadow of the Dam* (New York: Free Press, 2004), 236-239.

173 "In Haydenville 37 families": SDR, May 19, 1874.

173 "electrifying": *Boston Morning Journal,* May 18, 1874.

173 "somebody [was] responsible": HG, May 19, 1874.

174 "at a moment": HG, May 19, 1874. When Governor Hayden had been alive, he had kept the level of the reservoir to a certain height, but that level was not maintained after his death in November 1873. In light of this, one could argue that the pressure upon the dam from the reservoir in the spring of 1874 was indeed unusual, and that, too, merited investigation.

174 "The reservoir . . . is said to have been": *New York Tribune,* May 18, 1874.

Notes

174 "a fine-looking old gentleman": SDR, May 18, 1874.

175 "nearly all [were] distracted": *New York Tribune*, May 18, 1874.

175 "the night that followed was black": SDR, May 18, 1874.

175 "owners preferred to remain": PDP, May 19, 1874.

176 "The whole county is awake": NYT, May 17, 1874.

176 "How many broken hearts:" HG, Sep. 3, 1921.

176 "a cool, sweet Sabbath dawn": SDR, May 18, 1874.

177 "his empty mill site": "John Paul" in *Full and Graphic Account*, 37.

178 "Lumber wagons": HG, May 19, 1874.

178 "Such a Sunday": SDR, May 18, 1874.

178 "the number of teams": SDU, May 18, 1874.

178 "several teams spilled": *Boston Evening Journal*, May 19, 1874.

178 "My carriage wheels": *New York Herald*, May 19, 1874.

178 "Nearly all the visitors": NYT, May 18, 1874.

179 "It is true": *Greenfield* (Mass.) *Gazette & Courier*, May 25, 1874.

179 "of culture and European travel": *The Daily Graphic*, May 18, 1874.

180 "I looked back and the factory was gone": All dialogue from *The Daily Graphic*, May 18, 1874.

181 "on the spot": Brockett, *Silk Industry in America*, 71.

181 "Directly after breakfast": E. H. R. Lyman to A. A. Low, May 18, 1874. Low Family Papers, MS 391, New York Historical Society.

181 "[Skinner's] mill and everything connected": Ibid.

182 "had friends": Ibid.

183 "[Skinner] claims to be poor now": RGD, New York, vol. 239, p. 1514.

183 "I said to Mr. Skinner": *New York Herald*, May 25, 1874.

183 "The feeling on his behalf": PDP, May 19, 1874.

183 "When, if ever": HG, May 19, 1874.

184 "the flood has taken everything": HG, Jun. 2, 1874.

184 "When a factory": HG, May 19, 1874.

184 "send up a committee": SDR, May 18, 1874.

184 "dismissed his operatives": *New York Sun*, May 18, 1874.

185 "It is stated": *Boston Daily Globe*, May 19, 1874.

185 "Mr. H. L. James notifies his help": SDU, May 18, 1874.

185 "I have lost all I had": *New York Herald*, May 18, 1874.

185 "We have but just begun": HG, May 19, 1874.

186 NOTICE: HG, May 19, 1874.

186 "One can have but a faint idea": *Boston Daily Globe*, May 18, 1874.

187 "should be purchased": *Greenfield Gazette & Courier*, May 25, 1874.

187 "On [Sunday], charity offered": ESH, "the Haydenville Flood."

187 "jestingly searching": *New York Herald*, May 18, 1874.

187 "laughingly remarked": SDU, May 18, 1874.

Notes

188 "in some places": *Boston Morning Journal,* May 18, 1874.

188 "if we are only prepared": SAS to Belle Skinner, May 3, 1882, SFP.

Chapter 9

189 "There was a strike among the workmen": *New York Herald,* May 18, 1874.

189 "The frosts had started the earth": *Boston Evening Transcript,* May 18, 1874.

189 "I cannot attach particular blame": *The Daily Graphic,* May 18, 1874.

190 "Whatever may have been the cause": *New York Herald,* May 18, 1874.

190 "the work as a whole": SDR, May 18, 1874.

190 "did not take a great deal of interest in it": NFP, May 30.

191 "the very lowest": HG, Aug. 12, 1873.

191 "Scarcely one of the mills": HG, Sep. 5, 1865

191 "Does the mill run or not": WS to SAS, n.d, (pre-1874), SFP.

191 "an experiment . . . so successful": Richard E. Greenwood, "A Brief Assessment of the Historical Significance of the Woonasquatucket River Valley." http://www .woonasquatucket.org/history.php. Jun. 26, 2009.

192 "with all the powers": April 1865: *Acts and Resolves Passed by the General Court of Massachusetts in the Year 1865* (Boston: Wright & Potter, State Printers, 1865), 549 .

192 "the notion widely held today": Fenwick English, ed., *The SAGE Handbook of Educational Leadership: Advances in Theory, Research, and Practice* (Thousand Oaks, CA: SAGE Publications, 2005), 217.

195 "We can fix it afterwards": SDR, May 29, 1874.

195 "stronger, larger and more expensive dam": SDR, May 21, 1874.

196 "considerable experience": SDR, May 19, 1874.

196 "common engineering knowledge": Betsy Hunter Bradley, *The Works: The Industrial Architecture of the United States* (New York and Oxford: Oxford University Press, 1999), 16.

197 "Earth": SDR, May 28, 1874.

197 "wet and slushy": SDR, May 28, 1874.

199 "concerning the personal liability": Record Book of the Williamsburg Reservoir Company, entry for May 14, 1867, Forbes Library, Northampton, MA.

199 "admissible evidence": SDR, May 25, 1874.

199 "he knew nothing of": SDR, May 28, 1874.

199 "hath neglected and refused": *Commonwealth vs. William Skinner Capias* Docket 58 1864 Book 1 Page 1865, Records of the Hampshire County Superior Court, Archives of the Suffolk County Courthouse, Boston, MA.

200 "the reservoir [was] considered": SDU, May 27, 1874.

200 "Mr. Skinner thinks": Ellen Littlefield to Elizabeth Littlefield, Oct. 10, 1869, Littlefield Letters, SFP.

200 "as high as comfort will allow": NFP, April 11, 1874.

201 "But if we had gone over to it": BDG, May 18, 1874.

Notes

201 "that numberless suits": SDU, May 18, 1874.

201 "[The] sadness of the event": *New York Herald,* May 18, 1874.

201 "Owners of property": BDG, May 18, 1874.

201 "If it be true": As quoted in SDR, May 19, 1874.

202 "proper safeguards against failure": *Worcester Spy,* quoted in SDR, May 19, 1874.

202 "incapacity": *New York World,* May 18, 1874.

202 "While the state provides": *Worcester Gazette,* quoted in SDR, May 19, 1874.

202 "There are many reservoirs": HG, May 19, 1874.

202 "In certain parts of hilly New England": *Harper's Weekly,* Jun. 6, 1874.

202 "the model American commonwealth": *New York World,* May 18, 1874.

203 "Nothing since war times": *Berkshire County Eagle,* May 21, 1874.

203 "As the newspaper is becoming": SDR, May 19, 1874.

203 "It is a grave matter": As quoted in SDR, May 19, 1874.

203 "It is proper to await an investigation": Ibid.

205 "Public opinion": *San Francisco Chronicle,* May 18, 1874.

205 "The same general tone": SDR, May 26, 1874.

205 "We cannot charge God": Reverend John F. Gleason, "The Morning Sermon," delivered at the Williamsburg Congregational Church, May 24, 1874, Meekins Library, Williamsburg, MA.

206 "It is hoped": *New York Herald,* May 18, 1874.

206 "curious visitors": *New York Tribune,* May 19, 1874.

206 "For a few days": ESH, "the Haydenville Flood."

206 "was lugged off": HT, Jun. 24, 1874.

207 "secreted in dwellings": SDR, May 29, 1874.

207 "appeals were immediately made": SDR, May 19, 1874.

207 "The entire line of the valley": *New York Sun,* May 19, 1874.

207 "seemed for a second overjoyed": *Boston Morning Journal,* May 19, 1874.

208 "that he would be unable": NYT, May 20, 1874.

208 "that the statement made": Ibid.

209 "the immediate necessities": SDR, May 19, 1874.

209 "for clothes for seven boys": Ibid.

210 "saying he was under": Recollection of Fred Warner, in Hubbard, *Skinner Family Reunion,* 21.

211 "men of means and business and leisure": NYT, May 19, 1874.

211 "take the entire charge": SDR, May 19, 1874.

Chapter 10

214 "a careful examination": NYT, May 20, 1874.

215 "of high repute": *New York Tribune,* May 20, 1874.

215 "Frank, ready, [and] decisive": SDR, Jun. 1, 1874.

215 "slid off as though": SDR, May 20, 1874.

Notes

215 "This dam was not built": Dialogue from NYT, May 20, 1874.

215 "all sods, muck and everything": SDR, May 25, 1874.

215 "as strong as a single shaft of granite": SDR, May 18, 1874.

215 "scraped [the cement] out": HG, May 26, 1874.

216 "The accident": NYT, May 20, 1874.

216 "Look here": BDG, May 20, 1874.

216 "were not what they should have been": SDR, Jun. 1, 1874.

217 "Mr. Reporter": BDG, May 20, 1874.

217 "the loss to the town": *Boston Morning Journal*, May 20, 1874.

217 "a damage to highways": Ibid.

217 "So far as the committee": SDR, May 29, 1874.

218 "Mr. Skinner states": SDR, May 20, 1874.

219 "A manufacturer who had suffered severely": BDG, May 20, 1874.

220 "The pitiable condition": HT, May 20, 1874.

220 "Wanted": HT, May 9, 1874.

220 "the present restoration": HT, May 20, 1874.

221 "new and commodious buildings": Ibid.

221 "declared their intention": Ibid.

222 "We are not pleading": Ibid.

222 There is a wide range of duties: SDR, May 20, 1874.

223 "considerably enlarge": Ibid.

223 "crooked around a tree": NFP, May 30, 1874.

224 "Do you solemnly swear": *General Statutes of the Commonwealth of Massachusetts,* 2nd ed., 1873, edited by William A. Richardson and George P. Sanger (Boston: Wright and Potter, 1873), 848–49.

224 "a very intelligent body": HG, May 26, 1874.

224 "ruined": WCS, 1874 Diary, entry May 20, WHS.

225 "operatives and young girls": NYT, May 21, 1874.

226 "which sounded like iron": Recollection of Fred Warner, in Hubbard, *Skinner Family Reunion,* 20.

227 "What Mr. Skinner will do": BDG, May 21, 1874.

228 "To use [Mr. Skinner's] own expression": PDP, May 21, 1874.

228 "so shockingly mangled": *Boston Morning Journal,* May 21, 1874.

228 "was spent by the survivors": PDP, May 21, 1874.

Chapter 11

229 "considerably improving": SDR, May 22, 1874.

230 "Mr. Skinner has a natural pride": SDR, May 22, 1874.

230 "More than half the people": HG, May 26, 1874.

230 "torches and lanterns": John Paul (Charles H. Webb), *John Paul's Book* (Hartford and Chicago: Columbian Book Co., 1874), 561.

230 "never did like": Ibid., 562.

231 "It has rained all day": WS to WCS, May 4, 1898, SFP.

231 "to connect the divided people": SDU, May 23, 1874.

231 "They came most opportunely": HG, May 26, 1874.

232 "It is now written": HT, May 23, 1874.

232 "The inhabitants that live": Ibid.

232 "until to-day": Reverend Gleason, "The Morning Sermon."

233 "The vacant pews": HG, Sep. 3, 1921.

233 "generous tide": Reverend Gleason, "The Morning Sermon."

233 "Let it rise to Skinnersville": Ibid.

234 "intended to be": HG, Jun. 30, 1874.

234 "for a small sum": SDU, May 26, 1874.

234 "[didn't] propose to remain idle": SDR, May 26, 1874.

235 "The main building": Ibid.

236 "in a dainty manner": *Memorial. Charles Delano* (Northampton, MA: Hampshire Bar, 1883), 24.

237 "When heroes are called for": *New York Evening Post,* May 20, 1874.

237 "Whittier and Longfellow": *Western Hampden Times,* May 20, 1874.

237 "sorter throwin' his eye": HG, May 26, 1874.

237 "year in and year out": SDR, May 26, 1874.

238 "an electrical stir": Ibid.

238 "very clever": RGD, Massachusetts, vol. 46 p. 187.

238 "You are a mill owner in Williamsburg": SDR, May 26, 1874.

238 "out of mercy": Ibid.

239 "a long roll of answers": Ibid.

239 "in obedience to the jury": Ibid.

239 "moved that Mr. A. T. Lilly": Record Book of the Williamsburg Reservoir Company, entry for May 14, 1867.

239 "take such measures": Ibid.

240 "I am now convinced": WS to Eleanor Skinner, Jul. 3, 1894, Gibson Family Papers, Vaughan Homestead Foundation, Hallowell, ME.

240 "vitally interested": SDR, May 28, 1874.

240 "after the most wearisome repetitions": Ibid.

240 "terse, characteristic and satisfactory": Ibid.

240 "rough-and-ready": SDR, May 27, 1874.

240 "a handsome looking man": SDR, May 28, 1874.

241 "He had nothing to do": Ibid.

241 "the most profane man": Ira Glackens, *William Glackens and the Ashcan Group; the Emergence of Realism in American Art* (New York: Crown Publishers, 1957), 53.

241 "always cussing and damning": NFP, May 30, 1874.

241 "quiet but persistent questioning": SDR, May 27, 1874.

Notes

242 "if he was present": SDR, May 28, 1874.

242 "he must have forgot himself": NFP May 30, 1874.

242 "exactly swear": SDU, May 28, 1874.

242 "Mr. Skinner takes the matter": SDR, Oct. 14, 1888.

243 "one of the most important inquests": *Boston Morning Journal*, May 21, 1874.

243 "it has to deal": SDR, May 28, 1874.

243 "give such superintendence": SDR, May 27, 1874.

243 "he supposed it was not right": SDR, Jun. 1, 1874.

243 "if he had had any power": SDR, May 29, 1874.

243 "that he would not trust": Ibid.

244 "that there was great danger": SDR, May 28, 1874.

244 "There wasn't a great deal of conscience in that": SDR, Jun. 1, 1874.

244 "he thought they knew": SDR, May 27, 1874.

245 "You cannot tell": SDR, Jun. 1, 1874.

245 "over one hundred thousand dollars": SDR, May 21, 1874.

245 "the party left feeling satisfied": *New Haven Palladium*, May 23, 1874.

246 "The general relief committee": HG, Feb 2, 1875.

247 "money will be given": *Worcester Daily Spy*, May 29, 1874.

247 "If you give somebody a tent": Disaster relief expert Frederick Cuny, quoted in "Disaster Management" by Debra Shore, for the Disaster Management Center at the University of Wisconsin, Madison. http://dmc.engr.wisc.edu/Publications/Articles_and_Papers/Disaster_Managment.lasso, November 30, 2009.

247 "build cheap houses": NYT, May 22, 1874.

247 "These sums are": *Worcester Daily Spy*, May 30, 1874.

248 "[It] changes entirely": SDU, May 27, 1874.

248 "stricken from the relief book": SDR, May 29, 1874.

249 "The disbursement of relief": SDU, May 29, 1874.

249 "The generous contributions": SDR, Dec 16, 1883.

Chapter 12

251 "a great many of organzine": WCS, 1874 Diary, entry for May 23, WHS.

251 "in good condition": SDR, May 22, 1874.

251 "is said to be little inferior": Hummel, *Dyeing of Textile Fabrics*, 57.

251 "damp silk is less tenacious": Ibid., 58

252 "the slimy deposits": SDR, Jun. 3, 1874.

252 "what might seem to another": Recollection in William Skinner obituary, n.p., in *In Memoriam: William Skinner* (1902). Author's Collection.

252 "silk and silk soap": SDU, May 28, 1874.

253 "quite a good deal [of silk]": WCS, 1874 Diary, entry for May 23, WHS.

253 "several hundred dollars worth": Ellen Littlefield to Elizabeth Littlefield, May 31, 1874. Private Collection, Peabody, Mass.

Notes

253 "[on] a business trip": SDR, Jun. 1, 1874.

254 "There is no knowledge": RGD, New York, vol. 239, p. 1514.

256 "possessed plenty of labor": Matsui, *History of the Silk Industry* 47.

256 "awfully disgusted": WCS, 1874 Diary, entry for Jun. 5, WHS.

257 "The city was most suitable": Heusser, *History of the Silk Dyeing Industry,* 439.

258 "sympathy and consolation": WCS, 1874 Diary, entry for Jun. 5, WHS.

258 "the greatest potential mill development": Constance McLaughlin Green, *Holyoke, Massachusetts: A Case History of the Industrial Revolution in America* (New Haven: Yale University Press, 1939), 22.

258 "With profits the dominant motif": Ibid., 23.

259 "a six million dollar disaster": Dunwell, *Run of the Mill,* 85.

259 "[these] bankrupt cities": Ibid., 91.

259 "In the construction of the canals": Green, *Holyoke, Massachusetts,* 24.

259 "So admirable": Ibid., 24.

260 "an unusual drought": Ibid., 73.

260 "The spirit of hustle": George H. Allyn, "Sketch of Holyoke," in *Holyoke Daily Transcript, 1882-1912: Thirtieth Anniversary* (Holyoke, MA: Holyoke Daily Transcript, 1912).

261 "brilliant": Green, *Holyoke, Massachusetts,* 84.

261 "ample room": HT, May 20, 1874.

261 "We have been accused": HT, Jun. 10, 1874.

262 "The last month's freights": Ibid.

263 "Father went to Holyoke": WCS, 1874 Diary, entry for Jun. 6, WHS.

263 "A Blow to Their Worshippers": BDG, May 21, 1874

263 "enthusiastically confirmed": BDG May 27, 1874.

264 "the niggardliness of the men": SDR, Jun. 1, 1874.

265 "has bought the horse": SDR, May 30, 1874.

Chapter 13

267 "had the helping and counseling companionship": HT, Nov. 14, 1924.

267 "among the most attractive": HT, Jun. 3, 1874.

267 "the most brutal and atrocious crime": HT, May 6, 1874.

267 "kicked, beaten, [and] dragged": Ibid.

268 "This great structure": Judge J. P. Buckland, quoted in "The Holyoke Water Power Co." in *Holyoke Daily Transcript, 1882–1912: Thirtieth Anniversary.*

268 "to see the show": Edwin M. Bacon, *The Connecticut River and the Valley of the Connecticut* (New York: G. P. Putnam's Sons, 1911), 421.

268 "leaks were appearing": Green, *Holyoke, Massachusetts,* 28.

269 "10 a.m. Gates just closed": Federal Writers' Project, *Massachusetts: A Guide to its Places and People* (Cambridge, MA: Riverside Press, 1937), 249. Willimansett, Mass., is a town on the Connecticut River, south of Holyoke.

Notes

269 "by the constant action": Judge J. P. Buckland, quoted in "Holyoke Water Power Co."

269 "How different": HT, Jun. 13, 1874.

270 "Father and Mother": WCS, 1874 Diary, entry for Jun. 13, WHS.

270 "Father has not": Ibid.

271 "I was much alarmed at first": Lovisa Littlefield (Card) to Ellen Littlefield, May 28, 1874, Littlefield Letters, SFP.

272 "Will every girl": Author phone call with Elizabeth Pettus Losa, descendant of Ellen Littlefield, Sep. 17, 2007.

272 "Gingham is all the rage": Lovisa Littlefield to Chloe Littlefield, Apr. 4, 1869, Littlefield Letters, SFP.

273 "the skinflints": Lovisa Littlefield to Ellen Littlefield, Jun. 29, 1870, Huntley/Littlefield Collection, RCHS.

273 "I think if I were you": Elizabeth Littlefield to Ellen Littlefield, Aug. 13, 1870, Huntley/Littlefield Collection, RCHS.

273 "Mr. Skinner came around": Ellen Littlefield to Elizabeth Littlefield, April 10, 1870, Huntley/Littlefield Collection, RCHS.

274 "O. G. Spelman . . . is going to build again": WCS, 1874 Diary, entry for Jun. 14, WHS.

274 "We are pleased to hear": HG, Jun. 16, 1874.

275 "the largest car-works": Moses King, *King's Handbook of Springfield, Massachusetts* (Springfield, MA: James D. Gill, 1884), 319.

276 "to a grinding halt": "Wason Manufacturing Company," Mid-Continent Railway Museum. http://www.midcontinent.org/rollingstock/builders/wason2.htm. December 19, 2009.

276 "The city proper": Reverend Elias Nason, M.A. *A Gazetteer of the State of Massachusetts with Numerous Illustrations* (Boston: B. B. Russell, 1874), 566.

277 "as the essential base": Louis C. Hunter, *Waterpower: A History of Industrial Power in the United States, 1780–1930*, Vol. I (Charlottesville: University Press of Virginia, for the Eleutherian Mills-Hagley Foundation, 1979), 514.

277 "I have never seen": Nason, *Gazetteer,* 565.

278 "an age when some men": Dr. E. A. Reed, quoted in SDR, May 18, 1903.

278 "You stand either a success": WS to WCS, Oct 19, 1875, SFP.

278 "There is no such word as fail": SAS to WCS, Nov. 5, 1875, SFP.

278 "Behold her": *New Haven Evening Register,* Jun. 2, 1874.

279 "With the ample reservoir": James Leffel & Co., *The Construction of Mill Dams* (Springfield, OH: James Leffel & Co., 1874), 69.

279 "on the model": *Ousatonic Water Power Company: Dams and Canals (Derby Hydroelectric Project).* Report No. HAER No. CT-36, prepared by the National Park Service, Mid-Atlantic Region, Department of the Interior (Philadelphia, 1987), 4.

Notes

279 "every means": League of Women Voters of Shelton, *The Story of Shelton* (1980), http://www.electronicvalley.org/derby/quiz/pages/quiz13.htm. Dec. 21, 2009.

279 "furnished capital": Ibid.

279 "[was] likely to transfer": *Waterbury* (Conn.) *Daily American,* Jun. 25, 1874.

280 "Mother saw [teacher] Jo Sawyer": WCS, 1874 Diary, entry for Jun. 17, WHS.

280 "Improve your time": WS to WCS, May 5, 1874, SFP.

280 "soft strains of music": SDU, Jun. 17, 1874.

280 "It is a good thing": WCS, 1874 Diary, entry for Jun. 12, WHS.

281 "Mother enjoyed it very much": WCS, 1874 Diary, entry for Jun. 17, WHS.

281 "Nothing of any account": WCS, 1874 Diary, entry for Jun. 21, WHS.

281 "Well, is Skinner": HG, Jun. 30, 1874.

281 "The facts are": HG, Jun. 23, 1874.

282 "The people . . . are bound": NFP Jun. 27, 1874.

282 "Mr. Skinner was much affected": HG, Jun. 30, 1874.

283 "They believed . . . in dreams": Recollection of WCS, in Hubbard, *Skinner Family Reunion,* 24.

283 "one of the finest locations": SDR, Jun. 30, 1874.

284 "I've got my eye on a site": *Boston Sunday Post,* Jul. 7, 1929.

286 "To the Editor of the Republican": SDR, Jun. 29, 1874.

Chapter 14

287 "like news of the flood": HG, Jun. 30, 1874.

287 "serious loss": *Greenfield Gazette & Courier,* Jul. 6, 1874.

287 "All this of course": HG, Jun. 30, 1874.

288 "I thought he was going to stay": Ibid.

288 "Mr. Skinner has no occasion": Ibid.

288 "Why hadn't anyone come forward": Ibid.

289 "all were much interested": HG, Jul. 7, 1874.

289 "willing, and even anxious": Ibid.

290 "under the apprehension": HG, Jun. 30, 1874.

290 "to expend in that section": HG, Jul. 7, 1874.

290 "It appears that Holyoke": SDR, Jul. 3, 1874.

291 "Were Gov. Hayden living": HG, Jun. 2, 1874.

291 "from the contemplation of success": A. Forbes and J. W. Greene. *The Rich Men of Massachusetts: Containing A Statement of the Reputed Wealth of about Fifteen Hundred Persons with Brief Sketches of More than One Thousand Characters* (Boston: W. V. Spencer, 1851), intro., iii.

291 "Began poor": Ibid., 146.

292 "helped": RGD, Massachusetts, vol. 46, p. 162.

292 "sharp business man": RGD, New York, vol. 317, p . 300 a/7.

292 "feather[ing] his own nest": Ibid.

Notes

292 "over $300,000": RGD, Massachusetts, vol. 46, p. 162.

293 "very snug & good": Ibid., 187.

293 "The Northampton papers are amusing themselves": HT, Jul. 15, 1874.

293 "a favorable site": SDR, Jun. 30, 1874.

293 "so constructed": BMJ, May 20, 1874.

294 "not fully matured": SDU, Jun. 29, 1874.

294 "The verdict of the coroner's jury": HG, Jul. 7, 1874.

294 "delinquent": Ibid.

294 "far less": Ibid.

295 "[yielded] his own judgments": Ibid.

295 "guilty of great and manifest delinquency": Ibid.

295 "shared not a little responsibility": Ibid.

296 "As far as penalty is concerned": BDG, Jul. 6, 1874.

297 "Having entered": Louis H. Everts, *History of the Connecticut Valley in Massachusetts*, Vol. II (Philadelphia: privately printed, 1879), 918.

297 "Rain falls frequently and in profusion": HG, Jul. 14, 1874.

297 "It is about 4 o'clock": Ellen Littlefield to Elizabeth Littlefield, Jul. 12, 1874, Littlefield Letters, SFP.

297 "The damage done": *Western Hampden Times,* Jul. 15, 1874.

298 "The result was": *New Haven Register,* Jun. 10, 1874.

298 "I have scarcely seen Mr. Skinner": HG, Jun. 30, 1874.

298 "more prominent than any one": HG, Jul. 21, 1874.

299 "If the Goshen waters": Ibid.

299 "For many succeeding weeks": Recollection of Fred Warner, in Hubbard, *Skinner Family Reunion,* 21.

300 "The superiority of French silk braids": "Holyoke: The Young City of Western Massachusetts" in George Smith scrapbook (1876), Holyoke Public Library, Holyoke, MA.

300 "having a desire to excel": Ibid.

301 "Good silk is always good property": WS to WCS and Joseph Allen Skinner, Sep. 8, 1887, SFP.

301 "We have not finished": Ellen Littlefield to Elizabeth Littlefield, Jul. 12, 1874, Littlefield Letters, SFP.

302 "I will inclose a note": Ibid.

302 "I got the silk": Mary Tilley to Ellen Littlefield, Aug. 2, 1874, Huntley/Littlefield Collection, RCHS.

303 "It is the habit of Americans": Trollope, *North America,* 23.

303 "While the works are building": SDR, Jul. 22, 1874.

304 "several figures twice": SAS, 1871 Diary, entry for Jul. 24, SFP.

304 "splendid swimmer": WCS, 1890 Diary, entry for Jul. 12. Author's Collection.

304 "Belle & May were frightened": SAS, 1871 Diary, entry for Jul. 30, SFP.

Notes

304 "[I] felt that every breath": SAS to Belle Skinner, April 22, 1901, SFP.

304 "surrounded by the sea": NYT, May 24, 1874.

304 "It is in some respects": *Bridgeport* (Conn.) *Daily Standard,* Jun. 12, 1874.

305 "present[ed] the variety": Ibid.

305 "Where did all of these rocks come from?": HT, Jun. 3, 1874.

305 "remote from and ten feet above": HG, Jun. 16, 1874.

305 "not less than forty-eight tons": Ibid.

305 "had too much sense": WCS to SAS, Jul. 28, 1874, SFP.

306 "described children who refused": *Buffalo Creek Disaster: An Act of Man.* DVD. Filmed by Mimi Pickering, 1975 (Whiteberg, KY: Appalshop Films, 2006), part 1, time: 32:51.

306 "much decomposed": HG, Jun. 16, 1874.

306 "at a place not previously searched": HG, Jun. 30, 1874.

307 "I have only to shut my eyes": Fred Howard, Letter, Jun. 7, 1874, Private Collection, Leeds, MA.

Chapter 15

308 "[Holyoke] is not of an attractive appearance": "Holyoke: The Young City of Western Massachusetts," Smith scrapbook.

309 "sightly location": Fanny M. Johnson, "A Model Industrial City," *Bay State Monthly* 2, issue 5 (October 1885): 338.

309 "unsurpassed by [any other city hall]": "Holyoke: The Young City of Western Massachusetts," Smith scrapbook.

309 "straight, regular streets": Ibid.

309 "elevated tract of land": Ibid.

310 "great dam": HT, Jul. 22, 1874.

310 "superior pressed and sand brick": *Holyoke City Directory* (Holyoke, MA: 1876), 135.

310 "The walls of the basement": SDU, Aug. 3, 1874.

312 "I caught a run away horse": WS to SAS, Jul. 28, 1874, SFP.

312 "liked the place very much": WCS, 1874 Diary, entry for Jul. 23, WHS.

314 "All talk": HG, Aug. 11, 1874.

314 "Speak French": Eleanor Skinner to WCS, October 1873, SFP.

314 "This is the season": HG, Aug. 25, 1874.

314 "It is getting to be quite dusky": Ellen Littlefield to Elizabeth Littlefield, Jul. 23, 1874, Huntley/Littlefield Collection, RCHS.

314 "The projected new brass works": SDU, Aug. 18, 1874.

314 "Joel Hayden was in town": SDU, Aug. 25, 1874.

316 "assembled in crowds": HG, Aug. 11, 1874.

316 "Business is looking up in the village": HG, Aug. 18, 1874.

318 "In its original location": HT, Jun. 26, 1875.

Notes

318 "beautifully painted in party colors": Ibid.

319 "The most important thing": "In Moving Times," *Scribner's Monthly* 12, Issue 1 (May 1876): 127.

Chapter 16

321 "the employment of cheaper": Richard Dobson Margrave, *The Emigration of Silk Workers from England to the United States in the Nineteenth Century* (New York and London: Garland Publishing, Inc., 1986), 316.

321 "with ease 7,000 or 8,000 revolutions": Brockett, *Silk Industry in America,* 92.

321 "Our American silk manufacturers": Ibid., 91.

321 "a feeling of surprise much akin to awe": SDR, Oct 10, 1888.

323 "He . . . has been successful in business": RGD, Massachusetts, vol 46, p. 127.

323 "They had plenty of champagne": WCS, 1874 diary, entry for Sep. 2, WHS.

323 "it ha[d] not furnished enough water": HG, Sep. 1, 1874.

324 "Williamsburg wants water": HG, Dec. 15, 1874.

324 "supposed to be assisted": RGD, Massachusetts, vol. 36, p. 32.

325 "I never asked a man": *Hampshire County Journal,* Oct. 13, 1888.

325 "[The new silk mill] will give employment": SDU, Oct. 13, 1874.

325 "only a few employees": Green, *Holyoke, Massachusetts,* 143.

326 "asking him not to disappoint them": SDR, Dec. 21, 1874.

326 "Some of the residents": HT, Aug. 15, 1874.

327 "brought eighty-four cases": HT, Sep. 2, 1874.

327 "I could never think": Aurelia Damon to Ellen Littlefield, Jun. 20, 1875, Huntley/Littlefield Collection, RCHS.

327 "Holyoke has more and worse": Green, *Holyoke, Massachusetts,* 116–117.

328 "Going to hell": HT, Sep. 23, 1874.

329 "HAYDEN, GE—!": HT, Sep. 30, 1874.

329 "the negotiations were suddenly suspended": HT, Dec. 12, 1874.

329 "to avoid total loss of value": RGD, New York, vol. 317, p. 300 a/7.

331 "Pulled up stakes": WCS, 1874 Diary, entry for Oct. 2, WHS.

331 "no small share of public interest": HT, Jun. 26, 1875.

331 "there was a saying": HT, Jul. 6, 1959.

331 "in exactly its present condition": SDU, Oct. 24, 1874.

331 "could not be done": HT, Jun. 26, 1875.

331 "there rose up a race of prophets": Ibid.

332 "carefully calculated": Ibid.

333 "Mr. Skinner is indeed leaving us": NFP, Oct. 17, 1874.

333 "laying 600 feet of 4 inch gas pipe": SDU, Oct. 19, 1874.

333 "fire and burglar proof vault": SDU, Oct. 28, 1874.

333 "You have all written": Nina Skinner to Eleanor Skinner, Oct. 8, 1874, SFP.

334 "rumors [about] a big masquerade ball": HT, Oct. 7, 1874.

334 "to improve in manliness": Gordon Hall to WS, Sep. 1, 1875, SFP.

335 "splendid mill": SDU, Oct. 13, 1874.

335 "had a real interest": Bradley, *The Works,* 203.

336 "neatly furnished closet": HT, Dec. 12, 1874.

337 "as even as possible": Ibid.

337 "who worked at [spooling]": Lovisa Littlefield to Ellen Littlefield, Nov. 15, 1866, Littlefield Letters, SFP.

338 "of the best improved kinds": HT, Dec. 12, 1874.

338 "drew hot air currents upward": Bradley, *The Works,* 189.

Chapter 17

340 "the largest crowd": HG, Nov. 17, 1874.

341 "stood up amid deafening cheers": Ibid.

341 "It was eminently proper": Ibid.

342 "the Valley and its villages": SDR, Nov. 11, 1874.

342 "take years to replace": HG, Dec. 15, 1874.

342 "a rill so tiny": SDR, Nov. 11, 1874.

343 "that he will probably ere long": Ibid.

343 "lonely Skinnerville": Ibid.

344 "the pride of Skinnerville": Ibid.

344 "substantial": Ibid.

344 "Of the four villages": Ibid.

346 "They began to make silk": WCS, 1874 Diary, entry for Nov. 16, SFP.

Epilogue

349 "Time lost can never be regained": For one of many examples, see WS to WCS, Nov. 3, 1873, Archives of the Williston Northampton School, Easthampton, Mass.

349 "The smartest horse": HG, Jul. 11, 1871.

349 "It was an up-hill fight": *Hampshire County Journal,* Oct. 13, 1888.

350 "It will be an act of charity": Aurelia Damon to Ellen Littlefield, May 27, 1875, Huntley/Littlefield Collection, RCHS.

350 "Mr. Skinner complains bitterly": Helen Wood to Ellen Littlefield, Aug. 19, 1877, Huntley/Littlefield Collection, RCHS.

350 "had failed, gone insane": WCS, 1876 Diary, entry for May 11, SFP.

350 "The story about Father": Ibid., entry for May 16, SFP.

350 "a class of goods that [would] promise": RGD, Massachusetts, vol. 37, p. 498.

351 "Father's braid business": WCS, 1876 Diary, entry for May 12, SFP.

351 "Buying an imported silk": Wm. C. Wyckoff, *The Silk Goods of America,* 2nd ed. (New York: Silk Association of America, 1880), 31.

Notes

351 "The chief point": Ibid., 36.

351 "greatly to [the silk's] strength": "Skinner's Guaranteed Satin Lining," brochure, n.p. Author's Collection.

351 "an enviable reputation": *Modern Textiles* 37, no. 3 (Mar. 1956): 32.

351 "the most profitable part": RGD, Massachusetts, vol. 37, p. 498.

351 "doing as well if not better": Ibid.

351 "The sun finally burst through": *Hampshire County Journal,* Oct. 13, 1888.

352 "as proud a position": HT, Apr. 28, 1875.

353 "the world's largest single consumer": Christopher Clark, "The Travails of the Nineteenth Century American Silk Industry," in Marjorie Senechal, ed., *Silk Unraveled! Smith College Studies in History* 53 (2005): 97.

353 "This is a prosperous firm": RGD, Massachusetts, vol. 37, p. 600.

353 "It is seriously considered": WCS, 1876 Diary, entry for Jul. 10, SFP.

354 "spinning better and better cotton yarns": *Modern Textiles,* 37, no. 3 (Mar. 1956): 32.

354 "You can buy Skinner's Satin": William Skinner Mfg. Co. advertisement, *Ladies Home Journal* (April 1904).

355 "Our Best Satin": "Skinner's Guaranteed Satin Lining," brochure, n.p. Author's Collection.

355 "I am glad": WCS to Katharine Skinner, Aug. 15, 1882, SFP.

356 "subtle changes": Sharpe, *In the Shadow of the Dam,* 209.

356 "would take generations to complete": Ibid.

356 "Today is the 2nd Anniversary": WCS, 1876 Diary, entry for May 16, SFP.

356 "In the place of wealth": Everts, *History of the Connecticut Valley,* Vol. 1, p. 417.

357 "Rebuilding on such a large scale": RGD, New York, vol. 317, p. 300 a/7.

357 "criticized quite severely": RGD, Massachusetts, vol. 46, p. 347.

357 "establish[ed] the region in its position": Hannay, "Chronicle of Industry on the Mill River," 124.

357 "America's first silk stocking mill": Field et al., *American Silk,* 80.

358 "the finest residence in the city": HT, Jan 27, 1875.

358 "a handsome article": HT, May 26, 1875.

358 "beautifully dressed in white silk": HT, Sep. 11, 1875.

358 "His close attention to business affairs": SDU, Mar. 1, 1902.

358 "a huge man": Gibson, "Recollection of Grandfather Skinner."

358 "white as snow": HT, Feb. 28, 1902.

358 "I never saw anyone": Gibson, "Recollection of Grandfather Skinner."

358 "very good manager": RGD, Massachusetts, vol. 37, p. 498.

358 "newness": HT, Jan 13, 1875

359 "a live manufacturing place": HT, Jun. 13, 1874.

360 "Fellow citizens": HT, Oct. 19, 1898.

360 "no hungry man should be sent": Gibson, "Recollection of Grandfather Skinner."

360 "seemed to closely follow": SDU, Mar. 1, 1902.

360 "His gifts in a private way": SDR, Nov. 17, 1898.

360 "What Holyoke needs is soap": Remembrance of Mrs. W. G. Dwight, HT, Nov. 15, 1917.

360 "gave without reservation": *Western Massachusetts, A History, 1636–1925*, Vol. III (New York and Chicago: Lewis Historical Publishing Company, Inc., 1926), 440.

360 "usually had several wards": *Holyoke Telegram,* Feb. 28, 1902.

361 "I am feeling good": WS to WCS, n.d., SFP.

361 "the typical Englishman": SDU, Mar. 1, 1902.

361 "bitterly opposed": HT, Feb. 28, 1902.

361 "simply sent his sons to France": Ibid.

361 "unanimously nominated": HT, Oct. 5, 1888.

361 "Some men complain": SDR, Nov. 17, 1898.

362 "My observation": SDR, Nov. 18, 1898.

362 "felt like a boy": Belle Skinner to Katharine Skinner, Jan. 23, 1901, SFP.

362 "a severe attack of his malady": SDU, Mar. 1, 1902.

362 "just as the clock": Ibid.

363 "would rather have written": *The Athenaeum Journal of Literature, Science, The Fine Arts, Music, and The Drama.* Jan. to Jun., 1874 (London: Printed by Edward J. Francis, 1874), 387.

363 "The shock now that he is gone is severe": SDU, Mar. 1, 1902.

363 "William Skinner stood with Holyoke's first men": HT, Feb. 28, 1902.

363 "*Resolved:* That by the death of William Skinner": *Holyoke Telegram,* April 3, 1902.

363 "the biggest": SDU, Mar 1, 1902.

364 "His career": Ibid.

364 "It is known that he was a millionaire": HT, Mar. 19, 1902.

364 Indeed when factoring in profits: Based on percentage increases in the Consumer Price Index, the relative purchasing power of $3 million in 1902 would be approximately $80 million today. However, this does not give a sense of the economic status of $3 million at the time that Skinner died. According to the indicators at measuringworth.com, a leading website that calculates comparable figures over time, the equivalent financial status of that amount of money in 2012 would be just over $475 million. Samuel H. Williamson, "Seven Ways to Compute the Relative Value of a U.S. Dollar Amount, 1774 to present," MeasuringWorth, April 2012. www.measuringworth.com/uscompare/.

364 "with impressive ceremony": SDU, Mar. 3, 1902.

364 "See here, I don't want": Haru Matsukata Reischauer, *Samurai and Silk* (Cambridge, MA: The Belknap Press, Harvard University Press, 1986), 207.

365 "A large delegation": SDR, Mar. 4, 1902.

366 "a walk of several miles": *Silk* magazine (circa 1912). Author's Collection.

Notes

366 "the single corporate symbol": Craig P. Della Penna, *Holyoke: Images of America series* (Dover, NH: Arcadia Publishing, 1997), 37.

366 "Twenty-three years or more": Emelie M. Plourde, "From Paternalism to Professional Management: The Skinner Silk Mills, 1880–1938, Holyoke, Massachusetts." Volume I. Thesis, Smith College, Northampton, Mass. (1989), 61.

367 "We still fail to see": J. P. T. Armstrong, president of Corticelli, reporting for the Silk Association of America, as quoted in Field et al, *American Silk,* 83.

368 "Yesterday, I read": Reischauer, *Silk and Samurai,* 208.

368 "Today, as always": William Skinner & Sons, brochure: "100th Birthday Open House" (Holyoke, MA: Unity Press, 1948). Author's Collection.

368 "[who] had little interest": Dunwell, *Run of the Mill,* 158.

368 "first shipment[s] of merchandise by airplane": *The Knickerbocker Press,* May 28, 1928.

368 "in a wide range of fashionable shades": *The Delineator,* Oct. 1905.

369 "When Paris says 'Crepe Satin'": *Pictorial Review Fashion Book* (Winter 1928–1929).

369 "on the way out": *Modern Textiles,* 37, no. 3 (Mar. 1956): 66.

369 "moved over into synthetics": Ibid.

369 "the most famous name": *Photoplay* (Mar. 1931).

369 "made Skinner a household word": *Modern Textiles,* 37, no. 3 (Mar. 1956): 66.

370 "the costume designer was king": "The Backlot: Costume Designers." www.amctv.com/amc/behind/0,2867,CATO-56-CAT1–180-CAT2–277-SID-501,00.html. November 6, 2001. (Page obsolete.)

370 "perfect texture and draping qualities": *Photoplay* (Oct. 1931).

371 "giant textile house": "Case History: William Skinner & Sons" in *Fashion Trades* (Dec. 2, 1946).

372 "Talk of giving up . . . *NEVER*": WS to WCS, Oct. 19, 1875, SFP.

372 "What seemed to be": *Holyoke Telegram,* Feb. 28, 1902.

372 "to a lesser man": *Holyoke Evening Telegram,* Mar. 1, 1902.

372 "one of the greatest comebacks": *Boston Sunday Post,* Jul. 7, 1929.

373 "struck out on his own": *Reader's Digest* (Sep. 1956): 209.

373 "reconstructed to resemble": Kate Plass, Skinner Museum Collection Finding Aid, Mount Holyoke College Archives and Special Collections, South Hadley, MA, p. 3.

374 "Energy and pluck will win": WS to WCS, Sep. 30, 1875, SFP. Skinner frequently used the words *energy* and *pluck* to describe what he felt situations required. Many more examples may be found throughout his letters.

Selected Bibliography

Researching this book has been a journey of discovery and I only wish I could list all the incredibly illuminating sources that I have benefited from along the way. This bibliography has been limited to just those sources actually cited in the book, but I must nevertheless mention a few others up front, because to exclude them feels like denying some old and trusted friends their proper due.

My understanding of the Huguenots and their influence on Great Britain and the silk industry would have been incomplete without reference to *Huguenots in Britain and Their French Background, 1550–1800,* edited by Irene Scouloudi (Basingstoke, Hampshire: Macmillan, c1987); and *The Quiet Conquest: the Huguenots 1685–1985,* exhibition catalogue compiled by Tessa Murdoch (London: Museum of London, 1985.)

Spitalfields, England, has such a rich history. Some additional resources on the subject are *The Silk Weavers of Spitalfields and Bethnal Green,* catalogue by A. K. Sabin (London: Board of Education, 1931); *The Saving of Spitalfields* by Mark Girouard, Dan Cruickshank, Raphael Samuel, et al. (London: Spitalfields Historic Buildings Trust, 1989); and *Spitalfields,* Parts I–IV, from *The Copartnership Herald,* 1931–1932, available online at: www.casebook.org. For an explanation of Britain's forgery problem, I recommend Phil Handler's article "Forgery and the End of the 'Bloody Code' in Early Nineteenth Century England" in *The Historical Journal* 48, 3 (2005): 683–702. For a nineteenth-century description of Britain's silk industry, complete with illustrations, see *British Manufactures* by George Dodd (London, 1844), and for early silk dyeing, *The Silk Industry in Renaissance Venice* by Luca Mola (Baltimore: Johns Hopkins University Press, 2000).

Selected Bibliography

Two brief, enlightening overviews of silk production and the American silk industry are *The Story of Silk and Cheney Silks* by H. H. Manchester (New York: Cheney Brothers, 1924, revised edition) and *The Story of Silk* by Donald D. Leonard (New York: William Skinner & Sons, 1936). Regarding the study of early American fashion, *Textiles For Early Victorian Clothing, 1850–1880* by Susan W. Greene (Arlington, VA: Q Graphics Production Company, 2002) features actual fabric swatches, and *Survey of Historic Costume: A History of Western Dress*, 3rd ed., by Phyllis G. Tortora and Keith Eubank (New York: Fairchild Publications, 1998) provides in-depth information.

To appreciate the life of a mill worker in early nineteenth-century America, the following provide unusual detail: *Loom & Spindle* by Harriet Robinson (Kailua, HI: Press Pacific, 1976) and *A New England Girlhood* by Lucy Larcom (Gloucester, MA: Peter Smith, 1973). A thorough study of the labor history of Holyoke can be found in *Working People of Holyoke: Class and Ethnicity in a Massachusetts Mill Town, 1850–1960* by William F. Hartford (New Brunswick, NJ: Rutgers University Press, 1990). For further reading on the growth of mill villages and the urbanization of industry, I suggest *The Roots of Rural Capitalism: Western Massachusetts, 1780–1860* by Christopher Clark (Ithaca, NY: Cornell University Press, 1990) and *Industrializing America* by Walter Licht (Baltimore: Johns Hopkins University Press, 1995).

This story involved a great deal of genealogical research, and I am indebted to the online databases ancestry.com and familysearch.org and to the legion of researchers who have gathered all the information on those sites and made them available to the public. I have also gained much knowledge from the records in the Hampden and Hampshire Counties Registries of Deeds and Probate. They are invaluable resources for a researcher.

Archives

American Antiquarian Society, Worcester, MA
Archives and Special Collections, Amherst College, Amherst, MA
Baker Library Historical Collections, Harvard Business School, Boston, MA
Berkshire Athenaeum, Pittsfield, MA
Bridgeport Public Library, Bridgeport, CT
British Library, London
Connecticut Valley Historical Museum, Springfield, MA
Derby Public Library, Derby, CT
Forbes Library, Northampton, MA
Greenfield Public Library, Greenfield, MA
Guildhall Library, London
Hampshire County Superior Court Archives, Suffolk County Courthouse, Boston, MA
Historic Northampton, Northampton, MA
Holyoke Gas & Electric, Holyoke, MA
Holyoke Public Library, Holyoke, MA

Selected Bibliography

Macclesfield Silk Museums, Macclesfield, England
Meekins Library, Williamsburg, MA
National Archives and Records Administration, Northeast Region, Waltham, MA
New Haven Free Public Library, New Haven, CT
New York Historical Society, New York, NY
New York Public Library, Stephen A. Schwarzman Building, New York, NY
New York Public Library, Science, Industry and Business Library, New York, NY
Paterson Public Library, Paterson, NJ
Rensselaer County Historical Society, Troy, NY
Silas Bronson Library, Waterbury, CT
Skinner Museum Collection, Mount Holyoke College, South Hadley, MA
Sophia Smith Collection, Smith College, Northampton, MA
Thomas J. Dodd Research Center, University of Connecticut, Storrs, CT
Westfield Public Library, Westfield, MA
Worcester Public Library, Worcester, MA
University of Oregon Libraries, Eugene, OR
Vaughan Homestead Foundation, Hallowell, ME
W. E. B. Du Bois Library, University of Massachusetts, Amherst, MA
Williamsburg Historical Commission, Williamsburg, MA
Williamsburg Historical Society, Williamsburg, MA
Williamsburg Town Hall, Williamsburg, MA
Wistariahurst Museum, Holyoke, MA

Books, Articles, and Multimedia

Acts and Resolves Passed by the General Court of Massachusetts in the Year 1865. Boston: Wright & Potter, 1865.

Adrosko, Rita. J. *Natural Dyes and Home Dyeing.* Reprint. Mineola, NY: Dover Publications, 1971.

Archer, Thomas. *The Pauper, The Thief and The Convict: Sketches of Some of Their Homes, Haunts and Habits.* London: Groombridge and Sons, 1865. Courtesy of Lee Jackson, http://www.victorianlondon.org/.

The Athenaeum Journal of Literature, Science, The Fine Arts, Music, and The Drama. January to June, 1874. London: Printed by Edward J. Francis, 1874.

Bachman, Frank P. *Great Inventors and Their Inventions.* New York, Cincinnati, and Chicago: American Book Co., 1918.

"The Backlot: Costume Designers." www.amctv.com/amc/behind/0,2867,CATO-56-CAT1–180-CAT2–277-SID-501,00.html. November 6, 2001. (Page obsolete.)

Bacon, Edwin M. *The Connecticut River and the Valley of the Connecticut.* New York: G. P. Putnam's Sons, 1911.

Barlow, Alfred. *The History and Principles of Weaving by Hand and by Power.* 2nd ed. London: Sampson, Low, Marston, Searle & Rivington, 1879.

Selected Bibliography

Bayly, Thomas Haynes. *The Spitalfields Weaver: A Comic Drama.* First performed in 1838. London: Thomas Hailes Lacy, n.d.

Bell, William. *Hints to Emigrants, in a Series of Letters from Upper Canada.* Edinburgh: Printed for Waugh and Innes, 1824.

Bradley, Betsy Hunter. *The Works: The Industrial Architecture of the United States.* New York and Oxford: Oxford University Press, 1999.

Brockett, Linus P., M.D. *The Silk Industry in America. A History: Prepared for the Centennial Exhibition.* New York: Silk Association of America, 1876.

Buffalo Creek Disaster: An Act of Man. DVD. Filmed by Mimi Pickering, 1975. Whiteberg, KY: Appalshop Films, 2006.

Buxton, Thomas Fowell, Sir. *The Speech of Thomas Fowell Buxton, Esq. at the Egyptian Hall, on the 26th of November, 1816, on the subject of The Distress in Spitalfields: to which is added The report of the Spitalfields Association.* London: W. Phillips, 1816. *The Making of the Modern World.* Web. August 31, 2007.

Cantlie, James. *Degeneration Amongst Londoners.* London: Field & Tuer, 1885.

The City of Holyoke, Its Water Power and Its Industries, Holyoke, Massachusetts, U.S.A., 1876. Springfield, MA: Clark W. Bryan & Company, 1876.

Clark, Christopher, and Kerry W. Buckley, eds. *Letters from an American Utopia: The Stetson Family and the Northampton Association, 1843–1847.* Amherst, MA: University of Massachusetts Press, 2004.

Clark, Helen Burt. *Skinner Family Reunion.* New Rochelle, NY: The Knickerbocker Press, 1927.

Clark, Rev. Solomon. *Antiquities, Historicals and Graduates of Northampton.* Northampton, MA: Stearn Press, Gazette Printing Co., 1882.

Clark, Victor S. *History of Manufactures in the United States, 1607–1860.* Washington, DC: The Carnegie Institute of Washington, 1916.

Cobbett, William. *Cobbett's Advice to Young Men.* London: W. Nicholson & Sons, 1829.

———. *The Progress of a Plough-Boy to a Seat in Parliament, as Exemplified in the History of the Life of William Cobbett, Member for Oldham.* Edited by William Reitzel. London: Faber and Faber, 1933.

Coleman, Terry. *Going to America.* New York: Pantheon Books, 1972.

Commemorative Biographical Record of Tolland and Windham Counties, Connecticut. Chicago: J. H. Beers & Co., 1903.

Cowan, James. *Twelve Years of the Club.* Holyoke, MA: The Club, 1902.

Cox, Margaret. *Life and Death in Spitalfields, 1700–1850.* York, England: Council for British Archeology, 1996.

Dawson, Charles Carroll. *Saratoga: Its Mineral Waters and Their Use in Preventing and Eradicating Disease and as a Refreshing Beverage.* New York: Russell Brothers, 1874.

Della Penna, Craig P. *Holyoke.* Dover, NH: Arcadia Publishing, 1997.

Selected Bibliography

Deming, Phyllis Baker. *A History of Williamsburg in Massachusetts*. Northampton, MA: Hampshire Bookshop, 1946.

Devens, R. M. *Our First Century: Being a Popular Descriptive Portraiture of the One Hundred Great and Memorable Events of Perpetual Interest in the History of Our Country.* Springfield, Mass.: C. A. Nichols & Co., 1878. Courtesy of the Central Pacific Railroad Photographic History Museum. http://www.cprr.org/Museum/Our_First_Century.html. December 19, 2009.

Dickens, Charles. *American Notes*. New York: Modern Library, 1996.

Dickens, Charles. *Little Dorrit*. 1857. Reprint, New York: Penguin Books, 2003.

Dickens, Charles. *Selected Journalism 1850–1870*. New York: Penguin Books, 1997.

Dictionary of American Biography. New York: Charles Scribner's Sons, 1935.

The Domestic Dyer: being receipts for dying cotton and linen, hot and cold. New England: Printed for Domestic Uses, 1811. http://www.elizabethancostume.net/dyes/domesticdyer.html#12. December 8, 2008.

Dublin, Thomas. *Women at Work: The Transformation of Work and Community in Lowell, Massachusetts, 1826–1860.* 2nd ed. New York: Columbia University Press, 1993.

Dunwell, Steve. *The Run of the Mill*. Boston: David R. Godine, 1978.

Edelstein, Sidney. "Coppers, Kettles and Vats: Equipment in Early Dyehouses." From *The American Dyestuff Reporter* 44 (April 1955). http://www.elizabethancostume.net/dyes/vats.html. May 14, 2008.

Emrick, Robert P., comp. *Leeds: A Village Within the City of Northampton, Massachusetts*. Edited by James Parsons. Northampton, MA, 1999.

English, Fenwick, ed. *The SAGE Handbook of Educational Leadership: Advances in Theory, Research, and Practice.* Thousand Oaks, CA: SAGE Publications, 2005.

Everett, Griff, and Stephanie H. Hitchcock, Jane Middleton and Rosemary H. Timms. *Samuel Slater—Hero or Traitor? The Story of an American Millionaire's Youth and Apprenticeship in England.* Milford, England: Maypole Promotions, 2006.

Everts, Louis H. *History of the Connecticut Valley in Massachusetts*. Vols. I & II. Philadelphia: privately printed, 1879.

Federal Writers' Project. *Massachusetts: A Guide to its Places and People*. Cambridge: Riverside Press, 1937.

Feltwell, John, Dr. *The Story of Silk*. New York: St. Martin's Press, 1990.

Field, Jacqueline, and Marjorie Senechal and Madelyn Shaw. *American Silk: 1830–1930*. Lubbock, TX: Texas Tech University Press, 2007.

Forbes, A., and J. W. Greene. *The Rich Men of Massachusetts*. Boston: W. V. Spencer, 1851.

Full and Graphic Account of the Terrible Mill River Disaster. Springfield, MA: Weaver, Shipman & Co., 1874.

General Statutes of the Commonwealth of Massachusetts. 2nd ed., 1873. Edited by William A. Richardson and George P. Sanger. Boston: Wright and Potter, 1873.

Selected Bibliography

Gere, Henry S., ed. *An Historical Sketch of Haydenville and Williamsburg* (typescript prepared from *Hampshire Gazette* articles published 1860–61), reproduced for the Town of Williamsburg, MA, by Ralmon Jon Black, 1999.

Gibson, Richard. *The Art of Dyeing All Colors of Raw Cotton or Cotton Waste, for the Purpose of Working with Raw Wool: Also the Methods of Dyeing All Colors in the Piece.* Willimantic, CT: Joseph Rollinson, agent, 1861.

Glackens, Ira. *William Glackens and the Ashcan Group: The Emergence of Realism in American Art.* New York: Crown Publishers, 1957.

Glinert, Ed. *East End Chronicles.* New York: Allen Lane, 2005.

Godwin, George. *London Shadows.* London: George Routledge & Co., 1854. Courtesy of Lee Jackson. http://www.victorianlondon.org/.

Golin, Steve. *The Fragile Bridge: Paterson Silk Strike, 1913.* Philadelphia: Temple University Press, 1922.

Green, Constance McLaughlin. *Holyoke, Massachusetts: A Case History of the Industrial Revolution in America.* New Haven, CT: Yale University Press, 1939.

Green, Nancy L. "The Politics of Exile: Reversing the Immigration Paradigm." *The Journal of Modern History* 77 (June 2005): 263–89.

Greenfield, Amy Butler. *A Perfect Red.* New York: Harper Perennial, 2005.

Greenwood, Richard E. "A Brief Assessment of the Historical Significance of the Woonasquatucket River Valley." Woonasquatucket River Watershed Council. http://www.woonasquatucket.org/history.php. June 26, 2009.

Hale, William. *A Letter to Samuel Whitbread, Esq., M.P. Containing Observations on the Distresses Peculiar to the Poor of Spitalfields, Arising from Their Local Situation.* London: Williams and Smith, 1807. *The Making of the Modern World.* Web. August 31, 2007.

Hannay, Agnes. "Chronicle of Industry on the Mill River." *Smith College Studies in History* 21, nos. 1–4 (1935–1936): 1–142.

Heusser, Albert H. *The History of the Silk Dyeing Industry in the United States.* Paterson, N.J.: Silk Dyers' Association of America, 1927.

Holme, Ian. (2006), "Sir William Henry Perkin: A Review of His Life, Work and Legacy." Coloration Technology, 122: 235–251. doi: .10.1111/j.1478-4408.2006.00041.x February 11, 2008.

Holyoke City Directory and Business Advertiser, Combined with Directories of South Hadley Falls and Willimantic. Holyoke, MA: Transcript Book and Job Printing Establishment, 1876.

Holyoke Daily Transcript, 1882–1912: Thirtieth Anniversary. Holyoke, MA: Holyoke Daily Transcript, 1912.

Hummel, J. J., F. C. S. *The Dyeing of Textile Fabrics.* London: Cassell & Co., Ltd., 1890.

Hubbard, Martha Skinner. *Skinner Family Reunion.* New York: Knickerbocker Press, 1922.

Selected Bibliography

Hunter, Louis C. *Waterpower: A History of Industrial Power in the United States, 1780–1930. Vol. I, Waterpower in the Century of Steam.* Charlottesville: University Press of Virginia for the Eleutherian Mills-Hagley Foundation, 1979.

"In Moving Times." *Scribner's Monthly* 12, no. 1 (May 1876): 127–128.

James Leffel & Co. *The Construction of Mill Dams.* Springfield, OH: James Leffel & Co., 1874.

Johnson, Fanny M. "A Model Industrial City." *Bay State Monthly* 2, issue 5 (October 1885): 328–339. Courtesy of Cornell University Library, Making of America Digital Collection.

King, Moses. *King's Handbook of Springfield, Massachusetts.* Springfield, MA: James D. Gill, 1884.

Knight, Charles. *Knight's Cyclopaedia of London, 1851.* Vol. II. London: C. Knight, 1851.

League of Women Voters of Shelton. *The Story of Shelton.* 1980 ed. Excerpt. http://www.electronicvalley.org/derby/quiz/pages/quiz13.htm. December 21, 2009.

Leslie, Robert C. *Old Sea Wings, Ways and Words, In the Days of Oak and Hemp.* London: Chapman and Hall, Ltd., 1890.

Lilly, Alfred T. *The Silk Industry in the United States, From 1766 to 1874.* Boston: John Wilson and Son, 1875.

Low, Charles Porter. *Some Recollections by Captain Charles P. Low.* Boston: George H. Ellis Co., 1906.

Margrave, Richard Dobson. *The Emigration of Silk Workers from England to the United States in the Nineteenth Century.* New York and London: Garland Publishing, Inc., 1986.

Martineau, Harriet. *History of the Peace: Being a History of England from 1816–1854.* Vol. II. Boston: Walker, Wise & Co., 1865.

Matsui, Shichiro. *The History of the Silk Industry in the United States.* New York: Howes Publishing Co., 1930.

McCullough, David. *John Adams.* New York: Simon & Schuster, 2001.

Melville, Herman. *Moby-Dick: or, The Whale: The Writings of Herman Melville.* Evanston and Chicago: Northwestern University Press and the Newberry Library, 1988.

Memorial: Charles Delano. Northampton, MA: Hampshire Bar, 1883.

Miller, Kerby A. *Emigrants and Exiles: Ireland and the Irish Exodus to North America.* New York: Oxford University Press, 1988.

Nason, Rev. Elias, M.A. *A Gazetteer of the State of Massachusetts with Numerous Illustrations.* Boston: B. B. Russell, 1874.

O'Connell, Joe. "History of Delmonico's Restaurant and Business Operations in New York." http://www.steakperfection.com/delmonico/History.html. June 5, 2006.

Ousatonic Water Power Company: Dams and Canals (Derby Hydroelectric Project). Report: HAER No. CT-36, Prepared by the National Park Service, Mid-Atlantic Region, Department of the Interior, Philadelphia, 1987.

Selected Bibliography

Palmer, Alan. *The East End: Four Centuries of London Life*. New Brunswick, NJ: Rutgers University Press, 2000.

Paul, John. (Charles H. Webb). *John Paul's Book*. Hartford and Chicago: Columbian Book Co., 1874.

Plourde, Emelie M. "From Paternalism to Professional Management: The Skinner Silk Mills, 1880–1938, Holyoke, Massachusetts." Vol. I. Thesis, Smith College, Northampton, MA, 1989.

Reischauer, Haru Matsukata. *Samurai and Silk*. Cambridge, MA: The Belknap Press, Harvard University Press, 1986.

Reynolds, Terry S. *Stronger Than a Hundred Men: A History of the Vertical Water Wheel*. Baltimore and London: Johns Hopkins University Press, 1983.

Richardson, Briton. *An Address Upon the Silk Industry of the United States Delivered in the City of New York, October 28, 1869*. New York: S. W. Green, 1869.

Second Report from the Select Committee on Emigrant Ships. Vol. 13. House of Commons, 1854.

Senechal, Marjorie. *Northampton's Century of Silk*. Northampton, MA: 350th Anniversary Committee of the City of Northampton, 2004.

_____, ed., *Silk Unraveled! Smith College Studies in History* 53 (2005).

Sharpe, Elizabeth M. *In the Shadow of the Dam: The Aftermath of the Mill River Flood of 1874*. New York: Free Press, 2004.

Sheffield, Charles A., ed. *The History of Florence, Massachusetts*. Florence, MA: Charles A. Sheffield, 1895.

Shore, Debra. "Disaster Management." The Disaster Management Center, University of Wisconsin-Madison. http://dmc.engr.wisc.edu/Publications/Articles_and_Papers/Disaster_Managment.lasso. November 30, 2009.

Silk Association of America. *Annual Report of the Silk Association of America, 1873*. New York: Silk Association of America, 1873.

_____. *Annual Report of the Silk Association of America, 1874*. New York: Silk Association of America, 1874.

_____. *Annual Report of the Silk Association of America, 1875*. New York: Silk Association of America, 1875.

"Silk Manufacture of the United States." *Manufacturer and Builder* 2, no. 3 (March 1870): 82–83. Courtesy of Cornell University Library, Making of America Digital Collection.

Smiles, Samuel. *The Huguenots: Their Settlements, Churches, & Industries in England and Ireland*. London: John Murray, 1867.

Stowe, Harriet Beecher. "House and Home Papers," *Atlantic Monthly* 14, issue 81 (July 1864): 93–98. Courtesy of Cornell University Library, Making of America Digital Collection.

Thomas, Lately. *Delmonico's: A Century of Splendor*. Boston: Houghton, Mifflin, 1967.

Trollope, Anthony. *North America*. Edited by David Smalley and Bradford Allen Booth. New York: Alfred A. Knopf, 1951.

Vaughan, Virginia Mason. *Othello: A Contextual History*. Cambridge, England: Cambridge University Press, 1994.

Walker, Francis A., ed. *United States Centennial Exhibition 1876, Reports and Awards, Group IX*. Philadelphia: J. B. Lippincott & Co., 1877.

Warner, Frank, Sir. *The Silk Industry of the United Kingdom: Its Origin and Development*. London: Drane's Danegeld House, 1921.

"Wason Manufacturing Company." Mid-Continent Railway Museum. http://www.midcontinent.org/rollingstock/builders/wason1.htm. December 19, 2009.

Western Massachusetts, A History, 1636–1925. Vol. III. New York and Chicago: Lewis Historical Publishing Company, Inc., 1926.

Whitmarsh, Samuel. *Eight Years Experience and Observation in the Culture of the Mulberry Tree, and in the Care of the Silk Worm*. Northampton, MA: J. H. Butler, 1839.

Wyckoff, Wm. C. *The Silk Goods of America*. 2nd ed. New York: Silk Association of America, 1880.

Acknowledgments

I grew up with the photograph of a chateau on the wall in our living room. As one can imagine, I became very curious about this chateau, and when I was old enough to be verbally inquisitive asked my parents about it. My mother told me that my father had wanted to buy it in 1969 and she was relieved he hadn't been able to pull that off. My father, on the other hand, would go almost misty eyed when I asked him about it. He told me that my great-great-aunt Belle Skinner had owned the chateau, that it sat on a hill overlooking the valley of the Meuse, and the town in which it was situated, Hattonchâtel, almost disappeared after World War I. But Belle Skinner had rebuilt it, along with its chateau, and both exist to this day as a result of her efforts.

After college I began researching Belle Skinner's story and it wasn't hard to find relatives who were willing to talk about it. Belle was arguably the most famous person on the Skinner family tree. As I pieced together her war relief work, I continued to wonder what would compel this woman, then in her fifties and leading a comfortable life, to become so passionately involved in the restoration of a devastated village in a far-off valley?

I received a fellowship at the Five College Women's Studies Research Center at Mount Holyoke College to further my research and, after moving to nearby Northampton, discovered I had moved to the town where my great-great-grandmother Sarah Skinner (after whom I am named) had been born in 1834. I also learned for the first time that my ancestors had lived in Northampton as far back as the 1600s. I didn't feel an immediate connection to the place so much as astonishment that I had somehow landed there.

A friend decided to introduce me to the area and took me on a treasure hunt. He told me that a great flood had taken place here in the nineteenth century and that in the bed of the Mill River, which flowed down from the hills, you could still find bricks from the mills that had been washed away. He was right. You can also find bits of china and pottery and that day we even found a tarnished old silver spoon. Those bricks, that spoon, and the water that flowed about my ankles was my introduction to the Mill River Flood.

Back at Mount Holyoke College, poring over old newspapers and letters, I learned that the flood had taken place when Belle was eight years old, destroyed the village in which she'd been born and propelled her father to move his silk mill to Holyoke, where the family homestead still remained. Naturally I began researching the flood. This time, the only help relatives could offer was whatever might be found in their family storage. No one knew the details about the disaster.

If possible, even less was known about William Skinner, the founder of the family company and, I discovered, a central figure in the flood. Although everyone was familiar with William Skinner & Sons—my grandfather had been its last president, my father a vice-president, and other relatives trustees—no one could offer me leads on Skinner himself. He had died in 1902, too long ago for modern memory. Some colorful stories had persisted but he was mostly the mysterious patriarch who had left weighted words in his trail. ("Remember you are William Skinner's descendants. Make good in the world.")

One never knows how one will ultimately arrive at the story one is meant to tell. Or where it will lead. This one began in my childhood with visions of France and ended up taking me to the banks of the Mill River in 1874. The more I learned of the flood, of American silk, and of Skinner's life, the more I understand that Skinner was the subject I had to follow. Although I didn't end up telling her story, I owe this book partly to my great aunt Belle whose influence began the chase. Most significantly, of course, I owe its existence to my great-great-grandfather, so unfamiliar to me at the start, still not fully known, but whose impression upon me has become indelible. Thank you, William Skinner, for every single thing you've taught me.

In the course of writing this book, I have benefited from the help, guidance, support, friendship, scholarship, advice, and much-needed humor from a great many incredible and generous people. There is not enough ink to express my gratitude for all they have done for me, and I would like to make abundantly clear that any errors or mistakes in the previous pages are mine and mine alone.

In particular, I thank Rick Teller at the Northampton-Williston School, East-hampton, Mass.; Stephen T. Robinson at the W. E. B. Du Bois Library, University of Massachusetts, Amherst; Philip Eagle at the British Library; Lisa Wenner at the Meekins Library, Williamsburg, Mass.; Laura Smith at the Thomas J. Dodd Center, University of Connecticut Libraries; Abigail Thompson at the Baker Library Historical Collections, Harvard Business School; Kathryn Sheehan and the rest of the

Acknowledgments

staff at the Rensselaer County Historical Society, Troy, N.Y.; Julie Bartlett and Elise Bernier-Feeley at Forbes Library, Northampton, Mass.; Cheryl Harned at the Skinner Museum, Mount Holyoke College; Sarah Campbell and Jim Massery at the Holyoke History Room, Holyoke, Mass., and the incomparable Marie Panik at Historic Northampton in Northampton, Mass. For his special efforts in helping me locate the whereabouts of the only surviving editions of the *Holyoke Transcript* from the 1870s, I am deeply indebted to former Holyoke historian Devon Dawson.

Those editions of the *Holyoke Transcript* proved of incalculable significance, and I am so grateful to George Wilson, then publisher of the *Concord Monitor,* who had found himself their steward and allowed me unlimited access to them. I also thank Chuck Vincent, who provided me with my own room at the *Monitor's* facilities, brought the newspapers out from deep storage, and made sure I had everything I needed, including a thermos to keep my tea hot. (I still have that thermos.)

George's wife, Marilyn Dwight Wilson, came from a well-known Holyoke family, and she, along with her brother Donald R. Dwight, were kind enough to help me find locals who might assist in my research. John Newton, descendant of another well-known Holyoke family, sent me extremely helpful material on the Newton brothers, about whom comparatively little is known.

Elizabeth Pettus Losa, great-granddaughter of Ellen Littlefield, has preserved a profoundly rich collection of her family's papers and has organized, donated, and transcribed many of them. Early in my research, Elizabeth invited me into her home and with extraordinary faith loaned me pictures and documents from her private collection for use till the book came out. She then continued to send me new material as it surfaced. I am so glad the Littlefield sisters are a part of this book and Elizabeth made that possible.

Skinnerville remained a village of the past until I met Mary Elizabeth Noyes Waddell who grew up there in the 1930s in a house above the railroad tracks that had survived the disaster. Over a memorable lunch with her daughter Cheryl Elizabeth Waddell, who made the lunch possible, Mary brought to life for me a forgotten time.

For taking me on that treasure hunt so many years ago and introducing me to the Mill River Flood, I am forever indebted to Michael Beneville, a very special friend.

With her book *In the Shadow of the Dam,* Elizabeth M. Sharpe set the bar for anyone writing about the flood. I remember the first time I read her work as well as, years later, the day that Betty and I walked the path of the flood in Skinnerville together. Whether on the page or in person, she has been an influence throughout.

Faith Deering, entomologist, put a live silkworm into my hands for the first time, gave me my own silkworm cocoons, and explained sericulture in detail with a contagious passion. If not for her, my knowledge of the production of silk would be shallow at best.

Marjorie Senechal, Professor Emerita at Smith College, who is an expert on the history of American silk (among many other things), guided me toward resources at

Acknowledgments

the beginning of this project and at the end read the entire manuscript. Her input was critical, clarifying mistakes and offering valuable suggestions. I am humbled by her generosity.

During the middle of this project, I was extremely lucky to be introduced to John Diffley, then a recent graduate, who acted as a part-time assistant for me. Many cracks in this story were filled in because of John Diffley's careful research.

The staff at the Wistariahurst Museum, Skinner's former home, have done an astounding job modernizing its archives and assisted me in ways too numerous to count. Many thanks to the current team, Melissa Boisselle, Marjorie Latham, and Penni Martorell, as well as former members Carol Constant and Kate Navarra Thibodeau. A special thank you to Penni for her eleventh-hour assistance with images and information.

Relatives far and wide helped me in this endeavor, some of whom I knew, several of whom I met as a result of it. Christina Cook Bates sent me information on the Warners. Jeff Skinner was the first descendant of Thomas Skinner I ever knew. Bill, Clay and Peggy Armistead showed me photographs I'd never seen and continually offered to help in any way. William Hudnut IV duplicated a series of remarkable oral interviews. Charlie Cassidy sent me copies of some incredible lantern slides. William Skinner Kilborne, Jr. (Tawny to his friends), sent me a scrapbook that included a small, unknown journal and Allerton Kilborne passed along family stories. Elizabeth "Libbie" Skinner Hubbard Cook shared a wealth of family letters and Lisa Cook Reed became an unbelievable support. William Bicknell loaned me a treasure trove of diaries. Martha Logan Bicknell opened her house to me, a complete stranger, and hosted me for several wonderful days as I reviewed her collection of family papers. Jonathan Logan patiently answered several questions. Nancy Logan gave me so much information year after year that I am still breathless by the extent of it. She even did research for me on a trip to London and I thank her husband, my cousin Joseph Skinner Logan, for sacrificing some of his holiday as a result. Though we had never crossed paths, Ellen Gibson welcomed me like an old friend when I arrived at her parents' house, the Vaughan Homestead in Hallowell, Maine, and gave me carte blanche to look through everything the homestead might have.

Two relatives in particular stand out for their influence. George Gibson, publisher of Walker Books, was one of the first champions of this book. His early enthusiasm got this project off the ground. And my aunt, Belle Skinner Kilborne Taylor, has ever been a faithful friend, font of information, and source of encouragement.

For introducing me to the power of the written word at a very young age, I thank Ralph Greco, one of the greatest English teachers that ever lived. I also thank Glenda Thompson, another force in the classroom, for nourishing my progress as a writer.

Joan Feeney and Amanda Schatz Kitaeff gave me excellent advice when I decided it was time to show the manuscript to the world. Ann B. Murphy, Emily Majer, and Barbara Fimbel read the manuscript in part or in whole and helped push it forward. Jennifer Siegel, Jacqueline Rogers, and Brett Graff provided valuable last-minute assis-

Acknowledgments

tance. A small legion of people became involved in helping me decide on a title and I thank every one of them, especially Sheila Pietzrak and Ray Greenberg. I thank Isabel Livingston for the little red house where I finished the first draft and Patty Hinkein for the wonderful home where I brought the book to completion. Fellow artists and creators Robin Palmer, Rob Caldwell, Pamela Wallace, Stephen Reynolds, and Melora Kuhn (whose portrait of William Skinner hangs in my dining room) have been consistently supportive and, when I could have felt isolated in this process, shown me I wasn't alone. Jennifer S. Whittemore, Irena Ginsburg, Susanne Moss, Jess Kielman, Jennifer Cranna, and Reese Williams provided what I can best term "soul support," keeping my spirits up at various stages and, when I was overwhelmed by detail, blessedly reminding me of the bigger picture.

Melissa Weiner saw firsthand what writing this story involved. She went through much of it with me on a daily basis and offered unfailing belief, plus a great deal more. For her tremendous input, I thank her from the bottom of my heart.

Nor could I have come so far without the help of Ralmon Black and Eric Weber. Legendary for their knowledge of the disaster and all things Williamsburg-related, these two went above and beyond the call in doing everything in their power to give me all I needed so that I could get the story right. I cannot thank them enough.

Sandra Krein is another for whom an ocean of thanks would still be too shallow. A former director of Wistariahurst, a professional historian, and a great friend, Sandy provided fellowship, insight, suggestions, a sense of humor, and a place to stay, time and again. Much appreciation also goes to her husband, the patient Chris Krein, for listening to enough Skinner-related conversations to last a lifetime.

Rob McQuilkin, my agent and longtime friend, believed in this story from the beginning, when it was but a fragment of what it is now, and committed countless hours to its manifestation. He has been this book's biggest cheerleader, through thick and thin, and I couldn't have made it through without him. His assistant Christina Shideler deserves mention as well; she can work small miracles.

At Free Press, I am eternally thankful for my editor Leah Miller, for her confidence, kindness, and wisdom. She helped me bring this story into port with a guiding hand that amazes me still. For his faith in the promise of this story, I am indebted to Dominick Anfuso. And for their care with the book's production and publication, I am deeply grateful to Mara Lurie, Judith Ann Hoover, Eric Fuentecilla, Carla Jones, Elisha Jacobsen, Jackie Jou, and Jocelyn Kalmus. It is a privilege and an honor to be able to work with such talented people.

Finally, I thank my parents, George Briggs Kilborne and Lucie Peck Moffett. When he was alive, my dad did so much for me by teaching me about family and history. He introduced my imagination to the wonders of the past. My mom remains the foundation of my present. Without question she is the strongest person I know and has taught me the meaning of unconditional love. My mom is my hero.

Illustration Credits

Photographs and images from the Author's Collection: ii, 2, 5, 8, 10, 11, 12, 13, 14, 16, 18, 22, 25, 26, 27, 28, 29, 30, 31

Photographs courtesy of the Vaughan Homestead Foundation, Hallowell, ME: 1, 3, 19, 20, 21

Photographs and images courtesy of the Wistariahurst Museum, Holyoke, MA: 4, 9, 24, 32, 33, 34

Photographs courtesy of Elizabeth Pettus Losa: 6, 7

Photographs courtesy of the Williamsburg Historical Society, Williamsburg, MA: 15, 17

Map courtesy of the Holyoke Public Library, Holyoke, MA: 23

Index

Index

Index

Index

Index

Index

Pope, Alexander, 73
posttraumatic stress disorder, 306, 307
Pratt, William Fenno, 147, 317
prostitution in Whitechapel, 78
Protestants, French, 64–65

Quabbin Reservoir, 373

Ranhofer, Charles, 5, 18–19
raw silk, 13
    American importation of, 13, 115,
        365, 368
    cleaning of, 98–99
    cultivation of, 6–9, 10
    dyeing of, 73, 78–79, 90, 95–98,
        99–101
    Panic of 1873 and, 301
    throwing, 320
Reader's Digest, 372–373
red mulberry trees, 6
Reece, Rosamond, 114
Reed, Dr., 362
religious revival in America, 204–5
Rhodes, Willie, 36
Richardson, Briton, 18, 181, 256
Riochiro, Arai, 364–65, 368
Rixford, Nathan, 12
Ryle, John, 32

San Francisco Chronicle, 205
Saratoga, New York, 151
Sawyer, Jo, 280
Scribner's Monthly, 319
Sears, Mrs., 144, 273
sericulture, 6–7, 8–10, 88, 119
sewing machines, 106
    silk thread for, 35, 106–107
Shakespeare, William, 75
Sheffield Water Company, 204
Shelton, Edward N., 279
Shepherd's Hollow. *See* Leeds, Mass.

silk
    American vs. foreign, 13–15, 16,
        17, 21–22, 89, 150, 370–71
    decline in demand for, 68, 353
    importation of, 10–11, 16,
        138–39, 254
    Industrial Revolution and, 70
    manufacture of. *See* sericulture; silk
        mills, American
    weighted, 100–101
    on wooden spools, 35
    see also raw silk; silk thread
Silk Association of America
    on American silk linings, 351
    creation of, 17
    donations after flood, 209, 225–26
    first annual meeting of, 17, 158
    second annual meeting of, 3–5, 18,
        19, 20–23
    on Skinner, 363, 364
    third annual meeting of, 315
silk braids, woven, 350–51
silk dyeing, 73, 78–79, 90, 95–98,
    99–101
silk mills, American
    in the 1830s, 12–13
    in the 1840s, 13–15, 18, 88–90
    in the 1850s, 128, 129
    in 1873, 18, 21
    Civil War and, 16, 138–39
    cleanliness of, 121
    machinery for, 15, 128, 129, 130,
        320–21
    see also Skinner's Holyoke mill;
        Unquomonk Silk Mill
silk thread, 105–7, 115, 320, 367
silkworms, 6–9, 119
Singer, Isaac Merritt, 106, 107
Skinner, Ann, 103
Skinner, Belle, 25, 157
    education of, 334, 360

Index

Index

Index

About the Author

Sarah S. Kilborne is a writer, historian, musician, and editor. She holds a degree in philosophy from Yale University and has been a research fellow at the Five College Women's Studies Research Center at Mount Holyoke College. She is the author of two acclaimed books for children, *Peach & Blue* and *Leaving Vietnam: The True Story of Tuan Ngo*. Her grandfather, R. Stewart Kilborne, was the last president of William Skinner & Sons, one of the longest family-run textile companies in American history. She lives along the Hudson River in upstate New York.